THE BOUNDS
OF RACE

THE BOUNDS OF RACE

Perspectives on Hegemony and Resistance

Edited with an Introduction by

DOMINICK LACAPRA

Cornell University Press

ITHACA AND LONDON

First published 1991 by Cornell University Press.

International Standard Book Number 0-8014-2553-0 (cloth)
International Standard Book Number 0-8014-9789-2 (paper)
Library of Congress Catalog Card Number 91-11896

Printed in the United States of America

Librarians: Library of Congress cataloging information appears on the last page of the book.

⊗The paper in this book meets the minimum requirements of the American National Standard for Information Sciences—Permanence of Paper for Printed Library Materials, ANSI Z39.48-1984.

For the fellows and staff at Cornell's Society for the Humanities, in particular Mary Ahl and Agnes Sirrine. A special thanks to Skip Gates for helping to make 1987–88 a successful year.

Contents

Acknowledgments

The contributors to this volume gratefully acknowledge permission to reprint from the following sources.

An earlier version of Chapter 1, "The Master's Pieces: On Canon Formation and the Afro-American Tradition," by Henry Louis Gates, Jr., appeared in the February 26, 1989, *New York Times Book Review.* Copyright © 1989 Henry Louis Gates, Jr. Chapter 2, Hortense Spiller's "Moving On Down the Line," originally appeared in *American Quarterly* 40 (March 1988): 83–109, copyright © The American Studies Association. Chapter 5, Kwame Anthony Appiah's "Out of Africa: Topologies of Nativism," was published in the *Yale Journal of Criticism* 2 (1988): 153–78. Chapter 6, Françoise Lionnet's "Autoethnography: The An-archic Style of *Dust Tracks on the Road*," appeared as Chapter 3 of her book, *Autobiographical Voices: Race, Gender, Self-Portraiture.* Copyright © 1989 by Cornell University. Used by permission of the publisher, Cornell University Press. A version of Chapter 7, Anne McClintock's "'The Very House of Difference': Race, Gender, and the Politics of South African Women's Narrative in *Poppie Nongena*," appeared in *Social Text* 8/9 (1990). Chapter 10, José Piedra's "Literary Whiteness and the Afro-Hispanic Difference," is reprinted by courtesy of *New Literary His-*

tory 18 (1986–87), the University of Virginia. A shorter form of Chapter 11, Satya P. Mohanty's "Drawing the Color Line: Kipling, Baden-Powell, and Subjects of Race," appeared as "Kipling's Children and the Colour Line," in *Race and Class* 31 (1989).

Introduction

DOMINICK LACAPRA

The critical study of "race" is central to contemporary thought. The very concept of "race"—always to be read in quotes—is a feeble mystification with formidable effects: it is the crux of one of the most powerful ideological formations in history. To understand that ideology, its effects, and its intricate relations with such issues as class and gender is among the most forceful challenges facing history and criticism. Today racial ideology subsists in a troubled state, and its defects are more evident than ever before. But precisely for these reasons, its staying power and potential for inducing fanaticism are all the more incredible and intimidating. Indeed as societies become more complex and in certain respects more frustrating, the mesmeric appeal of a simplistic ideology may well increase. Such an ideology offers a shortcut to personal and collective identity that otherwise must be sought in a more self-questioning and problematic fashion.

The difficulty for us in analyzing the concept of race is to employ it with the required critical distance as we investigate the concept's uses and abuses over time. In the process, our very understanding of the concept may be refashioned and a beginning made in the attempt to work out a different manner of articulating both conceptual and sociocultural relations. Here the broader issue is how to avoid racial stereotyping or uncontrolled mythologizing and come to terms with race critically and transformatively without denying the historical and political need for people of color to find effective voices and to work out necessary subject-positions—indeed their need "to reclaim a legacy."

The very act of writing or speaking about race is fraught with difficulty even when one attempts to go about it in a critical and self-critical manner. For one thing, there is the risk of repeating in one's own approach the stereotypical features and debilitating consequences of one's objects of investigation. Indeed it is at present virtually impossible to write or say anything on the topic of race that is not in some way objectionable or embarrassing. This limitation applies particularly to those who are not "people of color," for one's own existential or "subject" position inflects what one says independently of the propositional content of assertions. It is decidedly difficult to overcome the tendency to privilege whiteness as the master-text—the valorized and often unmarked center of reference—and to identify the nonwhite as "other" or "different." It is equally difficult to avoid the growing tendency to substitute a commercialized exoticism or an anodyne, commodified discourse on race for problems of racial stereotyping and oppression.

Even in the best of circumstances, scholarship on race is itself currently an extremely sensitive and contested area wherein the pitfalls are often unavoidable. The dangerousness prejudicially ascribed to oppressed groups by their oppressors may, in disguised form, be displaced onto the seemingly elevated idea that newer modes and objects of study themselves endanger the canonical foundations of the Western tradition. On the part of the oppressed themselves, omissions of certain groups from the scope of analysis may be interpreted as an indication that their claims are somehow less valid or pressing than those of other groups. The absence of a noted scholar from the list of contributors to a collection may at times be seen as an implicit way of siding with a competing definition of the field.

Caveats and denials in such circumstances are never fully effective. But it is still worth noting that the coverage of issues in this book, while extensive, is in no sense exhaustive, and the absence of discussions of Native Americans, Chicanos, and Puerto Ricans should in no sense be interpreted as a delegitimating gesture. The book is more than the record of a conference, but its inspiration was in fact a conference held at Cornell University's Society for the Humanities, and its contents reflect the research interests of those

who were fellows in 1987–88. As acting director, I officially organized the conference, but in fact it was a very collaborative effort,
one of the goals of which was to give a public forum to work being
done in crucial areas of recent scholarship bearing on the issues of
race.

In one sense, I do not have a viable voice or position in addressing
many of the problems discussed in this volume. Still, my presence
may be taken as a sign of an increasingly obvious fact: it is vitally
important for all scholars and critics to listen attentively to, and
even attempt to enter into a mutually provocative exchange with,
the voices that sound in these pages, however difficult and problematic such an undertaking may be. I see at least three major implications of these essays for fields such as intellectual history,
literary criticism, and cultural studies—indeed for humanistic studies in general. First, the range of relevant texts must be expanded
beyond traditional canons to include writings and other artifacts
that would never appear in a conventional course of study focusing
on "great books" or "masterpieces" of the Western tradition. Second,
the very protocols of interpretation and the mechanisms of transmission in the study of canonical artifacts must themselves be transformed to make a prominent place for issues such as race, if only
by sensitizing the interpreter to the manner in which canonical
works or their reception may marginalize or otherwise frame such
issues. Third, the problem of reading or interpretation cannot be
posed in abstraction from significant historical contexts in which
texts and artifacts in general are produced, received, and appropriated; the contexts in question prominently include our own time
and the protocols we use in coming to terms with texts.

These implications are being explored on a number of fronts today
and have far-reaching consequences for existing humanistic disciplines. They betoken not only a state of crisis in the humanities but
the upsurge of newer possibilities that may take research in unforeseen or hitherto resisted directions. One justification for this
book is that the studies in it help to make implications for change
and possibilities for reorientation more evident, and they do so with
exemplary insight and rigor. They show how certain questions may
be raised within the scholarly arena and what happens to inquiry
when these questions come to have a strongly marked role. Whether
the focus is on a set of problems or a body of texts, a guiding objective
is to restructure modes of interpretation in terms of rereading the

existing canon, reaching out beyond its confines, and rethinking assumptions that often function implicitly to guide the work of its interpreters. Uppermost is an attempt to provide a subtle analysis of the variable role of racial ideologies in complex texts and social practices and to trace the intricate interplay between ideologically reinforced, hegemonic constraints and modes of resistance to them. This shared but differentially elaborated concern with the hegemonic and counterhegemonic effects of writing and reading should be of interest to all humanists and social scientists.

One particularly controversial issue confronted in these essays is how to conjoin critical theory and interpretation in an approach to problems that is historical and political without being narrowly historicist or propagandistic. While all of the contributors are committed to meticulous research, none of them is interested in the past for its own sake or beguiled by the idea that one may understand the past purely and simply in its own terms. With varying degrees of insistence and dialogic intensity, research in these essays engages interpretive problems in an awareness that the interpreter is implicated in his or her analysis and that interpretation has historical effects. For as we reconstruct the past and enter into an exchange with it, so we restructure ourselves and indicate the potentials of interaction in the present. In this sense, history itself is not frozen in amber or hypostatized as the simple opposite of theory; it is the necessary companion and counterpart of critical theoretical reflection in a mutual relation affecting one's understanding of historical processes, historiographical research, and textual interpretation. Thus there is in these essays a more or less pronounced effort to relate the investigation of the past to problems that have not been entirely transcended in the present. At times there is also an attempt to detect—in the phrase invoked by C. L. R. James—the future in the present.

The reader may find it useful to have an anticipatory sense of what each chapter will undertake. Once the volume has been read, the condensed accounts may in retrospect become schemata that are to be tested against closer readings. These "abstracts" were written in close collaboration with the authors and thus may to some extent be taken as expressions of authorial intention. But of course intention is overlaid by editorial work, and it has to be reassessed in terms of what the various chapters may be argued to do or to achieve. Hence even in the following brief accounts, one has a replay of the

problem of the interaction of voices and the functioning of hegemonic and counterhegemonic forces in which one is always involved, particularly with reference to the ideologically charged and
hotly contested concept of "race."

In "The Master's Pieces," Henry Louis Gates, Jr., himself modu-
lates adroitly between vernacular and scholarly voices as he addresses the difficult problem of establishing a canon of African-
American literature and relating it to hitherto dominant canons. He
confronts both the opposition of conservatives, such as William
Bennett and Allan Bloom, who want to return to a reinvigorated
canon of traditional "masterpieces," and the opposition of leftist
radicals who would like to rid the academy of all canons.

Gates argues pointedly that the choice confronting any collectivity is not between institutions and the absence of institutions. The
only real choice is the kind of institutions one shall have. He also
insists that before an identity can be fruitfully deconstructed, it may
in certain cases have to be constructed. Thus there is a need to forge
alternative canons that provide the oppressed with voices and her-
itages that are stakes in a struggle for long overdue places in the
academy and the larger society. Gates goes on to provide exceptional
insight into the concerns and principles involved in editing a landmark volume: the forthcoming *Norton Anthology of Afro-American
Literature*.

In "Moving On Down the Line: Variations on the African-
American Sermon," Hortense Spillers turns to one kind of noncanonical text with a long and sometimes moving history. She investigates the intricate role of religion for African-Americans through
a reading of the sermon as a complex, subtle text of popular culture.
She attempts to be attentive to the role of the ear in the reception
of sermons even as she offers a sophisticated analysis of texts whose
printed versions were often prompted by the desire of listeners to
have a record of what they heard. Spillers also evokes the way
churchgoers themselves hear in a double register by reading through
the preacher's delivery of lines of Scripture the intonations of narratives of insurgence and deliverance.

Spillers proceeds on the fundamental assumption that religious
sentiment and the documents of homiletics that inscribe it embody
the preeminent mode of discourse by which African-Americans envisioned alternative futures under conditions of captivity and
oppression. She provides extended analyses of two exemplary ser-

mons by the Reverend J. W. E. Bowen. Although she claims no broad influence for these sermons, she insists that, aside from their important inspirational role for Bowen's own congregation, the sermons shed light on the formal complexity of a popular discourse with a special function in the African-American community. Indeed the sermon may perhaps be seen as the initial event in the formation of a critical subject-position in a context where Christianity may have been the only available way for the African to gain historical purchase and a political voice. The sermon thus stands between worlds: worlds of religious devotion and secular protest, worlds of suffering and the hope of overcoming. In this context, the repeated discursive event with a known and anticipated ending becomes not a hollow variant of the repetition compulsion but a hallowed promise conveying a sense of necessary struggle and renewed urgency. The sermon also gives a different sense to listening and waiting as "meditative, medicinal" modes of empowerment that open auditors or readers to the "substance of things *hoped* for, the evidence of things *not* seen"—to what Spillers terms a "pregnancy of attentiveness."

In "Appropriating the Idioms of Science: The Rejection of Scientific Racism," Nancy Leys Stepan and Sander Gilman examine the theme of resistance and the difficulties of acquiring a "voice" in science. Their goal is to explore a terrain in the history of science that has been virtually unmapped. Focusing on African-Americans and Jews from 1870 to 1920, they investigate the ways in which the victims of scientific racism (and more generally of biological determinism) attempted to free themselves from charges of biological inferiority. Resistance and counterclaims were especially difficult for the victims of stereotyping to make because science was considered to be a universal, empirical, apolitical, nontheological, and uniquely objective form of knowledge unlike any other. If it was to register as effective or even as worth taking at all seriously, resistance to views seemingly sanctioned by science had therefore to be carried out in scientific language and in terms set by the dominant discourse. The struggle over meaning and self-definition was particularly difficult in view of the degree to which the dominant discourse established the terms of the debate and the high barriers it set to entry as a qualified participant. By the very definitions of scientific racism and sexism, the "inferior" were largely outside the making of science and therefore the defining of themselves. The language of science was itself a rather peculiar institution because of the special epistemological status it was granted and the way it was often encased in unexamined ideological assumptions taken to be definitive of science itself. Despite these difficulties, minorities did try to find a voice that enabled them to enter science, contribute to science, and criticize what they saw as unfounded descriptions of themselves by scientists.

Basing their argument on a close reading of a variety of texts in science written by minorities about their own racial and sexual identities, Stepan and Gilman draw up a short typology of the strategies used to counter the charges of biological difference and inequality. The criterion employed in drawing up their classification is the manner in which the resister related to the dominant discourse. The two polar possibilities are almost complete internalization of the terms set by the dominant discourse, at one extreme, and the basic questioning of existing "scientific" discourse, at the other. Between these extremes the authors explore a variety of other strategies of resistance. At any one time, multiple strategies were pursued simultaneously, often in contradictory fashion. What was possible for an individual or group varied enormously according to circumstances—intellectual and political resources, access to scientific education, social solidarities. Stepan and Gilman conclude by indicating that, while the dominant understanding of the scientific project was so strong at the turn of the century as to make fundamental alternatives largely unavailable, existing challenges to "scientific" racism were indispensable parts of psychological survival and political action for the oppressed.

In "The Color of Politics in the United States," Michael Goldfield offers his own interpretation and explanation of the thesis of American "exceptionalism" that has preoccupied analysts at least since the time of Alexis de Tocqueville. Goldfield maintains that the politics of the United States differs from that of other economically developed capitalist countries largely in the absence of an influential labor, social democratic, socialist, or communist political party. In this country, there exists no important, independent, class-based party with major support among poor and working-class people and with a primary concern for their interests within the political arena.

Few of the many theories dealing with American exceptionalism have highlighted the system of racial oppression (white supremacy) and racist attitudes (white chauvinism) of large numbers of influential whites in this country. Goldfield puts forth the hypothesis that white supremacy and white chauvinism provide the main explanation for the peculiarities of American politics from colonial times to the present. For Goldfield, the testing of this hypothesis requires a reformulation of questions and a reorientation of analytic attention. The critical periods to examine are not the "normal," more peaceful ones (it is no real challenge to try to explain why a working-class party was not formed in settled times), but those periods of working-class insurgency and popular protest when the formation of an independent class-based party was conceivable as a concrete possibility. The real question for him is not why mass, radical, broad-based, sometimes violent upsurges of the population have not happened (for they have and frequently), but why they have been so short-lived, why they were unsuccessful or repressed, and why they did not lead to a more enduring form of class-based organization. It is here that the questions of white supremacy and white chauvinism are found to be determining. In defending his provocative hypothesis, Goldfield takes sharp aim at psychocultural conceptions of race and argues for the greater adequacy of socioeconomic interpretations. He also tries to situate the ideology of racism and specify its historical origin and function without denying the value of close readings of its variable role in complex texts and cultural formations. Goldfield's emphasis is on a set of problems rather than on the interpretation of texts or the internal workings of ideology, but his causally oriented arguments are germane to the questions that preoccupy other contributors to this volume.

In "Out of Africa: Topologies of Nativism," Kwame Anthony Appiah notes that the issues of language and nation that are central to sub-Saharan African writers and critics are also those of American criticism. In this sense, Appiah's inquiry is not a voyage into the exotic or a flirtation with the distant Other but a rediscovery of what is—or should be—familiar. The appealing ideology of "nativism" is a simple reversal of Western hegemonic universalism, and it remains within the terms dictated by its adversary. Appiah offers a critique of the nativist response to the contemporary cultural situation of African literature and criticism: the response that calls for a return to precolonial roots. He argues instead for an approach that takes seriously the idea that literature is, in the formulation of Roland Barthes, "what is taught." Literature also reflects on the different purposes that may inform teaching with texts.

In particular, Appiah claims that a recognition of the role of colonialism in the creation of contemporary African literature is a crucial part of a responsible pedagogy, and that only through facing up to this history can we use the teaching of literature to complete the decolonization of the mind. Especially in approaching material for which we lack well-developed protocols of interpretation, we have the opportunity to reconsider the entire activity of reading and evaluating the comparative merits of texts. Appiah also emphasizes the different conditions of reading and teaching African literature in America and in Africa itself. In Africa, the reader or teacher must relate a text to precolonial forms of cultural production, to the colonial encounter, and to the invidious, internalized assumption of Western cultural superiority. In the American academy, the reading of African writing is—or ought to be—directed by somewhat different concerns, including the repudiation of racism, the fostering of genuine respect for the autonomy of the Other beyond facile forms of relativism, and the attempt to expand the horizons of the American imagination that does so much to affect events elsewhere.

In "Autoethnography: The An-archic Style of *Dust Tracks on a Road*," Françoise Lionnet argues that Zora Neale Hurston's autobiographical work should be read as an "autoethnographical" statement that explores the shifting boundaries of the racial self and the performative aspect of Hurston's project of self-portraiture. In this sense, *Dust Tracks* foreshadows Frantz Fanon's *Peau noire, masques blancs* (*Black Skins, White Masks*) and its visionary politics. Contrary to critics who approach Hurston's work with preconceived and Procrustean notions of autobiographical form—and criticize her for lack of "sincerity" and "truthfulness"—Lionnet suggests that *Dust Tracks* stages its own implicit theory of reading, and she attempts to base her own reading practice on Hurston's avowed methodology as essayist and anthropologist. She shows that the tensions at work in *Dust Tracks* are those between "an-archy" and community, history and memory, the individual and the collective, in short between particular and universal, and that Hurston redefines the limits within which such categories can and need be thought through.

By focusing on Hurston's need to feel grounded in a tradition that is itself dynamic and improvisational, Lionnet indicates how *Dust Tracks* is a historical allegory of the condition of New World blacks and a powerful attempt at reinterpreting our collective Greco-Roman and Afro-Mediterranean past. As such, *Dust Tracks* exemplifies the kind of hybridization or *métissage* of cultural forms that has become the challenging domain of "postmodern ethnography."

In " 'The Very House of Difference': Race, Gender, and the Politics of South African Women's Narrative in *Poppie Nongena*," Anne McClintock also turns to the problem of hybridized, heteroglossic "autobiography" and the interplay of voices through an analysis of an explicitly collaborative narrative. The day after Christmas in 1976, a black South African woman called "Poppie Nongena" arrived at the door of Elsa Joubert, a white Afrikaans writer. For six months Nongena would return to tell the story of her life in a series of taped interviews. The account of Nongena's resistance to the bantustan system appeared first in Afrikaans, then in English, and it took South Africa by storm. Yet despite the fact that the book is a searing portrayal of a black woman's ordeal under apartheid, it was widely and vigorously applauded in the white community as "apolitical." McClintock argues that the book's reception as apolitical was itself a political event with its own social logic, amounting to an act of national hygiene that attempted to sanitize the book's troubling and complicated politics. McClintock examines and refuses this flight into "aesthetics" by exploring the narrative in terms of the politics of reception, the politics of female authorship and (unequal) collaboration across races, and the politics of resistance within the black South African family.

McClintock provides a careful analysis of the relation between formal aspects of the text and the nature of women's resistance in a specific historical and social context. She reads the book in the light of current debates about women's narratives, specifically oral history and autobiography. She argues that the book throws into question notions of an essential, and inherently subversive, *écriture féminine* and suggests that this notion needs to be fundamentally historicized. She goes on to analyze in detail how the narrative of *Poppie Nongena* involves a communal interweaving of voices in which the marks of differential power and race relations remain prominent. The reader is denied the possibility of cathartic identification with a unified narrative subject or even with a clear-cut object of oppression. Instead the reader is put in the uncomfortable position of having to assume a fully implicated or complicitous relation to the narrative and to work out a political stance with respect to it. The dominant depoliticized reception of the text thus avoided or repressed precisely what it demanded of the reader.

McClintock concludes that the specific nature of the use of language in this text cannot itself be isolated or hypostatized; it must be understood as intimately bound up with the political project of transforming its context of engenderment.

In "Beyond the Limit: The Social Relations of Madness in Southern African Fiction," Stephen Clingman begins with the empirical observation of a simple yet startling fact: over the past one hundred years the theme of madness has recurred persistently in Southern African fiction (and, indeed, in colonial and postcolonial fiction more generally). The key analytic and interpretive insight may well be that the theme of madness in this body of fiction has to do with the setting up of inequitable limits in the colonial setting—economic, political, cultural, and symbolic. This process of confinement, besides setting up the terms of oppression of the colonized, produces an "anxiety of limits" in the oppressors (and perhaps in the oppressed, in a different form, as well). In this setting, the "political unconscious" is a potent force, relating to repression and the return of the repressed. The essay is, however, more than a simple positivistic, explanatory account of seemingly symptomatic features in "fictional" texts. It also inquires into the way texts reprocess and at times critically rework the contextual pressures that bear upon their writing and reception. And where an American audience may find more about class relations than it is used to in discussing racism, a radical South African audience, used to class analysis, will find more than is customary about the symbolic dimensions of historical process. From this point of view, fictional texts are also social relations that can produce unusual kinds of historical illumination.

Clingman investigates a broad and challenging range of fiction including Olive Schreiner's *Story of an African Farm*, William Plomer's *Turbott Wolfe*, Sarah Gertrude Millin's *God's Stepchildren*, Peter Abraham's *Path of Thunder*, Dorris Lessing's *Grass is Singing*, and Bessie Head's *Question of Power*. Throughout his analysis, he articulates a dissatisfaction with essentialistic formulations, whether these concern notions of literature, racism, white or black culture, or our conception of madness itself. He argues that the appearance of the latter phenomenon has to do with social relations and interactions; that it emerges from and relates to a specific history; and that racism in particular must be seen as an effect of, as well as a cause within, the colonial setting. Finally, Clingman suggests that in both black and white writing we are currently seeing

the breakdown of a dominant framework of reality in South Africa
and of the limits it has set up; he also considers the prospect of a
future without madness—at least of the old kind.

In "The Subversive Poetics of Radical Bilingualism: Postcolonial
Francophone North African Literature," Samia Mehrez notes that
one of the legacies of the French *mission civilisatrice* in North Africa
has been the creation of indigenous intellectual elites. Products of
the French colonial system of education, the members of elite groups
were referred to as *les évolués* (the evolved). Contrary to the assimilationist role assigned to them by the French colonizer, and in
keeping with many other examples of colonial situations, *les évolués*
became the vanguard of the resistance to, and contestation of, French
politicocultural domination—and that despite the initial unease,
ambivalence, even guilt about being the colonial/postcolonial, bi-
lingual/bicultural subjects that they were. In this context, decolonization could never be reduced to the physical ousting of the colonial
presence, nor could it devolve into a recounting of the evils of the
colonial period as opposed to the virtues of traditional culture.
Rather decolonization, aside from its more immediate political significance, requires an act of confrontation with a hegemonic system
of thought and practice that is in part internalized; hence it entails
a complex process of working through historical and cultural formations. It involves the contestation of all dominant forms and
structures and is an act of exorcism: a liberation from imposed self-
perceptions and self-representations as well as a constructive self-
criticism.

Mehrez examines the shifting strategies of contestation of the
dominant French culture as they are articulated in the works of two
major North African writers: the circumscribed yet often striking
textual operations of the Tunisian Albert Memmi and the more
radical, insistently hybridized overtures of the Moroccan Abdelkebir
Khatibi. Her goal is to highlight the role of a subversive poetics, one
that actively transforms imposed constraints (bilingualism/bicul-
turalism) into risky opportunities. Such a subversive poetics seeks
to create a new literary space for the bilingual, postcolonial writer.
It is a space that subverts hierarchies, whether they be linguistic or
cultural; it is a space where separate systems of signification and
different symbolic worlds are brought together in a relation of perpetual interdependence and intersignification. This poetics not only
challenges our conventions of reading; it also comes to question our

perceptions of institutions of knowledge and our disciplinary boundaries. Hence decolonization is not a one-sided endeavor; rather it is a process in which both colonizer and colonized are constantly written and rewritten.

In "Literary Whiteness and the Afro-Hispanic Difference," José Piedra explores certain facets of the imperial career of Spain, "the dark child of Europe, the light child of Africa." The notion of race is particularly elusive with reference to Hispanics; no "color" definition actually applies. Hence there has been a tendency to transfer the notion of an undefinable race to that of a definable language. As Piedra puts it, "To this day, language remains the relative dictator of Hispanidad." At first, nonwhites could write only as long as they did not address the issue of difference, and the earliest black writers who published in Vulgar Latin or in Castilian Spanish were preoccupied with neutral or white issues before they were able to address their own difference. Spain under Islamic domination attempted to Hispanize practically everybody it came in contact with by placing tools of linguistic validation—such as certificates of Hispanic selfhood, university degrees, and the grammatical competence granted by the first modern European linguistic primer—at the service of those entering the Hispanic racial orbit. Racist imperialism was disguised or justified as linguistic assimilationism, and rhetorical "whiteness" became the order of the day. In theory, if not always in practice, the language of Hispanic legitimacy could be learned, earned, and purchased by practically anyone, regardless of race. Thus, as Spain became a transatlantic empire, race was not an insurmountable obstacle to Hispanic assimilation. As was the case with future citizens "of color," however, the assimilated often had to go through indentured servitude or slavery as forms of "apprenticeship." The ultimate form of assimilation was to be able to write like a Spaniard, and the writing of literature was considered to be the foremost accomplishment.

Piedra illustrates the theoretical problem of the linguistic definition of the Hispanic "race" by tracing the evolution, from the sixteenth to the eighteenth century, of the ban against marginals writing literature. In order to break this bastion of prejudice, marginals Hispanized in what, to their minds, might have been an unsuspectedly thorough fashion. Still, at least subtle differences remained, and one may read in them the traces of resistance. It is not surprising that most examples of writing by marginals, both in print and in manuscript form, come from citizens under some service contract: Juan Latino, discreetly defending blackness while honoring the Habsburg dynasty with his literature; the unknown José Ventura, accused of refusing to be racially identified as nonwhite in order to write prose about the racial ambivalence of Hispanics; and the former slave Baltasar de Esquivel, celebrating in poetry the pleasures and pains of miscegenated love. Most of the writers Piedra discusses had direct or indirect dealings with the Inquisition as a literary "agency" that provided such writers with their first professional "critics." Writers found a paradoxical ally in the Inquisitorial trial as a public forum seemingly ready not only to hear their pleas but to scrutinize and preserve their literary efforts before determining whether they deserved punishment. The records of these most repressive of public performances serve us today as a repository of marginals' voices, even if often disguised as those of "honorary Hispanics," which often meant "honorary whites."

In "Drawing the Color Line: Kipling and the Culture of Colonial Rule," Satya P. Mohanty begins by delineating the ideological organization of Kipling's children's tales, in particular *The Jungle Books* and *Kim*. Mohanty's interest is less in the critical potential of Kipling's texts than in the manner in which they recycle and reinforce ideological currents. Situating these texts as exemplary of a kind of cultural-pedagogical project in the context of post–1857 colonial India, Mohanty analyzes the textual creation of racial meanings and values through new patterns of subjectivity, cultural identity, and narrative desire. The primary emphasis of the textual analysis is on the way the narrative generates and progressively structures desires, specific modes of perception, even subject-positions, in the process of refracting political realities and anxieties.

Mohanty proceeds to compare the so-called insular world of childhood in Kipling's work with the explicitly ideological project of Baden-Powell's Boy Scout movement. He traces a relationship between the fears and anxieties in the metropolitan (British) cultural imagination—generated by the 1857 revolt and the increased evidence of anticolonial sentiments and political movements in India—and a subterranean cultural desire to understand imperial selfhood as abstract and historically unspecifiable. This curious linkage between the historically concrete and the ideologically abstract gives a new twist to the theories of ideology proposed by thinkers such as Marx, Louis Althusser, and Fredric Jameson. The ideology of abstraction and the lack of specification are particularly convenient for the colonial rulers—in this case, the Anglo-Indian elite. Mohanty focuses on the process of "racialization," prominently including the construction of whiteness as an aspect of the relations between ruler and ruled. He concludes with some probing reflections about how best to "theorize" the problem of race, reflections that help situate the preceding chapters.

What emerges strongly in all contributions is the cross-disciplinary nature of this volume. Not only do the contributors represent the fields of philosophy, literary criticism, political science, intellectual and cultural history, and the history of science; but philosophers find themselves making points one might plausibly expect from literary critics or historians and vice versa. By their very nature, the analyses transgress disciplinary boundaries to become border incidents in thought that may prove to be particularly stimulating in carrying further our thinking about a vital set of issues. And the very type of unity they bring to the volume is dialogic: different contributions do not converge on a single dominant theme or "imperial" methodology but interact in thought-provoking ways by providing related angles of vision on a set of problems and allowing voices to resonate, at times contentiously, around shared concerns. This type of unity may be the only one possible and desirable for scholars who are themselves intently attuned to the often concealed or displaced relations between hegemony and difference. Indeed (as is altogether fitting in a relatively new and experimental area of research) the essays in their very intersections and divergences raise significant questions both for the reader and for the contributors themselves. The contributions also provide some basis for work that is not interdisciplinary in the sense of merely combining disciplines in their existing state, but genuinely cross-disciplinary in attempting to rethink and rearticulate the very nature of disciplines with respect to significant problems. One such problem is clearly that of the possibilities of historical and critical understanding in the wake of the recent proliferation of theoretical perspectives. Another is the necessary role of historical specification in tensely mediating between particularity and universality as well as in testing theory through the analysis of texts and contexts. By their strategies and objects of analysis, these essays may help point the way to theoretically informed modes of historical investigation and textual interpretation that indicate how the recent call for a "new historicism" may be answered in an intellectually cogent and politically useful manner—one alert to the variable interplay between hegemony and forces of resistance.

I

The Master's Pieces:
On Canon Formation and
the Afro-American Tradition

HENRY LOUIS GATES, JR.

William Bennett and Allan Bloom, the dynamic duo of the New Cultural Right, have become the easy targets of the Cultural Left— which I am defining here loosely and generously, as that uneasy, shifting set of alliances formed by feminist critics, critics of so-called minority discourse, and Marxist and poststructuralist critics generally, the Rainbow Coalition of contemporary critical theory. These two men symbolize for us the nostalgic return to what I think of as the "antebellum aesthetic position," when men were men, and men were white, when scholar-critics were white men, and when women and persons of color were voiceless, faceless servants and laborers, pouring tea and filling brandy snifters in the boardrooms of old boys' clubs. Inevitably, these two men have come to play the roles for us that George Wallace and Orville Faubus played for the Civil Rights movement, or that Nixon and Kissinger played for us during Vietnam—the "feel-good" targets, who, despite our internal differences and contradictions, we all love to hate.

And how tempting it is to juxtapose their "civilizing mission" to the racial violence that has swept through our campuses since 1986—at traditionally liberal Northern institutions such as the University of Massachusetts at Amherst, Mount Holyoke College, Smith College, the University of Chicago, Columbia, and at Southern institutions such as the University of Alabama, the University of Texas, and the Citadel. Add to this the fact that Affirmative Action programs on campus have meanwhile become window-dressing operations, necessary "evils" maintained to preserve the fiction of racial fairness and openness, but deprived of the power to enforce their stated principles. When unemployment among black youth is 40 percent, when 44 percent of black Americans cannot read the front page of a newspaper, when less than 2 percent of the faculty on campuses is black, well, you look for targets close at hand.

And yet there is a real danger of localizing our grievances; of the easy personification, assigning a celebrated face to the forces of re-action and so giving too much credit to a few men who are really symptomatic of a larger political current. Maybe our eagerness to do this reflects a certain vanity that academic cultural critics are prone to. We make dire predictions, and when they come true, we think we have changed the world.

It is a tendency that puts me in mind of my father's favorite story about Father Divine, that historic con-man of the cloth. In the 1930s, he was put on trial for using the mails to defraud, I think, and convicted. At sentencing, Father Divine stood up and told the judge: "I'm warning you, you send me to jail, something terrible is going to happen to you." Father Divine, of course, was sent to prison, and a week later, by sheer coincidence, the judge had a heart attack and died. When the warden and the guards found out about it in the middle of the night, they raced to Father Divine's cell and woke him up. "Father Divine," they said, "your judge just dropped dead of a heart attack." Without missing a beat, Father Divine lifted his head and told them: "I *hated* to do it."

As writers, teachers, or intellectuals, most of us would like to claim greater efficacy for our labors than we are entitled to. These days, literary criticism likes to think of itself as "war by other means." But it should start to wonder: have its victories come too easily? The recent turn toward politics and history in literary studies has transformed the analysis of texts into a marionette theater of the political, to which we bring all the passions of our real-world commitments. And that is why it is sometimes necessary to remind ourselves of the distance from the classroom to the streets. Academic critics write essays, "readings" of literature, where the bad guys (for example, racism or patriarchy) lose, where the forces of oppression are subverted by the boundless powers of irony and allegory that no prison can contain, and we glow with hard-won triumph. We pay homage to the marginalized and demonized, and it feels almost like we have righted a real-world injustice. I always think about the folktale about the fellow who killed seven with one blow.

Ours was the generation that took over buildings in the late 1960s and demanded the creation of black and women's studies programs, and now, like the return of the repressed, we have come back to challenge the traditional curriculum. And some of us are even attempting to redefine the canon by editing anthologies. Yet it sometimes seems that blacks are doing better in the college curriculum than they are in the streets.

This is not a defeatist moan. It is just an acknowledgment that the relation between our critical postures and the social struggles they reflect upon is far from transparent. That does not mean there is no relation, of course, only that it is a highly mediated one. In all events, I do think we should be clear about when we've swatted a fly and when we've toppled a giant.

In the swaddling clothes of our academic complacencies, few of us are prepared when we bump against something hard, and sooner or later, we do. One of the first lectures I ever gave was to a packed audience at the Howard University Honors Seminar, and my talk was one of those mistakes you don't make twice. Fresh out of graduate school, immersed in the arcane technicalities of contemporary literary theory, I was going to deliver a crunchy structuralist analysis of a slave narrative by Frederick Douglass, tracing the intricate play of its "binary oppositions." Everything was neatly schematized, formalized, analyzed; this was my Sunday-best structuralism, crisp white shirt and shiny black shoes. And the talk didn't play well— if you've seen an audience glaze over, this was double-glazing. Bravely, I finished my speech, and, of course, asked for questions. Long silence. Finally, a young man in the very back of the room stands up and says, "Yeah, brother, all we want to know is, was Booker T. a Tom or not?"

The funny thing is, this happens to be an interesting question, a lot more interesting than my talk was. And while I did not appreciate it at the time, the exchange did draw my attention, a little rudely perhaps, to the yawning chasm between our critical discourse and the traditions they discourse on. You know—is there a canon in this class? People often like to represent the High Canonical texts as the reading matter of the power elite. I mean, you have to try to imagine

James Baker curling up with the Four Quartets, Dan Quayle leafing through the *Princess Cassimassima*. What is wrong with this picture? Now, I suppose that Louis L'Amour or Ian Fleming are *possibilities*—but that carries us a ways from the High Canonical.

Obviously, some of what I am saying is by way of *mea culpa*, because I speak here as a participant in a moment of canon formation in a so-called marginal tradition. But my pursuit of this project has required me to negotiate a position between, on the one hand, William Bennett, who claims that black people can have no canon, no masterpieces, and, on the other hand, those on the critical Left who wonder why we want to establish the existence of a canon, any canon, in the first place.

When I think back to that Howard talk, I think back to why I went into literature in the first place. I suppose the literary canon is, in no very grand sense, the commonplace book of our shared culture, in which we have written down the texts and titles that we want to remember, that had some special meaning for us. How else did those of us who teach literature fall in love with our subject than through our very own commonplace books, in which we inscribed, secretly and privately, as we might do in a diary, those passages of books that named for us what we had for long deeply felt, but could not say?

I kept my diary from the age of twelve, turning to it to repeat those marvelous passages that named myself in some private way. From H. H. Munro and O. Henry—some of the popular literature we had on the shelves at home—to Charles Dickens and Jane Austen, to Victor Hugo and Guy de Maupassant, I found resonant passages that I used to inscribe in my book. Finding James Baldwin and writing down passages from his work at an Episcopal church camp during the Watts riots in 1965 (I was fifteen) probably determined the direction of my intellectual life more than did any other single factor. I copied down over and over verbatim his elegantly framed paragraphs, full of sentences that were at once somehow Henry Jamesian and King Jamesian, yet clothed in the cadences and figures of the Spirituals. I try to remind my graduate students that each of us turned to literature through literal or figurative commonplace books, a fact that we tend to forget once we adopt the alienating strategies of formal analysis. The passages in my commonplace book formed my own canon, just as I imagine each of yours did for you. And a canon, as it has functioned in every literary tradition, has served as the commonplace book of our shared culture.

The question I want to consider is this: how does the debate over canon formation affect the development of Afro-American literature as a subject of instruction in the American academy?

Curiously enough, the very first use of the word "canon" in relation to the Afro-American literary tradition occurred in 1846, in a speech delivered by Theodore Parker. Parker was a theologian, a Unitarian clergyman, and a publicist for ideas, whom Perry Miller described eloquently as "the man who next only to Emerson . . . was to give shape and meaning to the Transcendental movement in America." In a speech called "The Mercantile Classes" delivered in 1846, Parker laments the sad state of "American" letters:

> Literature, science, and art are mainly in [poor men's] hands, yet are controlled by the prevalent spirit of the nation. . . . In England, the national literature favors the church, the crown, the nobility, the prevailing class. Another literature is rising, but is not yet national, *still less canonized*. We have no American literature which is permanent. Our scholarly books are only an imitation of a foreign type; they do not reflect our morals, manners, politics, or religion, not even our rivers, mountains, sky. They have not the smell of our ground in their breath [my emphasis].

Parker, to say the least, was not especially pleased with American letters and their identity with the English tradition. Did Parker find any evidence of a truly American literature? "The American literature is found only in newspapers and speeches, perhaps in some novel, hot, passionate, but poor and extemporaneous. That is our national literature. Does that favor man—represent man? Certainly not. All is the reflection of this most powerful class. The truths that are told are for them, and the lies. Therein the prevailing sentiment is getting into the form of thoughts."[1] Parker's analysis, we see plainly, turns upon an implicit reflection theory of base and superstructure. It is the occasional literature, "poor and extemporaneous," wherein "American" literature dwells, but a literature, like English literature, which reflects the interests and ideologies of the upper classes.

1. Theodore Parker, *Social Classes in a Republic*, ed. Samuel A. Eliot (Boston, 1907), p. 32.

Three years later, in his major oration titled "The American
Scholar," Parker had at last found an entirely original genre of American literature:

> Yet, there is one portion of our permanent literature, if literature it
> may be called, which is wholly indigenous and original. . . . we have
> one series of literary productions that could be written by none but
> Americans, and only here; I mean the Lives of Fugitive Slaves. But as
> these are not the work of the men of superior culture they hardly help
> to pay the scholar's debt. Yet all the original romance of Americans
> is in them, not in the white man's novel.[2]

Parker was right about the originality, the peculiarly *American*
quality, of the slave narratives. But he was wrong about their inherent inability to "pay the scholar's debt"; scholars had only to
learn to *read* the narratives for their debt to be paid in full, indeed
many times over. Parker was put off by the language of the slave
narratives. He would have done well to heed the admonition that
Ralph Waldo Emerson had made in his 1844 speech, "Emancipation
in the British West Indies." "Language," Emerson wrote, "must be
raked, the secrets of slaughter-houses and infamous holes that cannot front the day, must be ransacked, to tell what negro slavery has
been." The narratives, for Parker, were not instances of greater literature, but they were the prime site of America's "original romance." As Charles Sumner said in 1852, the fugitive slaves "are
among the heroes of our age. Romance has no stories of more thrilling interest than" their narratives. "Classical antiquity has preserved no examples of adventurous trial more worthy of renown."[3]
Parker's and Sumner's divergent views reveal that the popularity of
the narratives in antebellum America most certainly did not reflect
any sort of common critical agreement about their nature and status
as art. Still, the implications of these observations upon black canon
formation would not be lost upon those who would soon seek to
free the black slave, or to elevate the former slave, through the
agency of literary production. (Johann Gottfried Herder's ideas of
the "living spirit of a language" were brought to bear with a venge-

2. Theodore Parker, *The American Scholar*, ed. George Willis Cooke (Boston,
1907), p. 37.
3. Charles Sumner, cited in *The Slave's Narrative*, Charles T. Davis and H. L.
Gates, Jr. (New York, 1985), p. xv.

ance upon eighteenth- and ninetenth-century considerations of the place in nature of the black.)

The relationship between the social and political subjectivity of the Negro and the production of art had been discussed by a host of commentators, including Hume, Hegel, and Kant, since Morgan Godwyn wondered aloud about it in 1684. It was probably Emerson's comments that generated our earliest efforts at canon formation. As Emerson said, again in his speech "Emancipation in the West Indies,"

> If [racial groups] are rude and foolish, down they must go. When at last in a race a new principle appears, an idea—*that* conserves it; ideas only save races. If the black man is feeble and not important to the existing races, not on a parity with the best race, the black man must serve, and be exterminated. But if the black man carries in his bosom an indispensable element of a new and coming civilization; for the sake of that element, no wrong nor strength nor circumstance can hurt him; he will survive and play his part. . . . now let [the blacks] emerge, clothed and in their own form.[4]

The forms in which they would be clothed would be those of literature, registered in anthologies that established the canon of black American literature.

The first attempt to define a black canon that I have found is that by Armand Lanusse, who edited *Les Cenelles*, an anthology of black French verse published at New Orleans in 1845—the first black anthology, I believe, ever published. Lanusse's "Introduction" is a defense of poetry as an enterprise for black people, in their larger efforts to defend the race against "the spiteful and calumnious arrows shot at us," at a target defined as the collective black intellect.[5] Despite this stated political intention, these poems imitate the styles and themes of the French Romantics, and they never engage directly the social and political experiences of black Creoles in New Orleans in the 1840s. *Les Cenelles* argues for a political effect—that is, the end of racism—by publishing apolitical poems, poems that share as silent second texts the poetry written by Frenchmen some three thousand miles away. The black poets were saying, "We are

4. "Emancipation in the British West Indies," *The Complete Writings of Ralph Waldo Emerson*, vol. 2 (New York, 1929), pp. 1137–38.

5. Armand Lanusse, ed., *Les Cenelles: A Collection of Poems by Creole Writers of the Early Nineteenth Century*, trans. Regine Latortue and Gleason R. W. Adams (1845; reprint, Boston, 1979), p. xxxviii.

just like the French—so, treat us like Frenchmen, not like blacks."
This was an apolitical art being put to uses most political.

Four years later, in 1849, William G. Allen published an anthology
in which he canonized Phillis Wheatley and George Moses Horton.
Like Lanusse, Allen sought to refute intellectual racism by the act
of canon formation. "The African's called inferior," he writes. "But
what race has ever displayed intellect more exaltedly, or character
more sublime?" Pointing to the achievements of Pushkin, Placido,
and Augustine, as the great African tradition to which Afro-
Americans are heir, Allen claims Wheatley and Horton as the exemplars of this tradition, Horton being "decidedly the superior
genius," no doubt because of his explicitly racial themes, a judgment
quite unlike that which propelled Armand Lanusse into canon formation. As Allen puts it, with the publication of their anthology:

> Who will now say that the African is incapable of attaining to intel-
> lectual or moral greatness? What he now is, degrading circumstances
> have made him. What he is capable of becoming, the past clearly
> evinces. The African is strong, tough and hardy. Hundreds of years of
> oppression have not subdued his spirit, and though Church and State
> have combined to enslave and degrade him, in spite of them all, he
> is increasing in strength and power, and in the respect of the entire
> world.[6]

Here, then, we see the poles of black canon formation, established
firmly by 1849: is "black" poetry racial in theme, or is black poetry
simply any sort of poetry written by black people? This quandary
has been at play in the tradition ever since.

I do not have time to trace in detail the history of this tension
over definitions of the Afro-American canon, and the direct relation
between the production of black poetry and the end of white racism.
It is sufficient to point to such seminal attempts at canon formation
in the 1920s as James Weldon Johnson's *The Book of American
Negro Poetry* (1922), Alain Locke's *The New Negro* (1925), and
V. F. Calverton's *An Anthology of American Negro Literature* (1929),
each of which defined as its goal the demonstration of the existence
of the black tradition as a political defense of the racial self against
racism. As Johnson put it so clearly:

6. William G. Allen, *Wheatley, Banneker, and Horton; With Selections from the
Poetical Works of Wheatley and Horton, and the Letter of Washington to Wheatley,
and of Jefferson to Banneker* (Boston, 1849), pp. 3, 7.

A people may be great through many means, but there is only one measure by which its greatness is recognized and acknowledged. The final measure of the greatness of all peoples is the amount and standard of the literature and art that they have produced. The world does not know that a people is great until that people produces great literature and art. No people that has produced great literature and art has ever been looked upon by the world as distinctly inferior.

The status of the Negro in the United States is more a question of national mental attitude toward the race than of actual conditions. And nothing will do more to change that mental attitude and raise his status than a demonstration of intellectual parity by the Negro through the production of literature and art.[7]

Johnson, here, was echoing racialist arguments that had been used against blacks since the eighteenth century, especially those by Hume, Kant, Jefferson, and Hegel, which equated our access to natural rights with our production of literary classics. The Harlem Renaissance, in fact, can be thought of as a sustained attempt to combat racism through the very *production* of black art and literature.

Johnson's and Calverton's anthologies "frame" the Harlem Renaissance period, making a comparison of their ideological concerns useful. Calverton's anthology made two significant departures from Johnson's model, both of which are worth considering, if only briefly. Calverton's was the first attempt at black canon formation to provide for the influence and presence of black vernacular literature in a major way. "Spirituals," "Blues," and "Labor Songs" each constituted a genre of black literature for him. We all understand the importance of this gesture, and the influence it had upon the editors of *The Negro Caravan*, the monumental anthology edited by Sterling Brown, Arthur Davis, and Ulysses Lee in 1940. Calverton, whose real name was George Goetz, announced in his introductory essay, "The Growth of Negro Literature," that the selection principles for his 1929 anthology were determined by his sense of the history of black literary *forms*, leading him to make selections because of their formal "representative value," as he put it. These forms, he continued, are *Negro* forms, virtually self-contained in a hermetic black tradition, especially in the vernacular tradition, where artistic American originality was to be found:

7. James Weldon Johnson, ed., *The Book of American Negro Poetry, Chosen and Edited with an Essay on the Negro's Creative Genius* (New York, 1922), p. vii.

It is no exaggeration whatsoever to contend that [the Negro's contributions to American art and literature] are more striking and singular in substance and structure than any contributions that have been by the white man to American culture. In fact, they constitute America's chief claim to originality in its cultural history.... The white man in America has continued, and in an inferior manner, a culture of European origin. He has not developed a culture that is definitely and unequivocally American. In respect of originality, then, the Negro is more important in the growth of American culture than the white man.... While the white man has gone to Europe for his models, and is seeking still an European approval of his artistic endeavors, the Negro in his art forms has never sought the acclaim of any culture other than his own. This is particularly true of those forms of Negro art that come directly from the people.[8]

And note that Calverton couched his argument in just that rhetoric of nationalism, of American exceptionalism, that had long been used to exclude, or anyway occlude, the contribution of the Negro. In an audacious reversal, it turns out that *only* the Negro is really American, the white man being a pale imitation of his European forebears.

If Calverton's stress upon the black vernacular heavily influenced the shaping of *The Negro Caravan*—certainly one of the most important anthologies in the tradition—his sense of the black canon as a formal self-contained entity most certainly did not. As the editors put it in the introduction to the volume:

We...do not believe that the expression "Negro literature" is an accurate one, and...have avoided using it. "Negro literature" has no application if it means structural peculiarity, or a Negro school of writing. The Negro writes in the forms evolved in English and American literature.... The editors consider Negro writers to be American writers, and literature by American Negroes to be a segment of American literature....

The chief cause for objection to the term is that "Negro literature" is too easily placed by certain critics, white and Negro, in an alcove apart. The next step is a double standard of judgment, which is dangerous for the future of Negro writers. "A Negro novel," thought of as a separate form, is too often condoned as "good enough for a Negro." That Negroes in America have had a hard time, and that inside stories of Negro life often present unusual and attractive reading matter are

---

8. V. F. Calverton, "The Growth of Negro Literature," in *An Anthology of American Negro Literature*, ed. V. F. Calverton (New York, 1929), pp. 3–5.

incontrovertible facts; but when they enter literary criticism these facts do damage to both the critics and the artists.[9]

Yet immediately following this stern admonition, we are told that the editors have not been too concerned to maintain "an even level of literary excellence," because the tradition is defined by both form and content: "Literature by Negro authors about Negro experience ...must be considered as significant, not only because of a body of established masterpieces, but also because of the illumination it sheds upon a social reality" (p. 7). And later, in the introduction to the section titled "The Novel," the editors elaborate upon this idea by complaining about the relation of revision between Frances Harper's *Iola LeRoy* (1892) and William Wells Brown's *Clotel* (1953), a relation of the sort central to Calverton's canon, but here defined most disapprovingly: "There are repetitions of situations from Brown's *Clotel*, something of a forecast of a sort of literary inbreeding which causes Negro writers to be influenced by other Negroes more than should ordinarily be expected" (p. 139). The black canon, for these editors, was that literature which most eloquently refuted white racist stereotypes (p. 5) and which embodied the shared "theme of struggle that is present in so much Negro expression" (p. 6). Theirs, in other words, was a canon that was unified thematically by self-defense against racist literary conventions, and by the expression of what the editors called "strokes of freedom"(p. 6). The formal bond that Calverton had claimed was of no academic or political use for these editors, precisely because they wished to project an integrated canon of American literature. As the editors put it,

> In spite of such unifying bonds as a common rejection of the popular stereotypes and a common "racial" cause, writings by Negroes do not seem to the editors to fall into a unique cultural pattern. Negro writers have adopted the literary traditions that seemed useful for their purposes.... While Frederick Douglass brought more personal knowledge and bitterness into his antislavery agitation than William Lloyd Garrison and Theodore Parker, he is much closer to them in spirit and in form than to Phillis Wheatley, his predecessor, and Booker T. Washington, his successor.... The bonds of literary tradition seem to be stronger than race. (Pp. 6–7)

9. Sterling Brown, Arthur P. Davis, and Ulysses Lee, eds., *The Negro Caravan: Writings by American Negroes* (New York, 1941), p. 7.

Form, then, or the community of structure and sensibility, was called upon to reveal the sheer arbitrariness of American "racial" classifications, and their irrelevance to American canon formation. Above all else, these editors sought to expose the essentialism at the center of racialized subdivisions of the American literary tradition. If we recall that this anthology appeared just thirteen years before *Brown* v. *Board of Education*, we should not be surprised by the "integrationist" thrust of the poetics espoused there. Ideological desire and artistic premise were one. Afro-American literature, then, is a misnomer; "American literature" written by Negroes more aptly designates this body of writing. So much for a definition of the Afro-American tradition based on formal relationships of revision, text to text.

At the opposite extreme in black canon formation is the canon defined by Amiri Baraka and Larry Neal in *Black Fire*, published in 1968. This canon, the blackest canon of all, was defined by both formal innovations and by themes: formally, individual selections tended to aspire to the vernacular or to black music, or to performance; theoretically, each selection reinforced the urge toward black liberation, toward "freedom now" with an up-against-the-wall subtext. The hero, the valorized presence, in this volume is the black vernacular: no longer summoned or invoked through familiar and comfortable rubrics such as "The Spirituals" and "The Blues," but *embodied, assumed, presupposed*, in a marvelous act of formal bonding often obscured by the stridency of the political message the anthology meant to announce. Absent completely was a desire to "prove" our common humanity with white people, by demonstrating our power of intellect. One mode of essentialism—African essentialism—was used to critique the essentialism implicit in notions of a common or universal American heritage. No, in *Black Fire*, art and act were one.

I have been thinking about these strains in the formation of a black canon because I was part of a group that edited still another anthology, in yet another attempt at canon formation, the *Norton Anthology of Afro-American Literature*. The editing of this anthology had been a great dream of mine for a long time. I am most excited about the fact that the anthology defines a canon of Afro-American literature for instructors and students at any institution that desires to teach a course in Afro-American literature. No one will ever again be able to use the unavailability of black texts as an excuse not to teach our literature. A widely available anthology functions in the academy to *create* a tradition, as well as to define and preserve it. The *Norton Anthology* opens up a literary tradition as simply as one opens the cover of a carefully edited and ample book.

I am not unaware of the politics and ironies of canon formation. The canon that we define will be "our" canon, one possible set of selections among several possible sets of selections. In part to be as eclectic and as democratically "representative" as possible, most other editors of black anthologies have tried to include as many authors and selections (especially excerpts) as possible, in order to preserve and "resurrect" the tradition. I call this the Sears and Roebuck approach, the "dream book" of black literature.

We have all benefited from this approach to collection. Indeed, many of our authors have only managed to survive because an enterprising editor was determined to marshal as much evidence as she or he could to show that the black literary tradition existed. While we must be deeply appreciative of that approach and its results, our task is a different one.

Our task in editing the *Norton Anthology* was to bring together the "essential" texts of the canon, the "crucially central" authors, those whom we feel to be indispensable to an understanding of the shape, and shaping, of the tradition. A canon is often represented as the "essence" of the tradition, indeed, as the marrow of tradition: the connection between the texts of the canon is meant to reveal the tradition's inherent, or veiled, logic, its internal rationale.

None of us is naive enough to believe that "the canonical" is self-evident, absolute, or neutral. It is a commonplace of contemporary criticism to say that scholars make canons. But, just as often, writers make canons, too, both by critical revaluation and by reclamation through revision. Keenly aware of this—and, quite frankly, aware of my own biases—I attempted to bring together as the *Norton Anthology*'s period editors a group of scholar-critics (five black women, five black men, one white man), each of whom combines great expertise in her or his period with her or his own approach to the teaching and analyzing of Afro-American literature. I attempted, in other words, to bring together scholars whose notions of the black canon might not necessarily agree with my own, or with each other's. I wanted to gather a diverse array of ideological, methodological, and theoretical perspectives, so that we together might produce an anthology that most fully represents the various definitions of what it means to speak of the Afro-American literary tradition, and what it means to *teach* that tradition. My own biases toward canon formation are to stress the formal relationships that obtain among texts in the black tradition—relations of revision, echo, call and response, antiphony, what have you—and to stress the vernacular roots of the tradition. For the vernacular, or oral literature, in my tradition, has a canon of its own.

Accordingly, let me add that the *Norton Anthology* features a major innovation in anthology production. Because of the strong oral and vernacular base of so very much of our literature, we included a cassette tape along with our anthology—precisely *because* the vernacular has a canon of its own, one that has always in its turn informed the written works of the tradition. This means that each period section includes both the printed and spoken text of oral and musical selections of black vernacular culture: sermons, blues, spirituals, rhythm and blues, poets reading their own "dialect" poems, speeches—whatever! Imagine an anthology that includes Bessie Smith and Billie Holliday singing the blues, Langston Hughes reading "I Have Known Rivers," Sterling Brown reading "Ma Rainey," James Weldon Johnson, "The Creation," C. L. Franklin, "The Sermon of the Dry Bones," Martin Luther King speaking "I Have a Dream," Sonia Sanchez, "Talking in Tongues"—the list of possibilities was endless, and exhilarating. We will change fundamentally not only the way that our literature is taught, but the way in which any literary tradition is even conceived. So much of our literature seems dead on the page when compared to its performances. In our anthology we wanted to incorporate performance and the black and human voice.

My pursuit of this project required me to negotiate a position between, on the one hand, William Bennett, who claims that black people can have no canon, no masterpieces, and, on the other hand, those on the critical Left who wonder why we want to establish the existence of a canon, any canon, in the first place.

On the right hand, we face the outraged reactions of those custodians of Western culture who protest that the canon, that transparent decanter of Western values, may become—whisper the word—*politicized*. But the only way to answer the charge of "politics" is with an emphatic *tu quoque.* That people can maintain a straight face while they protest the irruption of politics into something that has always been political from the beginning—well, it says something about how remarkably successful official literary histories have been in presenting themselves as natural objects, untainted by worldly interests.

I agree with those conservatives who have raised the alarm about our students' ignorance of history. But part of the history we need to teach has to be the history of the very idea of the "canon," which involves (though it is hardly exhausted by) the history of literary pedagogy and of the very institution of the school. Once we understand how they arose, we no longer see literary canons as *objets trouvés* washed up on the beach of history. And we can begin to appreciate their ever-changing configuration in relation to a distinctive institutional history.

Universal education in this country was justified by the argument that schooling made good citizens, good American citizens: and when American literature started to be taught in our schools, part of the aim was to show what it was to be an American. As Richard Brodhead, a leading scholar of American literature, has observed, "no past lives without cultural mediation. The past, however worthy, does not survive by its own intrinsic power." One function of "literary history," then, is to disguise that mediation, to conceal all connections between institutionalized interests and the literature we remember. Pay no attention to the men behind the curtain, booms the Great Oz of literary history.

Cynthia Ozick once chastised feminists by warning that *strategies become institutions.* But isn't that really another way of warning that their strategies, heaven forfend, may *succeed?*

Here we approach the scruples of those on the cultural Left, who worry about the price of success. "Who's coopting whom?" might be their slogan. To them, the very idea of the canon is hierarchical, patriarchal, and otherwise politically suspect. They would like us to disavow it altogether.

But history and its institutions are not just something we study, they are also something we live, and live through. And how effective and how durable our interventions in contemporary cultural politics will be depends upon our ability to mobilize the institutions that buttress and reproduce that culture. The choice is not between institutions and no institutions. The choice is always, What kind of

institutions shall there be? Fearing that our strategies will become
institutions, we could seclude ourselves from the real world and
keep our hands clean, free from the taint of history. But that is to
pay obeisance to the status quo, to the entrenched arsenal of sexual
and racial authority, to say that they should not change, or become
something other, and, let us hope, better than they are now.

Indeed, this is one case where we have got to borrow a leaf from
the Right, which is exemplarily aware of the role of education in
the reproduction of values. We must engage in this sort of canon
deformation precisely because William Bennett is correct: the teaching of literature *is* the teaching of values, not inherently, no, but
contingently. It is—it has become—the teaching of an aesthetic and
political order, in which women and people of color were never able
to discover the reflection or representation of their images, or to
hear the resonances of their cultural voices. The return of "the"
canon, the high canon of Western masterpieces, represents the return
of an order in which my people were the subjugated, the voiceless,
the invisible, the unrepresented, and the unrepresentable. Who
would return us to that medieval never-never land?

The classic critique of our attempts to reconstitute our own subjectivity, as women, as blacks, and so on, is that of Jacques Derrida.
"This is the risk. The effect of Law is to build a structure of the
subject, and as soon as you say, 'well, the woman is a subject and
this subject deserves equal right,' and so on—then you are caught
in the logic of phallocentricism and you have rebuilt the empire of
Law." To expressions such as this, made by a critic whose stands
on sexism and racism have been exemplary, we must respond that
the Western male subjects have long been constituted historically
for themselves and in themselves. And, while we readily accept,
acknowledge, and partake of the critique of *this* subject as transcendent, to deny us the process of exploring and reclaiming our
subjectivity before we critique it, is the critical version of the grand-
father clause, the double privileging of categories that happen to be
preconstituted. Such a position leaves us nowhere, invisible, and
voiceless, in the republic of Western letters. Consider the irony:
precisely when we (and other Third World peoples) obtain the complex wherewithal to define our black subjectivity in the republic of
Western letters, our theoretical colleagues declare that there ain't
no such thing as a subject, so why should we be bothered with that?

In this way, those of us in feminist criticism or African-American criticism who are engaged in the necessary work of canon deformation and reformation, confront the skepticism even of those who are allies on other fronts, over this matter of the death of the subject and our own discursive subjectivity.

So far I have been talking about social identity and political agency as if they were logically connected. I believe that they are. And that has a lot to do with what I think the task of the Afro-American critic today must be.

Simone de Beauvoir wrote that one is not born a woman. No, and one is not born a Negro; but then, as Donna Haraway has pointed out, one is not even born an organism. Lord knows that black art has been attacked for well over a century as being "not universal," though no one ever says quite what this might mean. If this means an attack against *self-identification*, then I must confess that I am opposed to "universality." This line of argument is an echo from the political Right. As Allan Bloom writes:

> The substantial human contact, indifferent to race, soul to soul, that prevails in all other aspects of student life simply does not usually exist between the two races. There are exceptions, perfectly integrated black students, but they are rare and in a difficult position. I do not believe this somber situation is the fault of the white students who are rather straightforward in such matters and frequently embarrassingly eager to prove their liberal credentials in the one area where Americans are especially sensitive to a history of past injustice.... Thus, just at the moment when everyone else has become "a person," blacks have become blacks...."They stick together" was a phrase once used by the prejudiced, by this or that distinctive group, but it has become true by and large of the black students.[10]

Self-identification proves a condition for agency, for social change. And to benefit from such collective agency, we need to construct ourselves, just as the nation was constructed, just as the class was, just as *all* the furniture in the social universe was. It is utopian to think we can now disavow our social identity; there is no other one to take its place. You cannot opt out of a Form of Life. We cannot become one of those bodiless vapor trails of sentience portrayed on that "Star Trek" episode; though often it seems that the universalists

10. Allan Bloom, *The Closing of the American Mind* (New York, 1987), pp. 91–92.

want us to be just that. You cannot opt out of history. History may be a nightmare, as James Joyce suggested, but it's time to stop pinching ourselves.

But there is a treacherous non sequitur here, from "socially constructed" to essentially unreal. I suppose there is a lurking positivism in the sentiment, in which social facts are unreal compared to putatively biological ones. We go from "constructed" to "unstable," which is one non sequitur; or to "changeable by will," which is a bigger problem still, since the "will" is yet another construction.

And theory is conducive to these slippages, however illegitimate, because of the real ascendancy of the paradigm of dismantlement. Reversals do not work, we are told; dismantle the scheme of difference altogether. And I do not deny the importance, on the level of theory, of the project; it is important to remember that "race" is *only* a sociopolitical category, nothing more. At the same time, in terms of its practical, performative force, the proclamation of non-existence of the Negro sounds like another version of the old darky joke about the Negro in the chicken coop.

Maybe the most significant thing, here, is the tension between the imperatives of agency and the rhetoric of dismantlement. Here is an example: Michel Foucault says, and let us take him at his word, that the "homosexual" as life form was invented sometime in the mid-nineteenth century. Now, if there is no such thing as a homosexual, then homophobia, at least as directed toward people rather than acts, loses its rationale. But one cannot respond to the discrimination against gay people by saying, "I'm sorry, I don't exist; you've got the wrong guy." The simple historical fact is that the Stonewall uprising on Christopher Street was necessary, concerted action was necessary to resist the very structures that, as it were, called the homosexual into being, that subjected certain people to this imaginary identity. To reverse Audre Lorde, *only* the master's tools will ever dismantle the master's house.

Let me be specific. Those of us working in my own tradition confront the hegemony of the Western tradition, generally, and of the larger American tradition, specifically, as we set about theorizing about our tradition, and engaging in attempts at canon formation. Long after white American literature has been anthologized and canonized, and recanonized, our attempts to define a black American canon—foregrounded on its own against a white backdrop—are often decried as racist, separatist, nationalist, or "essentialist." At-

tempts to derive theories about our literary tradition from the black
tradition—a tradition, I might add, that must include black vernacular forms as well as written literary forms—are often greeted by
our colleagues in traditional literature departments as misguided
attempts to secede from a union that only recently, and with considerable kicking and screaming, has been forged. What is *wrong*
with you people, our friends ask us in genuine passion and concern;
after all, aren't we all just citizens of literature here?

Well, yes and no. It is clear that every black American text must
confess to a complex ancestry, one high and low (that is literary and
vernacular), but also one white and black. There can be no doubt
that white texts inform and influence black texts (and vice versa),
so that a thoroughly integrated canon of American literature is not
only politically sound, it is *intellectually* sound as well. But the
attempts of scholars such as Arnold Rampersad, Houston Baker,
M. H. Washington, Nellie McKay, and others to define a black American canon, and to pursue literary interpretation from within this
canon, are not meant to refute the soundness of these gestures of
integration. Rather, it is a question of perspective, a question of
emphasis. Just as we can and must cite a black text within the larger
American tradition, we can and must cite it within its own tradition,
a tradition not defined by a pseudoscience of racial biology, or a
mystically shared essence called blackness, but by the repetition
and revision of shared themes, topoi, and tropes, a process that binds
the signal texts of the black tradition into a canon just as surely as
separate links bind together into a chain. It is no more, or less,
essentialist to make this claim than it is to claim the existence of
French, English, German, Russian, or American literature—as long
as we proceed inductively, from the texts to the theory. For nationalism has always been the dwarf in the critical, canonical chess
machine. For anyone to deny us the right to engage in attempts to
constitute ourselves as discurseive subjects is to engage in the double
privileging of categories that happen to be preconstituted.

In our attempts at canon formation we are demanding a return to
history in a manner scarcely conceived of by the New Historicists.
Nor can we opt out of our own private histories, which Houston
Baker calls the Afro-American autobiographical moment, and which
I call the auto-critography. Let me conclude with a personal expe-
rience, one that I had forgotton until just recently.

Early in 1988, I was listening to Hortense Spillers, the great black feminist critic, read her essay, "Mama's Baby, Papa's Maybe." Her delivery, as usual, was flawless, compelling, inimitable. And although I had read her essay in manuscript, I had never before felt— or heard—the following lines:

> The African-American male has been touched . . . by the *mother*, handled by her in ways that he cannot escape, and in ways that the white American male is allowed to temporize by a fatherly reprieve. This human and historic development—the text that has been inscribed on the benighted heart of the continent—takes us to the center of an inexorable difference in the depths of American women's community: the African-American woman, the mother, the daughter, becomes historically the powerful and shadowy evocation of a cultural synthesis long evaporated—the law of the Mother—only and precisely because legal enslavement removed the African-American male not so much from sight as from *mimetic* view as a partner in the prevailing social fiction of the Father's name, the Father's law.
>
> Therefore, the female, in this order of things, breaks in upon the imagination with a forcefulness that marks both a denial and an "illegitimacy." Because of this peculiar American denial, the black American male embodies the *only* American community of males which has had the specific occasion to learn *who* the female is within itself, the infant child who bears the life against the could-be fateful gamble, against the odds of pulverization and murder, including her own. It is the heritage of the *mother* that the African-American male must regain as an aspect of his own personhood—the power of "yes" to the "female" within.[11]

How curious a figure—men, and especially black men, gaining their voices through the black mother. Precisely when some committed feminists or some committed black nationalists would essentialize all "others" out of their critical endeavor, Hortense Spillers rejects that glib and easy solution, calling for a revoicing of the master's discourse in the cadences and timbres of the Black Mother's voice.

As I sat there before her, I recalled, to my astonishment, my own first public performance, when I was a child of four years. My mom attended a small black Methodist church in Piedmont, West Virginia, just as her mom had done for the past fifty years. I was a fat little kid, a condition that my mom defended as "plump." I remember that I had just been given a brand-new gray suit for the occasion, and a black stingy-brim Dobbs hat, so it must have been Easter,

---

11. Hortense Spillers, "Mama's Baby, Papa's Maybe: An American Grammar Book," *Diacritics* 17 (Summer 1987): 80.

because my brother and I always got new hats for Easter, just like my dad and mom did.

At any rate, the day came to deliver my Piece. What is a Piece? A Piece is what people in our church called a religious recitation. I don't know what the folk etymology might be, but I think it reflects the belief that each of the fragments of our praise songs, taken together, amounts to a Master Text. And each of us, during a religious program, was called upon to say our piece. Mine, if you can believe it, was "Jesus was a boy like me, and like Him I want to be." That was it—I *was* only four. So, after weeks of practice in elocution, hair pressed and greased down, shirt starched and pants pressed, I was ready to give my Piece.

I remember skipping along to the church with all of the other kids, driving everyone crazy, saying over and over, "Jesus was a boy like me, and like Him I want to be." "Will you shut up!" my friends demanded. Just jealous, I thought. They probably don't even know their Pieces.

Finally, we made it to the church, and it was packed—bulging and glistening with black people, eager to hear Pieces, despite the fact that they had heard all of the Pieces already, year after year, like bits and fragments of a repeated Master Text.

Because I was the youngest child on the program, I was the first to go. Miss Sarah Russell (whom we called Sister Holy Ghost— behind her back, of course), started the program with a prayer, then asked if Little Skippy Gates would step forward. I did so.

And then the worst happened: I completely forgot the words of my Piece. Standing there, pressed and starched, just as clean as I could be, in front of just about everybody in our part of town, I could not for the life of me remember one word of that Piece.

After standing there I don't know how long, struck dumb and entranced by all of those staring eyes, I heard a voice from near the back of the church proclaim, "Jesus was a boy like me, and like Him I want to be."

And my mother, having arisen to find my voice, smoothed her dress and sat down again. The congregation's applause lasted as long as its laughter as I crawled back to my seat.

For me, I realized as Hortense Spillers spoke, much of my scholarly and critical work has been an attempt to learn how to speak in the strong, compelling cadences of my mother's voice. To reform core curricula, to account for the comparable eloquence of the African,

the Asian, and the Middle-Eastern traditions, is to begin to prepare
our students for their roles as citizens of a world culture, educated
through a truly human notion of "the Humanities," rather than—
as Bennett and Bloom would have it—as guardians at the last frontier
outpost of white male Western culture, the Keepers of the Master's
Pieces.

And for us as scholar-critics, learning to speak in the voice of the
black female is perhaps the ultimate challenge of producing a discourse of the critical other.

2

Moving On Down the Line: Variations on the African-American Sermon

HORTENSE J. SPILLERS

> Let us stand with both feet upon the shoulders of the past and gather before us the events of today as an horoscope of time; and we will be able to detect and depict, in the gray dawn of the new morning, the events that will transpire and to read *between the lines* the story of the age. (Emphasis mine)
>
> —From "What Shall the Harvest Be?" preached by Rev. J. W. E. Bowen; 1892

On a late July Sunday a few years ago, following an observance of the midday office, I stood shyly spectating beneath the dome of Milan's Cathedral of San Carlo. But at least twelve months would pass before I understood why the moment might have provided me a useful hesitation. Remembering from childhood how Southerners—en route to New York especially—were warned not to betray their comical foreignness, I almost laughed out loud that I was not only about to look, but look *way* up, toward a distance farther—it felt—from the earth plane than the most brazen astronaut travels. The ceiling of Il Duomo de San Carlo requires that the observer virtually assume a supine posture in order to see it properly. One is compelled to topple over backward in a dizzying effort to grasp that

incredible distance between self and topmost, floor and apex. The
neck strains, the whole torso falls back, and, even now, I recall not
seeing entirely that single clear path of zooming light that hooks
two distant points in a geometry of sudden recognition. This momentary parallelism, which flattens out the perpendicular human
plane, seems adapted to the functions of humility: the "I" repeats
the gestures of a crucifixion as the eye travels—startled—upward,
in a sudden nausea of helplessness.

But I didn't know any of that until, months later, reading through
some of the sermons on which this essay is based, I concocted this
analogy: what the feast of the gaze is to the great churches of Europe,[1]
built in early Christian centuries with the money of the Prince, the
feast of hearing is to the church of the insurgent and the dispossessed,
whose "Prince" is surrounded by "clouds and darkness...his pa-
vilion...dark waters and thick clouds." In the church of the Prince,
ecclesiastical architecture accomplishes the project of awe through
the play of light, the immediated spaces along the line of horizontal
vision, the sweep, the curve of the soaring angle.[2] The *eye* initiates
a vault, a leap of faith. In the church of the Insurgent, the hierarchy
of the ecclesia, of the political body, is razed, as nuance is stripped
down to its bare, necessary minimum. In this church of democratic
forms, attested by a far humbler architectural display, the listening
ear becomes the privileged sensual organ, as the sermon attempts
to embody the Word. Between eye and ear, there is not much to
choose regarding human status in the places of the Holy. We are
small there. But through the Protestant sermon's rhetoric of admonition, through the African-American's sermon of exhortation,
"I" improve; "I" "hear"/"have" the Word, at last, in a gesture of
intervention that the physical and psychic violence of the North
American slave trade neither anticipated, nor could ward off. The

1. One of the most significant readings by an American of European culture,
reflected in the architecture of its churches, is provided in Henry Adams's classic
study, *Mont-Saint Michel and Chartres*.

2. I have adopted a contextual meaning of this term from Robert Plante Armstrong, *The Powers of Presence: Consciousness, Myth, and Affecting Presence* (Philadelphia, 1981), pp. 31ff. Armstrong's term "im-media/im-mediate(d)" refers to the
symbolic system that cues "through a semantic construct" an existential analogue,
that is, the literary arts "that proceed through the employments of the names of
meanings to the evocation of subsequent analogic states" (p. 34). For my own purposes, I use the term *immediated* to mean those recessed spaces of architecture that
affect consciousness with suggestions of mystery, inward-turning, the hidden.

African-American church, therefore, sustains a special relationship of *attentiveness* to the literal Word that liberates.

In this case, the churchgoer hears double, or in excess, because it is between the lines of Scripture that the narratives of insurgence are delivered. We address here the requirements of literacy as the ear takes on the functions of "reading."

This essay pursues, then, a fundamental assumption: the religious sentiment and the documents of homiletics that inscribe it bring into play the preeminent mode of discourse by which African-Americans envisioned a transcendent human possibility under captive conditions. It is no accident, either of language or intent, that African-American preachers in the twentieth century have variously chosen the "Eagle" as the figurative embodiment of a thematics of liberation.[3] But just as the Eagle in its emblematic history conflates notions of freedom under military might, just as it elides in a distinct visual field a protocol of the imperialistic and the free, the African-American's relationship to Christianity and the state is marked completely by ambivalence; we could even say that at moments such a relationship gropes toward a radically alternative program. For instance, on November 2, 1845, J. W. C. Pennington—whose powerful narrative of captivity instantly yokes the contents of literacy and conversion to the very same epiphanic instance—preaches a "farewell" sermon on the occasion of his imminent two-year departure from the pulpit of the Fifth Congregational Church of Hartford,

3. The "Eagle" sermon is to the African-American Church what the oikotype is to the folk narrative. See Roger D. Abrahams, *Deep Down in the Jungle: Negro Narrative Folklore from the Streets of Philadelphia* (Hatboro, Penn., 1964). This popular sermonic motif, usually appearing under the title "The Eagle Stirs Her Nest," is featured in sermons preached in various regions of the country, by various preachers, over time. Though the details of the sermon differ according to individual circumstance, the narrative essentially concerns a story of mistaken identity: an eagle turns up in a chicken coop; acquires the behavior of its surroundings, and the farmer of the yard eventually discovers the error. The Schomburg Collection, New York Public Library, New York City, holds in its archives of sermons Rev. E. O. S. Cleveland's "The Eagle Stirring Her Nest" (1946). One of the most celebrated versions of the "Eagle" is preached by the late Rev. C. L. Franklin of Detroit and is available on Chess Records. My family's church in Memphis was pastored from about 1948 to the present by the Rev. L. D. McGhee, Sr. Growing up, I heard this sermon preached once a year. It is obviously a piece of the repertoire that ministers of an older generation—and apparently all of them Baptist—kept at hand.

Connecticut.[4] Developing the rhetorical pivot of the sermon around a central dramatic question—"Does the Bible condemn slavery without any regard to circumstances, or not?"—Pennington *thunders*, we might imagine:

> If you stand commended to the guidance of the Word of God, you are bound to know its position in reference to certain overt acts that crowd the land with curses. Take the last and greatest of the curses that I named above. I mean slavery. Is the word of God silent on this subject? I, for one, desire to know. My repentance, my faith, my hope, my love, and my perseverance all, all, I conceal it not, I repeat it, all turn upon this point. If I am deceived here—if the word of God does sanction slavery, I want another book, another repentance, another faith, and another hope![5]

Pennington's urgent address, just as that of many of the documents of printed religious narratives and sermons from this community of texts, marks the central paradox of an American identity that seeks transformation, has so far evaded resolution, and stays urged toward a dialectical movement.[6] These documents provide systematic access to a spate of discourse that intersects at least two culture maps at an overwhelming problematic: the African-American, long before the barred subject of Lacanian discourse brought it to our attention,

4. For Pennington's narrative, see "The Fugitive Blacksmith; or, Events in the History of James W. C. Pennington, Pastor of a Presbyterian Church, New York, Formerly a Slave in the State of Maryland," in *Great Slave Narratives*, ed. and intro. Arna Bontemps (Boston, 1969), pp. 192–269. The impact of literacy, as the gateway to the "pre-generic myth," is illuminated in Robert B. Stepto's "Teaching Afro-American Literature: Survey or Tradition," in *Afro-American Literature: The Reconstruction of Instruction*, ed. Dexter Fisher and Robert B. Stepto (New York, 1978), pp. 8–25.

5. *A Two Years' Absence or a Farewell Sermon, preached in the Fifth Congregational Church, by J. W. C. Pennington*, Nov. 2, 1845 (Hartford, 1845), pp. 3–31; 22–23. The Moorland-Spingarn Collection, Howard University, Washington, D.C.

6. My work on the rhetoric of Afro-American sermons involves the study of some 300 manuscripts, gathered from the Schomburg Collection of the New York Public Library, New York City, and the Moorland-Spingarn Research Center of Howard University, Washington, D.C. This survey is confined to printed documents preached and narrated by black religious figures from Jupiter Hammon's "A Serious Exhortation" (1782) up to Randall Albert Carter's "Morning Meditations and Other Selections" (1917). The latter marks a strategic and rather arbitrary cut-off point. After World War I, the electronically recorded sermon was possible; that media shift provides this material with another dimension, beyond the immediate aims of my project.

becomes the hyphenated proper noun that belongs neither "here," nor "there." This deferment of place provides the background thematic of this essay, which tracks, more precisely, some of the narrative implications of the stories that certain African-American preachers tell and have told through their sermons and how their parishioners "read" and "hear" them.

The issues that Pennington raises in his address relate very specifically to his own fugitive status, narrated in his autobiography. Pennington's story of escape, conversion, and literacy links contrastive narrative energies to a single line of inquiry: for the captive personality to learn to "read" is not only "mastery" of the inherited texts of his or her culture, but also its *subversion*, or a seeking after those moments that enable a different, or "thickened" reading. The auditors of Pennington's sermon(s) are called upon to perform essentially the same task as Pennington, and that is to read/hear a Gospel message that would now incorporate the "stolen" man or woman. This "drama of a tremendous striving," to borrow W. E. B. Du Bois's more urgent formulation, everywhere insinuates itself into the project of literacy for African-Americans, inasmuch as it defines their fundamental relationship to dominant culture. In that regard, African-American sermons offer a paradigmatic instance of reading as process, encounter, and potential transformation.

Fleeing the scene of captivity and dismemberment is not only Pennington's story and not just the actual move that has brought on the heat of the farewell sermon. It is the thematic implied across the discourse of these sermons. It further suggests the hoped-for definitive motion, I believe, of African peoples in the New World, less "new" now and still delinquent in the fleshing out the vision of a Christian "City on a Hill."[7] The sermon documents addressed here provide an imaginative field of inquiry into the strategies of African survival, evinced on a hostile landscape of social and polit-

7. The colonial outcome of this thematic lends shape to Sacvan Bercovitch's significant study of aspects of an American identity, *The Puritan Origins of the American Self* (New Haven, Conn., 1975). A brilliant counterreading is pursued in the opening chapter of Houston Baker's *Blues, Ideology, and Afro-American Literature* (Chicago, 1984). The magisterial work of Annette Kolodny opens up the entire field of inquiry into origins of American culture to the voices of women: see Kolodny's *The Lay of the Land: Metaphor as Experience and History in American Life and Letters* (Chapel Hill, N.C., 1975); and *The Land Before Her: Fantasy and Experience of the American Frontiers, 1630–1860* (Chapel Hill, N.C., 1984).

ical praxis. We would not exaggerate the case in observing that the sermon, as the African-American's prototypical public speaking, locates the primary instrument of moral and political change within the community. But at crucial times, the sermon not only catalyzes movement, but *embodies* it, *is movement*. We vividly observe such instances in the public career of at least two contemporary figures of recent national life, in the persons of Martin Luther King, Jr., and Malcolm El-Hajj Malik El-Shabazz.[8] Whether or not we encounter the sermon in its customary social context, as the driving words of inspiration and devotion, or in its variously secular transformations and revisions as urgent political address, we perceive it fundamentally as a symbolic form that not only lends shape to the contours and outcome of African-Americans' verbal fortunes under American skies, but also plays a key role in the psychic configurings of their community.

How this is so is not entirely clear to me, but "figuring" it out is the crucial "reading" and execution of my own involvement in the collective. Because the captive's exposure to American Protestantism was more or less immediate, and because she or he came to the New World with, already, a profound religious capacity from the Old World, "religion" for black Americans has never been anything *but* complicated. The sermon, I believe, not only gestures toward these forces, but in a sense, *knots* them up, proffers a syntactic possibility for reading them. The program of reading, hearing, and listening to the sermons yields no metaphor that applies, at once, to all three. But one might say that unknotting this fabric of a complicated national identity brings all three into related play.

I regard African-American sermons as a paradigm of the structure of ambivalence that constitutes the black person's relationship to and apprenticeship in American culture. These documents provide a means for examining the broad and unspoken tensions of that relationship. But what is the risk, though we have considerable prec-

8. Though the forceful contemporaneity of these two figures requires no documentation, I would note one of the most recent studies of King's career: David J. Garrows's *Bearing the Cross: Martin Luther King, Jr., and the Southern Christian Leadership Conference, a Personal Portrait* (New York, 1986). In addition to Alex Haley's co-written *Autobiography of Malcolm X* (New York, 1965), John Henrik Clarke's collection of critical essays, *Malcolm X: The Man and His Times* (New York, 1969), remains one of the best sources for Malcolm X studies.

edent here, for removing the sermon from its accustomed scene—
an architecture that marks it in a more or less isolated spatial economy; a social relationship among discrete subject-positions in a lapse
of difference; a participatory configuration not entirely unlike that
between "audience" and "stage," and above all else, out of the eye
of the storm, so to speak?[9] If James Cone is right, then the best way
to study a sermon is to hear one and to hear it in the customary
context of ritual and consecration.[10] In short, I am as aware as Cone
that an "analysis" of sermons not only scandalizes people who grew
up "in church," but that an analysis also renders sermons, perhaps,
anti-sermons, for an exhortation not heard becomes something else
entirely—maybe. Though we reenact it and though it participates
in a material and commercial dimension when subjected to print
and the bookseller, how might we now describe its new status? To
try and answer those questions, we cannot ask the sermon itself,
since its mission has little to do with the mundane. Yet in trying
to respond to its contents, both on its own ground and against one's
own immediate situation, we are trapped somewhere between the
church doors and the library.

We tread, then, a discursive boundary that must be reached by
certain elaborately observed mediations, hardly exhausted in this
writing: the sermons that I address here are all written and preserved
in that manner and all of them were preached before the twentieth
century. Because the oral/spoken sermon is granted, at the moment,
privileged status in African-American life and thought, we must seek
a place for the written/spoken documents.[11] An American com-

9. The classic reading of the Puritan sermon in the colonial experience is provided
by Perry Miller in his two-volume work, *The New England Mind: From Colony to
Province* (Cambridge, Mass., 1953), and *The New England Mind: The Seventeenth
Century* (New York, 1939). Emory Elliott's *Power and the Pulpit in Puritan New
England* (Princeton, N.J., 1975) rereads the Puritan context against current modes of
literary/theoretical analysis.

10. James Cone, *God of the Oppressed* (New York, 1975).

11. The study of Afro-American oral sermons, or the unwritten, recorded ones,
has attracted a number of researchers. Among the most noted studies are Charles V.
Hamilton, *The Black Preacher in America* (New York, 1972); Henry H. Mitchell,
Black Preaching (Philadelphia, 1970); William H. Pipes, *Say Amen, Brother: Old-
Time Negro Preaching, a Study in American Frustration* (rpt. Westport, Conn., 1970);
Bruce A. Rosenberg, *The Art of the American Folk Preacher* (New York, 1970).
Though the following texts do not focus on sermons, they provide a historic context
for "reading"/"hearing" them: James H. Cone, *Black Theology and Black Power*
(New York, 1969); Arthur Huff Fauset, *Black Gods of the Metropolis: Negro Religious*

munity that reads itself primarily as "oral" and "musical" and remains, in its critical/theoretical disposition, divided between "folklore"/"vernacular" on the one hand, the "literary"/"theory" on the
other, is presently called upon to rethink itself. We have yet to
examine fully the dramatic encounters of New World Africans as
texts and the impact of the latter on the cultural development of
strangers in a strange land. Ages ago, in this land, the book for the
black person was a mysterious (and therefore) precious formula to
be known, precisely because his or her captors did not want them
to know, and the captors actually enacted antiliteracy laws! In that
regard, the "folk" are simply the *thousands* who would immerse
themselves in the knowledge of the world, and that would include,
I suppose, even those illiterate preachers who learned the Gospel by
heart.

The occasion, then, to look at some of the written documents,
now transformed from an immediate vocality into a delayed, or
muted one, long removed from the literal day and the immediate
history of their writing and publication, offers certain advantages.
Black American apprentice-culture and its aftermath problematize
along different lines of stress, as we must now consider the possibilities of the Book—some of the leaves torn out, albeit—as one
other shaping (and powerful) metaphor in a situation that has been
too long narrated as basically *text-deprived*. The written sermons
draw another line of inquiry, intrude another dimension of discursive possibility into our thinking.

Because these sermons were preserved as a writing, they were not
only intended for particular congregations, but to be disseminated
to a larger audience of readers and students of the sermon. We currently have no information regarding the intellectual habits of consumption for a national black readership, but taking two of the
sermons of Rev. J. W. E. Bowen, for example, we might say that his
series of "plain talks" were meant for the "colored people of America." It is doubtful that these particular documents reached their

---

Cults in the Urban North, new intro. by John Szwed (Philadelphia, 1980); C. Eric
Lincoln, ed., *The Black Experience in Religion: A Book of Readings* (Garden City,
N.Y., 1974); Joseph R. Washington, Jr., *The Politics of God: The Future of the Black
Churches* (Boston, 1969). My own study of the sermon style of Martin Luther King,
Jr. (in *The Black Scholar* 3 [September 1971] and reprinted in Lincoln, *Black Expe-
rience in Religion*) led to the writing of my dissertation on the subject, "The Fabrics
of History: Essays on the Black Sermon," Brandeis University, 1974.

putative target, or that their influence stretched much wider than the congregation to which they were preached. But certainly for *that* audience, they served an inspirational function as published material. Historiographically, the sermon documents in their preserved state are useful for rather different reasons: they not only shed light on the habits of public discourse evolved by particular communities, but also suggest an element of self-consciousness intruded on a form popularly thought of as "spontaneous." The written sermon suggests that *no* sermon is without contrivance, or a considerable degree of forethought. If that is so, then the "folk" sermon is actually misnamed, if by "folk" we mean devised on the spot, or plucked from thin air. Not that a written sermon might not sustain an important element of the extemporaneous, but that the sermon itself, written down, or "remembered" from other sermonic practice, inscribes the self-conscious pursuit of form. The written documents imply a certain class of *readers* who might have been, for the most part, the sermons' hearers. In their overlap, these functions induced, we might imagine, the rise of a religious readership that consumed the popular religious journals of the late nineteenth century and the literature produced by the Sunday School movement of the same era.

In offering the student a community of texts and propositions, the sermons help to sketch a concept of "community" in its various and dynamic transmutations. On closer reading, one perceives that the initial "community" of this paragraph seems settled, while the subsequent one stays open to a kind of crisis. But in truth, all "community" in this writing falls into suspension, and we inquire if either version does not, in fact, acquire its density, in part, by an element of the arbitrary. A "community of texts and propositions" offers one way of avoiding "tradition," which appears to gain dominant ground through notions of the dynastic, the hierarchical, and the prior. But "community" seems to hold out the possibility of intervention, of inclusion. For example, the sermons about which I write here are drawn from a "community" at the fundamental level of data—the material belongs to an alphabetical file, photocopied for scholarly use, and comes from two separate archives, both of them located on the East Coast of the United States. Most of them conform to this geographical region, delivered in eastern cities and towns from North Carolina to Vermont. I would not claim here any "master code" sermon, though there are "masterful" documents/performances among them. A different pair of archives, from another part of the country, would soundly intrude upon any conceptual narrative that valorized notions of the "traditional." Though one inevitably privileges one sermon by talking about it and not another, I would much prefer to leave this survey exposed to trends and forces that I have not yet considered, or about which I have no information.

If the possibilities of the survey are virtually endless, we might say that any assertion concerning pieces of it is compromised. The student, however, must be willing to settle for an aspect of an imagined totality, just as one particular thematizing might speak metonymically for the whole that never appears. But is the whole as much a fiction as the part-for-whole in this case? As a totality, or "part-for-whole," a "community" of subject-positions is always a partial effect of some putative plenitude. Yet we *need* the fiction of "community" in order to speak at all. I must say that a few of the familiar terms and assumptions of a currently discredited Western metaphysic—primarily, the stability and primacy of a subject-position and the capacity of a text to *mean*—are reclaimed in this writing as (1) an "imitation" of the material that I address; (2) in order to set this configuration of discourse in place for other and different readings; (3) to suggest that in certain places, at this table, for instance, the subject suspects that it lives on. But just as the concept of "community" takes on complications for this writer, it offers different occasions for analytical discourse *within* the sermons and for those who preach them.

If we think of "community" as the elaboration of a "critical mass" differentiated from others that surround it, then the African-American community in the United States becomes at once distinct within the larger field of American culture and distinct from that series of geopolitical moments that constitute its racial, or African, origins. This precisely segmented portion of American cultural content designates what I have identified before as a *hyphenated* national identity divided in the first instance both from its new situation and severed from the old one. We can either read "community" as homogeneous memory and experience, laying claim to a collective voice and rendering an apparently unified and uniform Narrative, or we might think of it as a content whose time and meaning are "discovered," but a meaning, in any case, that has not already been decided. In other words, "community," in the latter instance, becomes *potentiality*; an unfolding to be attended. One

might go on to say, then, that African-American community articulated in these documents becomes, at times, a systematic elaboration of a particular historical order that one makes up as she or
he goes along, with whatever comes to, and is already at hand; at
other times, an invention of the dominant culture (to the extent
that the violence of captivity has been imposed on the subject).
Needless to say, these processes and positionalities are simultaneous
and progressive, inasmuch as "inner" and "outer" converge in this
case on the subject. By way of this inquiry, we see more clearly that
human culture is both a groping and a given. It is precisely in this
paradoxical sense that "community" for African-Americans has
been an enablement *and* an accommodation.

As an enabling postulate, the sermons provide a strategy of identity for persons forced to operate under a foreign code of culture;
they offer an equipment not only for literacy, but a ground for her-
meneutical play in which the subject gains competence in the interpretation and manipulation of systems of signs and their ground of
interrelatedness. The "reader" of the culture is involved in the interpretation of both texts and "texts"—those actual densities of social
meaning that converge on the terrain of power relations. This latter
"reading" takes place "within" and "outside" texts, while it mandates a wider grasp of relationships than a specific reading might
call for. In other words, reader-as-captive is confronted with what
is spoken and written as well as the immeasurable repertoire of
implications and responses ("nowhere" necessarily inscribed, or ma-
terialized) out of which the situation of dominance and subordination arises. This "reader," then, in participatory readership, is *given*
a history at the same time that she or he seeks to fabricate one. (In
one notable instance, for example, the domestication of Scripture is
achieved as a series of nationalist narratives in which the personas
of Genesis "speak" in the "voices" of the preacher.)[12]

The sermons, preached across denominational and doctrinal differences, actually help create the sense of "a people" forged from a
background of divergent and originating African families. Against a
pattern of radical discontinuity—in every sense, a *rupture* among

---

12. William Hatcher, a white Virginia journalist, contemporaneous with the slave
preacher Rev. John Jasper, has left transcriptions of several of Jasper's sermons: *The
Unmatched Negro Philosopher and Preacher* (New York, 1908). See chapter 3 of
Spillers, "The Fabrics of History."

African languages and "natal communities,"[13] the sermons assert
the same story with significant variation: the liberating word that
Pennington wishes *his* Bible to speak is none other than the "Good
News" of divine force working in the captive situation to free it.
Acting coterminously with this program of cultural development,
however, is the subversive motion of a narrative "underdevelop-
ment." Christianity, in its ability to stand in for "civilization," "patriarchy," "hierarchy," "enlightenment," "progress," "culture"—a
series of lexical items that inaugurate one of the grammars of otherness—renders a text for dominant culture. Since we will spend
the better portion of this essay looking at sermons that offer a narrative of "development," we might examine now a couple of instances that intrude upon this description.

On July 17, 1794, Samuel Magaw delivered the inaugural sermon
of the African Church of Philadelphia. In Richard Allen's "Life Experiences," which sketches the early history of what becomes the
African Methodist Episcopal Church in the United States, there is
no record of this sermon event, nor does Bishop Daniel A. Payne's
History of the African Methodist Episcopal Church carry a reference
to it in Payne's opening chapter.[14] "A Brief History of St. Thomas's
Church," appended to Allen's short "Life," does note this sermon
in a calendar of church events.[15] Remarkable for its structure of
assumptions that both incorporate and eject African personality
from the body of Christianity, Magaw's sermon is brilliantly developed around the topos of light and its generative schema. Magaw
prays that this congregation will keep a lively remembrance of the
mercy that has been proffered to them, for they have been called

13. Barbara Christian's term for "race" moves us much closer to the cultural scene
that illuminates the making of "race" as a social construct: *Black Women Novelists:
The Development of a Tradition, 1892–1976* (Westport, Conn., 1980).

14. "The Life Experience and Gospel Labors of the Rt. Rev. Richard Allen, to which
is annexed the rise and progress of the African Methodist Episcopal Church in the
United States of America. Containing a narrative of the yellow fever in the year of
our Lord 1793. With an address to the People of Color in the United States. Written
by Himself and published by request," intro. by George A. Singleton, the Schomburg
Collection. Bishop Daniel A. Payne, *History of the African Methodist Episcopal
Church* (Philadelphia, 1922).

15. "Chronology of St. Thomas' M. E. Church" carries a full entry on this sermon
and notes Rev. Samuel Magaw as the rector of St. Paul's Church (cataloged in the
Schomburg Collection with Allen's "Life Experience").

"out of the darkness of paganism, and the bondage of ignorance and error into the clear light of Gospel Revelation."[16] The sermon offers an exemplary exposition in the use of binary modes. We see in operation not only the play of contrarieties, but a contradiction that takes on teleological status: the fixed otherness, for which the "world" of "pagan" stands and for which African personality and its progeny materialize, situates in natural opposition to Judeo-Christian culture.

These hallowed and hollowed signifieds, or subjects without verbs, so to speak, show essentially no historical movement (just as Hegel, in the nineteenth century, declared for all of the African continent south of Egypt, and for the whole of the Americas with its indigenous populations). Magaw's sermon invites attention to those structures of belief that make it possible to install African/African-American person on the landscape of social praxis as the very embodiment of anomie, as that almost-human principle that occupies the vestibular culture—"The people that walked in darkness have seen a great light" (Isaiah 9:2). From one point of view, seeing is not believing, or *seeing* alone falls short of the Promised Land. Yet St. Thomas's congregants, according to Magaw, have been prepared for a total beneficence under the rule of Christianity, despite their dark-skinned selves.

To take a different case, we situate Magaw's words in perspective with those of William Miller, from a sermon delivered on the occasion of the abolition of the African slave trade, January 1, 1810, to the African Church of New York:

> I cannot forego the satisfaction of expressing my acknowledgment to my brethren, for having conferred on me the honor of addressing them from the pulpit, on an occasion so auspicious to Africans as the celebration of a day, the contemplation of which is sufficient to inspire the heart of every African with fervent gratitude to the throne of grace, for having directed the councils of our legislature and the parliament of Great Britain, to the consideration of the deplorable and ignominious condition of Africans and their descendants; and in opening a

16. Samuel Magaw, "Discourse Delivered July 17, 1794, in the African Church of the City of Philadelphia, on the occasion of opening the said church, and holding public worship in it the first time. . . . Divine service introduced with select scripture passages, and a special prayer, and then proceeding in its usual offices, having been performed by James Abercrombie" (Philadelphia, W. W. Woodward), pp. 9–24, the Schomburg Collection.

way for their relief, by prohibiting that abominable traffic, the Slave Trade.[17]

Miller goes on to evoke the litany of a great African past, pointing out that the decline and abasement of African peoples were largely initiated by the Moors and exploited by the Europeans. As Miller approaches the closure of the sermon, we encounter that structure of semantic attention that would suggest this document as an able candidate for a "confounded" or complicated reading. In other words, "Africa" in this sermon demarcates a site of degradation at the same time that Miller embraces it as a point of cultural origin. In fact, Miller appears to approach the sociopolitical sensibilities of the Black Nationalist movement of the 1960s in imagining "Africa" in continuity with African-Americans in the Diaspora. "Our *improved* state in the arts" implies a "before" and "after" that link continental African culture and the current situation of African-Americans to the same spatiotemporal modality.

As a step toward "raising" the Africans, he would have it, Sierra Leone was carved out of the West Africa coast by Great Britain in 1789, and numbers of missionaries sent there "for the identical purposes of civilizing and improving the continent." Then, says Miller, "although we cannot, consistent with our feelings, thank the oppressors of our forefathers for bringing them to the civilized world, yet when we compare our improved state in the arts to the state of improvement and civilization in Africa, we are ready to cry to God, individually, like David, 'It is good for me that I have been afflicted, that I may learn thy statutes, the law of thy mouth is better unto me than thousands of pure gold and silver.' "[18]

Conceding little or nothing to a contemporary sensibility and "self-consciousness" that delight in the "undecidability" of the current order of things, from literary historiography, to gender and sexual positionalities, Miller's address poses its own embarrassment of riches. Situated in an abeyance of closure, Miller appears to speak out of both sides of his mouth, and it seems that this double-speaking precisely characterizes African-American apprentice-culture and its

17. William Miller, "A Sermon on the Abolition of the Slave Trade Delivered in the African Church, New York on the First of January, 1810 ... Published by request of the Committee" (New York, 1810), pp. 3–16, the Spingarn Collection.
18. Ibid.

latter-day manifestations. Miller is not alone in the use of certain major figures of thought available to him regarding continental Africans in their autochthonous cultural enterprise. Alongside Miller's sermon, we could place Jupiter Hammon's "Winter Piece" and some of Phillis Wheatley's shorter poems from the same era of writing and history in the mid-to-late eighteenth century.[19]

Yet to dismiss these writings as inadequate political response would generate, in turn, its own critical inadequacy. We are called upon instead to try to grasp more completely the "Rule of Gospel Order" in the life of an unfolding national purpose, whose religious impulse tends toward the enthusiastic. "The intense emphasis upon conversion," Albert Raboteau argues, "the primary characteristic of evangelical, revivalistic Protestantism, tended to level all men before God as sinners in need of salvation. This tendency opened the way for black converts to participate actively in the religious culture of the new nation as exhorters, preachers, and even founders of churches, and created occasions of mutual religious influence across racial boundaries whereby blacks converted whites and whites converted blacks in the heat of revival fervor."[20] The charismatic itinerancy of England's methodist preachers—among them, George Whitefield, the subject of address of one of Phillis Wheatley's eulogies—provides an impetus to revivalistic religion in the pre-Revolutionary colonies of North America.[21] But as vulnerable as the captive community was to the will of its captors, there was no sparing its members from the influences—for good or ill—of a democratic religious force. Historians point out that the Great Awak-

---

19. Jupiter Hammon, "A Winter Piece: Being a Serious Exhortation with a call to the Unconverted: And a short Contemplation on the Death of Jesus Christ written by Jupiter Hammon, a Negro Man belonging to Mr. John Lloyd, of Queen's Village, on Long Island, now in Hartford. Published by the author with the assistance of his Friends" (Hartford, Conn., 1782), the Moorland Collection. William H. Robinson's *Early Black American Poets* carries Phillis Wheatley's "On Being Brought to America" and several other Wheatley poems under the category "Formalist Poets" (Dubuque, Iowa, 1969). See also M. A. Richmond's *Bid the Vassal Soar: Interpretive Essays on the Life and Poetry of Phillis Wheatley and George Moses Horton* (Washington, D.C., 1974).

20. Albert J. Raboteau, *Slave Religion: The "Invisible" Institution in the Antebellum South* (New York, 1978), p. 152.

21. See Robinson, *Early Black American Poets:* "On the Death of the Rev. Mr. George Whitefield." See also "Phillis Wheatley's Methodist Connection" by Samuel J. Rogal, in *Black American Literature Forum* 21 (Spring/Summer 1987): 85–97.

ening of the mid-eighteenth century demarcates one of four crucial
stages in the Christianizing of Africans.[22]

We observe that the period engendered its own paradoxes: as the
"free" community contemplated its own liberational plan, the captive community became immured in its condition, as the slave codes
of various southern states assured that conversion and manumission
were not synonymous. It must be true, however, that the "Rule of
Gospel Order" became the flaming sword that cut two ways. If the
captive could make the Gospel "speak" his or her own state, then
the subversion of dominance was entirely possible. So powerful a
force must therefore reduce the "world" to a single human order.
Read from this perspective, an "unchristian" "Africa" lost its use
for the captive person, now "freed" by the Single and Singular Truth.
Even though the erasure of ethnicity from its capital place in the
social configuration strikes the contemporary mind as a blunder, we
recognize that the impact of "race" conceals the profound question
of culture. By 1794, the year of Magaw's address to the Philadelphia
church; by 1810, the year of William Miller's "schizophrenic" embrace and denial of "Africa," the black person in the United States
is already adrift between two vast continents, both in his or her body
and brain.

Because a contemporary audience has no ready analogy with
which to gauge the impact of kerygmatic religion, the world view
purported by certain of these sermons appears alien, and perhaps
"ambivalence," as the controlling metaphor of my own conceptual
narrative, is nothing more than a different term for emotional distance. But if by ambivalence we might mean that abeyance of closure, or *break* in the passage of syntagmatic movement from one
more or less stable property to another, as in the radical disjuncture
between "African" and "American," then ambivalence remains not
only the privileged and arbitrary judgment of a postmodernist imperative, but also a strategy that names the new cultural situation
as a *wounding*. We recall the undeniable catachresis buried in "African Methodist Episcopal Church" itself, for example, as historic
and narrative cross-purposes elide into an imagined unity of religious
organization and praxis.

22. Sydney E. Ahlstrom, *A Religious History of the American People* (New Haven,
Conn., 1972), p. 3, "The Century of Awakening and Revolution" and p. 6, "Slavery
and Expiation."

Because Christianity identifies the cultural ground upon which one stands and for that reason, precisely, is not always immediately visible, we might assume that the "crisis of faith" has no particular efficacy in this analysis, but how is it possible, or is it possible, to bracket "belief" in reference to a structure of human attention that looks back, ultimately, to the primary text of Judeo-Christian synthesis? To questions that might best be negotiated by sacred theology and the vastly empowered patriarchal traditions of hermeneutics and interpretation, reverting, in turn, to the first post-Christian centuries and the canonical urgencies to establish the right texts and ground for legitimation?[23] The response that I would sketch to this self-inquiry scatters in different directions. (1) If one accepts the posture of critical insurgency, then the contradictions of *speaking through* the alien and foreign notation are visibly raised; (2) but the posture of a critical insurgency must be achieved. It cannot be assumed. Essentially, the test of "belief" that is crucial to our purposes here has less to do with the Word of God, or words pertaining to God, than with the words and texts of human community in their liberational and enslaving power, refracted in the Gospel. We stand here. Without doubt, the Good News that the New World African understood and preached, in its radical *this*-worldliness, speaks to us in ways that we had not anticipated, and that is to say, that the words and texts of human encounter, of which the Gospel provides an Ur-text, render the most powerful and dangerous "making" that we can imagine. The insurgent critical activity acting upon that encounter becomes the very Gospel reenacted both in its transformative potential and as it actually arises in the inclusionary praxis of an altered social scene. Is it too much to say that the African could not *but* have become a Christian in the sociopolitical context of the United States, as a *strategy* for gaining his or her historical

23. An impressive array of feminist scholarship has effected powerful intervention on the assumptions that cluster around patriarchist religion. Among these are included Mary Daly, *Beyond God the Father: Toward a Philosophy of Women's Liberation* (Boston, 1973); Rosemary Radford Ruether, *Sexism and God-Talk: Toward A Feminist Theology* (Boston, 1983). Ruether and Rosemary Skinner Keller are also the general editors of Harper and Row's *Women and Religion in America* series. Its first volume was published in New York in 1981: *The Nineteenth Century: A Documentary History*.

ground and humanation here? And is the preacher and the sermon the first-run event of an African *critical* subject-position in such a context? These questions loom before us in an investigation that straddles this (our current situation in the world) and that (the ever-deferred perfections of a *becoming*). Between worlds stands the sermon. With both feet planted in the actual mess of human being, the sermon would convince the chicken that it is an eagle.

In trying to find a way, over time, to address this often familiar material now made alien by our own habits of language and current critical practices, one decides that the sermon reenacts a ritual and necessary fable, a fable whose actants and end are already known. An aspect of the sermon's miracle is that its audience already knows that there are no suspended or ironic conclusions to the tales that sermons project. In fact, there is only *one* sermonic conclusion, and that is the ultimate triumph over defeat and death that the Resurrection promises. In this case, the processes of hearing/reading lose their character of uncertainty in the Single Surprise that matters. I would go so far as to say that this rewarded anticipation of an outcome is the most prominent feature of temperament in a reading/auditory variable that distinguishes an African-American readership from other constituent reading communities trained in and on the economies of irony. It is important to add that these communities of readers are often interchangeable; they do not stay fixed. The sermon itself has formal success only to the extent that the preacher knows that his or her "readers" *choose* to agree with the sermon "contract"—to obey the rules of listenership that obtain in the situation.

One of those "rules" of behavior would suggest to the reader/hearer that the sermon's repetitive character does nothing to mitigate the suspenseful eschatology that the Gospels inscribe concerning the life, career, and death of Jesus Christ. The annual Protestant sermons of the Christmas and Easter rituals, for example, in their insistence on mercy and forgiveness, do not suffer because the hearer knows the story both "by heart" and from the Book, but appear to gain prestige for the narratives they tell by way of this process. To say the same thing over and over again not only induces a headache of conviction, but creates a *fellowship* of belief. The ritual narrative in this way bears an element of infection; everyone is compelled toward the same story.

Roland Barthes called the revelation of an already anticipated subject and outcome the "hermeneutic narrative." He wrote, "Just as any grammar, however new, once it is based on the dyad of subject and predicate, noun and verb, can only be a historical grammar, linked to classical metaphysics, so the hermeneutic narrative, in which truth predicates an incomplete subject, based on expectation of and desire for its imminent closure, *is dated*, linked to the kerygmatic civilization of meaning and truth, appeal and fulfillment."[24] The sermons addressed here demarcate an incomparable "hermeneutic narrative," and it would appear that they succeed precisely because they project an incomplete subject, engendered in the expectation of and desire for the imaginably blissful end of truth. But as *dated* as this narrative process is, and more, as "unprogressive" as the relevant reading sensibilities are, the "hermeneutic narrative" for the sermon's "readers" matches—perfectly—the "end" of the world; in the black community, this is Freedom, and the "beginning."

To say that these sermons exert a pull on the hearer is to reassert what we already know, but the dynamics of this exertion remain somewhat unclear. No narrative genre appears to depend so solidly upon the cooperative agency at work in others. The sermon seeks to *inculcate* its words; to make them enter the hearer, and this would account for the rhetorical tenacity of the form, as we will see shortly in two of J. W. E. Bowen's performances. The sermon's rhetoric of admonition appears to behave on a contrastive analogy with dramatic form. Whereas the latter marks a verbalization through a material scene, a sermon inscribes a verbalization that substitutes "hearer" for "stage." To that extent, the "scene" of the sermon opens into an interior space, and here it seeks to enact and reenact its narrative urgencies against an invisible scenic apparatus. In the interior of the listener, doubt is subjected to severe criticism, as the sermon is grounded, without apology, in the conviction of human error. In the interior space, a repertoire of feeling is aroused to heightened consciousness. Though the sermon embodies a particular form, its primary function may well be transcultural, subject to a number of narrative and thematic variations, for it is public discourse, ideologically sanitized, it would seem, that cannot execute its program without a hearer, in this case, a "reader."

Even though the confrontation with the small, helpless self is accomplished in the Protestant sermon of the insurgent through the

24. Roland Barthes, *S/Z*, trans. Richard Miller (New York, 1974), p. 76, my emphasis.

rhetoric of admonition, the confrontation itself becomes enabling, because the relationship between pulpit and parishioner has shifted: *both* subject-positions now occupy a common ground of inquiry, a common ground of suffering.

In order to demonstrate how certain black sermons call forth the interpretive project as it points both toward this world and the transcendent human possibility, I would like to look closely at two sermons from the Reverend J. W. E. Bowen's "What Shall the Harvest Be?" Even though I have examined these texts as if they were literary documents, I have also attempted to situate my own hearing, first of all, within the imagined context of the particular setting of the church and, second, within the immediate history of the climate in which these sermons were rendered. What one loses as a participant on the spot one gains after the fact. As a writing, Bowen's sermons offer a remarkable analogy and reading of *history as process*, in specific reference to African-Americans. As spoken address, they are not recoverable to a listening ear, except that I have "repeated" them according to the dictates of my own readerly responses. In other words, Bowen's "voice" and "personality" are none other than a current articulation for the strategies of a specific cultural management. On balance, the net result for different audiences, far removed in time and circumstance, might be amazingly similar: a certain reading/hearing of history ordains *struggle*, or *movement* as the key text of human community in general and African-American community in particular.

These sermons provide a demonstration of the rhetoric of admonition; but they also suggest, as a result, how the symptoms of "hermeneutic narrative" bring its lost, wounded subject into view. Moving on down the line, Bowen anticipates the future as he comprehends past and present in a narrative sweep that "explains" the inexplicable. Is it not at least ironic, if not altogether devastating, that the Christian witness, insinuating itself throughout the colonial experience and parallel to the captivity and enslavement of some 10 million African persons in the New World, not only attracted the religious loyalties of much of that captive population, but also described the primary discourse of its radically altered historic situation? Operating under a vivid fiction of the "powers of presence," these sermons *make it all right*.[25] But isn't *that* the trouble, that

25. See note 2.

we must become reconciled to death? In the closing sections of this essay, I will attempt to provide a systematic reading of Bowen's response.

William J. Simmons's *Men of Mark: Eminent, Progressive, and Rising* was published in 1887 and carried some 1,300 biographical entries, which provided, in Ernest Kaiser's words, "a much needed dictionary of Negro biography . . . of nearly all of the great and near-great Negro men of history."[26] This work's publication occurred in Bowen's thirty-second year, at which time he was preaching in Newark, New Jersey, but *Men of Mark* makes no note of him. We can only guess, then, how Bowen might have been characterized in the hortatory rhetoric of Simmons's late-century prose. It is important to observe that, even though death interrupted the biographer's plan to make a comparable volume of black American women, both Simmons and Bowen conceive of history as a grand affair of men. From this point of view, a race, a people must think its way back through the *fathers*, if they will claim their rightful human place. This version of history becomes less odd, once we contemplate it in the light of the African-American male's peculiar status in a decidedly phallocentric, slaveholding America: for all intents and purposes, *banished* (not absent) from their issue, African-American males were moved to make themselves twice over—once, with regard to female and family, whom they are theoretically obligated to protect, and again, in light of the phallic economies of naming and empowerment by which standard they are measured, *qua* male. It is probably no simple sexist maneuver (if any such gesture can ever be called merely simple) that drives a William Simmons to collect information *first* on black American men, which would exhaust two or three volumes of paperback on today's market, or a J. W. E. Bowen to found his narratives of history on a reconstituted, reconstructed male subject. We might say that men of their class, of their generation, did the right thing for the wrong reasons, or the wrong thing for reasons that seemed right to them, given the cultural imperatives of high heterosexism under which they operated.[27] In other words, I am

26. Kaiser quotes from William J. Simmons in his preface to *Men of Mark: Eminent, Progressive, and Rising* (Cleveland, Ohio, 1887).

27. Wilson J. Moses, in "The Lost World of the Negro, 1895–1919: Black Literary and Intellectual Life before the 'Renaissance,'" *Black American Literature Forum*

prepared for Bowen's "problem" with the pronouns and the man-
noun and would consider this problematic fit for another study.

Cornel West's impressive work on the points of intersection between aspects of revolutionary Christianity and Marxist thought
would help us place Bowen's ministry. West identifies four distinct
phases of "black prophetic theology" in the United States. His second stage, designated the "Black Theology of Liberation as Critique
of Institutional Racism," covers the period 1864–1969, which embraces Bowen's years. Occupying a little over a century, West's second movement comprehends the careers, also, of Francis L. Grimké,
Howard Thurman, and Martin Luther King, Jr., among others. Because Martin Luther King won renewed respect for the national black
clerical community, these years are among the most crucial of
West's outline. The period "found black prophetic Christians prin-
cipally focusing attention on the racist institutional structures in
the United States which rendered the majority of black people politically powerless (deprived of the right to vote or participate in
governmental affairs), economically exploited (in dependent positions as sharecroppers or in unskilled jobs), and socially degraded
(separate, segregated, and unequal eating and recreational facilities,
housing, education, transportation, and police protection)."[28] It is
against this background of social and political deprivation that the
African-American pulpit of these years becomes, in certain notable
instances, a different version of the church militant.

We recall that 1892, for example, the year that Bowen preached
these sermons to his members of Washington, D.C.'s Asbury Methodist Episcopal Church, is not very far removed from 1878 and the
congressional compromise that brought to closure the Union's military occupation of the Old Confederacy and generated the entire
configuration of backlash that would essentially revoke Fifteenth
Amendment rights and other constitutional guarantees granted to
the newly emancipated. Out of this violent turnaround which mod-
ulated into the southern "Reign of Terror," in the awful, new specter
of the Klansman's robe and lynching rope, much of contemporary
United States history is engendered. It is safe to say that the pulpit

---

21 (Spring/Summer 1987): 61–85, looks at some of the issues that contextualized the
period in which Bowen preached.

28. Cornel West, *Prophesy Deliverance! An Afro-American Revolutionary Christianity* (Philadelphia, 1982), pp. 102–3.

of the 1890s and the turn of the century—whose merciful God was evoked to bear witness against the invidious protocol of racist doctrine, pursued by the national press and excoriated in the sermons of D.C.'s Francis Grimké—was embattled in every sense by the social and political ecologies in which the Church Insurgent is situated.[29]

The 1928–29 edition of *Who's Who in Colored America* records Bowen's December 1855 birth in New Orleans.[30] Some five degrees were conferred on him, including the Doctors of Philosophy and Divinity, both from the Gammon Theological Seminary (now absorbed into Atlanta's Interdenominational Theological Center). A teacher of remarkable versatility, Rev. Bowen also served Gammon in top administrative posts between the late 1890s and the late 1920s. Writer and editor, Bowen became a prominent figure of the official establishment of the Methodist Episcopal Church. According to Carter G. Woodson, Bowen missed election to the regular bishopric of the church by a hair.[31] Into this recorded eminence, John Hope Franklin intruded a note of terror: during the month of September 1906, one of the most sensational race riots in the country occurred in Atlanta. On the riot's second day, "Dr. J. W. E. Bowen, the president of Gammon, was beaten over the head with a rifle butt by a police official."[32]

Years earlier, Bowen was ministering to the congregants of Asbury Methodist Episcopal Church, and during the months of January and February 1892 he delivered the series of sermons that his Official Board would request him to disseminate: "Resolved: That the Official Board heartily endorse and unanimously approve of the ideas

29. Together, the Schomburg and the Moorland-Spingarn Collections carry a number of Grimké's sermons. Carter G. Woodson's *Works of Francis James Grimké*, 4 vols. (Washington, D.C., 1942) explores, in addition to the sermons, the addresses, meditations, thoughts, and letters. Volume 1 provides a study of Grimké's life. Related to Sara and Angelina Grimké on the "black" side of this white South Carolina slaveholding family, Grimké became one of the most eminent Afro-American figures of the turn of the century and beyond. Grimké preached through the 1930s and, like W. E. B. Du Bois, gives the impression of having lived "forever." The intensity of Grimké's sermons "burns" the consciousness in a manner comparable to J. W. E. Bowen's.

30. *Who's Who in Colored America: A Biographical Dictionary of Notable Living Persons of African Descent*, ed. Joseph J. Boris (New York, 1929), p. 43.

31. Carter G. Woodson, *The History of the Negro Church* (Washington, D.C., 1921), p. 275.

32. John Hope Franklin, *From Slavery to Freedom*, 3d ed. (New York, 1969), p. 441.

expressed by our pastor... in the series of sermons entitled 'What Shall the Harvest Be?' delivered in our Church during the past four weeks; and we unite in requesting him to publish the same pamphlet form for distribution with the conviction that a general reading of the same will produce a healthful moral effect upon us as a people."[33]

Sermonic form in general is not shy, nor does it believe that ego-particularity matters very much. In the case of the African-American pulpit, the Gospel remains the greatest glory of a democratic governance, and vice versa. The sermon invests in the fundamental belief that the Gospel and democracy are complementary forces and that a message emphatically delivered actually generates conviction. In the case of Bowen's sermons, his parishioners, at least, equate "healthful moral effect," assertive speaking, and the unitarian appeal of a free peoplehood. The notion that once "the people" read these sermons they will be changed reenforces the sense of urgency out of which the texts come.

Many of the written sermons of African-American preachers found their way to print and a wider public because their audience first made the request.[34] We might assume, however, that the minister spoke, in the initial instance, from a text already prepared, as Coretta Scott King observed about her husband's celebrated address, "I Have a Dream," delivered at Lincoln's Memorial in 1963.[35] Because the sermon appears to "think" itself as "message," its seams cannot show. In other words, the sermon is successful to the extent that it conceals its efforts to *be* a text. This is appropriate behavior for words that proffer themselves as a divine prosthesis and as the crucial strong words in the formal history of a people. Because we now have the capacity, as in King's case, to compare a written text with the electronically recorded one, we can better conjecture the play of mediation between the premeditated word and the extemporaneous tongue that literally "arises," unexpectedly, on the cutting

33. J. W. E. Bowen, "A National Sermon; or a series of plain talks to the Colored People of America, on their Problems" (Washington, D.C., 1902), pp. 12–87, the Schomburg Collection. This quotation is from p. 12; hereafter page numbers are cited in the text.

34. Some of the sermons of this survey are published as "practice," or paradigmatic sermons, for example, James Walker Hood's "The Negro in the Christian Pulpit; or two characters and two destinies, as delineated in twenty-one practical sermons" (Raleigh, N.C., 1884), the Spingarn Collection.

35. Coretta Scott King, *My Life with Martin Luther King, Jr.* (New York, 1969), p. 239.

edge of the hot, crowded, public event. In Bowen's case, the stutters, the haltings, the play and plasticity of the human face "in motion" with its speaking, the peculiar dynamics of the voice in occasional "forgetfulness" of the paragraph in front of it, have been excised from the page; no meddling and meticulous editorial hand, of either the preacher, or any of the auditory, has left its mark.

In response to his board's request, Bowen assumes a typical pose of theatrical modesty, publicly witnessed, as the "disclaimer" marks out its own discursive ground: "The writer of these sermons makes no such pretentious claim as to have sounded the depths or to have given the final word upon the vital questions herein touched upon. All that can be claimed is that they are the honest convictions of an honest student of history and of the affairs of men, delivered for the good of the race" (p. 12). As we have observed before, this modulation of a theological praxis into a key of social and political militance effects common ground between the ministries of such figures as J. W. E. Bowen and Martin Luther King more than fifty years later. More precisely, we might argue that the already political and historic matrix of theological discourse and practice is clearly revealed at certain points of spatiotemporal impression. Bowen makes his own intentions quite clear: "I call particular attention to the 'Manhood Problem' as the one that takes priority in importance and consideration. I also refer to what is popularly known as the 'Negro Problem,' and to its all-comprehending feature. 'Political Equality,' as secondary and as existing only because the first and great problem remains unsolved. I believe that the solution of the first will dissipate the second as the sun scatters the morning dew" (pp. 12–13).[36]

Clearly, Bowen alludes in the "Preface" to the necessity for a systematic ontological dimension concerning the life and thought of African-Americans, but it is not until W. E. B. Du Bois writes his *Souls of Black Folk* (1903) that the question of manhood acquires a radically different formulation. The Du Boisian "double-consciousness," with its Hegelian overtones, proposes at once a paradigm shift and a different discursive code through which "colored," "Negro," "black" might be restated. With Du Bois, "black," as a

36. Alain Locke's celebrated 1925 volume, *The New Negro* (New York), a miscellany of critical and creative work by Afro-Americans, suggests a contrast between the "New Negro" and the "Negro Problem."

preeminent situation of culture, gains contemplative status that will
be elaborated some decades later in the stunning fictional project of
Ralph Ellison's *Invisible Man*. In the absence of an epistemic formula that might have provided a more adequate reading of the prob-
lematics of culture and society, Bowen, near the turn of the century,
dramatically offers, nonetheless, the critical content of an agonistic
and "hermeneutic" narrative that re-visions human society by way
of African-American person. We might restate Bowen's interrogation
along the lines of an analogy: if Hegel wished to make philosophy
"speak German," then Bowen, in these sermons, projects the processes of humanation as they "speak" and iconize as "black." He
narrates the fundamental human rhythm, as we have already observed, as a *movement* of the spirit through history, metaphorically
configured as a progression from "darkness" to "light." Inasmuch
as every human community must negotiate this motion, African-
Americans are enjoined to confront their future as an inevitable
overcoming. But in the structure of "What Shall the Harvest Be?"
this motion *toward* . . . is dramatically focused as "struggle."

Bowen's idea of historic movement in struggle is explored system-
atically in the second sermon of the series, "The Disciplinary Character of Affliction," wherein he asserts for "discipline" and
"punishment" the "iron hand of law" that brings a nation or race
to maturity. Passing through successive periods of growth, a nation
or race, like man, like *a* man, "must subject itself to the discipline
peculiar to the periods, each in its order, that it may become a fit
heir to the blessings and fruits of the following, and in order that it
may realize the possibilities of each to its fullest extent" (p. 33). The
law must be "engraved" upon the conscience, just as "violence,
unrestraint, sensuality, and disrespect for law must be beaten out
of the racial system with the iron hand of law" (p. 34). A race, in
order to reach this high conception of law, "requires many years of
discipline and years of affliction." This disciplinary regime prepared
the Puritan nation for July 4, 1776, and January 1, 1863, "the might-
iest days in the Christian calendar since the birth of Christ." Without its "afflictions, trials, wars, defeats, deaths, and successes, and
withal its juridical morality," the "full realization of its majority
among the nations of the world" could not have been accomplished
(pp. 35–36).

Bowen not only has before him the "rise" of the United States
and the ancient history of Israel, attested by Scripture, but also

intimations of a great African past, whose legendary script is invoked in the opening sermon of this four-part series. Both the "Negro Problem" and the "Manhood Problem" are linked, through a series of mediating questions, to a narrative of the "fallen" continent/man. Against this interrogation, interlocking several parts—"whether the Negro will vindicate for himself a right to stand among the thinking nations of the world, and to claim citizenship by contributing to the thoughtful and material products of civilization in the republic of thought" (p. 23)—Bowen infers a *counternarrative* that leans on the American Negro's regaining his "pristine position in arts and sciences, in literature and history, in architecture and philosophy; the position that he held in his original home: whether he will come back to the heights from which he had fallen; to a civilization second only to this Christian civilization in that it lacked the touch of a divine afflatus" (pp. 23–24).

   This swerve off the trajectory of culture development, which, for Bowen, culminates in the plight of the American Negro, makes for no simple rupture. It has exploded, in fact, an originating continuity:

> For, be it remembered, that in his original home there reigned once "all the pomp and magnificence of oriental splendor; that the grandest ruins of antiquity are here; that architecture has here been carried to a perfection which baffled the skill of modern artisans; that here flourished large and beautiful cities filled with literary, military and commercial men; that Europe is indebted to Africa for letters and arts; that Greece even traces her civilization to Egypt; and that while all Europe was covered with gross darkness, Africa was radiant with science and literature. Astronomy was taught in African schools before Germany had heard of a schoolhouse. Africans were clothed in purple and dwelt in palaces when Englishmen covered themselves with skins of wild beasts and crawled into low mud huts nothing superior to those now occupied by the Kaffirs and Hottentots." This is the second or manhood problem, and I ask what people under the sun has its equal? [Pp. 23–24]

This text of History, covered over now by the radically altered situation of the African in the New World, belongs, astonishingly, to the past *and* the future. It is past-oriented in the procession of past/past-progressive tense verbs that crowd the quoted excerpt of the citation; the adverbial marker, "once," the distinguishing "not now" of the fairytale, clearly evinces a reversal of script in the current one out of which Bowen's address gains efficacy. But this spectacular narrative orients also toward the future, belonging to the "golden age . . . before us, somewhere in the dim tracery of the future" (p. 18). "Upon the shoulders of [this] past," Bowen and congregants stand to gain the capacity to "detect and depict, in the gray dawn of the new morning," events to come (but now *repeated*) and "to read between the lines the story of the age" (p. 22).

To "augur" is "reading" deeply, as Bowen, in the hortative mood— "let us stand"—mandates the visionary and the literate response. In this moving overlap of a double-seeing, the American Negro, the African-American "reads" what his or her culture has made "dim" and what they can barely detect between the lines of script that "come up" into view. It is this making the text plain in this series of "plain talks" that Bowen addresses in these sermons.

Bowen's found *and* made text participates in opposing realities, but those realities are antipathetic, in his view, because human society remains intransigent to providential will, made plain in the Scripture. Though divine order has already written the answer to the "Manhood Problem" and the "Negro Problem," by implication, the race itself must bring it to bear. Two propositions obtain here. On the one hand, Bowen asserts that "God has hidden somewhere in the unrevealed future the solution of all these problems which so vex and disturb us today" (p. 26). On the other hand, a people "that would be free must strike the first blow: and this race, if it is to be counted, must resolutely set itself to the answering of the question, What shall *we* do for ourselves? It must give up the unreasonable and unhistorical basis of expecting to have its future made for it, and begin with might and main to write its own history and make its own future" (pp. 27–28, Bowen's emphasis).

"Writing" and "making," as different aspects of the same visionary moment, are literally and figuratively determined. But these processes of making are not at all polite activity, nor must we assume that the rule of kindness oversees their production. Writing the collective self into history belongs to the offices of affliction, as Bowen would see it, and even though we might use a different *lexis* for the agonistic now, we understand the same thing in reference that Bowen understood—no human community is admitted to fellowship, or the essential right to "self-determination," without undergoing the ways and means of confrontational violence.

If African-Americans have been "taught" anything under the regimes of New World domination, it adheres in the very close analogy between dominant behavior and the *shape* of information in which it is conveyed.[37] If "I am" captive and under dominance, there can be no doubt of this "reading" in the woundings and rendings of "my" flesh. As African-Americans read their own history in the United States, the *wounded, divided* flesh opens itself to a metaphorical rendering both for the principle of self-determination and as a figurative economy for its peculiar national encounter. In other words, one seeks an adequate expression of equivalence, in "reading" the culture, between the situation of captivity and its violent markings. The *imprint* of words articulates with "inscriptions" made on the material body, so that an actual "reading" of captivity brings us to consider those changes in the very tissue-life of the organism; to consider those differences of nuance inflicted on individual and collective identities, which help create the American regime of difference that only the Gospel, from a certain perspective, can reconcile or satisfy. We do not wonder, then, that the narratives of ancient Israel shadow Bowen's sermons, nor are we surprised that the narratives, specifically, of the wonderful deliverance of the Jews from their Egyptian overlords, render a central metaphor of African-American religious expression. Though "Old Pharoah" is situated in a specific historical sequence, "it" has the power to come again. This repetitive potential underscores Bowen's vision of history and the figures of an instrumental, cleansing violence that bolster it.

The procession of suffering configured in Bowen's narrative marks the human scene as fateful movement. At the same time, we are bound to an outcome that is both known and delayed: "The sorrowful chapter of our afflictions, when held up before the light of Revelation, reveals between the lines the grand story of the divine purpose" (p. 23). This intersticial narrative—read in an interface between the given text of the apocalyptic vision and the unwritten texts of future, ordained by it—becomes precisely the "invisible" line that the collective must make manifest; must "practice," must "write" into history as its own powerful tale of human freedom. *This* speaker and his hearers/readers now embody the content of a different narrative that would make positively distinct the *African* element of an American identity. At the same time "human"/"humanity" is now read in the light of "African-American." As an unex-

---

37. The problematic of the analogical dimensions of art is explored in the opening chapter of Armstrong's *Powers of Presence.*

plored narrative resource, black personality elaborates human freedom as a single chapter of "transition" between the "beginning" and the "end."

"The Disciplinary Character of Affliction," the second sermon in the series, not only provides the high point, but also distinguishes itself as a testing ground for Bowen's gifts. Energized by the tensions of this particular moment in the culture career of black Americans and called upon to display the full range of sermonic mastery for which his own career has prepared him, Bowen reaches toward the forceful concision that will urgently declare the meaning and import of his ministry. He pleads, he prays, he urges, he hopes, he knows, in a supreme agitation of feeling that conveys its message the long distance between an immediate history and the present. We read this climactic movement in three parts:

(1) It seems to be in the very constitution of affairs that affliction is necessary to bring out our virtues. All races before us that have made a history worth reading, have had to suffer and to write it with the crimson ink that came from their veins. The Asiatic nations of ancient history and the European nations, likewise, all have been obligated to pass through the fires of afflictions, discipline and punishment to purify their gold. [P. 39]

(2) I am a strong believer in the future destiny of greatness for my people. I believe that God has kept hid from us all, what he has in store for us; and that in the future, when the race shall have been purged in the furnace of afflictions, and its virtues shall sparkle like burnished silver; when it shall reveal the elements of character that God can trust; and when it shall have divested itself of the filthy rags of that black civilization, whose noxious stench is an offense in the nostrils of God and of good men; yea, a thousand times, when the carcasses of those who have come up from the land of slavery, and upon which may be found the marks of the curse, and even when this present generation, so worthless, helpless, and godless in so many cases, have all rotted in the wilderness of forgetfulness, and a new generation shall spring forth whose feet shall catch the first rays of yon rising sun, and whose God shall be the "Lord of Lords and King of Kings"; then, and not till then, will the crown of honor, glory, power, and victory adorn his sable brow. [Pp. 43–44]

(3) I repeat, my hope is fixed. And standing upon the top of this present Mt. Nebo, and letting my eyes sweep through the dark past up along the shores of the river we have crossed, and now into the wilderness with our churches, school-houses, trade schools, and various Christian and civilizing agencies; with faith in God, I am certain that I see,

through the thick darkness that envelops us, the gray rays of a new morn, and I hear the tramp of a new civilization and the music of its *avant-courier* joyfully shouting: "There's a good time coming, boys, a good time coming."

And rising in my meditations upon the afflictions of my fathers that made them groan, I hear the united voice of all nations that have preceded us as the voice of many waters, saying: "For our light affliction, which is but for a moment, worketh out for us a far more exceeding and eternal weight of glory." And rising still higher, I listen again, and the voice of prophecy rings with the distinctness of a clarion note and with the sweetness of an angelic harp and the melody of a heavenly lyre: "Though thou hast lain among the pots, yet shall ye be as the wings of a dove covered with silver and her feathers with yellow gold." [Pp. 46–47]

The power of delay, achieved in the second passage by impacted modification and the parallelism of noun and number, is appropriate to the conflated sense of time that the speaking assumes. "When ... Then," in rapid movement through violent change in the corporate body, is nearly subjunctive, except that the insistence of the future/future-progressive tense slides it into decree. It is the language of the public document (the courts of civil and criminal law); the oracular pronouncement (Lincoln at Gettysburg); the reverberative prohibition, spoken (the fiery speech of the Ten Commandments), not mindful of locale or weather, and above all else, it is the discourse of primary certainty that banishes all doubt to the realm of the inconsequential: "But they that wait upon the Lord shall renew their strength; they shall mount up with wings as eagles; they shall run, and not be weary; and they shall walk, and not faint." The Baptist songbook, in a clerical organization even less hieratic than Bowen's Methodist Episcopal Church, extends Isaiah to read, therefore, "teach us, Lord, teach us, Lord, how to wait." Hearing through a kind of palimpsest of voices, the female hearer/reader, in a turmoil of alternatives, eventually recognizes that the tongue, in the general, in this specific, instance, "belongs" to Father.[38] The power of enunciation and decree assimilates to the phallic mightiness. But Bowen is also black; knows that the "carcasses ... from the land of slavery"

38. An illuminating inquiry into the symbolic import of the voice and the ear is provided in a fascinating fictional narrative of conceptualization in Thomas G. Pavel, "In Praise of the Ear (Gloss's Glosses)" in *The Female Body in Western Culture: Contemporary Perspectives*, ed. Susan Rubin Suleiman (Cambridge, Mass., 1986), pp. 44–68.

and the "marks of the curse" are not only metaphorical, but a cor-
poreality turned back upon its tropic possibilities with a vengeance.
Brought to a common coronation—"the crown of honor, glory,
power and victory [upon] his sable brow"—what is the common
ground of the discretely embodied sexualities between speaker and
hearer/reader within a shared historic destiny that has stripped gender distinctions just about down to nil?

In the third passage, "I see . . . I hear" invite momentary confusion,
compete for equal time in a strained figurative move that would
comprehend—as in an Adamic vision—what is past and what is to
come. But the power of the gaze relinquishes to the ear, and could
it be said in this case that "we encounter in awe the transcendent
attentive breath moving upon the surface of the waters"?[39] The
posture of *waiting*—profoundly associated with the female—that
my generation of political activists and scholars generally regard as
inappropriate passiveness in the face of danger, assumes here an
entirely different thrust. The listening, the waiting to which Bowen
refers are *meditative*, a term that shows root kinship with *medicine*—having to do with notions of thinking about, caring for, curing.
From this angle, hearing, listening, waiting, meditating give way to
a deep height, if we could say so, of activity omnipresent in its
"everywhereness." But it becomes the empowered seeing of the
blind one, or more precisely, the Pauline situation of "faith"—the
"substance of things *hoped for*, the evidence of things *not* seen."
Even though from our current point of view the sciences of medicine
designate a more or less apodictic certainty, the profession seems
to adhere—in its deepest motivations—to the optimism of the cure,
the stochastic game of healing. The "Doctor of Philosophy" *waits*
as long as the "Doctor of Medicine," but Bowen occupies the midst
of an overlapping ground that conflates these social tasks. "Rising
in [his] meditations upon the afflictions of his fathers that made
them groan," he is quickened to the mother's powerful hearing, the
philosopher's "concernful care" that opens him, in effect, to a *pregnancy of attentiveness*. We are signaled, in turn: *this man*, in *caring
for* his kin, the literally wounded ones, takes upon himself the "let-
terings," the "writings" of the dismembered person.

In the context of domination, African-Americans, in the split between "homes," inhabit the subject-position whose corporate body
is shattered between worlds. In the first excerpt from Bowen's end-

39. Ibid., p. 49.

ing, these rifts on the surface of the body situate in general and specific figurative reference: "All races before us" in the making of a "history worth *reading*" have had to write it "with the crimson ink that came from their veins." But this "writing of the flesh" is inscribed—"engraved" is Bowen's word—on a physical/material actuality that throws meditation on the image into confusion, even resistance, as the metaphor dissolves on the very ground of its concatenation. About fifty years before Bowen's address, Frederick Douglass laid hold of a terrible juncture—elements in a syncretic fusion *meet* with the body's wreck and the autobiographical topic that has enabled its saying. Douglass wrote, "My feet have been so cracked with the frost that the pen with which I am writing might be laid in the gashes."[40]

If we think of the cultural situation of African-Americans as a wounding, or a writing in [the] blood, the ground of such conjecture traces back to those branded and marked bodies that Bowen "remembers." In meditating on the breaking point, Bowen, as well as other preachers and "caretakers," whose address, in various forms, compels attention, arrives at the place where others have stood. At this place of fracture, we listen attentively for the moving line that is made articulate to living. In this case, the sermonic word does not soar; it does not leap, it never leaves the ground. It *scatters* instead through the cultural situation and, like the force of gravity, holds us fast to the mortal means. Bound to this earth by the historical particularity of the body's wounding, the community comes face to face with the very limit of identity—the indomitable; irremediable "otherness" of death, metaphorized, in this instance, by the institution of slavery. But this apparent fatality, in binding speakers and hearers/readers to the material situation, quickens us all the more to the radicalizing move. It seems to me that it is the role of the sermon to replay not only *this* narrative, but its *outcome* on the other side of disaster, as Bowen's "good time coming" would have us believe. Against this single passion—to repeat, to remember— the narratives of African-American history and becoming are read and interpreted.

40. An examination of Douglass's "syncretic phrasing" is offered in Robert B. Stepto's *From Behind the Veil: A Study of Afro-American Narrative* (Urbana, Ill., 1979), p. 20. Chapter 5 of Frederick Douglass's 1845 *Narrative* (New York, 1968, p. 43) gives the context for this quotation.

3

Appropriating the Idioms of Science: The Rejection of Scientific Racism

NANCY LEYS STEPAN
SANDER L. GILMAN

This chapter considers some writings of minority groups, as they responded to and resisted the claims of scientific racism. In exploring the relationship between language and resistance we focus on two very different groups of individuals stereotyped as different and inferior in the biological, medical, and anthropological sciences, namely African-Americans and Jews. We concentrate specifically on the period of transition to modern science between 1870 and 1920, when the claims of scientifically established inferiority were pressed most insistently by the mainstream scientific community. Our analysis reveals a body of literature by minorities and the marginal *about* the sciences of themselves that has been virtually untouched by historians of science. What did the men and women categorized by the biological and medical sciences as racially distinct and inferior say about the matter? How did they respond to the claims made about them in the name of science?

Limitations of space have made us very selective with materials. Examples have been chosen for their effective illustration of points, and the goal is to open up a problem for discussion in the history of science and racism that has hitherto been almost entirely ignored.

The Problem Defined

This paper derives from a consideration of two intertwined issues: the centrality of scientific racism to the Western intellectual tradition, and the absence of sustained criticism of scientific racism from within mainstream science in the period under study. Historians have long been aware of the existence of scientific racism in Western societies, especially its intensification and institutionalization in the second half of the nineteenth century. Scientific racism was significant because it provided a series of lenses through which human variation was constructed, understood, and experienced from the early nineteenth century until well into the twentieth century, if not until the present day.[1] We assume in this paper that the races that peopled the texts of science in the past were "artifactual," constructed categories of social knowledge. These categories had material weight in the lives of individuals and groups; racial identities were embodied in political practices of discrimination and law, and affected people's access to education, forms of employment, political rights, and subjective experience. Scientific language was one of the most authoritative languages through which meaning was encoded, and as a language it had political and social, as well as intellectual, consequences.[2]

In studying the history of scientific racism, we have been struck by the relative absence of critical challenges to its claims from within mainstream science. This absence is in itself an interesting problem in the sociology of scientific knowledge, since controversy and contention are often taken to be characteristic of science and the route by which empirical certainty is established. When it came to the sciences of race difference, however, disagreements tended to be minor and technical.[3] Since racial science was invariably a science

1. On scientific racism, see Nancy Stepan, *The Idea of Race in Science: Great Britain, 1800–1960* (London, 1982); George Mosse, *Toward the Final Solution: A History of European Racism* (New York, 1981); and Stephen Jay Gould, *The Mismeasure of Man* (New York, 1981).

2. For an interesting discussion of how ideological/linguistic formulations of race have material consequences, see K. J. Anderson, "Cultural Hegemony and the Race-Definition Process in Chinatown, Vancouver: 1880–1980," *Environment and Planning: Science and Society* 6 (1988): 127–49.

3. Before 1850 there was an active tradition of scientific antiracism, albeit one with its own racialist condescensions. See Stepan, *The Idea of Race*, chaps. 1–2. After

of inequality, produced by European men in an age of widespread racism, to a large (but not predetermined) extent the scientists' own racial identities and identifications prevented them from asking critical questions about their own science—its assumptions, its methods, its content. The concepts within racial science were so congruent with social and political life (with power relations, that is) as to be virtually uncontested from inside the mainstream of science.[4]

One place one encounters a "critical tradition" in relation to scientific racism is in the writings of those stereotyped by the sciences of the day. These writings had a problematic relation to the mainstream, since by the very definitions of racial science the stigmatized were largely outside, or at the margins, of science. Their exclusion was part of the very process of the construction of the sciences of difference and inequality, a result of the scientific expectation that the so-called lower races served mainly as objects of study, but not as scientific truth-seekers themselves. Yet many individuals reacted to scientific racism by actively seeking to enter the relatively closed circle of science, or to use its tools and techniques, to define and defend themselves.

There is far more writing by such individuals than is generally recognized by historians of science. Much of the historical work of uncovering the "struggles and strategies" (in Margaret Rossiter's words) of minority writers, as they confronted a hostile and ste-

---

1850, critics of scientific racism and/or sexism from within science were often themselves in one way or another members of marginal groups (for example, Franz Boas in the United States was Jewish). As for the "technical" disagreements about race, many disputes arose among scientists about *which* measurement accurately demonstrated the essential differences between human races—facial angle, cephalic index, overall brain weight, brain volume, or some other index. These disputes generated a large literature, but the fundamental principle underlying the science of race difference—that some measurement would indeed reveal categorically the essential racial types—was generally accepted.

4. As an example, one could contrast the caution, care, and argumentative skill with which Darwin defended his general position on the evolution of species by natural selection, with the broad assumptions and lack of caution with which he discussed male and female differences in the human species in the *Descent of Man*. On this point see Susan Mosedale, "Science Corrupted: Victorian Biologists Consider the 'Woman Question,'" *Journal of the History of Biology* 11 (1978): 1–55; and Evelleen Richards, "Darwin and the Descent of Woman," in *The Wider Domain of Evolutionary Thought*, ed. D. Oldroyd and I. Langham (Dordrecht, Holland, 1983), pp. 57–111.

reotyping science of race, remains to be done. Our purpose here is to reflect generally on such writing, and to present some examples of the the "textual" strategies we have uncovered.[5]

The problem of resistance to imposed meaning and identity in the human sciences is only beginning to be articulated by scholars. The situation contrasts markedly with the issue of social and political resistance, long considered an essential part of historical analysis, for example in the brilliant work on slave revolts and runaway slave communities, or the fight for black or female suffrage. These studies are indispensable to the study of intellectual resistance, since the capacity to formulate challenges to dominant discourses is closely tied to the political and social resources of the groups making the challenges. Often, the strategies of intellectual resistance—struggles over meaning—mirror or are part of the same process of political struggle. Confronting scientific racism necessitated acquiring a degree of control over the elements of an intellectual idiom, their reassemblage and employment for new ends. How could science be used to transform the racial valuations built into discussions of human variation? Can we discern in the writings of minorities a variety of different tactics, and if so, what were they? As a genre of writing, does it have distinctive features? What effect did the resistance of minorities to negative scientific claims have on the dominant discourse? What does the study of such writings offer the historian of scientific change?

In the history of science, the reasons for theoretical neglect of such questions are rather straightforward. The temptation to think of science as a neutral and universal form of knowledge is still strong, despite many years of criticism of traditional scientific epistemology. By thinking of science as objective, scientists have been in a position to dismiss areas of knowledge from the past that are now viewed as obviously out of date and biased—such as scientific racism—as nothing but "pseudoscience." Studying the resistance of men and women to what has been labeled a pseudoscience is then seen as a narrow endeavor, of interest primarily to the "victims" themselves, but not central to the story of modern science. Fur-

---

5. Margaret W. Rossiter, *Women Scientists in America: Struggles and Strategies to 1940* (Baltimore, 1982). Our focus in this paper is not on the many groups categorized as "inferior" races but on those few individuals with access to education or scientific writings who challenged the claims about their "race."

thermore, calling scientific racism a pseudoscience also allows scientists to refuse to confront the issue of the inherently political nature of much of the biological and human sciences, and to ignore the problem of the persistence of racial metaphors of inferiority in the sciences of today.

Critical approaches from outside the history of science have been more useful to our work on oppositional, cognitive strategies, even though scientific writing usually lies outside their purview. Antonio Gramsci's explorations of cultural hegemony and the role of the "organic" intellectual in his *Prison Notebooks;* the deconstructionists' attacks on essentialism and metaphysics, and their emphasis on the radically heterogeneous nature of the text; Michel Foucault's projects on the inherently political character of knowledge, his analysis of power as something dispersed discursively through entire systems of discourses and practices, and the problematic character of resistance from within the regime of power and knowledge; recent analyses of minority writing that examine the degree to which female and minority literary traditions represent explicit or implicit subversions of the dominant discourse: all of these developments are relevant to analyzing scientific racism.[6] Our study can be seen as a contribution to the debate about how people use languages to constitute themselves as self-conscious subjects, or find a self-representation that is not sexualized or racialized.[7] Our work is distinctive in its focus on science as an especially weighty discourse of identity, whose appropriation by oppositional groups was extremely problematic. The period from 1870 to 1920 has been chosen on purpose because, as we shall show, science acquired its modern epistemological, institutional, and cultural forms during this period.

6. Gramsci's *Prison Notebooks* has many striking passages: see Michael Walzer, "The Ambiguous Legacy of Antonio Gramsci," *Dissent* 35 (Fall 1988): 444–56. Also valuable is Edward Said's work on Orientalism, especially his comments in "Orientalism Reconsidered," in *Cultural Critique* 1 (Fall 1985): 89–108, and his introduction in Said and Christopher Hitchens, eds., *Blaming the Victims: Spurious Scholarship and the Palestinian Question* (London, 1988), pp. 1–19. See also the two issues on the theme "The Nature and Context of Minority Discourse," in *Cultural Critique* 6 (Spring 1987) and 7 (Fall 1987); Gayatri Chakravorty Spivak, *In Other Worlds: Essays in Cultural Politics* (New York, 1987); and Henry Louis Gates, Jr., *Figures in Black: Words, Signs, and the "Racial Self"* (New York, 1987).

7. See the reflections of Joan Wallach Scott, in *Gender and the Politics of History* (New York, 1988); Teresa de Lauretis, "The Technology of Gender," in *Technologies of Gender* (Bloomington, Ind., 1987), pp. 1–30.

Our interest in this paper lies in the interplay between these cultural forms, scientific racism, and scientific resistance. Strategies and meanings are always historically specific and cannot be given transcendant value; our focus throughout is on a particular kind of discourse in a particular moment in history, and the strategies open to resisting individuals and groups.

The Authority of Modern Science

Responding to scientific racism was peculiarly difficult because of certain characteristics of the emerging discourse of science itself. Our argument is that from the mid-nineteenth century onward, scientific claims could be effectively rebutted only by scientific discourses to which resisting groups stood in an especially disadvantaged and problematic position.

Our period situates scientific racism in a moment of elaboration and institutional embodiment of modern science and its epistemology. It was the time in which, as Morrell and Thackray have remarked in their history of the British Association for the Advancement of Science (BAAS), science became consolidated as "the dominant mode of cognition of industrial society." As a mode of cognition, science was conceptualized as "a sharply edged and value-neutral domain of knowledge"—as an apolitical, nontheological, universal, empirical, and uniquely objective (in part because uniquely methodological) form of knowledge unlike any other.[8] The result was the self-definition of science as *the* nonpolitical, unbiased arena of knowledge.

This conceptualization was not a "natural" outcome of the unproblematic study of nature, but a social outcome of a process whereby science was historically and materially constituted to have certain meanings, functions, and interests. In a complex series of innovations, science's epistemological claims were given definition and institutional representation in the form of new scientific societies and organizations sharply delimited from other institutions. These innovations were tied not only to industrialization, but to the politics of class, and the closing of ranks of bourgeois society in the

8. Jack Morrell and Arnold Thackray, *Gentlemen of Science: Early Years of the British Association for the Advancement of Science* (Oxford, 1981), p. 32.

face of challenges from the working class in the 1830s and 1840s. Race and gender were also crucial to the construction of modern science, in that science was defined as "masculine" and European in its abstraction, detachment, and objectivity.[9]

Morrell and Thackray point out that appeals to an impersonal "nature" are common in times of turmoil; what made the mid-nineteenth century distinctive was the successful institutionalization of a particular view of that "nature."[10] The processes of boundary setting were contested at many points, since they meant the delegitimization of many areas of knowledge and redefinition of those areas as "nonscience" or "pseudoscience." Morell and Thackray, for instance, demonstrate that between 1832 and 1870, as the BAAS created a new ideology of science, practitioners in fields of inquiry ruled "unscientific" were excluded from the association and thereby from representation within "science." Areas fraught with moral and/or political controversy kept a place within the boundaries of science only when purged of those concerns, as scientists adopted the value-neutral, empirical language now seen as defining science itself. Science as a form of knowledge separated itself from other knowledge systems; in the process, the dichomoties between the pure and the impure (or the applied sciences), the rational and the irrational, the objective and the subjective, the hard and the soft, the male and the female, were given material form. Such polarities, and the institutional boundaries that created and maintained them, were not the inevitable results of a nature merely "discovered" and described; they were the products of active institution creation, demarcation setting, and the successful use of political and cultural resources to achieve these ends.[11]

9. The relation of gender to the emergence of modern scientific epistomology has been explored by a number of historians. See Carolyn Merchant's The Death of Nature: Women, Ecology and the Scientific Revolution (San Francisco, 1980); and Londa Schiebinger, The Mind Has No Sex? Women in the Origins of Modern Science (Cambridge, 1989).

10. In Britain, science was represented as a "gentlemen's" pursuit (hence the title of Morrell and Thackray's book). Class and gender exclusions from science followed from the social structure of science. The long persistence of the "amateur" in science—one consequence of the gentlemanly and aristocratic nature of British high culture—made British science organizationally distinctive and postponed professionalization. For American science, see Alexandra Oleson and John Voss, The Organization of Knowledge in Modern America, 1860–1920 (Baltimore, 1979); for aspects of the new epistemology in Vienna, see Erna Lesky, Die Wiener medizinische Schule im 19. Jahrhundert (Graz, 1965).

11. Boundary setting in areas of knowledge other than science was not dissimilar—

The formation of the scientific *text* as a new, standardized cultural genre, replacing the more open, varied, metaphorically porous, literary forms of science, is a further aspect of scientific modernization that bears on the problem of the responses to scientific racism. It was in the late nineteenth century that the modern scientific text as we know it stabilized to become the standard, accepted form of writing in nearly all branches of the natural sciences. We are referring here to the scientific paper—the short, depersonalized, empirical paper that is still the hallmark of science today. In a persuasive account of the scientific paper as a cultural and literary genre that emerged in the specific, historically contingent conditions of the late nineteenth century, Gyorgy Markus argues that the scientific text served normative goals, and through its form—its depersonalized authorship, its demand for a peculiarly competent scientific reader—successfully satisfied the expectations of science for constant innovation and accumulation of knowledge.[12] The neutral style of the scientific paper, the absence of a strong, individualized, authorial "I," the emphasis on the factuality of nature, on a nature revealed by specific methods (experimental, technical)—all these features rendered the scientific text problematic for the nonscientific writer and reader and successfully circumscribed the process of contestation.

The new cultural genre of science was an added impediment to opposition in the realm of scientific racism, since it delegitimized the cultural forms of the earlier period.[13] The scientific text became more sharply distinguished from the literary; in the process the range of literary repertoires of meaning—the opportunity for literary play

---

between "high" and "low," elite and popular, the canonical and noncanonical in literature and the visual arts, for example. An especially interesting analysis is Andreas Huyssen's "Mass Culture as Woman: Modernism's Other," in *After the Great Divide: Modernism, Mass Culture, Postmodernism* (Bloomington, Ind., 1986), chap. 3.

12. Gyorgy Markus, "Why Is There No Hermeneutics of Natural Sciences? Some Preliminary Theses," *Science in Context* 1 (March 1987): 5–51. In a very different vein, see Mary Louise Pratt, "The Face of the Country," *Critical Inquiry* 12 (Autumn 1985): 119–43, on the emergence of the informational, depersonalized, scientistic form of travel literature as a new genre in the late eighteenth century, a form whose lack of vivid and personalized narrative was resisted by the continued use of older forms of travel literature as heroic adventures of personal and geographical discovery.

13. The neutral, universal forms of science disguise the way science is nevertheless grounded on the metaphors and practices of racism and sexism. See for example Luce Irigaray's "Is the Subject of Science Sexed?" *Cultural Critique* 1 (Fall 1985): 73–88.

and hermeneutics—was reduced. One thinks, for example, of the charged and metaphoric language of Charles Darwin's *Origin of Species* compared to the dry, limited vocabulary of the sciences of evolution by the 1920s and 1930s. Darwin could not keep control over the metaphors he introduced (such as natural selection, struggle for survival, survival of the fittest). Nearly every term he used was multivalent and was appropriated in selective and varied ways by very different groups for very different purposes.[14] Though Darwin endeavored in later editions of *The Origin of the Species* to reduce the metaphoric ambiguities of his science, his attempts failed, and until well into the twentieth century Darwinism served as a meta-discourse that opened up, rather than merely closed off, the discussion of nature. By the 1900s in the physical sciences, and by the 1920s in the biological sciences, however, the metaphors of scientific language had become much more tightly controlled. The modern scientific text had replaced the expansive scientific book, and the possibilities of multivalent meanings being created out of scientific language were thereby curtailed.

The Marginalization of Moral/Political Argument in Science

The result of the various processes of transformation of science that accompanied industrialization and modernization was that, from 1870 to 1920, science became both more specialized and authoritative as a cultural resource and language of interpretation. It began to replace theological and moral discourse as the appropriate discourse with which to discuss nature. Science also encroached heavily on political discourse, as many political issues were transposed into the realm of neutral "nature," the scientists' province. The outcome was a narrowing of the cultural space within which, and the cultural forms by which, the claims of biological determinism could be effectively challenged.

The effects of this narrowing can be seen in the marginalization

14. See Gillian Beer, *Darwin's Plots: Evolutionary Narrative in Darwin, George Eliot, and Nineteenth-Century Fiction* (London, 1983); Robert M. Young, *Darwin's Metaphor: Nature's Place in Victorian Culture* (Cambridge, 1985); Ted Benton, "Social Darwinism and Socialist Darwinism in Germany: 1860–1900," *Rivista di Filosofia* 73 (1982): 79–121.

and delegitimization of a number of forms of oppositional writing that had been used before about 1860. We will give a few examples. One was to keep in the foreground the moral issues of rights and justice, and to refuse to separate them from scientific ones. These rights, belonging to individuals as members of the human family, rights debated in political and theological terms until the 1850s and 1860s, were increasingly reduced to questions about the racial "natures" of individuals, questions that scientists now claimed had objective, neutral answers. Moral rights were thereby translated into matters of anatomy and physiology.

In the mid-1800s, African-Americans, confronting a "purely factual" science whose message was apparently ever more racialistic in its conclusions concerning themselves, tried to resist the process of reduction and "naturalization" associated with science. In 1854, for instance, the abolitionist Frederick Douglass, in an address titled "The Claims of the Negro Ethnologically Considered," attacked the scientific racists by questioning their logic, their data, and their conclusions concerning the supposed gulf separating the white and black races. He proved to his audience that anatomically and craniologically the similarities between the Negro and the white race far outweighed the differences, that the human species was one, and that the Negro could therefore claim full membership in the human family. But at the end of his address, Douglass made a crucial move from the discourse of anatomy to the discourse of morality and rights: "What, if...the case [of anatomical similarity between whites and blacks] is not made out? Does it follow, that the Negro should be held in contempt?" He answered with a resounding "No," because the title to freedom, liberty, and knowledge was not a question of "natural" difference or similarity, but an issue of natural rights and morality. "It is registered in the Courts of Heaven, and is enforced by the eloquence of the God of all the earth." Douglass here asked a question that would virtually disappear from science: What difference does difference make to human rights? Douglass's answer was that it made no difference, because equality and rights were moral, political, and religious issues.[15] The silence of most scientific texts on this matter after 1860 suggests the power of sci-

15. The speech was a commencement address before the literary societies of Western Reserve College (Rochester, N.Y., 1854). Reprinted in Philip S. Foner, ed., *The Life and Writings of Frederick Douglass*, 5 vols. (New York, 1975), 2: 289–309.

ence to occupy the terrain formerly held by moral discourse, and to disguise the political projects that helped constitute the scientific field.

African-American intellectuals continued to infuse discussions of race with theological, moral, and political concerns. They continued, especially, to evoke the older tradition of Christian monogenism long after it had lost ground as an acceptable *style* of scientific argumentation in mainstream science. Christian monogenism was one of the few powerful traditions linked to science on which they could draw in self-defense; moreover, theological discourse was one of the most significant intellectual productions of the black community. A notable example of the genre is the work of the Harvard-trained physician and Pan-Africanist Dr. Martin R. Delany. He used the Mosaic story of the Deluge to structure a scientific study of race unity in his *Principia of Ethnology* (1879). His strategy made sense within the black tradition but it rendered his book a cultural and linguistic hybrid unlike white scientific writings on race in the same period, a hybrid reflected in its very title, half-English and half-Latin. Religiously oriented ethnography survived as a form because it served the political and psychological needs of the African-American. Isolation from the norms of science meant that those norms were less internalized. The creation of a different narrative form resisted the conventions of science, but as a strategy of resistance, theological arguments had the disadvantage of seeming illegitimate or "unscientific" when measured by the canons of mainstream science.[16]

Another strategy of resistance was the employment of wit, irony,

16. Martin R. Delany, *Principia of Ethnology: The Origin of Races and Color, with an Archeological Compendium of Ethiopian and Egyptian Civilization from Years of Careful Examination and Enquiry* (Philadelphia, 1879). A great deal could be said about the survival of older cultural scientific forms among groups who needed to resist the growing racialism and the narrowing of the languages within which racialism was expressed in the transition period from about 1830 to 1930. For example, Casely Hayford's *Ethiopia Unbound: Studies in Race Emancipation* (1911), the first African novel, fused fiction with factual "studies" to create a tale of black emancipation and power. Other uses of monogenism by blacks were less religious in tone. A powerful statement was made by C. V. Roman, *American Civilization and the Negro* (Freeport, N.Y., 1971, rpt. of 1916 ed.); the chapter "Racial Differences" engaged directly in rebutting racialism and Roman used the scientific argument for monogenism as the necessary and sufficient foundation for political and moral equality. The survival of traditional environmentalist explanations of difference, dating back to the Enlightenment, is also worth exploring.

or parody. These literary devices became marginalized and delegitimized in the second half of the nineteenth century precisely because they did not fit the depersonalized, nonauthorial style of modern science. As a style, humor had the advantage of distancing and subverting the claims of science, thereby serving as a strategy of empowerment. An exceptional use of the ironic voice is found in an anonymous article in the black American periodical, the *Anglo-African Magazine*, in 1860. The article, which was almost certainly the work of the black Scottish-trained physician Dr. James McCune Smith, is especially interesting because it represents, as far as we know, the first account of Darwinian ideas by an African-American. Titled "A Word for the Smith Family," the article put Darwin's new science to witty use to defend the unity and success of the black people named Smith. The very commonness of the name Smith was taken as proof of the evolutionary success of black people, who were shown to have thrived, adapted, and multiplied through natural selection and the struggle for survival. The theory of common descent was also used implicitly to poke fun at the pretensions of all the white Smiths who thought they were distinct and superior to black Smiths. All Smiths, the author suggested, were linked together in an evolutionary kinship.[17]

Wit and irony gave a writer control and power over language and content. Parody could perform a similar task of distancing in relation to the claims of science. But all three literary (or cultural) styles, because they impressed directly the author's own personality on the text, had less and less place in scientific discourse as the century wore on. As strategies of resistance, they too became marginal to the scientific enterprise.[18]

17. "A Word for the 'Smith' Family," *Anglo-African Magazine* 2 (March 1860): 77–83. In addition to its irony, the article is interesting for the accurate account of the main points of Darwin's themes in relation to human beings, and for the association McCune Smith makes between Darwinism and monogenism. Within a few years, Darwinism would be successfully integrated into scientific polygenism and put to the service of disunity and inequality. Black writers often resisted Darwinism for this reason, and because it destroyed the religious basis of ethnnology and anthropology by stressing humankind's common heritage with animals.

18. For an interesting account of the uses of parody as a strategy of resistance to medical authority and expertise, as well as the limits of this strategy in the face of increasing success and professionalization of science, see Judith R. Walkowitz, "Science and Seance: Transgressions of Gender and Genre in late Victorian London," *Representations* 22 (Spring 1988): 3–29.

Using the Scientific Idiom

Despite the continuing resort to political and moral written arguments to challenge the claims of the scientific racists, the professionalization of science made such tactics less effective. By the last third of the century, effective strategies of resistance were often structured by the dominant discourse. Science's conceptual categories, rhetorical styles, and methodologies were adopted.

Of course, science had always been used as a source of ideas and arguments by people challenging the conventional wisdom and dominant ideologies of their day. Feminists in the eighteenth century defended the rights of women in the language of Newton; artisanal socialists in the early nineteenth century called upon Lamarckian evolutionism to serve their antibourgeois, confrontational needs.[19] After the mid-1800s, however, writers were forced to use the sciences of the day more narrowly to challenge scientific claims if they wished to have a hearing within science. As minorities moved into the scientific arena, their own competencies in the scientific idiom grew, as did their ability to meet science on its own terms. It is no surprise, then, to find that evolutionism, hereditarianism, the new Mendelism, and even "eugenics" (which in the United States was racist almost by definition) were embraced by African-Americans, Jews, and other minorities to counter the charges of racial inferiority.[20] The cultural forms of scientific texts were imitated in a necessary process of identification with the norms and standards of

---

19. Lois N. Magner, "Women and the Scientific Idiom: Textual Episodes from Wollstonecraft, Fuller, Gilman and Firestone," *Signs* 4 (1986): 61–80; Adrian Desmond, "Artisan Resistance and Evolution in Britain, 1819–1848," *Osiris*, 2d ser., 3 (1987): 77–110.

20. As we show later, the use of idioms of science usually associated with, or carrying, racialist meanings, such as eugenics, demanded a huge effort of transformation of meanings. Some examples of the use of the language of eugenics by African-Americans can be found in the black *Journal of the National Medical Association (JNMA)*; see, for example, Dr. John A. Kenney, "Eugenics and the School Teacher," *JNMA* 7. 4 (1915): 253–59; Dr. Barnett M. Rhetta, "A Plea for the Lives of the Unborn," *JNMA* 7. 3 (1915): 200–205; C. V. Roman, "Some Ramifications of the Sexual Impulse," *JNMA* 12. 4 (1920): 14–17. In nearly every case, African-American doctors accepted the importance of good heredity in health and emphasized the need for care in reproduction. They called this "eugenics." At the same time, they rejected the anti-black and sterilization themes characteristic of white eugenics. Many women and Jews also embraced the themes and conclusions of eugenics.

science. Blacks produced texts of blackness, with anthropological illustrations of heads, cranial measurements, and scientific tables of racial health and illness.[21] Jewish scientists particularly used scientistic representations of self because of their greater access to scientific education and greater commitment to the norms of science.

The use of science to dismantle the claims of science involved the authors in complex processes of transformation of the meaning of terms. Any discussion of the critical responses to scientific racism in the late nineteenth and early twentieth century must acknowledge how the need to meet science on its own terms limited the nature of the response. This was also true of other discourses—for example, literary discourse—but scientific discourse was distinguished by its high barriers of entry.[22] By the end of the nineteenth century, professionalization separated science from both "high" literary culture and popular culture. Science acquired technical procedures and practices, as well as new vocabularies unfamiliar to the nonscientist; these could only be acquired in the professional scientific academy. Only the trained scientist, it was claimed, was able to speak coherently and legitimately about scientific matters. Disciplinary boundaries were a further disincentive to the kind of critical inquiry that dismantling scientific racism and sexism required.[23]

21. For an example, see The Health and Physique of the Negro American, ed. W. E. Burghardt Du Bois (Atlanta, 1906), especially its plates of "Typical Negro-Americans" prefacing the text.

22. For valuable work on the problem of how dominant discourses in literature structure minority writing and the degree to which the Jewish, female, and black literary traditions represent implicit or explicit forms of resistance to the dominant discourse, see Sandra M. Gilbert and Susan Gubar, The Madwoman in the Attic: The Woman Writer and the Nineteenth-Century Literary Imagination (New Haven, Conn., 1979); Mary Poovey, The Proper Lady and the Woman Writer: Ideology as Style in the Works of Mary Wollstonecraft, Mary Shelley and Jane Austen (Chicago, 1984); Deirdre David, Intellectual Women and Victorian Patriarchy (Ithaca, N.Y., 1987); Henry Louis Gates, Jr., Figures in Black; and Sander L. Gilman, Jewish Self-Hatred: Anti-Semitism and the Hidden Language of the Jews (Baltimore, 1986).

23. A sign of this separation was the translation of increasingly specialized knowledge of great cultural, symbolic, and material power into more accessible forms for the general public. Journals such as Nature and Popular Science Monthly were established to carry out this task of translation, initially by scientists themselves. The social circumstances in which successful attacks on scientific racism and sexism could be made also need to be studied in far greater detail. When disciplinary structures are not stabilized, or where new fields come into being that are not fully professionalized, the opportunities for minorities in science are increased.

Exclusion from the academy meant exclusion from the authoritative use of the idioms of science. Whenever racial minorities and women wrote critically about the sciences of themselves, their writing ran the risk of being ignored or dismissed because it came from "outside" professional science, and was therefore by definition "unscientific." Furthermore, resisting the claims of scientific racism by pointing out its subjective, metaphorical, particular, or politically biased nature (namely, that science was articulated around notions of race) was extraordinarily difficult because many minority writers shared the belief of the mainstream scientists in science as a progressive, instrumental, and objective form of knowledge. Given the epistemological status of science, to admit that race, especially one's own, was an issue in science was to make the writer immediately less than fully "objective" and therefore less than fully "scientific."[24] For the African-American or Jew writing *as* a scientist, or from *within* science, the writer's own status as objective observor of nature was at stake. The problem of both using science as a language of self-assertion and identity, while exposing its essentially *political* character in relation to racial claims, was rarely addressed by resisting groups because rarely recognized.[25]

Some Tactics and Responses to Scientific Racism

In relation to the terrain and idioms of science, different groups were very differently situated. Access to education and the languages of science varied, and was indeed a part of the social construction *of* race as a category of human and political difference. Yet even when the barriers were very great, as was the case for African-Americans, critical engagement with scientific racism long predated

24. The defensive tone characteristic of critical writing by minorities is explained by the high barriers to entry science had erected. See Evelyn Fox Keller, "The Gender/ Science System: or, Is Sex to Gender as Nature Is to Science?" *Hypatia* 2 (Fall 1987): 37–49.

25. This problem *is* addressed, however, by feminists writing on science today. As Rossiter (*Women Scientists*) and others have noted, accepting the prevailing ideology of science as unmarked by gender did not protect women and/or minorities in science from discrimination and exclusion. Instead, it only perpetuated and masked the material conditions of that exclusion.

the Civil War; the way this critical response influenced black periodical writings is relatively unstudied. Jews as a group had far greater access to education in general and were strongly attracted to the scientific professions. In some branches of science, in fact, Jews made up 6 to 10 percent of all scientists, a figure much higher than their total representation in the population.[26]

What is not generally realized is the degree to which Jews themselves engaged with racial science, because of its potentially harmful implications for themselves as a "race." Their cultural production has barely been studied in the context proposed here. As Jews (and other groups stereotyped in the biological and social sciences of the day) were drawn more deeply into the sciences of racial difference, whether in measuring themselves as a race by craniometry and other methods, or by comparing one fraction of the Jewish "race" with another, or by commenting on or contesting the thesis of Jewish pathology and illness, they were tempted simultaneously to embrace and reject the field: to embrace science's methods, concepts, and the promise it held out for discovering knowledge, and to reject, in a variety of ways, the conclusions of science as they appeared to apply negatively to themselves.

Audre Lorde has stated that "the master's tools will never dismantle the master's house."[27] Yet our studies suggest that when minorities took on the matter of racial science, in the idioms of science, that science was inevitably changed. Even for the most

26. According to Willie Pearson, about 950 African-Americans earned doctorates in the natural sciences between 1876 and 1976; the percentage of all natural scientists who are African-American has remained the same for over a century, namely 1 percent. About 1 percent of all PhDs in the social sciences in the United States are African-American. See Willie Pearson, Jr., *Black Scientists, White Society and Colorless Science: A Study of Universalism in American Science* (Millwood, N.Y., 1985), pp. 31–33. For the size of the African-American medical population in the period under study, see Todd Savitt, "Entering a White Profession," *Bull. Hist. Med.* (1987): 516. By 1920, African-American physicians represented 2.7 percent of all doctors, compared to only 0.9 percent in 1890. European medical schools opened to Jewish males at the very beginning of the emancipation of the Jews, with the Act of Tolerance of 1782 promulgated by Joseph II of Austria. Jews tended to be clustered in the medical specialities with the lowest status (for example, syphilology, dermatology, and so on); when Ferdinand von Hebra took over the dermatological clinic in Vienna in the 1860s, he was able to recruit only Jewish assistants. See Monika Richarz, *Der Eintritt der Juden in die akademischen Berufe* (Tübingen, 1974), pp. 28–43; and Erna Lesky, *Die Wiener medizinische Schule im 19. Jahrhundert* (Graz, 1978).

27. Quoted in Barbara Johnson, *A World of Difference* (Baltimore, 1987), pp. 1–2.

oppressed, science created spaces for self-definition and self-representation. It is these interstices—or more precisely, the strategies that created them—to which we turn now.

Our discussion takes the form of a simple typology. One of the typology's functions is to draw attention to a variety of responses to scientific racism and a range of textual materials that are usually overlooked. By providing a simple classification of these materials, we show that despite the individuality of the responses, despite the very different social experiences of the writers analyzed, despite the fact that "race" was not a unitary category but had multiple meanings, certain similarities in textual strategies can be found in minority responses. These similarities indicate the power of scientific racism to map the terrain within which, and the terms by which, resistance and challenge could be carried out. Recurring tropes, recurring techniques of reenvisioning identity, certain patterns in the tactics of re-representation, characterize the critical tradition we examine.

The kinds of responses illustrated here are not exhaustive or mutually exclusive. We find that a writer employed a number of responses or strategies, either simultaneously or successively over the course of a writing career. Since the dominant ideology of scientific racism was itself heterogeneous, and fueled by contradictory impulses, so were the resisting discourses that echoed, commented upon, and modified them. "Cannibalization," disarticulation and reassemblage, and the employment of multiple modes of attack were the tactics that made sense.[28] Our typology, then, is a highly dynamic one, employed mainly to point out how responses placed the writer in different relations to the dominant discourse, with varying consequences psychologically, intellectually, and scientifically.

28. Obviously, the social differences fracturing race (and gender) affected the emphases within the dominant discourse of "natural" difference, as it was applied to particular groups. Thus both black males and Jewish males were described in nineteenth-century anthropological and medical science as "female" in traits and character. How African-Americans and Jews supposedly manifested this femaleness was distinctive. Any study of the reactions to racial science must be alert to the nuances and emphases within the scientific stereotypes, since the responses were fundamentally structured by them, echoing, commenting upon, and modifying the specifics of particular themes. See Desmond ("Artisan Resistance") for the use of the word "cannibalization" to mean the selective use of elements of science whereby "stolen fragments were ... re-constituted" in such a way as to legitimate an alternative program.

The most pernicious effect of racial science was the profound *internalization* of the negative terms and norms of the discourse itself. Insofar as resisting discourses are necessarily tied to, reflective of, and constructed in similar terms to dominant discourses, "internalization" is to a certain extent characteristic of all strategies of intellectual resistance. "Internalization" here, however, means more than this—we refer to the very profound psychological and social introjection of negative images and meanings contained in the stereotypes, in the contruction and understanding of one's self-identity. Such internalization was recognized by the stereotyped people as a common and profoundly problematic outcome of stereotyping discourses. "In the psychology of the human mind, suggestion plays an important part," wrote the African-American George Parker in 1908: "If it be true that as a man thinketh, so he is, then the self-making power becomes proportionately more powerful when applied to a whole race. For years it has been constantly affirmed and re-affirmed that races of African blood have contributed nothing to humanity's store of knowledge and civilization, and this incessant affirmation has produced a conviction of truth not only in the minds of those who affirm it, but also in the minds of those whom it wrongs."[29]

The psychological processes of identification with and internalization of the dominant discourses of "otherness" are extremely complex and varied. Gilman has discussed the fragmentation of identity that internalization of the norms of "otherness" entails, and the conflicts that arise when we use on ourselves the discourse that labels us as different and unacceptable.[30] Our interest here is in the special weight of scientific discourses of otherness and inequality on individual and group self-consciousness in the late nineteenth and early twentieth centuries, in which the self was understood and represented through a preexisting, racialized science. Absolute application, without qualification, of the dominant discourse to one-self or to one's group is for rather obvious reasons relatively rare. Psychologically the outcome is extreme and potentially devastating self-hatred. The publication of one such self-hating text, by the Jewish student of philosophy Otto Weininger in 1903, was followed a

29. George W. Parker, "The Negroid Line in History," *American Methodist Episcopal Review* 25 (October 1908): 28.
30. See Gilman, *Jewish Self-Hatred.*

few months later by his suicide. Weininger, a student of the Viennese philosophers Laurenz Müller and Friedrich Jodl, attempted to combine a biology of human sexuality with a philosophy of sexual and racial identity. His self-inflicted death, in the house in which Beethoven had died, reveals the profound conflict he experienced when biological determinism came into direct contact with self-definition.

No matter how bizarre Weininger's attempt to place himself within the discourses of race may appear to be, in his own times he was undertood as a scientific investigator whose ideas, though controversial, were nevertheless taken as contributions to scholarship, not as examples of psychosis. His well-known text was called *Sex and Character*, a title not unrelated to the problem of internalization. For even in the case of such self-hating texts, it is evident there must always be a way out of extreme negative self-stereotyping, whether or not the step is taken. As a male author, Weininger tried to rescue himself from complete negativity by projecting onto the the female sex all the most negative qualities found in the science of biological determinism. Women were portrayed as biologically predisposed to illness, hysteria, and to an inferior and incomplete form of speaking and thinking. Such strategies of internalization and projection in principle provide a form of psychological rescue for the author. But for Weininger, both homosexual and Jewish, it proved a failure.[31]

The choice of the female as the site of negative projection in Weininger's text was not idiosyncratic but deeply structured by the stereotyping discourses of the day, as is shown in texts by male authors writing in very different social and racial circumstances. For example, the African-American William Hannibal Thomas wrote *The American Negro* in 1901, just two years before Weininger's book, during the height of American scientific racism. Thomas's work provoked an immediate angry reaction within the African-American intellectual community. Kelly Miller, professor of math-

---

31. Otto Weininger's *Sex and Character* appeared in English translation in 1906. Weininger conceived of both sex and racial character as a continuum; qualities of maleness and femaleness were, therefore, not absolutes, and both aspects could be found in an individual. Nevertheless, the extreme end of the continuum of sex, the female, was postulated as unchangeable and negative. Freud was one scientist who ackowledged the basic validity of Weininger's concept of bisexuality. See Peter Heller, "A Quarrel over Bisexuality," in *The Turn of the Century: German Literature and Art, 1890–1915*, ed. Gerald Chapple and Hans H. Schulte (Bonn, 1981), pp. 87–116.

ematics at Howard University, commented that the book had been "more widely noticed than any other recent work on the race problem," and he drew attention to its similarity to Jewish self-hating texts.[32]

Thomas, a Northerner who went to the South to study the Negro and did not like what he found, wrote a text that might have been produced by the most racist white scientist. Yet here too processes of projection, of "self-rescue," and re-representation similar to those in Weininger can be discerned, despite the differences in personality, nationality, and the terms of the dominant, scientific, stereotyping discourse. First, Thomas maintained that the women of the Negro race embodied all of the corrupting sensuality that scientists had attributed to the entire Afro-American race. In this way Thomas implicitly exonerated the male author from the most negative aspects of the stereotyping discourse of science. Second, like Weininger, Thomas attempted to shift the definition of "race" away from a permanent, outwardly visible "sign" such as color, to a subjective, psychological condition within. To Thomas, the term "Negro" referred negatively to a "characteristic form of thought and action" (the equivalent to Weininger's "psychological constitution" of Jewishness), so that any person, of whatever hue, who exhibited such characteristic traits was to be considered a "Negro." The inclusion of all people of a particular color (such as blackness) in the same category was an unjust classification "which acts with great severity against a saving remnant of good men and true women."[33] By projecting blackness onto women and away from color per se, the mulatto author both internalized the terms of racialized and scientized discourse, and distanced himself from complete application of the negative elements of racialist discourse to himself.

A second response to racial science was to accept the terms set by the dominant discourse, but to change the valuations attached

32. William H. Thomas, *The American Negro: What He Was, What He Is, and What He May Become: A Critical and Practical Discussion* (New York, 1901). Chapter 5, "Characteristic Traits," is of special interest. Kelly Miller, "Review of W. Hannibal Thomas' Book 'The American Negro,' " *Hampton Negro Conference* 5 (July 1901): 64–74; the quotations are from pp. 64–65. See also Du Bois's review in *Book Reviews by W. E. B. Du Bois*, comp. and ed. Herbert Aptheker (Millwood, N.Y., 1977), pp. 1–3. Other reviews were by Charles W. Chesnutt, "A Defamer of His Race," *The Critic* (April 1901): 350–51; Charles T. Walker, "Reply to William H. Thomas: The Twentieth Century Slander of the Negro Race—Address" (New York, n.d.).

33. Thomas, *American Negro*, p. xxiii.

to them. The significance of biological race differences was accepted, but the "inferior" element in the hierarchy revalued and renamed. This strategy entailed a transvaluation of the terms of the dominant discourse. For example, blackness became an oppositional structure to whiteness, and negativity was thereby transformed into positivity.

Once again, this kind of strategy is familiar in discourses other than scientific ones; we mean to call attention here to the authority of scientific language in structuring such reversals. We call this strategy "transvaluation" because in such writing the response was always couched in terms similar to the dominant discourse, so that one mythology of identity was in a sense replaced by another. Though as a type, the form of writing moved the resisting author further away from total acceptance or accommodation to the dominant discourse of difference, the terms of the dominant discourse were very far from being transcended. In addition, the reverse stereotype that was created had many of the disadvantages of stereotyping in general—it failed to give space to individuality and variation, and could therefore be circumscribing. Furthermore, the simple process of transvaluation of the terms from negative to positive was not always convincing, since the resisting minority voice was always in a position of lesser legitimacy than that of the dominating voice. For the writer, however, such transvaluations often had considerable weight. Reactive and defensive though transvaluations may have been, the result was often empowerment. Upon the basis of such reversals, political solidarities were created. At times, too, they could result in telling criticisms of the science of race of the times.[34]

Since the strategy of reversal and transvaluation echoed the dominant discourse—indeed it appropriated the binary opposition upon which the dominant terms themselves depended—these reversals had somewhat predictable forms. What is important is to connect the use of such reversals to the politics of discrimination and assimilationism. When patterns of discrimination and negative stereotypes circulated widely in discourses, a dialectical politics of self-segregation, solidarity, and reversals was set in motion. We can see this clearly in the use of reversals and transvaluations in the

---

34. Gates, *Figures in Black*, emphasizes the reactive and negative side of such reversals, and the bizarre stereotypes that can result.

African-American intellectual and political tradition. The "romantic racialism" espoused by some white abolitionists before the Civil War (a romanticism that included a great deal of condescension, as George Fredrickson has remarked), was embraced by African-American writers themselves in periods of intensified racism. August Meier notes the appearance of such racialism in the 1890s, at a time when anti-immigration sentiment was growing and racial categorization and exclusion were widespread.[35] Marcus Garvey's Back to Africa movement involved this kind of reversal and transvaluation.

These reversals were sometimes grounded in the idioms of science. W. E. B. Du Bois, in an early (1897) and controversial statement, "The Conservation of Races," countered the charge of biologically based racial inferiority of the black population by asserting a distinctive and positive psychic-biological identity for African-Americans.[36] Anthony Appiah, in a recent commentary on Du Bois's text, describes this transvaluation as the "classic dialectic," in that it is the antithesis to the thesis of the "American Negro denial of difference." Instead of rejecting the biological concept of race of the time, Du Bois accepted it and proposed that the different biological races of the world were complementary and necessary to each other. Appiah remarks that, as the dialectic required, Du Bois's reevaluation occurred "in the face of the sciences of inferiority."[37]

35. George M. Fredrickson, *The Black Image in the White Mind: The Debate on Afro-American Character and Destiny, 1817–1914* (New York, 1971), pp. 97ff. August Meier, *Negro Thought in America, 1880–1915: Racial Ideologies in the Age of Booker T. Washington* (Ann Arbor, Mich., 1966), pp. 22ff.

36. W. E. B. Du Bois, "The Conservation of Races" (1897), in Andrew G. Paschal, ed., *A W. E. B. Du Bois Reader* (New York, 1971), pp. 19–31. An earlier statement of the theme is Du Bois's Harvard Address of 1890, where he posited the African-American as the opposite race to the Teuton, and suggested that the Teuton needed the more submissive Negro for the full development of civilization. See his *Against Racism: Unpublished Essays, Papers, Addresses, 1887–1961*, ed. Herbert Aptheker (Amherst, Mass., 1985), p. 16.

37. Anthony Appiah, "The Uncompleted Argument: Du Bois and the Illusion of Race," *Critical Inquiry* 12 (Autumn 1985): 21–35. A similar example is provided by Kelly Miller's "The Artistic Gifts of the Negro," in his *Race Adjustment: Essays on the Negro* (New York, 1908), pp. 246–57. The political context of Du Bois's embrace of biology was not only scientific racism, but the need to oppose Booker T. Washington's accommodationism. In a period in which there was much discussion of "pure races," of race sentiment as binding nations together, of the need to preserve the integrity of race, it is not surprising to find many minorities embracing for themselves these notions. Du Bois's "biologism" was exceptional in his overall en-

The results of such transvaluations of a binary opposition were complex. Reversals sometimes involved not only racial "essences" but the narrative histories of self and the group. For instance, B. F. Lee, in an article on "Selection, the Environment and the Negro's Future," argued, as Du Bois did later, that race was not effaced or altered by changes in the environment. Lee posited the "Ethiopian" as a noble type of race which, through its "wonderful primitive instinct of adaptation" would survive to take its turn as the ruling race, when dark skin, as well as all the other traits of the Negro, would become "the highest concept of the beautiful."[38]

Among Jewish scientists, transvaluations were often tied closely to scientific anti-Semitism and the politics of antiassimilationism, especially Zionism. Theodor Herzl set the tone when he accepted the pejorative label "Oriental" for the Jews of Europe, and turned it into the basis for a new political ideology, Zionism. Martin Buber's emphasis on the positive racial identity of the Jew, or Max Nordau's call for a "muscle Jew," must be read in this context and seen as the antithesis of stereotyped Jewish feminization, weakness, mental illness, and degeneracy.[39]

A third response to scientific racism moved the speakers even further from the dominant discourses. This textual strategy involved "recontextualizations." Writings of this kind were associated with a growing empowerment of minorities in science, an increased familiarity with its idioms and technologies, and, therefore, a new authority in challenging the claims of science on its own terms.

Two rather different aspects of the process of recontextualization can be discerned. First, the tools of science were used either to prove that the supposed factual data upon which the stereotypes of racial inferiority were based were wrong, or to generate new "facts" on which different claims could be made. Second scientific reasoning was used to question the *explanation* of the facts. "Recontextuali-

---

deavor; he is generally known for his steadfast opposition to biological racism. Other strategies employed by Du Bois in countering scientific racism are discussed later.

38. B. F. Lee, "Selection, Environment and the Negro's Future,"*AME Church Review* 20. 4 (1904): 388–90. The rewriting of African history, from one of nullity or "blank darkness," to use Christopher Miller's arresting title (*Blank Darkness: Africanist Discourse in French* [Chicago, 1985]), to a densely filled history of African civilization, is another aspect of the process of reversals.

39. See Gilman, *Jewish Self-Hatred*, p. 291.

zation" resulted in new interpretations, new narratives of self and identity, which amounted to a scientific counterdiscourse.

For example, the high mortality and morbidity figures of Afro-Americans were cited repeatedly by white physicians as evidence of "racial" susceptibilities and in exoneration of white inaction in the face of the poverty and misery of the black population. Two issues confronted the Afro-American scholar. Were the facts and figures of mortality and morbidity correct? And, to the extent that accurate information about the Negro was available, what was the meaning of the statistics? A superb example of the process of re-contextualization was Dr. Kelly Miller's sophisticated critique of the highly racialistic tract on supposed Negro racial inferiority by the statistician Fredrick Hoffman, *Race Traits and Tendencies of the American Negro.*[40] The German origin of the author made him, Hoffman said, "impartial" in his approach. The factual, impersonal form in which Hoffman couched his argument also made the book's impact powerful. It was, said Miller, "by far the most thorough and comprehensive treatment of the Negro problem, from a statistical standpoint, which has yet appeared."[41] As a *scientific* statement, it demanded an answer in scientific terms.

Miller's long review of Hoffman's work was the first paper to be published by the newly founded American Negro Academy, estab-lished in 1897 in Washington, D.C., as a forum for intellectual dis-cussion, and more specifically to refute or challenge the assertions of white scientists.[42] Miller used the occasion to point out the many errors in Hoffman's data. Hoffman's main thesis was that the Negro race was dying out in America because of racially based morbidity exacerbated by conditions of political "freedom." Miller, using data collected from a wide variety of sources from several cities, showed that the African-American population had actually grown in abso-

40. Fredrick L. Hoffman's book was published for the American Economic Asso-ciation. Hoffman, *Race Traits and Tendencies of the American Negro* (New York, 1896). A short variation of this tract appeared earlier as "The Vital Statistics of the Negro," *The Arena* 24 (1892): 529–42.

41. Kelly Miller, "A Review of Hoffman's *Race Traits and Tendencies of the American Negro,*" *The American Negro Academy, Occasional Papers, No. 1* (Wash-ington, D.C., 1897), pp. 3–36.

42. Alfred A. Moss, Jr., *The American Negro Academy: Voice of the Talented Tenth* (Baton Rouge, 1981), gives a detailed account of this institution.

lute numbers, that its birthrate was greater than that of whites in many places, and that the data "proving" the death of the black race were so selectively assembled by Hoffmann as to be completely fallacious.

Miller also recontextualized the actual statistics of death and disease, establishing a very different understanding of the meaning of the figures. Here the most significant figures concerned high black morbidity and mortality from diseases such as tuberculosis, which Hoffman, in keeping with the science of race of the times, presented as the result of innate racial susceptibilities to illness and degeneration. Miller used comparable data on working-class whites in Europe to make the case that high rates of disease and death were a function not of innate racial susceptibilities but of social conditions (whites in parts of Europe were as poorly off in housing, employment, education, medical care and health as African-Americans). Miller also neatly turned to advantage some of Hoffman's own arguments and data—for instance, by citing Hoffman's assertion that 50 percent of all Negro children who died under the age of five received *no* medical attention. Miller's conclusion was that the Afro-American should not be discouraged by scientific inquiry, for "it is a condition and not a theory that confronts him."[43]

W. E. B. Du Bois's *The Health and Physique of the Negro American* (1906), was the first of the Atlanta University publications on black Americans that was supervised by Du Bois himself, after he was invited to Atlanta in 1897. This project was more ambitious than Miller's in that it not only attacked the data on which many of the claims of the white scientists were founded, but collected new data as a means of narrating in a new way the history and condition of the Afro-American people.[44] Du Bois was the most imposing black intellectual of the time, and a pioneer of the new sociology, which he saw as an essential tool in the fight against racism. In addition to combing the U.S. Census records for information, Du Bois arranged to have measured, craniometrically and otherwise, some 1,000 students at Hampton Institute in Atlanta, in strict accordance with the techniques of contemporary racial science.

43. Miller, "Review of Hoffman's *Race Traits*," p. 36.
44. See Du Bois, *Health and Physique*. Du Bois "singlehandedly initiated serious research in blacks in America" says Elliot Rudwick, in "W. E. B. Du Bois as Sociologist," in *Black Sociologists: Historical and Contemporary Perspectives*, ed. James E. Blackwell and Morris Janowitz (Chicago, 1974), p. 46.

On the existing data on blacks, the study attacked the conclusions concerning the supposed low brain weights of African-Americans, showing they were based on insufficient numbers (the total number of Afro-American brains that had been measured and weighed in America at the time was 500, from which generalizations about more than 20 million persons of Negro descent in the West had been formed). Furthermore, Du Bois pointed out that no account was given of the age, stature, social class, occupation, nutrition, or cause of death of the individuals whose heads and brains had been measured, all of which separately or together affected the structure of the brain. In cases in which morbidity and mortality rates in the Afro-American race were accepted as correct, Du Bois recontextualized the data, emphasizing social conditions, economic environment, and the political realities of discrimination, as their cause. The evidence showed, for instance, that tuberculosis was "not a racial disease but a social disease," and that high infant mortality in the cities was "not a Negro affair, but an index of social conditions." "If the population were divided as to social and economic conditions the matter of race would be almost entirely eliminated," the report concluded.[45]

Jewish scientists also produced a plethora of statistical data of their own—on Jewish disease rates and head shapes—in order to contribute to, and rewrite, the scientific study of their own identity. Of special interest were the scientific data on the supposed high rates of illness. As trained scientists, many employed by municipal and state mental hospitals, Jewish physicians were in a position to gather their own data on rates of mental illness, and to recontextualize the problem as one not of biology but of the history of Jews in Europe. Raphael Becker, a student of Eugen Bleuler and resident physician of the Zurich University psychiatric clinic, for example, produced a monograph that was widely cited by Jews, demonstrating that the higher incidence of mental illness among Western European Jews compared with non-Jews was the result of a "Jewish inferiority

---

45. Du Bois, *Health and Physique*, p. 89. Several white scientists contributed data to the Atlanta University publications. Du Bois revised drastically the themes of African-American difference put forward in the Atlanta University publication no. 2, which had been published in 1897 before Du Bois became director of the conferences and publications on the Negro. In the second publication, the excessive Negro mortality and morbidity were attributed not to the environment but to ignorance of health laws and immorality, a theme that reflected the self-help outlook of the period.

complex," itself a product of "two thousand years of persecution."[46] Biological race, Becker asserted, was not the causal factor. Other Jewish scientists challenged the existing information on supposed Jewish mental illness, much as Miller had challenged the data on black racial susceptibilities to disease, and set out to gather their own, more accurate, statistics.

By such recontextualizations, rejection of the *meaning* of the dominant scientific discourses of difference could be achieved, and efforts at explanation could be steered in innovative directions.[47] The new social sciences, with their growing identity as "sciences," their accessibility, and their early connection to reform projects, were important weapons in the fight against biological racism and sexism, although they could also be used in the elaboration of racial and sexual stereotypes.

Another form of recontextualization was "universalization," whereby a trait or character labeled as peculiar to one race and designated as negative, was relabeled instead as a universal trait of all human beings, so that the racial marker was removed as a sign of inferiority. We see it at work in Delany's universalization of color in his *Principia of Ethnology*, where he argued that the black skin, the supposed "sign" of black inferiority, was the result not of features unique to the black race, but merely of a subtle elaboration of a universal, underlying color process in the skin shared by all human beings. The blackness of the black was therefore only a "concentrated" form of something universal in humans. As Delany put it, "The color of the blackest African is produced by *identically the same* essential coloring matter that gives the 'rose cheeks and ruby

46. Raphael Becker, *Die jüdische Nervosität: Ihre Art, Entstehung und Bekämpfung* (Zurich, 1918).

47. The noted Swedish sociologist Gunnar Myrdal, in studying the problem of American racism and its grounding in the idioms of science, gave pride of place to the new social sciences in dismantling racism, and noted that from the beginning black social scientists took the stand that the American dogma of race inequality was a scientific falsehood. See Gunnar Myrdal, *An American Dilemma: The Negro Problem and Modern Democracy*, 2 vols. (New York, repr. 1972), 1:93. Myrdal's emphasis on the liberating effects of the social sciences reflects the time in which he was writing (the late 1930s and 1940s); he could not foresee how many of the stereotypes of race would be reformulated, following the collapse of the older biological discourse of racism, in the new languages of sociology, cultural and social anthropology, and developmental political science.

lips' to the fairest and most delicately beautiful white lady."[48] Similarly we see a strategy of universalization in the rejection, early in the twentieth century, of the very concept of "tropical" diseases, which scientists in the newly emerging discipline of "tropical medicine" attributed to tropical places and "tropical" (racially dark or racially mixed) peoples.[49] Some Latin American physicians removed the stigma of tropicalization by embracing a "universal" theory of disease causation, namely germ theory. A racial theory of illness was thereby replaced by a nonracial theory of disease etiology.[50]

A last category we want to discuss is one that, theoretically at least, moves the writer to a position of greatest distance from the terms of the dominant discourse. This category involves the creation of an "alternative ideology" that serves to place the minority writer outside the terms of the discourse of scientific racism. Such an alternative ideology functions as (and produces) a genuine oppositional discourse or set of discourses, but this is accomplished not through the appropriation and reassemblage of elements of the existing science, but by positing a radically different world view, with different perceptions of reality, goals, and points of reference. It effectively dissolves the relevance of the stereotyping discourse of science, by conceptualizing the issue of human variation in different, and essentially egalitarian, terms.

It is interesting to ask whether the individuals and groups in the period we have been examining could have created such alternatives to science, and thereby "stepped outside" the discourse and ignored science's claims about human difference and inequality. Today such alternatives seem attractive and even possible. In our so-called postmodern world, many of the projects of modernism are under attack. Among them is science itself, and its epistemology. Thomas Kuhn's investigations into scientific paradigms, the "strong program" in the social construction of science, the study of the fundamental metaphors that structure science, the feminist examination of gender in the development of scientific epistemology—all of these themes are part of the postmodern reevaluation of science, and all cast doubt

48. Delany, *Principia of Ethnology*, p. 23, Delany's italics.
49. See Thomas E. Skidmore, *Black into White: Race and Nationality in Brazilian Thought* (New York, 1974), p. 183.
50. See Nancy Stepan, *Beginnings of Brazilian Science: Oswaldo Cruz, Medical Research, and Policy, 1880–1920* (New York, 1976), pp. 57–58.

on the claims of science to be a value-free, apolitical, universal, or purely empirical form of knowledge. The consensus that once underlay the scientific enterprise has gone, and questions arise about the relativity of scientific knowledge, the fundamentally political character of science, the problems of its rationalistic claims. The fragmentation of the consensus surrounding scientific positivism, a fragmentation that is itself a product of political and social changes since the 1950s, has in turn created political and intellectual possibilities for seeing science in new ways and of imagining a science put to different political ends.

In the period between 1870 and 1920, however, the consensus about science was relatively strong. As we noted earlier, until the middle of the nineteenth century, several world views and discourses about human identity, difference, and destiny competed for cultural and political authority. Theological and political discourses, for example, rivaled science for legitimacy, and potentially offered alternative world views for the representation of human variation along lines different from that of the new scientific racism. By the middle of the century, however, science replaced other discourses in the authoritative representation of the facts of nature. As science acquired status as the preeminently empirical, value-free, and objective type of knowledge, its power to settle political issues concerning "nature" was increased. Theological, ethical, and political approaches to what scientists now presented as problems of mere empirical nature were reduced in their authority. Thus scientists effectively removed from science the most powerful defense against scientific racism and sexism—namely, the assertion that individual and group variation made no difference to issues of justice and rights. As Douglass had said, rights were grounded not in putatively neutral "facts" of different natures, but on other, political and moral, principles.

This is not to say that men and women stereotyped as different and inferior in the sciences of the late nineteenth century, and denied equality and fair treatment on the grounds of their "natures," stopped talking about and fighting for rights—for equal treatment in the law, for political representation, or the right to education. The politically motivated and biased characters of the charges made against them by supposedly "objective" scientists were often intensely felt by the stereotyped. Even as minorities at the turn of the century pinned their hopes on the possibilities inherent in the sciences for uncovering the truth about themselves, many of them saw clearly that racial science violated the standards of neutrality, and that scientists' ideas were fundamentally marked by the relations of power between the dominating and the dominated. The African-American physician, monogenist, and trenchant critic of scientific racism C. V. Roman, in 1916 (quoting the French journalist, Jean Finot) wrote: "The science of inequality is emphatically a science of white people. It is they who have invented it, and set it agoing, who have maintained, cherished, and propagated it, thanks to *their* observations and *their* deductions."[51]

To the mainstream scientists, however, such criticisms were contaminated by their language of engagement and passion, and by their source in the stereotyped or injured parties. By the norms of modern science, passion was taken to be an inappropriate stance in relation to nature and scientific argument. Science called for detachment, neutrality, a depoliticization of the terms of the debate, and the achievement of the suitably scholarly tone—even in matters of such extreme urgency and political consequence as one's own individuality and meaning. This meant, therefore, that when the stereotyped engaged in the scientific study of difference, they too found it difficult to introduce the question asked by Douglass—what difference does difference make?—and to transform the discourses of science into ones of morality and politics.[52]

What we are arguing is that in the era of the successful establishment of science as an epistemologically neutral and instrumentally successful form of knowledge, standing "outside of" or ignoring science was very difficult. With the triumph of "positive" science and positivist ideology, even those with the most radical intellectual and political philosophies and programs—alternative world views—

---

51. C. V. Roman, *American Civilization and the Negro* (Philadelphia, 1916), p. 149. Jean Finot, a naturalized Frenchman of Polish birth, wrote two of the more remarkable antiracist and antisexist books of the late nineteenth and early twentieth centuries: *Race Prejudice*, trans. Florence Wade-Evans (Miami, 1969, rpr. of Eng. ed. of 1906), and *Problems of the Sexes*, trans. Mary J. Safford (New York, 1913).

52. This difficulty remains within the field of sex differences. Usually the argument about sex or gender difference is couched in terms of "the actual facts of difference," whether the issue is brain anatomy or function, hormonal or reproductive differences, or differences in psychic or mental operations. What is rarely broached within science is why apparently small differences between the sexes (often so small they remain disputed matters to this day) are nevertheless seen as neutral *answers* to complex problems of modern social life.

tended to exempt science from their criticisms and to posit science as the one positive form of knowledge that escaped contamination from political and personal factors. A hard-hitting critique of science, as itself a political form of knowledge reflective of power, was, relatively speaking, absent.[53]

Operating within the circle of science, expressing themselves in the terms of the debate set by science, the stereotyped groups' best defense in the heyday of scientific racism was, as we have seen, to use science to point out the errors, the questionable data, and the specious logic of the discourses on human difference and inequality. The dominant discourse of race within science was not without its contradictions and fractures; it did not and could not wholly determine how individuals saw themselves. Even within the confining space and languages of science, Afro-Americans and Jews found opportunities to represent themselves in alternative yet "scientific" terms. In acting *as* scientists and intellectuals, in insisting on gaining a foothold within the scientific academy, even if on "separate and unequal" terms, they kept open and contested arenas of knowledge that otherwise might have become completely "naturalized" and uncontested.

It is true that the challenges mounted by the minorities we have examined here often made relatively little difference to mainstream science. The white, male academy usually ignored the contributions of minorities to the sciences of themselves. For instance, only one of W. E. B. Du Bois's many articles on the sociology of the African-American was published in the journal of the new profession of sociology, *The American Journal of Sociology*, even during the time when the journal was actively involved in the discussion of race (and even though its editors shared to some degree the antiracist outlook of Du Bois).[54] Similarly, Jewish scientific writing on the

53. For example, Marxists treated science as an unproblematical and highly desirable feature of modern society. The most important exceptions to the relative dearth of strong criticism of the political agendas of science were the socialist scientists, who maintained that science was part of a complex political and social system.

54. Challenges to scientific racism rarely came from within mainstream science, or from those individuals whose own status was most closely tied to science. Resistance came from the marginalized and works critical of biological determinism were rarely accepted by well-known publishers of scientific books; critics rarely held chairs of science in universities; and works of criticism were rarely reviewed seriously except

Jewish race and self-identity was more important to Jews themselves than to the establishment circles of science.

But despite the apparently marginal status of the counterwriting produced by Afro-Americans and Jews within scientific racism before the 1930s, their efforts were not without significance. Their work created modes of representation and knowledge essential for the stereotyped themselves. Swedish sociologist Gunnar Myrdal, for instance, in his massive study of race in America in the late 1930s undertaken very much in the spirit of an objective and scientific investigation, found that he was able to call upon a long tradition of scientific work produced by African-American physicians, educators, and social scientists about their own identity, meaning, and status. Myrdal remarked upon the environmentalist emphasis found in these black scientific studies of the Negro, in contrast to the innatist tendencies of the white academy. That emphasis gave black writing, he said, a much more modern tone than white writings of the same period. Myrdal also stressed that black intellectual resistance to the dogma of Negro racial inferiority had a significant impact on the black community itself. By being widely disseminated in the black press, their counterformulation of the issue of race had emerged as a fundamental belief of all black communities, he said, allowing them to refuse to accommodate themselves to white beliefs.[55] The history of resistance to dominant scientific discourses of inequality suggests that, for the stereotyped, challenges to intellectual discourses of difference and inequality were indispensable to their psychological survival and political action.

---

by the stereotyped. On Du Bois, see Blackwell and Janowitz, *Black Sociologists*, pp. 50–52.

55. Myrdal, *American Dilemma*, 1:96.

4

The Color of Politics in the United States: White Supremacy as the Main Explanation for the Peculiarities of American Politics from Colonial Times to the Present

MICHAEL GOLDFIELD

Many people have tried to discover and explain the nature, essence, or mainsprings of American politics. What makes this country tick? What are its defining, paradigmatic, idiographic characteristics? Stated another way, what is peculiar or exceptional about the United States in comparison with other economically developed capitalist countries (namely, Japan, Australia, New Zealand, Canada, Britain, and those in Western Europe)?

This question might at first glance seem particularly inappropriate for someone trained as a social scientist. It might seem eminently more suited to broad, impressionistic cultural and literary analysis—the question does not conform to the rigorous hypothesis testing commonly associated with modern social science (at least in the minds of its practitioners). Yet one might in good faith believe that the questions about the essence of American politics are worthy of a different methodology. The distinctive features of U.S. culture, the amalgamation of frontier images in politics (from Ronald Reagan on horseback to former Tennesee Senator Estes Kefauver's raccoon-skin cap), violence, movie westerns, rock music, blue grass, blues and jazz, American individualism and pragmatism, not to mention white racism, national chauvinism, and imperialist hubris all seem to lend themselves to such an analysis. One prominent political scientist, perhaps in recognition of the cogency of such an approach, has written a serious paper on this topic addressed to the specific issue of why there is no soccer in the United States.[1]

Without denying the validity of various forms of analysis of American cultural distinctiveness, one may also concentrate on a whole series of precise, often quantifiably measurable differences that help identify the peculiar nature of U.S. society and its political life. We might start by noting that this country is, of course, the wealthiest, most powerful capitalist country in the world—a fact supported by a large array of indicators, despite its relative material decline since the heyday of the post–World War II period. Yet despite this aggregate wealth, the extremes of individual poverty and affluence, particularly the grinding poverty of millions of people, disproportionately nonwhite and female, are found in no other developed country. Crime and violence and other signs of social disintegration are well known and pervasive. These conditions, particularly as they affect the poorest, darker-skinned members of our society, have dramatically worsened in the last decade.[2] To see similar conditions, one must go to economically underdeveloped countries and cities, perhaps Colombia, Calcutta, or Algiers. In spite of the large number of economically disadvantaged citizens in the United States, the nation has less social welfare, more limited national health care, less comprehensive unemployment insurance, and weaker higher educational support than far less wealthy capitalist countries. In terms of social organization, the United States has a comparatively weak trade union movement (particularly with respect to membership), although there is a long history of strikes

1. Andrei S. Markovits, "Why Is There No Soccer in the United States? Variationen zu Werner Sombarts grosse Frage," *Leviathan, Zeitschrift für Sozialwissenschaft* 15 (December 1987): 486–525.

2. This point has been forcefully and convincingly argued by William Julius Wilson, *The Truly Disadvantaged* (Chicago, 1987), among others. See also Lawrence Mishel and Jacqueline Simon, *The State of Working America* (Washington, D.C., 1988).

and conflict.[3] Finally, although it touts itself as the paradigm of democracy, the United States has among the lowest rates of voter participation in elections, completely skewed by class and race. And there are many who argue that high-level uniform voter participation is a central de facto (substantive) as opposed to de jure (that is, formal) criterion for democracy.[4]

Those writers who have focused on the distinctiveness of political life in the United States have invariably highlighted our lack of a labor, social-democratic, socialist, or communist party with significant electoral and organizational support. Unlike all other developed capitalist countries, the United States has no substantial, independent working-class party. The key question, then, is why working-class politics is so undeveloped. Attempts to explain this apparently unique feature of U.S. society have been manifold for over a century. Analysts have ranged across the political spectrum, from Marxists (including Marx, Engels, Lenin, and Trotsky, who tried to explain the reasons for the historical, temporary retardation of the U.S. working-class movement), to more conservative commentators who have argued that the United States was not merely exceptional, but a permanent, enduring proof to the falsity of Marxist prognosis.[5]

Here is a sampling of explanations for "American exceptionalism."

3. Michael Goldfield, *The Decline of Organized Labor in the United States* (Chigao, 1989), pp. 127–32, 11, 15, 16, 39–40.

4. See for example, Walter Dean Burnham, "The Appearance and Disappearance of the American Voter," *The Current Crisis in American Politics* (Oxford, 1982); and Frances Fox Piven and Richard A. Cloward, *Why Americans Don't Vote* (New York, 1989).

5. Daniel Bell, *The End of Ideology* (New York, 1960); Clark Kerr et al., *Industrialism and Industrial Man* (Cambridge, Mass., 1960). The idea of "American exceptionalism" owes its genesis to a debate within the Communist party of the United States and the Communist International (or Commintern) during the late 1920s. Jay Lovestone and his associates, who took over the leadership of the Communist party in 1927, albeit with strong minority opposition, attempted to justify the weakness of their party and its need for a "nonrevolutionary" American approach on the basis of the historic strength and adaptability of U.S. capitalism. His opponents in the U.S. party, eventually supported by the Commintern, accused him of a break with Marxism which they labeled "American exceptionalism." During the late 1920s and the 1930s, large numbers of U.S. intellectuals, many of whom would eventually become prominent academics, were involved in the radical movement; they provided the transmission belt for the terminology to become absorbed into the mainstream of academia.

1. Alexis de Tocqueville and Werner Sombart identified the supposedly more democratic, egalitarian features of U.S. society as the reason for the absence of developed working-class politics.

2. Others, like Stephen Thernstrom, point to alleged higher rates of social mobility.

3. Geographic mobility and uprooting of the poorest members of the working-class population has also been cited as a key factor. The transient character of the worst-off parts of the population precluded the formation of stable working-class communities, the basis in many other countries for enduring left working-class politics.

4. Louis Hartz, in his classic *The Liberal Tradition in America*, argues for the importance of a nonfeudal past in this country and the acceptance by the general population of a strong belief in Lockean individualism. These factors are sometimes said to be reflected in the frontier images and the Horatio Alger myth.

5. Some assert that workers have historically had higher wages here. Or, in the words of Sombart, in the United States, "All Socialist utopias came to nothing on roast beef and apple pie."[6]

6. The historian Frederick Jackson Turner and his followers have pointed to the existence of a frontier in the Western United States as a "safety valve" for working-class frustration and discontent.

7. Political scientist Theodore Lowi has stressed the federal structure of U.S. politics as the main obstacle to the formation of an influential working-class party.

8. Others have located working-class failures in a lack of solidarity rooted in the historic ethnic diversity of the country.

9. Still others have argued for the centrality of early white manhood suffrage, gained more easily here than in Europe and other countries.

10. The savage repression of working-class radicals by the state and the extreme nature of capitalist opposition to working-class politics and organization are cited by some analysts.

11. In a global, anti-Marxist argument, Kerr, and others claim that sharp class conflict is a feature not of developed capitalist society, but of emerging preindustrial society.[7]

12. And the list goes on.[8]

6. Alexis de Tocqueville, *Democracy in America*, 2 vols. (New York, 1956). Stephen Thernstrom, *Poverty and Progress* (New York, 1975). Louis Hartz, *The Liberal Tradition in America* (New York, 1955). Werner Sombart, *Why Is There No Socialism in the United States?* (White Plains, N.Y., 1976), p. 106.

7. Frederick Jackson Turner, *Frontier and Section: Selected Essays* (Englewood Cliffs, N.J., 1961). Theodore J. Lowi, "Why Is There No Socialism in the United States? A Federal Analysis," *International Political Science Review* 5: (1984): 369–90. Kerr et al., *Industrialism*.

8. I first became aware of the arguments over American exceptionalism from a pithy and cogent pamphlet by Theodore Allen ("Can White Workers—Radicals—Be Radicalized?" Ann Arbor, Mich., 1968), where a brief analysis of many of the foregoing explanations is presented. See also Allen, *The Kernel and the Meaning* (Verso, forth-

All these theories are in my view defective. Those that are not totally misleading or wrong provide at best only partial insights.[9] Here, let me merely note that social mobility studies have shown little difference between the United States and other capitalist countries during the relevant comparable historical periods.[10] White manhood suffrage was extremely limited before the Civil War, and in the South after 1900. From the dawn of the twentieth century until the 1960s, disenfranchisement affected poor whites almost as much as it did blacks in the South.[11] The issue of white male suffrage, of course, never touches on the disenfrachisement of nonwhites, women before their enfranchisement in 1920, and noncitizen immigrants. Feudalism was long gone in Europe before working-class movements emerged there. Finally, the frontier (whatever its impact in an earlier time)—has long since departed from the U.S. landscape.

Reconceptualization of the Problem

The problem of American exceptionalism must be posed differently. There have been many times in U.S. history when mass, radical, broad-based, sometimes violent, working-class upheavals took place. These struggles have sometimes had both the breadth and intensity of uprisings in other countries that led to the establishment of independent working-class political organization. The real question then (and here I follow the lead suggested in Allen) is not why such struggles have not taken place (since, of course, they have—no matter how deeply buried and suppressed this information is in many standard presentations of U.S. history), but why they were so comparatively short-lived, why they were repressed or un-

---

coming). A comprehensive discussion of many of these and other theories may also be found in Seymour Martin Lipset, "Why No Socialism in the United States?" in S. Bailer and S. Sluzard, eds., *Sources of Contemporary Radicalism* (Boulder, Colo. 1977); convenient excerpts for many positions are available in a collection by John Laslett and Seymour Martin Lipset, *Failure of a Dream!* (Garden City, N.Y., 1974).

9. Broad critiques of these theories may be found in Allen "Can White Workers—Radicals—Be Radicalized?" and in Lipset "Why No Socialism?" See also Ian Katznelson, *City Trenches* (New York, 1981).

10. Lipset and Reinhold Bendix, *Social Mobility in Industrial Society* (Berkeley, Calif., 1964).

11. V. O. Key, *Southern Politics in State and Nation* (Knoxville, Tenn., 1949).

successful, why they did not lead to the formation of a more enduring form of class-based organization.[12] To place this question in historical perspective I want to mention some of the broad insurgencies that have occurred in this country.

Protest and struggle by the lower classes can be traced to the very beginnings of the Anglo-American colonies on these shores. Colonial society was shaken by a series of lower-class revolts between 1660 and 1680, many of these taking place in Virginia, the wealthiest, most populous, most important colony, the home to the families of most of the future Founding Fathers. The underlying causes of the rebellions were the oppressive conditions of labor and life of the current and newly freed bond servants. Their circumstances and opportunities were held in check by the colonial elite, a corrupt, avaricious group of large tobacco planters who completely controlled the colonial government. The most significant revolt during the early colonial period was Bacon's Rebellion in 1676. Nathaniel Bacon, himself a member of the colonial elite but involved in a dispute with the governor, was pressed by the logic of events to offer freedom to servants and slaves who would join him; he forced the House of Burgesses to pass a series of democratic measures, burned Jamestown to the ground (after Governor Berkeley had accused Bacon of treason), then temporarily forced the governor and his allies to flee. Edmund Morgan, discussing the class resentment in Virginia, argues, "It is questionable how long Virginia could have continued on this course, keeping men in servitude for years and then turning them free to be frustrated by the engrossers of land, by the collectors of customs, by the county courts, by their elected representatives, by the council, and, above all, by the king himself"[13]

The period of Reconstruction between 1868 and 1876 is not generally regarded as one of labor struggle in the South. The key text for this interpretation is W. E. B. Du Bois's *Black Reconstruction.* Du Bois describes the development of a surprisingly united black and white laboring class in the South, struggling for political influence in Reconstruction state governments and for economic equality against the former planter class and its allies. A parallel labor move-

12. Allen, "Can White Workers—Radicals—Be Radicalized?"

13. Edmund Morgan, *American Slavery, American Freedom* (New York, 1975), p. 246, quotation from p. 292.

ment (which conceived of itself as national) was developing in the North, with few ties to the drama in the South.[14]

In 1877, a year that historian Robert Bruce calls the year of violence, rail centers throughout the country were aflame, as workers, their families, and other citizens battled troops.[15] In many cases these troops were the same military units that had just been withdrawn from the South, ensuring the defeat of Reconstruction at the hands of the Ku Klux Klan (KKK) and other planter-supported vigilantes. The armories that disfigure many U.S. cities were first built in 1877 in order to have ready arms to defeat working-class insurgencies in railroad towns.

From 1886, when hundreds of thousands of workers struck for the eight-hour day and bloody Haymarket saw eight working-class leaders framed for police murder, to 1894, when Eugene V. Debs led hundreds of thousands of railroad workers in the Pullman strike, the U.S. army was used at least 328 times to suppress strikes.

During the 1880s and 1890s, under the leadership of the Colored Farmers Alliance, the Farmers' Alliance, and the People's (Populist) Party, when crops were selling well below their costs of production, black and white farmers briefly joined hands to fight against banks, railroad magnates, and trusts.

As both a leader and a reflection of opposition to the government, the Socialist party, with its extensive press and elected government officials, rolled up large presidential votes in 1912 and 1920. With Debs as the Socialist candidate, the party's total in 1912 reached over 700,000 or 6 percent of the vote, and in 1920, the tally was almost a million.

During the 1930s, depression and anger led to insurgency in almost every downtrodden sphere of society, among African-Americans, farmers, the unemployed, students, and intellectuals. Most dramatic were the massive worker upheavals, culminating in the creation of integrated industrial unions in major industries. New constituencies entered the political arena realigning the country's electoral process, even as they created influential state-level and local left-wing third parties.

The struggles of the 1960s and early 1970s, whose motor force

14. See, for example, David Montgomery, *Beyond Equality: Labor and the Radical Republicans, 1862–1872* (New York, 1970).
15. Robert V. Bruce, *1877: Year of Violence* (Chicago, 1959).

was the African-American Freedom Movement, inaugurated what might be called a second period of Reconstruction. This movement stimulated and gave birth to the massive student and antiwar demonstrations, the movement for women's equality and liberation, and the militant organization of federal, state, and local governmental employees.

The history of labor and popular movements, of course, is replete with examples of narrowness, national chauvinism in the guise of patriotism, male supremacy, and most of all of white racism, even polluting some of the aforementioned upheavals, staining some of the finest examples of militant, solidaristic, multiracial, ethnic, and gender struggles and organization. Now, I will argue that racism and ethnic chauvinism, or at the very least insensitivity to the importance of solidarity in the fight against white supremacy have been instrumental in the defeat or failure of many of these movements. But that is only one strand. The main enigma is that U.S. labor and social history is filled with inspiring examples of African-American and white working-class solidarity. It is certainly not merely a history of race hatred and lack of solidarity by white workers.

Modern scholars have amassed evidence that suggests black and white laborers in the early colonial period accepted each other as equals. As Edmund Morgan concludes: "Black and white serving the same master worked, ate, and slept together, and together shared in escapades, escapes and punishments." This familiarity was reflected in many of the revolts, including Bacon's Rebellion. As we saw, although Bacon himself was a member of the colonial elite and certainly a racist with respect to Indians, the logic of events had forced him to declare freedom for all the black and white servants and slaves who would follow him. Both African-Americans and whites responded in large numbers. Even after the untimely death of Bacon allowed the rebellion to dissipate greatly, more than 100 black and white followers stuck together to the end, refusing to yield.[16]

---

16. Morgan, *American Slavery, American Freedom,* p. 155. Bacon's thousands of supporters were only demobilized by trickery. This was accomplished through the skilful and deceitful maneuvering of Governor Berkeley's representative Captain Thomas Grantham. According to Wilcomb E. Washburn, Grantham approached the last group of "400 English and Negroes in arms." "Most of the men he persuaded to disperse to their homes, but eighty Negroes and twenty English refused to deliver the arms." Wilcolm Washburn, *The Governor and the Rebel* (Chapel Hill, N.C.,

During the Civil War, there were significant numbers of white loyalists in the South. Theodore Allen estimates that one out of twenty white Southern soldiers fought for the North. This fact was largely ignored until recently by most Civil War historians, whose sympathies for the Confederacy are well known. A largely white county in Mississippi, Jones County, seceded from the Confederacy, engaging in guerilla warfare against the Confederate rebel armies.[17]

Numerous local labor movements provide examples of interracial solidarity, even in the face of strong racist public opinion. Among the most impressive were the unions in New Orleans between 1880 and the 1920s, where black and white laborers, led by the city's dock workers, displayed strong mutual support, including joint participation in the 1893 general strike.[18] Also successful during the 1880s and 1890s, going against the increasing informal and legally enforced patterns of segration in the South were the Knights of Labor with their many local assemblies, meetings, and strikes jointly involving both African-American and white workers.[19] Even the Populists at times understood and practiced an impressive degree of solidarity during the 1890s. As C. Vann Woodward reports in his biography of the Populist leader Tom Watson,

> At a time when Georgia led all states in lynching, Watson announced that it was the object of his party to "make lynch law odious to the people." And in 1896 the Populist platform of Georgia contained a plank denouncing lynch law. In the campaign of 1892 a Negro Populist who had made sixty-three separate speeches for Watson was threatened with lynching and fled to him for protection. Two thousand armed white farmers, some of whom rode all night, responded to Watson's call for aid and remained on guard for two nights at his home to avert the threat of violence.[20]

1957), p. 88. All of this attests to the interracial character of Bacon's armed minions. See Allen, "Class Struggle and the Origin of Racial Slavery," *Radical America* 9 (May–June 1975): 41–63, for a detailed analysis.

17. Allen, *The Invention of the White Race* (Verso, forthcoming); V. O. Key, *Southern Politics*, p. 328.

18. Robert Wallace Shugg, "The New Orleans General Strike of 1892," *Louisiana Historical Quarterly* 21 (April 1938): 547–60; David Paul Bennetts, "Black and White Workers: New Orleans, 1880–1900" (Ph.D. diss., University of Illinois, 1972); Daniel Rosenberg, *New Orleans Dockworkers: Race, Labor, and Unionism, 1892–1923* (Albany, N.Y., 1988).

19. See, for example, Peter Rachleff's *Black Labor in Richmond, 1865–1890* (Chicago, 1989).

20. C. Vann Woodward, *Tom Watson: Agrarian Rebel* (New York, 1934), p. 44.

During the early part of the twentieth century, the Industrial Workers of the World (IWW) with their program for organizing all oppressed labor, organized black and white workers together in the North and South. In Phildelphia, between 1913 and the early 1920s, the IWW maintained their organization of dock workers (approximately 50 percent African-American, and 50 percent white) in the face of racist appeals from both employers and American Federation of Labor (AFL) unions. Between 1910 and 1913, the IWW successfully maintained an organization of 35,000 Southern timber workers in Lousianna, Texas, and Arkansas. The timber workers, with a membership evenly divided between black and white, often defied Jim Crow barriers in the deep South, to provide integrated democratic meetings.

From shortly after the time of its founding in the 1880s until the 1940s, most of the craft unions in the American Federation of Labor (and most of the independent union like those in railroad) had racially discriminatory policies of one form or another. The major exception to this general trend was the United Mine Workers (UMW). From the turn of the century on, with varying degrees of success, the UMW attempted to organize both black and white workers throughout the coal districts of the North and South. Very early they had constitutional clauses with penalities for discrimination. In 1924, with the rise of the Klan, they added a clause outlawing KKK membership. The UMW had many black officials, including local presidents in areas of low African-American concentration. Black officials were, of course, also prominent in those areas of high African-American concentration in the mining regions of Alabama and parts of West Virginia.[21]

By the 1930s a large number of industrial unions were organizing black and white workers together, and championing the fight against the special oppression of their Afro-American members. These unions, either under left-wing leadership or with a large leftist influence, included the Mine, Mill, and Smelter Workers, the Packinghouse Workers, several maritime unions, longshoremen on the

21. For widely differing perspectives on the depths of egalitarianism in the UMW see Herbert Gutman, "The Negro and the United Mine Workers of America," in Julius Jacobson, ed., *The Negro and the American Labor Movement* (Garden City, N.Y., 1968); chap. 10 in Stirling Spero and Abram Harris, *The Black Worker* (New York, 1968); and Herbert Hill, "Myth-Making as Labor History," *International Journal of Politics, Culture and Society* 2 (Winter, 1988): 132–200.

West Coast, as well as the unions in auto, electrical, and farm and construction equipment.

During the late 1960s and early 1970s, hundreds of African-American worker organizations developed throughout the country, whose apex was reached with the short-lived League of Revolutionary Black Workers in Detroit. These groups eventually generated a strong degree of support by white workers, culminating in a series of wildcat strikes against Chrysler Corporation in 1973 led by African-American radical workers. And in a lesser political act, although not totally devoid of political significance, white workers in Michigan, Wisconsin, California, and other places joined with their African-American brethren to vote for Jesse Jackson.

In this extended preface, I have pointed out a range of possibilities and problems related to the theme of the peculiarity of American politics and the low level of sustained class organization. Next I want to sketch out some key episodes or turning points in U.S. history, showing the centrality of race in politics. My analysis will focus on the ideology of white supremacy, on both its semiautonomous character and its roots in the political economy. My burden will be to show the importance of white supremacy for American exceptionalism, to indicate its superiority in comparison to the Hartzian argument about American individualism.

Theories of Race

The first task is to look at several theoretical approaches to analyzing race. Biological theories of racial superiority, inferiority, and hierarchy were dominant through the 1920s, but these theories have been largely discredited and, thus, will not be discussed here. More popular today is the theory that Allen calls the psychocultural approach. This view, while rejecting the superiority of any particular group, argues among other things that race prejudice and racial oppression are natural, rooted in deep-seated psychological needs for cultural identity; thus, racism is a set of attitudes, either innate or transmitted. Hence, white racism and racial slavery were the inevitable consequences of British culture and the search for a colonial identity. Carl Degler, Winthrop Jordan, and perhaps Gunnar Myrdal are representative of this approach; each has done important research, some of which in my opinion casts doubt on their central theses. Nevertheless, the psychocultural approach historically has been dominant in the study of race, only recently challenged by mainstream scholars. Hartz's emphasis on the centrality of the "liberal tradition" is also rooted in the psychocultural methodology. The challenge to this view has come from those holding a socioeconomic approach which, while giving a certain independent weight to cultural and psychological features, argues that they are neither primary, nor completely autonomous. Rather, race and racial oppression are rooted in changing economic and social conditions, often in the economic needs of ruling classes. This approach is reflected in the work of Eric Williams, Oliver Cox, W. E. B. Du Bois, Mary and Oscar Handlin, Lerone Bennett, William Julius Wilson, Theodore Allen, and perhaps Edmund Morgan.[22]

The truth, I believe, does not exist in the golden mean. Although I disagree with various socioeconomic analyses, I will attempt to show that this general approach is largely correct and that the psychocultural perspective is wrong in essential aspects. Even within the tradition of those who emphasize socioeconomic factors, however, there are telling differences.

The proper place to start is to return once more to the beginning, with the development of colonialism in the New World. During the sixteenth and seventeenth centuries the Portugese, Spanish, Dutch, French, and English began to explore and settle the Americas. Supported by investors and their respective governments, each nationally affiliated contingent of explorers and settlers sought to discover wealth and amass fortunes, both for themselves and their various sponsors. Aside from the initial large amounts of gold stolen from the Aztecs and other Indian tribes by the Spanish and other early expeditions, the main wealth in the New World turned out to be the vast quantities of fertile land. The productive use of this land, however, required labor. Unlike in England and various parts of Europe where a ready supply of labor was available in the form of peasants and former serfs who had been forced from their hereditary land, in the Americas labor had to be imported. The Portuguese, Spanish, and Dutch with small populations at home could supply

22. Allen, "Class Struggle," p. 19. Degler's views may be seen in his *Neither Black nor White: Slavery and Race Relations in Brazil and the United States* (New York, 1971). Michael Omni and Howard Winant, *Racial Formation in the United States* (New York, 1986) also falls into this broad approach with its extensive emphasis on the cultural aspects of race.

very few laborers from their domestic reserves. They soon began to rely on Africans who had been bought, kidnapped, stolen, or captured from their homeland. The English, with their huge surplus of unemployed laborers, dispossessed churchmen, paupers, beggars, vagabonds, thieves, highway robbers, pickpockets, prostitutes, and despised "riff raff," were the only colonizing power with a huge labor surplus to send to the Americas. And, this they did by enticement (including the promise of eventual free parcels of land or, in New England, religious freedom) and coercion (sentencing and kidnapping). The distinctive feature of colonial labor on the Anglo-American mainland throughout the seventeenth century was that it was made up of British and European indentured servants. These laborers would eventually be referred to as "white," although before 1680 the term was not a common one for racial or ethnic identification.[23]

As a number of historians have argued (including the Handlins, Morgan, Bennett, and Allen), slavery, bondage, and servitude were not originally racial in the United States. The original group of African bond servants (those who first arrived in 1619 in the Virginia colony and those that soon followed them to the Anglo-American mainland colonies) seem to have been freed after their terms were served in the same manner as their British and European brethren. It was only in the period from 1680 to 1710 that hereditary lifetime African slavery was first regularly instituted. And, in order for this slavery to become institutionalized, the early English tolerance as expressed in the words and actions of explorer Francis Drake, early British colonial leader Richard Hakluyt, and in the easy relations between African and "white" bondsmen had to be defeated. As recent historical research makes clear, the passage of Irish, English, and European bond servants to the New World was as horrific and deadly as that later suffered by African slaves. The conditions of labor for the Africans and non-Africans when they arrived were equally oppressive. As Edmund Morgan explains in describing the working conditions of African-American bond servants, "There is no evidence before 1660 that they were subjected to more severe discipline than other servants." Even sexual relations seem to have been on a relatively equal basis. "In 1649 William Watts, a white

23. Allen, "Slavery, Racism, and Democracy," *Monthly Review* 29 (March 1978): 57–63. See Winthrop Jordan, *White over Black* (New York, 1977), p. 95.

man, and Mary, a Negro servant, were required to do penance for fornication, like any other couple, by standing in the church at Elizabeth River with the customary white sheet and white wand."[24] And, as Lerone Bennett argues, "It was not at all unusual for a white master to force a white woman servant to marry a black male servant. Nor was it unusual for a white master to give a black man a position of authority over white male and white female servants."[25]

These facts bode ill for the psychocultural interpretation. In addition, if long-standing racial prejudice was central, why were not Jews and the historically despised and abundant Irish laborers enslaved? Further, if the prejudices on the Anglo-American mainland were traceable to long-term attitudes rooted in English culture, why was the color line so sharp in the Anglo-American colonies, but so fluid in the British Carribean, where there was a clear social place for the children of mixed parentage? And, casting the net wider, we might ask, why in Brazil did there exist social mobility for Afro-Brazilians? These clear, unambiguous facts are the reefs on which the fanciful project of psychoculturalism must ultimately be shipwrecked.

To maintain and increase their wealth, British colonialists, American capitalists, merchants, and plantation owners not only needed laborers, they needed to control them. And, the many rebellions between 1660 and 1680, some interracial, many largely "white" (both former bondsmen, now free, and present bondsmen), of which Bacon's rebellion was the most important, "convinced" the plantation owners and other elites that a "white" racial identity was central. Theodore Allen presents a compelling argument for this case.[26] He argues that what is needed to maintain control of the laboring population in a colony is a social buffer. It was the numerical ratio of poor whites to blacks that led to the creation of a "white" social buffer and the sharp drawing of the color line in what was to become the United States. Where few whites lived, as in Haiti, Barbados, and Brazil, it was necessary to create other forms of social buffers, mulattoes where their numbers were sufficient, free blacks where they were not. This I believe, following Allen, is the key to some of the central differences in racial and skin color

24. Morgan, *American Slavery, American Freedom*, pp. 154, 155.
25. Lerone Bennett, *The Shaping of Black America* (Chicago, 1975), p. 18.
26. Allen, "Class Struggle."

classifications in South Africa, Brazil, the Anglo-Carribean, and various former Spanish colonies.[27]

The centrality of slavery to the subsequent development of the early colonial economy is partially reflected in the fact that Virginia in particular and the South in general were the most prosperous, most rapidly growing part of the country. Not only was the South dependent on slavery, but a good deal of the economic health of the Northern Anglo-American colonies was dependent on their commercial dealings with the wealthier South.[28]

The economic importance of slavery did not merely stand by itself, but asserted itself in colonial politics. Slavery was to be a pivotal issue in the formation of the Union. Despite the growing antislavery sentiment in the North after the 1750s in the form of activities by Quakers, increasing opposition to the international slave trade, the formation of abolition and manumission societies, the rising agitation and petitions of free African-Americans, and the outspoken statements of a small number of colonial leaders (Benjamin Franklin was the most prominent), serious consideration for the plight of African-American slaves at the time of the American Revolution was minimal. The spirit of 1776 had already developed what W. E. B. Du Bois called the "American blindspot." Southern elites knew that every bit of their affluence was completely dependent on African slavery. Without it, they would be impoverished. The South Carolinians were quite lucid on this point at the Constitutional Convention. For example, a representative from South Carolina, General Pinckney, stated that without slaves, "South Carolina would soon be a desert waste." Rawlin Lowndes, a delegate from South Carolina who opposed ratification because he thought that the Constitution jeopardized slave property, stated: "Without negroes, this state would degenerate into one of the most contemptible in the union . . . Negroes are our wealth, our only natural resource." The enthusiastic participation of most Southerners in the formation

27. A parallel argument is given by George Fredrickson, *White Supremacy* (New York, 1981) in his chapter "Race Mixture and the Color Line," comparing the United States and South Africa.

28. Virginia was to be soon displaced, but not by a Northern colony. According to Donald Robinson, by the middle of the eighteenth century, "South Carolina was the richest colony on the mainland," and not fortuitously, "slavery there the harshest." Robinson, *Slavery in the Structure of American Politics, 1765–1820* (New York, 1979), pp. 55–56.

of a national government had one absolute qualification: black slavery could not be affected. Northern political elites, of course, knew this; there could be no Union without their acceptance of slavery in the South. No Northern leader of any importance at the Constitutional Convention ever seriously suggested that the freedom fought for in the Revolution should apply to black people in the South.[29]

Yet, this complete capitulation in accepting the legality of slavery did *not* eliminate it as a major issue. While the Continental Congress rejected the South Carolinian attempt to place the adjective "white" in the Constitution, it acceded or compromised on almost every other demand. Sectional disputes on how to regard Negro slavery came up over taxation (1783) and representation (1787). The Founding Fathers made a final compromise on July 12, 1787, by assigning three-fifths representation for both issues. And this compromise had momentous consequences. As Robinson's argues,

> It gave constitutional sanction to the fact that the United States was composed of some persons who were "free" and others who were not. And it established the principle, new in republican theory that a man who lived among slaves had a greater share in the election of representatives than the man who did not. With one stroke, despite the disclaimers of its advocates, it acknowledged slavery and rewarded slaveowners. It is a measure of their adjustment to slavery that Americans in the eighteenth century found this settlement natural and just.[30]

The centrality and dominance of racial slavery and the hegemony of white supremacy throughout the land is perhaps nowhere more clearly seen than in the complete capitulation of Northern delegates over the 1787 Fugitive Slave Law. Any black person in any state in

29. See ibid., pp. 210, 242, 141. Thus, the vaunted federalism of U.S. politics may be traced back to the desires of the Southern ruling class to preserve their particularly oppressive and remunerative forms of exploitation based on white supremacy, without northern interference. These federalist stances extended far beyond the slavery era. They can be seen, for example, in the 1930s with Southern political opposition to nationally uniform minimum wages and relief rates; they were also reflected in the 1950s and 1960s in the opposition to federal civil rights directives, including Arkansas governor Orval Forbus's initial defiance of President Eisenhower at Little Rock in 1957 and former Alabama Governor George Wallace's long-term resistance to integration.

30. Robinson, *Slavery in the Structure of American Politics*, p. 201.

the Union, if she or he were accused of being a fugitive slave must be captured and sent back to the place from whence they supposedly escaped. Thus the North permitted its free black citizens to be captured by Southern slave owners with the help of Northern officials and delivered up to the whims of the slaveocracy and its judicial officials. No right to a hearing prior to transfer was provided. Robinson suggests that Northern delegates might have successfully taken a stand on this and other slave-related issues had they so desired.[31] Gouverneur Morris of New York was probably the only delegate who argued against these laws on abolitionist grounds. Benjamin Franklin, who missed virtually all of the proceedings because he was in Europe, demanded in 1790 through a petition the immediate ending of the slave trade. The vehemence and self-confidence of the attacks against him by Southern representatives suggest that the standard interpretation of this period—that the Founding Fathers including the Virginians in this period, before the invention of the cotton gin and the Haitian Revolution, hoped that slavery would soon die out—is completely off the mark.

Slavery remained a central issue from the founding period throughout the first part of the nineteenth century not because abolition was a dominant political issue, but because slavery was the focal point of sectional conflict. The sectional conflict primarily revolved around whether the plantation capitalists of the South or the merchant and industrial capitalists of the North would control the national government. Though tariffs, foreign policy, and a host of related issues were involved, the key determining issue was whether slavery would be extended to the new territories, first east of the Mississippi, then to the huge expanses west of the great river. The outcome of this struggle would eventually determine who would control the fortunes of the nation and what would be the primary method by which labor would be exploited in the country as a whole. Yet, it is clear that opposition to the extension of slavery implied, neither in theory nor practice, an opposition to the already existing slavery of the South.

The issue of slavery in the territories began early. It arose in 1790 at the time of the Southwest Ordinance and again in 1798 with the organization of the Midwestern territories under the Northwest Ordinance. The question was discussed heatedly after the revolt of the

31. Ibid., pp. 232–33.

"Black Jacobins" in Haiti led by Toussaint L'Ouverture in 1791.[32] In 1803, the Louisiana Purchase raised the issue again with renewed vehemance. It was temporarily resolved in 1820 with the Missouri Compromise. During the Senate debates over this latter bill, Rufus King denounced slavery itself; his attack was reprinted in pamphlet form. One of those who read the pamphlet was a remarkable slave named Denmark Vessey who would organize an underground insurrectionary network involving thousands. The issue of slavery in the territories was debated with increased fury between 1846 and 1847 over the Wilmot Proviso. The question of statehood for Texas and the war with Mexico, both supported heavily by slaveowners, fueled the fire. The extension of slavery was settled temporarily again by the Clay-Webster Compromise of 1850 and a new Fugitive Slave Law. The conflict raged on over the 1854 Kansas-Nebraska Act and with the vehemently proslavery 1857 Dred Scott decision.

And the discourse often took a far from genteel form. The proslavery vigilantes and thugs had been so brutal to independent white farmers in Kansas that the massacre of a group of those vigilantes by John Brown and his men in 1856 at Oswatomie, Kansas, did not lead to a backlash. Instead, the event reinvigorated abolitionists and underscored the fact that proslavery forces could only be stopped by violence. After four years of civil war, Kansas was declared a free state in 1858. In 1859, John Brown again electrified the nation. With a small band of men, Brown attacked the Harpers Ferry federal arsenal, seizing wagon loads of arms to begin launching armed slave insurrection in the South. The plan nearly succeeded and if it had, Afro-American slaves might have been liberated by their own armed guerilla struggle and the subsequent course of U.S. history would undoubtedly have been different. Instead Brown was captured. He was hanged and martyred. His last prophetic words, which were to serve as an inspiration to Union troops in the coming war, were as follows: "I, John Brown, am quite certain that the crimes of this guilty land will never be purged away but with blood."[33] The most popular song of the ensuing Civil War was to become "John Brown's Body."

How central was the turn to a reliance on African slavery during the late seventeenth and early eighteenth century in the Southern

32. C. L. R. James, *The Black Jacobins* (New York, 1963).
33. W. E. B. Du Bois, *John Brown* (New York, 1962), p. 365.

colonies? Its significance, not merely to North America's future, but to the whole development of the world economy, was stated succinctly by Karl Marx:

> Without slavery you have no cotton; without cotton you have no modern industry. It is slavery that gave the colonies their value; it is the colonies that created world trade that is the pre-condition of large-scale industry. Thus slavery is an economic category of the greatest importance.
>
> Without slavery North America, the most progressive of countries, would be transformed into a patriarchal country. Wipe North America off the map of the world and you will have anarchy—the complete decay of modern commerce and civilization. Cause slavery to disappear and you will have wiped America off the map of nations.[34]

Specific figures underscore the phenomenal growth in the production of cotton and the crucial role of the system of Afro-American slavery that produced it:

1791—9,000 bales of cotton
1800—79,000
1822—1/2 million
1831—1 million
1840—2 million
1852—3 million
1861—5 million

This exponential increase in cotton production supplied the raw materials for Britain to become the workshop of the world.[35] Besides creating pressure for newer, more fertile lands to the west, it created a greater demand for more slaves. To control and maintain the labor supply that produced this enormous wealth, an elaborate system of white supremacy in law, economic hierarchy, and personal relations had to be developed. The whole system was justified by a racist ideology of extreme white chauvinism, an ideology that developed a life of its own. For the entire structure of white supremacy and

34. Friedrich Engels comments in a footnote that this statement by Marx was correct for 1847. It was only as the North began to industrialize in the 1850s and produce meat and corn for export that the abolition of slavery became economically possible. Both the quote and footnote by Engels are on page 112, Karl Marx, *The Poverty of Philosophy* (1847; Moscow, n.d.).
35. W. E. B. Du Bois, *Black Reconstruction* (Cleveland, Ohio, 1964), p. 4.

its racist ideology to gain legitimacy, they both had to be extended to the North and West. As Du Bois argues, the free African-American in the United States, unlike in the Carribean or Brazil, particularly the educated or skilled free African-American, was a grave threat to the ideology of white supremacy:

> As slavery grew to a system and the Cotton Kingdom began to expand into imperial white domination, a free Negro was a contradiction, a threat and a menace. As a thief and a vagabond, he threatened society; but as an educated property holder, a successful mechanic or even professional man, he more than threatened slavery. He contradicted and undermined it. He must not be. He must be suppressed, enslaved, colonized. And nothing so bad could be said about him that did not easily appear as true to slaveholders.

To enforce this rigid system of white supremacy, Du Bois argues that "gradually the whole white South became an armed and commissioned camp to keep Negroes in slavery and to kill the black rebel."[36] The shadow of the plantation became so firmly entrenched, not merely in the South, but in the North and the country as a whole, that by 1857 it seemed to many only natural when the Supreme Court upheld the Dred Scott decision, asserting that African-Americans had no rights that whites were bound to respect.[37] Newspapers and other periodicals in the South and the rest of the country were part of the ideological apparatus that saturated the nation with white chauvinist filth, justifying as natural, necessary, even noble, the stench of the New Orleans slave markets, the sting of the lash, and even the slave-breeding farms in Virginia and other border states.

Only the socioeconomic approach allows one to fully integrate an understanding of gender and class oppression with an understanding of the domination of racial oppression. For example, such a framework offers a clear explanation of the sexual exploitation of African-American women by Euro-American men as a particular variant of the traditional forms of ruling-class male supremacist domination.

With the development of great factories in the North, Northern workers faced the full range of brutal features of early industrialization in capitalist societies: low wages, insecure livelihoods, ac-

36. Ibid., pp. 7, 12.
37. Frederick Douglass, *The Life and Times of Frederick Douglass* (New York, 1962), p. 293.

cidents, injuries, disfigurement and crippling, disease, early death, child labor, and repression of their attempts at organization. Yet the Northern workers' movement, including the bulk of its radical wing, was peculiarly obtuse to the plight of African-Americans in the South. Thus, the pre–Civil War abolitionist movement, with its black and white supporters, and the pre–Civil War white workers' movement had hardly any point of intersection.

Du Bois describes the situation:

> Here then, were two labor movements: the movement to give the black worker a minimum legal status which would enable him to sell his own labor, and another movement... to increase the wage and better the condition of the working class... largely composed of foreign immigrants, and dispute with the new American capitalism the basis upon which the new wealth was to be divided. Broad philanthropy and a wide knowledge of the elements of human progress would have led these two movements to unite and in their union to become irresistible. It was difficult, almost impossible, for this to be clear to the white labor leaders of the thirties. They had their own particularistic grievances and one of these was the competition of free Negro labor [and] they could easily envision a new and tremendous competition of black workers after all the slaves became free. What they did not see... was that this competition... would continue... if the Negro continued as a slave worker. On the other hand, the Abolitionists did not realize the plight of the white laborer, especially the semiskilled and unskilled worker.

White labor leaders suffered from a blindspot. They preached the doctrine of Free Soilism, an illusory escapist solution to the plight of labor that had a "whites only" tag on it. Until the early 1850s when Joseph Wedemeyer and other radical followers of Karl Marx who understood the importance of abolition for the white workers, gained some small influence in the white workers' movement, labor leaders as a whole were more interested in freedom from Afro-Americans than in freedom for them. The rallying cry of Free Soilism in 1845 was the Wilmot Proviso, which barred slavery from the new territories, but suggested that land rights should be reserved for whites only. Such an approach was counterposed to the more radical and more realistic approach offered by Frederick Douglass for Kansas in 1854. Douglass argued that 1,000 free black homesteading families settling in Kansas would put up a "wall of living fire" through which slavery could not pass.[38] He argued that this approach would provide a more certain and more peaceful approach to stopping the spread of slavery.

With such a divided movement, questions naturally arise about why the system of racial slavery fell. Certain key aspects of the answer have already been noted. It is, of course, true that Northern capital had benefited greatly from the profits of slavery. Yet the North's future and continued expansion was being threatened and undermined by the spread of slavery and the national political dominance of Southern slaveholders.[39] This conflict, whose armed struggle began in Kansas in 1854, led to the Civil War. And, as with Bacon's Rebellion, the North, in order to win the war, in order to undermine the economic base of the South, to gain willing troops, to gain moral authority and so to lessen the chance of a British intervention on the side of the Southern rebellion, was reluctantly drawn by the logic of events to free the slaves. By this chain of circumstances, which included first and foremost the actions as well as the presence of the Afro-American slaves themselves, did Jubilee Day arrive.[40]

While Northern labor held back, failing to appreciate the momentous worldwide significance of the war to free the slaves, the South itself was not monolithic in its support of slavery. Few seces-

---

38. Du Bois, *Black Reconstruction*, pp. 20–21. Frederick Douglass, *The Life and Writings of Frederick Douglass*, 5 vols. (New York, 1950), 2: 311–14.

39. Frederick Douglass argues that the crisis was brought to a head by the increasingly truculent actions of the slaveholders themselves. He cites the annexation of Texas "for the avowed purpose of increasing the number of slave states and thus increasing the power of slavery in the Union," "the perfidious repeal of the Missouri Compromise when all its advantages to the South had been gained and appropriated, and when nothing had been gained by the North—the armed and bloody attempt to force slavery upon the virgin soil of Kansas," the attempts to drive from public life those hostile to slavery, including William H. Seward and Charles Summer, and the growing brazenness of many Southern leaders in demanding that slavery be spread to every state in the union (Douglass, *Life and Times*, pp. 292–95). It is also interesting that Marx, in a careful analysis of Southern statements and actions, argued that the real purpose of the Civil War on the part of the South was to make all labor in the United States slave labor: Karl Marx and F. Engels, *The Civil War in the United States* (New York, 1969), pp. 4, 61, 72–83, 280. Thus, Marx concluded that the "slaveholders' rebellion was to sound the tocsin for a general holy crusade of property against labor" (p. 280).

40. For accounts that emphasize this latter theme see Du Bois, *Black Reconstruction*, and Eric Foner, *Reconstruction* (New York, 1988).

sion conventions obtained real, noncoerced majorities.[41] Even during the Civil War, a surprising number of Southern whites were loyalists. Northern labor in general missed its chance to support and gain strength from abolitionism before the war, during it, and in its aftermath. And this failure to recognize their proletarian allies is a central theme of Du Bois's book *Black Reconstruction.*

Du Bois convincingly argues that the movement to reconstruct the South was a vast radical democratic, progressive labor movement. The 1867 South Carolina Reconstruction convention had a majority of black and white propertyless delegates. Large numbers of Southern whites (unlike their Northern counterparts) supported radical Reconstruction measures, including full equality for African-Americans. Du Bois quotes Provisional Governor Perry of South Carolina, who was quite fearful of this growing unity and its implicit threat to property. He argues that Perry actually feared a proletarian revolution, a remark that perhaps says more about Du Bois than Perry (even the great W. E. B. Du Bois, with his penetrating insights and analyses, occasionally bent the bow too far back). But Du Bois was not far off the mark. In 1868, the black representatives were expelled from the Georgia legislature. In the succeeding election, radical whites ran on the central platform plank of reversing this decision and won overwhelmingly. For those who remain skeptical of the overwhelmingly progressive, radical democratic nature of Reconstruction, let me mention one paradigmatic fact. White supremacy has always been accompanied by male supremacy; South Carolina, where slavery was harshest, proved no exception. The Reconstruction convention there dramatically enlarged the rights of women, even giving the state its first divorce law.[42] And, I would argue, following Charles Fourier and Marx, that the status of women is perhaps the surest most universal indicator of the progressive social development of a society.

Still, Northern labor ignored the great proletarian drama that was taking place in the South. This obtuseness extended to the first national worker organization, the National Labor Union (NLU), formed in the immediate postwar period. The lack of solidarity with labor in the South was particularly evident in William Sylvis, the

41. Marx was one of the first to assemble the data for this assertion and to analyze its significance (Marx and Engels, *Civil War*, pp. 228–32).
42. Du Bois, pp. 390, 412, 396.

leader of the NLU, so revered in much radical historiography. Du Bois contrasts Sylvis's stance unfavorably with that of Karl Marx who had a lucid understanding of the plight of the former slaves and their relationship with the white workers of the North.[43]

For Du Bois, the period of Reconstruction represented a missed opportunity for changing the face of U.S. politics, for erasing the exceptional nature of American society. It was not the ideology of American individualism that blocked this alternative, but the ideology of racism and the white blindspot. In Du Bois's view, after the Civil War it was in the South that "the greatest opportunity for a real national labor movement" existed. "Yet the labor movement, with but few exceptions, never realized the situation. It never had the intelligence or knowledge, as a whole, to see in black slavery and Reconstruction, the kernel and meaning of the labor movement in the United States." This opportunity for a unified labor movement North and South, black and white, was missed, while the Southern labor movement, led by the forces of Reconstruction, was crushed by planter-led extralegal violence. The withdrawal of federal troops in 1876 with the Hayes-Tilden Compromise sealed its fate. Northern white workers, by failing to oppose the crushing of Reconstruction, thus went into their battles in 1877 totally isolated. They not only lost a valuable ally in Southern labor, but also strengthened immeasurably the Southern opponents of labor, thus assuring that they would face the implacable hostility of the federal government in their great struggles. According to Du Bois, even revolutionary socialists failed to realize in the early 1870s that the greatest potential for their "successful rooting" in the working class lay with the Southern worker.[44]

The immediate post–Civil War period would have been an especially propitious one for the empowerment of labor because of the sharp divisions between Northern and Southern capitalists. After the war, Southern planters acted like they had been the victors, sending Confederate officers to Congress, disenfranchising and

43. Ibid., pp. 357–58. Marx presented his views and analyses on numerous occasions. Representative are his remarks in *Capital,* where he states: "In the United States of America, every independent workers' movement was paralyzed as long as slavery disfigured a part of the republic. Labour in a white skin cannot emancipate itself where it is branded in a black skin." Karl Marx, *Capital* (New York, 1977), p. 414.

44. Du Bois, *Black Reconstruction*, pp. 353, 360.

reclaiming their land from African-American homesteaders, even opposing Northern capitalists at the national level. Northern capitalists, including the owners of the major newspapers, supported radical Republicans and used radical black Reconstruction to help blunt planter dominance. By 1869, the Union Pacific and Central Pacific railroads joined in driving in the Golden Spike at Promontory Point, Utah; before long, cattle were heading from Texas and the West to Chicago. As their economic and political hegemony in the nation became secure, the importance of Reconstruction for Northern capitalists diminished. Interest was lost in preventing the counterrevolution in the South. Nevertheless, the interests of Northern capital provide no valid excuse for the blindness of Northern labor. As Du Bois points out, labor unions entered "into the great war of 1877 against Northern capital unsupported by the black man, and the black man went his way in the South to strengthen and consolidate his power, unsupported by Northern labor." Du Bois asks, "Suppose for a moment that Northern labor had stopped the bargain of 1876 and maintained the power of the labor vote in the South; and suppose that the Negro with new and dawning consciousness of the demands of labor as differentiated from the demands of capitalists, had used his vote more specifically for the benefit of white labor, South and North?"[45]

Northern labor proved too weak to organize itself as a class without its Southern and black allies. Although Afro-Americans in the South felt the brunt of the counterrevolution, the white farmers and workers also lived and labored under oppressive and exploitative conditions. Poor Southern whites, however, were fully mobilized only after Reconstruction had been defeated. Their circumstances led to the strength of Southern populism in the 1880s and 1890s, whose white leaders and members early realized that they could not succeed without their Afro-American brethren. Yet the violence, lynching, murder, corruption, and electoral fraud that had been permitted in the 1870s proved too overwhelming to dislodge. This level of violence and extreme disregard for human life embedded in the fabric of Southern social and political life during this period is certainly not unrelated to the present violent nature of U.S. society, as

45. Ibid., p. 367.

evidenced in our high rates of assault, murder, police brutality, and capital punishment.[46]

The crushing of Southern populism by the late 1890s under the battle cry of white supremacy created the impetus for a determined group of plantation owners and their entourage of black-belt whites to dominate not merely the African-Americans of their region, but the rest of the whites in the South too. Poor whites as well as blacks were disenfranchised and controlled. While black–white wage differentials in the South remained the highest in the nation (indicating the privileged position of poor whites), the wages of Southern whites remained the lowest among whites in the nation. As in colonial and antebellum times, a determined group of white supremacist planters and their allies (including many Southern industrialists) forced their racial policies on the rest of the nation until the years following World War II. Not only did radicalism become problematic in much of the South, but liberalism faltered as well. Thus, one answer to Sombart's old question, "Why No Socialism" in the United States? may be the rejoinder, "Why No Liberalism in the South?" And, here the dominance of racist Dixiecrat elites and their use of white supremacy and white chauvinist ideology to dominate white as well as black labor must prove central to the full answer.

At the turn of the century, few, even including radical groups, comprehended the significance of white supremacy and how the development of a unified class struggle and an independent labor movement required a frontal assault on it. Du Bois, who wrote in *The Souls of Black Folk* in 1903 that "the problem of the 20th

46. As Frederick Douglass argues, such undemocratic, brutal, uncivilized, and oppressive behavior in the South was—contrary to the claims often made about the "gentility" of slave society—the norm for the slaveocracy. He cites the "mobocratic demonstrations against the right of free speech" in Congress, the display there "of pistols, bludgeons, and plantation manners" (Douglass, *Life and Times*, p. 292). These and other actions shocked the "not so genteel" people from the North: "No one act did more to rouse the North to a comprehension of the infernal and barbarous spirit of slavery and its determination to 'rule or ruin,' than the cowardly and brutal assault" in the Senate against Charles Sumner by Preston S. Brooks, a congressman from South Carolina. "Shocking and scandalous as was this attack, the spirit in which the deed was received and commended by the community was still more disgraceful. Southern ladies even applauded the armed bully for his murderous assault upon an unarmed northern Senator, because of words spoken in debate! This more than all else told the thoughtful people of the North the kind of civilization to which they were linked and how plainly it foreshadowed a conflict on a larger scale" (p. 294).

century is the problem of the color line," was one of those few.[47] The attitudes of labor groups ranged from the racist craft unions that echoed or capitulated to white supremacist filth to the mine workers who recognized the need to organize blacks and whites together, but who did not grasp the strategic importance for labor of fighting the entire system of white supremacy. Even the IWW, which challenged Jim Crow practices in the South, did so because they doggedly and courageously refused to let local customs prevent their reaching the most downtrodden workers, not because they intended to challege white supremacy itself. The Socialist party was even more mixed. Many of its leaders, including Socialist congressman from Milwaukee Victor Berger, aped the racism of Samuel Gompers and the AFL.[48] The more radical, progressive leaders, epitomized by Eugene V. Debs, offered at best benign neglect. Debs asserted, "We have nothing special to offer the Negro, and we cannot make separate appeals to all the races."[49] The Socialist party, barely able to organize immigrant industrial workers during the years before World War I, did not reflect seriously on the plight of Afro-Americans.

A decisive change in the political orientation of radicals took place during the 1920s. Greater attention focused on both the condition of African-Americans and the role of white supremacy in holding back working-class struggle. Partly spurred by the first important grouping of African-American Marxists, initially arising around the *Messenger* magazine, later around Cyril Briggs's African Black Brotherhood, and then supported and encouraged by the early Communist International (whose Russian Bolsheviks had made the fight against national and racial oppression their hallmark), the question of African-American oppression finally moved to center stage in radical, working-class strategy.

Communist party activity in the late 1920s and early 1930s put special emphasis on the fight against white supremacy; the party highlighted political activity among African-Americans in the South. The intensity and missionary zeal with which they pushed forward their political stance left even other radicals aghast. In 1929

47. See W. E. B. Du Bois, *The Souls of Black Folk* (New York, 1903).
48. For a compelling analysis of the racist policies of Gompers and other top AFL leaders, see Gwendolyn Mink, *Old Labor and New Immigrants in American Political Development* (Ithaca, N.Y., 1986).
49. Spero and Harris, *The Black Worker*, p. 405.

during a major strike at the all-white Gastonia, North Carolina, textile mills, they raised the fight against racial oppression as a central demand, even including Afro-American organizers in their organizing group. Their agitation was not without its impressive moments; at one point, white textile workers mobilized to save black organizer Otto Hall from a lynch mob. In 1931, the Communists came to the aid of the Scottsboro Boys, nine black youths accused of raping two white women with whom they were riding on a freight train. The Scottsboro case not only became a focal point of mass activity in this country, but received worldwide attention. African-American Communist agitators emerged in major cities around the country, while the intransigent commitment of white Communist party activists to fighting racial discrimination earned grudging admiration from conservative African-American newspapers. As historian Mark Naison notes, "Not only Jews felt moved by the Party's position: Finnish, Polish, Hungarian, Irish, Italian, and Slavic Communists became passionate exponents of the Party's position on the Negro question."[50] Communist commitment to the fight against racism was so impressive that the party recruited members of the secondary leadership of Marcus Garvey's nationalist United Negro Improvement Association during 1929 and 1930.

The Communists extended their activities to the organization of black sharecroppers in the heart of the black-belt South. They successfully organized large concentrations of African-American workers into the Mine, Mill and Smelter Workers in the Birmingham area, into the Food and Tobacco Workers, the Packinghouse Workers, and the Maritime Workers unions. It was almost a sine qua non during the 1930s that wherever militant, interracial unionism with strong stances and a willingness to struggle for the equality of black workers existed, one would almost invariably find the Communist party. So dominant and uncompromising was their orientation that even liberals and moderates within the Congress of Industrial Organizations (CIO) movement were forced to adopt egalitarian rhetoric, even while complaining about Communist party "disruptions" over issues of black equality.[51]

50. Mark Naison, *Communists in Harlem during the Depression* (Chicago, 1983), p. 49.
51. For more detailed information and references, see Goldfield, "The Decline of the Communist Party and the Black Question in the U.S.," *Review of Radical Political Economy* 12 (Spring 1980), and Goldfield, "Recent Historiography of the Com-

If this thrust within the labor movement had continued unabated, forming a merged labor and civil rights movement, the South might have been organized by industrial unions, and racist Dixiecrat control might have been broken in the 1930s and 1940s by a united black-led working-class movement; much later pain could have also been spared. But that was not to be. The Communists ultimately backed off from their new approach. Although they did not completely abandon the struggle against racial discrimination, their new-found support for President Franklin Roosevelt led them to look for broader coalitions. In the South this often meant electoral alliances with "liberal" Dixiecrat New Deal supporters. I believe that a direct line can be traced to the moderation of Communist and CIO racial policies and the failure of Operation Dixie, labor's unsuccessful attempt to organize the South after World War II. Militant African-American workers and left-wingers (and these were often the same) were excluded from Operation Dixie and later purged from the labor movement, ensuring that the labor movement of the 1930s remained only a regional phenomenon of the Northeast, Midwest, and West Coast. Thus, Dixiecratic control of Southern politics and the national Congress would see that class-based political alternatives would be marginalized or crushed. In this political environment, accompanied by anti-Soviet hysteria and Cold War and a long period of U.S. prosperity, organized labor became increasingly conservative politically.

Yet the question of African-Americans would still not go away. In the 1950s and 1960s the Black Freedom movement reemerged. And it is this movement that is crucial to understanding U.S. politics since then: the antiwar movement, the student movement, the women's movement, the unionization of local, state, and federal-level public sector employees and the resultant liberal impulses within the Democratic party, all owe much to the African-American movement. The backlash of the 1970s and 1980s from George Wallace and Richard Nixon to Ronald Reagan and George Bush must be understood as the reaction to the second wave of Reconstruction. This backlash of the 1970s through 1990s also signifies a recurrent political theme, the short-sightedness of whites, particularly poor and working-class whites. Recall the flag-waving construction work-

munist Party U.S.A.," in Mike Davis, Fred Pfeil, and Michael Sprinker, eds., *The Year Left* (London, 1985), vol. 1, pp. 315–58.

ers of the late 1960s. They now belong to the most devastated unions and industry in the country. This period was not without its rays of interracial hope, however. Black caucus movements of industrial workers in the late 1960s paved the way for the integrated, radical, black-led labor insurgencies of the early 1970s.

Despite the setbacks and the seemingly unlikely prospects for the near-future development of a broad independent, influential, class-based movement and political party, we are not, I believe, back at square one. I say this despite the recent ascendancy of the right, not only in the Republican party, but also among Democrats; despite the ominous rise in racist incidents on campuses and in cities. The situation of labor and the poor is hardly ascendant, with declines in living standards of both black and white workers, with rising populations and the worsening of conditions of the ghetto poor, with the dramatic decline in strength of trade unions. Yet the legacy of the 1960s and the second Reconstruction ushered in a new era in America; for the first time in U.S. history, no progressive person can deny the importance of the issues of chauvinism and inequality. The bulwark of Southern reaction in the political arena has been sharply undermined—despite continued violence, such as the 1979 assassination of anti-Klan demonstrators in Greensboro, North Carolina. Society can no longer afford to uphold explicitly racist propositions in law or rhetoric: witness the 1988 Title 7 Civil Rights Bill override, the defeat of Ronald Reagan's nominee for the Supreme Court Robert Bork, the increased respect in the media for Jesse Jackson, even the lip service paid to civil rights issues by George Bush. Today, there exists a window of opportunity, albeit with all the contradictions that have always accompanied such situations historically. And if black and white workers can be unified in common struggle (hints of such a tendency emerged during the Jackson campaign of 1988), then perhaps the question of American exceptionalism and the notion of American individualism will be buried once and for all.

5

Out of Africa:
Topologies of Nativism

KWAME ANTHONY APPIAH

Au delà du refus de toute domination extérieure, c'est la volonté
de renouer en profondeur avec
l'héritage culturel de l'Afrique,
trop longtemps méconnu et refusé.
Loin d'être un effort superficiel ou
folklorique pour faire revivre quelques traditions ou pratiques ances-
trales, il s'agit de construire une
nouvelle société dont l'identité
n'est pas conférée du dehors.[1]

Beyond the refusal of all exterior
domination is the urge to reconnect
in a deep way with Africa's cultural
heritage, which has been for too long
misunderstood and rejected. Far
from being a superficial or folkloric
attempt to bring back to life some of
the traditions or practices of our
ancestors, it is a matter of construct-
ing a new African society, whose
identity is not conferred from
outside.

—Cardinal Paul Zoungrana

I

In 1985—in an issue whose cover article reviewed the *Dictionary
of American English* under the title "One Language, Highly Divisible"—the *New York Times Book Review* carried a critique of Robertson Davies's novel *What's Bred in the Bone*. Larry McCaffery's
gentle attack on Robertson Davies took him to task for having writ-

1. The epigraph is cited by Valentin Mudimbe, "African Gnosis. Philosophy and
the Order of Knowledge: An Introduction," *African Studies Review* 28 (June–September 1985): 164.

ten a novel that was insufficiently Canadian, too immersed in British "cultural motifs, symbols and methodology." Anyone who needed to know *why* Davies should have sought, in his writing, to express the juridical fact of his Canadian citizenship, could find an answer implicit in the review of the dictionary. For the reviewer of the *Dictionary of American English*—Stuart Flexner, himself the editor of *The Dictionary of American Slang*—finished by observing that the *Dictionary of American English* "makes us proud of our scholars, our language and our country." McCaffery's challenge to Davies— the challenge of an American professor of American literature—was clear enough: "Why is it," the message went, "that *you* are not proud of *your* language and *your* country?" One could read on through this issue of the *Book Review* for signs of the centrality and the interdependence of issues of nation and language and literature in these times. McCaffery's review is followed immediately, for example, by a discussion of Leonard Thompson's *The Political Mythology of Apartheid*, a work that seeks to examine the changing stories that Afrikaners have told of their origins...stories in which the linguistic and cultural differentia that separate them from other English-speaking "whites" play a crucial role.[2]

But then, of course, one could read almost any issue of the *Book Review* (indeed, almost any issue of the *New York Times*) for such signs. In this country and around the world, so much of our writing and, more especially, of our writing about writing touches on the issue of the nation and its language, on the conjunction captured almost at the start of modern theories of the nation in the Herderian conception of the *Sprachgeist*.[3] For intellectuals everywhere are now

---

2. Larry McCaffery, "Painter, Forger, Miser, Spy," Review of Robertson Davies's *What's Bred in the Bone* (New York, 1985); Stuart B. Flexner, "One Language, Highly Divisible," Review of *The Dictionary of American English* (New York, 1985); Vincent Crapanzano, "Inventing the Afrikaner Past," Review of Leonard Thompson's *The Political Mythology of Apartheid* (New Haven, 1985), all appeared in the *New York Times Book Review*, December 15, 1985, pp. 6–7; 1, 33–34; 7, respectively.

3. In his *Über die Neure Deutsche Literatur: Fragmente* of 1767, Johann Gottfried Herder first put forward the notion that language, far from being (as the received Aristotelian tradition had it) the merely material cause of a literary work, is not just "a tool of the arts and sciences" but "a part of them; whoever writes about the literature of a country must not neglect its language." The notion of the *Sprachgeist*— the living "spirit" of the language—embodies the thought that language is more than the transparent medium through which a nation communicates with itself. As Hans

caught up—whether as volunteers, draftees, or resisters—in a struggle for the articulation of their respective nations.

The power of the idea of the nation in the nonindustrialized world
is more than a consequence of the cultural hegemony of the Europeans and Americans whose ancestors invented both the idea and
most of the world's juridical nationalities. As Benedict Anderson
has argued—in his elegant *Imagined Communities*—though the national idea was introduced to much of the world by way of contacts
with European imperialism, the appeal of the idea to the "natives"
soon outran the control and the interests of the metropole.[4] African
and Asian intellectuals do not believe in national self-determination
simply because it was forced upon us, because it was imposed as a
tool of our continued neocolonial domination: rather, the idea of
the nation provided—first for the local elite, then for the newly
proletarianized denizens of the colonial city and finally even for a
peasantry attempting to come to terms with their increasing incorporation into the world system—a way to articulate a resistance
both to the material domination of the world empires and to the
more nebulous threat to precolonial modes of thought represented
by the Western project of cultural hegemony.

I begin with these observations on one issue of an (emblematically)
American newspaper because I want to insist at the start on the
extent to which the issues of language and nation that are so central
to the situation I want to discuss—that of sub-Saharan African writers and critics—are also the problems of American criticism. This
is not a voyage into the exotic, a flirtation with a distant Other.
Voltaire or one of his *philosophe* comrades in a European culture
before the heyday of the world empires once said that when we
travel, what we discover is always ourselves. It seems to me that
this thought has, so to speak, become true. In the world after those
world empires, a world where center and periphery are mutually

---

Kohn has written, for Herder a "nationality lived above all in its civilization; its
main instrument was its language, not an artificial instrument, but a gift of God, the
guardian of the national community and the matrix of its civilization. Thus language,
national language, became a sacred instrument; each man could be himself only by
thinking and creating in his own language. With the respect for all other nationalities
went a respect for their languages." Hans Kohn, *The Idea of Nationalism* (New York,
1967), pp. 431–32.
    4. Benedict Anderson, *Imagined Communities: Reflections on the Origin and
Spread of Nationalism* (London, 1983).

constitutive, political life may be conceived of (however misleadingly) in national terms, but what Voltaire might have called the life of the mind cannot. If I seek to situate my discussion of the African situation with a few elements of context, then, it is in part so that you can recognize how much of that situation is familiar territory.

That the territory *is* so familiar is a consequence of the way in which intellectuals from what I will call, with reservations, the Third World, are a historical product of an encounter with what I will continue, with similar reservations, to call the West. Most African writers have received a Western-style education; their ambiguous relations to the world of their foremothers and forefathers and to the world of the industrialized countries is part of their distinctive cultural (dis)location, a condition that Abiole Irele has eloquently described in "In Praise of Alienation."[5] Of course, there are influences that run from the precolonial intellectual culture to those who have received colonial or postcolonial educations in the Western manner. Nevertheless, in sub-Saharan Africa, most literate people are literate in the colonial languages; most writing with a substantial readership (with the important exception of Swahili) is in those languages; and the only writing with a genuinely subcontinental audience and address is in English or in French. For many of their most important cultural purposes, African intellectuals, south of the Sahara, are what we can call "europhone."

There *are* intellectual workers—priests, shamans, griots, for example—in Africa and Asia (and some in South America and Australasia, too) who still operate in worlds of thought that are remote from the influences of Western literate discourse. But we surely live in the last days of that phase of human life in culture; and whether or not we choose to call these people "intellectuals"—and this strikes me as a decision whose outcome is less important than recognizing that the decision has to be made—they are surely *not* the intellectuals who are producing the bulk of what we call Third World literature, nor are they articulating what we call literary theory or criticism. Literature, by and large, in sub-Saharan Africa means europhone literature (except in the Swahili culture area, where Swahili

5. F. Abiole Irele, "In Praise of Alienation," inaugural lecture delivered on November 22, 1982, at the University of Ibadan, Nigeria. F. Abiola Irele was a professor of French and the head of the Department of Modern Languages.

and the colonial languages are active together.) And what matters in its being europhone is more than its inscription in the languages of the colonizers.

For language here is, of course, a synecdoche. When the colonialists attempted to tame the threatening cultural alterity of the African (whether through what the French called *assimilation*, or through the agency of missionary "conversion") the instrumentalities of pedagogy were their most formidable weapon. So that the problem is not only, or not so much, the English or the French or the Portuguese language as the cultural hegemony that it represents. Colonial education, in short, produced a generation immersed in the literature of the colonizers, a literature that often reflected and transmitted the imperialist vision.

This is no new thing: literary pedagogy played a similar role in Roman education in the provinces of that empire, an empire that still provides perhaps our most powerful paradigm of imperialism. John Guillory has recently focused our attention on a standard—dare I say, magisterial—treatment, by R. R. Bolgar in *The Classical Heritage and Its Beneficiaries*, of the process in which "the legions withdraw and are replaced by schools." "As the protective might of the legions weakened, so the imperial government came to rely to an ever greater extent on its intangible assets.... Steel was in short supply ... so the provinces were to be grappled to the soul of Rome by hoops of a different make."[6]

The role of the colonial (and, alas, the postcolonial) school in the reproduction of Western cultural hegemony is crucial to African criticism because of the intimate connection between the idea of criticism and the growth of literary pedagogy: for (as John Guillory reminds us) the role of literature, indeed, the formation of the concept, the institution of "literature," is indissoluble from pedagogy. Roland Barthes expressed the point in a characteristic apothegm: " 'l'enseignement de la littérature' est pour moi presque tautologique. La littérature, c'est ce qui s'enseigne, un point c'est tout."[7]

---

6. Cited in John Guillory, "Canonical and Non-Canonical: A Critique of the Current Debate," *ELH* 54 (1987): 499. This essay will surely come to be seen as a definitive analysis.

7. " 'The teaching of literature' is for me almost tautological. Literature is what is taught, that is all." Roland Barthes, "Reflections sur un manuel," in Tzvetan Todorov and Serge Doubrovsky, *Enseignement de la littérature* (Paris, 1971), p. 170.

Abstracted from its context, this formulation no doubt requires some qualifying glosses. But one cannot too strongly stress the fact that what we discuss under the rubric of modern African writing is largely what is taught in high schools all around the continent. Nor should we ignore the crucial psychological importance of the possibility of such an African writing. The weapon of pedagogy changes hands simply because we turn from reading John Buchan and Joseph Conrad and Graham Greene to reading Peter Abrahams, Chinua Achebe, and Ayi Kwei Armah, to begin an alphabet of writers in the Heinemann African Writer's series, which constitutes in the most concrete sense the pedagogical canon of anglophone African writing. We see the formation of a counterhegemonic discourse and the possibility of a counterhegemonic pedagogy as the decolonized subject people write themselves, now, as the subject of a literature of their own. The simple gesture of writing for and about oneself—there are fascinating parallels here with the history of Afro-American writing—has a profound political significance.

Writing for and about ourselves, then, helps constitute the modern community of the nation; but we do it, largely, in languages imposed by "the might of the legions." Now that the objects of European imperialism have at last become the subjects of a discourse addressed both to each other and to the West, European languages and European disciplines have been "turned," like double agents, from the projects of the metropole to the intellectual work of postcolonial cultural life.

But though officially in the service of new masters, these tools remain, like all double agents, perpetually under suspicion. Even when the colonizer's language is creolized, even when the imperialist's vision is playfully subverted in the lyrics of popular songs, there remains the suspicion that a hostile *Sprachgeist* is at work. Both the complaints against defilement by alien traditions in an alien tongue and the defenses of them as a practical necessity (a controversy that echoes similar debates in situations as otherwise different as, say, the early twentieth-century Norwegian debate over "New Norwegian" and the nineteenth-century German Jewish debates over Yiddish) seem often to reduce to a dispute between a sentimental Herderian conception of Africa's languages and traditions as expressive of the collective essence of a pristine traditional community, on the one hand, and, on the other, a positivistic conception of European languages and disciplines as mere tools; tools that can be cleansed of the accompanying imperialist—and, more specifically, racist—modes of thought.

The former view is often at the heart of what we can call "nativism": the claim that true African independence requires a literature of one's own. Echoing the debate in nineteenth-century Russia between "Westerners" and "Slavophiles," the debate in Africa presents itself as an opposition between "universalism" and "particularism," the latter defining itself, above all else, by its opposition to the former. But there are only two real players in this game: us, inside; them, outside. That is all there is to it.

Operating with this topology of inside and outside—indigene and alien, Western and traditional—the apostles of nativism are thus able to mobilize the undoubted power of nationalist rhetoric. And, I believe, we shall have the best chance of redirecting that power if we challenge not that rhetoric of the nation but the topology that it presupposes, the opposition it asserts.

II

Consider, then, that now-classic manifesto of African cultural nationalism, *Toward the Decolonization of African Literature.* This much-discussed book is the work of three Nigerian authors—Chinweizu, Onwuchekwa Jemie, and Ihechukwu Madubuike—all of them encumbered with extensive Western university educations. Chinweizu, a widely published poet and quondam editor of the Nigerian literary magazine *Okike,* was an undergraduate at Massachusetts Institute of Technology (MIT) and holds a doctorate from the State University of New York, Buffalo; and he has emerged (from a career that included time on the faculty at MIT and at San Jose State) as one of the leading figures in contemporary Nigerian journalism, writing a highly influential column in *The Guardian* of Lagos. Jemie holds a Ph.D. from Columbia University in English and Comparative Literature, is also a distinguished poet, and has published an introduction to the poetry of Langston Hughes. And Ihechukwu Madubuike—who has been Nigeria's Minister of Education—studied at Laval in Canada, the Sorbonne, and the State University of New York, Buffalo. All three critics have taught in

Black Studies programs in the United States—in their preface they thank the Department of Afro-American Studies at the University of Minnesota and the Black Studies Department at Ohio State University for "supportive clerical help." If their rhetoric strikes responsive chords in the American ear, we shall not find it too surprising.

Not that their language fails to incorporate Nigerian elements. The term *bolekaja*—which means "Come down, let's fight"—is used in western Nigeria to refer to the "mammy-wagons" that are the main means of popular transportation; and it reflects "the outrageous behaviour of their touts." In their preface, Chinweizu, Jemie, and Madubuike call themselves "*bolekaja* critics, outraged touts for the passenger lorries of African literature." They write, "There comes a time, we believe, in the affairs of men and of nations, when it becomes necessary for them to engage in *bolekaja* criticism, for them to drag the stiflers of their life down to earth for a corrective tussle. A little wrestle in the sands never killed a sturdy youth." But it is clear that it is not really the "sturdy youth" of African criticism that they take to be at risk; for the work of the succeeding chapters is to wrestle the critical ethnocentrism of their Eurocentric opponents to the ground in the name of an Afrocentric particularism. If this is to be a struggle to the death, Chinweizu and his compatriots expect to be the survivors. They assert, for example, that "most of the objections to thematic and ideological matters in the African novel sound like admonitions from imperialist motherhens to their wayward or outright rebellious captive chickens. They cluck: 'Be Universal! Be Universal!' " And they condemn "the modernist retreat of our poets into privatist universalism [which] makes it quite easy for them to shed whatever African nationalist consciousness they have before they cross the threshold into the sanctum of 'poetry in the clouds.' And that suits the English literary establishment just fine, since they would much prefer it if an African nationalist consciousness, inevitably anti-British, was not promoted or cultivated, through literature, in the young African elite." Thus, when the British critic, Adrian Roscoe, urges African poets to view themselves as "inheritors of a universal tradition of art and letters and not just as the recipients of an indigenous legacy," he reaps the nationalists' scorn. For their central insistence is that

"African literature *is* an autonomous entity separate and apart from all other literature. It has its own traditions, models and norms."[8]

Now we should recognize from the start that such polemics can be a salutary corrective to a great deal of nonsense that has been written about African literature, by critics for whom literary merit is gauged by whether a work can be inserted into a Great White Tradition of masterpieces. It is hard not be irritated by high-handed pronouncements from critics for whom detailed description of locale amounts to mere travelogue, unless, say, the locale is "Wessex" and the author is Thomas Hardy; for whom the evocation of local custom amounts to mere ethnography, unless, say, they are the customs of a northern English mining town and the author is D. H. Lawrence; and for whom the recounting of historical event amounts to mere journalism, unless the event is the Spanish Civil War and the author is Hemingway.

What Chinweizu and his colleagues are objecting to, in other words, is the posture that conceals its privileging of one national (or racial) tradition against others in false talk of the Human Condition. It is not surprising, then, that Chinweizu and his colleagues also endorse T. S. Eliot's view that "although it is only too easy for a writer to be local without being universal, I doubt whether a poet or novelist can be universal without being local too."[9] And here, of course, it is plain enough that "universal" is hardly a term of derogation. For it is characteristic of those who pose as antiuniversalists to use the term "universalism" interchangeably with "pseudouniversalism"; and the fact is that their complaint is not with universalism at all. What they truly object to—and who would not?—is Eurocentric hegemony *posing* as universalism. Thus, while the debate is couched in terms of the competing claims of particularism and universalism, the actual ideology of universalism—and if

---

8. Chinweizu, Onwuchekwa Jemie, and Ihechukwu Madubuike, *Toward the Decolonization of African Literature* (Enugu, Nigeria, 1980), pp. xiv and note, 89, 151, 147, 4.

9. Eliot is cited in ibid., p. 106. When Chinweizu et al. assert, typically, that "there was in pre-colonial Africa an abundance of oral narratives which are in no way inferior to European novels," they presuppose the universalist view that there is some (universal) value-metric by which the relative excellence of the two can be gauged (p. 27).

"pseudo-universalism" receives the brunt of our polemics, we must have in reserve a conception of universalism *simpliciter*—is never interrogated; and, indeed, is even tacitly accepted.

The appeal of this nativist rhetoric is most easily understood in the context of the subcontinent's politicolinguistic geography. We should begin with the fact that more than half of the population of black Africa lives in countries where English is an official language and almost all the rest of Africa is governed in French or Arabic or Portuguese. Both francophone and anglophone elites not only use the colonial languages as the medium of government, but they know and often admire the literature of their former colonizers, and have chosen to make a modern African literature in European languages. Even after a brutal colonial history and nearly two decades of sustained armed resistance, the decolonization in the mid-1970s of Portuguese Africa left a lusophone elite writing African laws and literature in Portuguese.

Yet at the same time, with few exceptions outside the Arabic-speaking countries of North Africa, the language of government is still the first language of a very few and is securely possessed by only a small proportion of the population. In most of the anglophone states even the educated elites learned at least one of the hundreds of indigenous languages as well as—and always before—English. In francophone Africa there are now elites that speak French better than any other language, and whose French is particularly close in grammar, if not always in accent, to the language of metropolitan France. But even in those nations French is not confidently possessed by anything close to a majority.

It is precisely this combination of a europhone elite and a noneurophone populace that makes for the appeal of nativism. That the European languages (and, in particular, the dialects of them in which elite writing goes on) are far from being the confident possession of the populace does not, of course, distinguish Third World literature—the writings that are taught—from the bulk of contemporary European or American taught writings. But the fact that contemporary African literature operates in a sphere of language that is so readily identifiable as the product of schooling (schooling that is fully available only to an elite) invites the nativist assimilation of formal literature to the alien. This association is reinforced by the recognition that there is, in Africa as in the West, a body of distinctive cultural production—over the whole range of popular culture—that *does* have a more immediate access to the citizen with less formal education.

So, for example, there are certainly strong living practices of oral culture—religious, mythological, poetic and narrative—in most of the thousand and more languages of sub-Saharan Africa; and there is no doubt as to the importance of the few languages that were already (as we say) reduced to writing before the colonial era. But we must not fall for the sentimental notion that the "people" have held on to an indigenous national tradition, that only the educated bourgeoisie are "children of two worlds." At the level of popular culture, too, the currency is not a holdover from an unbroken stream of tradition; indeed, it is like most popular culture in the age of mass production hardly national at all. Popular culture in Africa encompasses Michael Jackson and Jim Reeves; and when it picks up cultural production whose sources are geographically African, what it picks up is not usually in any plausible sense traditional. Highlife music is both recognizably West African and distinctly *not* precolonial; and the sounds of Fela Kuti would have astonished the musicians of the last generation of court musicians in Yorubaland. As they have developed new forms of music, drawing on instrumental repertoires and musical ideas with a dazzling eclecticism, Africa's musicians have also done astonishing things with a language that used to be English. But it is *as* English that that language is accessible to millions around the continent (and around the world).

III

If we are to move beyond nativist hand-waving, the right place to start is by defamiliarizing the concepts through which we think the issues of literary pedagogy. Too often, attempts at counterhegemonic cultural analysis are short-circuited by a failure to recognize the historicity of the analytical terms—"culture," "literature," "nation"—through which the sociopolitical margin is produced as an object of study. So it is as well to remind ourselves of the originary twinning of literature with nationalism, both of which are essentialized through narrative. We are familiar, from Ernest Renan, with the selective remembering and forgetting of the past that undergirds group identity. And recent historiography has stressed again and

again the ways in which the "national heritage" is constructed
through the invention of traditions; the careful filtering of the rough
torrent of historical event into the fine stream of an official narrative;
the creation of a homogeneous legacy of values and experience.[10]

In the specific context of the history of "literature" and its study,
recent debates have also left us attuned to the ways in which the
factitious "excavation" of the literary canon can serve to hypostatize
a particular cultural identity. The official constitution of a national
history bequeaths us the nation; and the discipline of literary history,
as Michel de Certeau has aptly remarked, "transforms the text into
an institution"—and so bequeaths us what we call literature.[11]

Raymond Williams once noted that as the term "literature" begins
to acquire its modern semantic freight, we find "a development of
the concept of 'tradition' within national terms, resulting in the
more effective definition of 'a national literature.' "[12] "Literature"
and "nation" could hardly fail to belong together: from the very start
they were made for each other. Once the concept of literature was
taken up by African intellectuals, the African debate about literary
nationalism was inevitable.

So that what we see in *Toward the Decolonization of African
Literature* is, in effect, the establishment of a "reverse discourse":
the terms of resistance are already given us, and our contestation is
entrapped within the Western cultural conjuncture we affect to dispute. The pose of repudiation actually presupposes the cultural institutions of the West and the ideological matrix in which they, in
turn, are imbricated. Railing against the cultural hegemony of the
West, the nativists are of its party without knowing it.[13] Indeed, the

10. Ernest Renan's influential essay "Qu'est-ce qu'une nation" in *Oeuvres Com-
plètes*, vol. 1 (Paris, 1947), pp. 887–906, is the *locus classicus* of attempts to define
nationality through a "common memory." For recent work on the invention of
traditions see, for example, Eric Hobsbawm and Terence Ranger, *The Invention of
Tradition* (Cambridge, 1983).

11. Michel de Certeau, *Heterologies: Discourse on the Other*, trans. Brian Massumi
(Minneapolis, 1986), p. 32.

12. "The sources of each of these tendencies can be discerned from the Renaissance,
but it was in the eighteenth and nineteenth centuries that they came through most
powerfully, until they became, in the twentieth century, in effect received assumptions." Raymond Williams, *Marxism and Literature* (Oxford, 1977), p. 47. See also
Louis Montrose, "Of Gentlemen and Shepherds: The Politics of Elizabethan Pastoral
Form," *ELH* 50 (1983): 433–52; and Michel Beaujour, "Genus Universum," *Glyph* 7
(Baltimore, 1980), pp. 15–31.

13. Real agon, as Ernesto Laclau and Chantal Mouffe remind us, "always consists

very arguments, the rhetoric of defiance, that our nationalists muster are, in a sense, canonical, time-tested. For they enact a conflict that is *interior* to the very nationalist ideology that provided the category of "literature" its conditions of emergence: defiance is determined less by "indigenous" notions of resistance as by the dictates of the West's own Herderian legacy—its highly elaborated ideologies of national autonomy, of language and literature as their cultural substrate. Nativist nostalgia, note well, is largely fueled by that Western sentimentalism so familiar after Rousseau; few things, then, are less native than nativism in its current forms.

In the debate among African intellectuals, then, we see recapitulated the classic gestures of nation formation in the domain of culture. Surely this is exactly as we should expect. In postcolonial discourse the project of nation formation—what used to be, in the eighteenth century, the attempt to define (and thus to invent) the "national character"—always lies close to the surface. But, as any Americanist would remind us, the emergence of American literature in the nineteenth century was circumscribed by just such concerns, coupled with a strong sense of being at the periphery vis-à-vis the European center. So it is with a sense of recognition that one turns from the rhetoric of postcolonial criticism today to read, say, William Carlos Williams's anxious observation: "Americans have never recognized themselves. How can they? It is impossible until someone invent the original terms. As long as we are content to be called by somebody's else's terms, we are incapable of being anything but out own dupes."[14] In their ideological inscription, the cultural nationalists remain in a position of counteridentification (to borrow Michel Pêcheux's convenient schematism), which is to continue to participate in an institutional configuration—to be subjected to cul-

---

in the construction of a social identity—of an overdetermined subject position—on the basis of the equivalence between a set of elements or values," a cultural commonality, which is, obversely, a common cultural difference. As they argue: "Only if it is accepted that the subject positions cannot be led back to a positive and unitary founding principle—only then can pluralism be considered radical. Pluralism is *radical* only to the extent that each term of this plurality of identities finds within itself the principle of its own validity, without this having to be sought in a transcendent or underlying positive ground for the hierarchy of meaning of them all and the source and guarantee of their legitimacy." Laclau and Mouffe, *Hegemony and Socialist Strategy* (London, 1985), p. 167.

14. William Carlos Williams, *In the American Grain* (1951; rpr. New York, 1956), p. 226. This remark is in an essay on Edgar A. Poe.

tural identities—they ostensibly decry. For Pêcheux the more radical move is toward what he terms disidentification, in which we are no longer invested in the specific institutional determinations of the West.[15]

Once we lay aside the "universalism" that Chinweizu and others rightly attack as a disguised particularism, we can understand how an Afrocentric particularism—Chinweizu's cultural nationalism— is itself covertly universalist. Nativism organizes its vaunted particularities into a cultural-institutional determination (corresponding to "culture" used in an implicitly normative, and positive sense) that is an artifact of Western modernity. While Western criteria of evaluation are challenged, the way in which the contest is framed is not. The "Eurocentric" bias of criticism is scrutinized; but not the way in which its defining subject is constructed. For to acknowledge *that* would be to acknowledge that outside is not outside at all; so that the topology of nativism would be irretrievably threatened.

Ideologies succeed to the extent that they are invisible, in the moment that their fretwork of assumptions passes beneath consciousness; genuine victories are won without a shot being fired. Inasmuch as the most ardent of Africa's cultural nationalists participates in naturalizing—universalizing—the value-laden categories of "literature" and "culture," the triumph of universalism has, in the face of a silent *nolo contendere*, already taken place. The Western emperor has ordered the natives to exchange their robes for trousers: their act of defiance is to insist on tailoring them from homespun material. Given their arguments, plainly, the cultural nationalists do not go far enough; they are blind to the fact that their nativist demands for cultural production inhabit a Western architecture.

I think that once we see the larger context more clearly, we will be less prone to the anxieties of nationalism, less likely to be seduced by the rhetoric of ancestral purity. In 1968, Frantz Fanon exposed the artificiality of the nativist intellectual, whose ersatz populism only estranges him from the *Volk* he venerates: "He sets a high value on the customs, traditions, and the appearances of his people, but his inevitable, painful experience only seems to be a banal search

15. Michel Pêcheux, *Language, Semantics and Ideology* (New York, 1982), pp. 156–59.

for exoticism. The sari becomes sacred, and shoes that come from Paris or Italy are left off in favor of pampooties, while suddenly the language of the ruling power is felt to burn your lips."[16] Inevitably, though, the "culture that the intellectual leans toward is often no more than a stock of particularisms. He wishes to attach himself to the people, but instead he only catches hold of their outer garments." Fanon does not dismiss the products of the modern cultural worker in the colonial or postcolonial era; but he urges that the native poet who has taken his or her people as subject "cannot go forward resolutely unless" the poet "first realizes the extent of his estrangement from them."[17] The intellectuals betray their estrangement by their fetishistic attitude toward the customs, folklore, and vernacular traditions of their people; an attitude which, Fanon argues, must, in the end, set the intellectual against the people in their time of struggle.

One focus of this estrangement that has not, perhaps, been sufficiently appreciated is the very conception of an African identity. Although most discourse about African literature has moved beyond the monolithic notions of *négritude* or the "African personality," the constructed nature of the modern African identity (like all identities) is not widely enough understood. Terence Ranger has written of how the British colonialist's "own respect for 'tradition' disposed them to look with favour upon what they took to be traditional in Africa."[18] British colonial officers, traveling in the footsteps of Lord Lugard (and with the support of that curious creature, the gov-

16. Frantz Fanon, *The Wretched of the Earth* (New York, 1968), pp. 221, 223–24, 226. For Ngugi, wa Thiong'o, the cause of cultural nationalism led him to write in Gikuyu, eschewing the languages of Europe. In fact, he insists of his europhone compeers that "despite any claims to the contrary, what they have produced is not African literature," and he consigns the work of Chinua Achebe, Wole Soyinka, Ousmane Sembene, and others to a mere hybrid aberrancy that "can only be termed Afro-European literature." Ngugi wa Thiong'o, "The Language of African Literature," *New Left Review* 150 (1985): 125. So it is interesting to note that, despite his *linguistic* nativism, he does not eschew innovations rooted in Western expressive media. Recently he explained some of the effects he achieved in his latest Gikuyu novel, *Matigari ma Njirugi*, by the happy fact of his being "influenced by film technique. . . . I write as if each scene is captured in a frame, so the whole novel is a series of camera shots." Interview with Ngugi wa Thiong'o by Hansel Nolumbe Eyoh, *The Journal of Commonwealth Literature* 21.1 (1986): 166.

17. Terence Ranger, "Invention of Tradition in Colonial Africa," in Hobsbawm and Ranger, *The Invention of Tradition*, p. 212.

18. R. S. Rattray, *Ashanti Law and Constitution* (London, 1929).

ernment anthropologist) collected, organized, and enforced these "traditions." Such works as R. S. Rattray's *Ashanti Law and Constitution* had the effect of monumentalizing the flexible operations of precolonial systems of social control as what came to be called "customary law."[19] Ironically, for many contemporary African intellectuals, these invented traditions have now acquired the status of national mythology; and the invented past of Africa has come to play a role in the political dynamics of the modern state.

"The invented traditions imported from Europe not only provided whites with models of command but also offered many Africans models of 'modern' behavior. The invented traditions of African societies—whether invented by the Europeans or by Africans themselves in response—distorted the past but became in themselves realities through which a good deal of colonial encounter was expressed." So it is, Ranger observes, that "those like Ngugi who repudiate bourgeois elite culture face the ironic danger of embracing another set of colonial inventions instead."[20] The English, who knew all about nations, could extend a similar comprehension to its stand-in, the "tribe," and that could mean inventing tribes where none quite existed before. The point extends beyond the anglophone domain. In Zaire, we find that a sweeping linguistic division (between Lingala and Swahili) is a product of recent history, an outcome of worker stratification imposed by the Belgian administration.[21] Indeed, the very invention of Africa (as something more than a geographical entity) must be understood, ultimately, as an outgrowth of European racialism; the notion of Pan-Africanism was founded on the notion of the African, which was, in turn, founded not on

---

19. Ranger, in Hobsbawm and Ranger, *The Invention of Tradition*, pp. 212, 262.

20. Al-Amin M. Mazrui has argued, to the point, that "empirical observations have tended to suggest a shift towards increasing ethnic consciousness, despite the reverse trend towards decreasing ethnic behaviour. Losing sight of such observations necessarily culminates in the distortion of the nature of tribal identity and in the mystification of cultural revival as an aid to tribal identity. In fact, this tendency to mystify tribal identity is precisely the factor which has made imperialist countries realise that there is no conflict of interest in their sponsoring all sorts of parochial tribal cultural festivals in the guise of reviving African cultural heritage, while attempting to infuse our societies with a 'new' cultural ethos that will be conducive to further consolidation of neocolonial capitalism in Africa." Al-Amin M. Mazrui, "Ideology or Pedagogy: The Linguistic Indigenisation of African Literature," *Race and Class* 28 (Summer 1986): 67.

21. Johannes Fabian, *Language and Colonial Power* (Cambridge, 1986), pp. 42–43. The dominance of Swahili in many areas is, itself, a colonial product (p. 6).

any genuine cultural commonality but on the very European concept of the Negro.[22] "The Negro," Fanon writes, is "never so much a Negro as since he has been dominated by whites."[23] But the reality is that the very category of the Negro is at root a European product: for the "whites" invented the Negroes in order to dominate them. Simply put, the overdetermined course of cultural nationalism in Africa has been to make real the imaginary identities to which Europe has subjected us.

IV

As John Wisdom used to observe, "every day, in every way, we are getting meta and meta." It was inevitable, in such an age, that the debate should have been translated to a higher register. Certainly the claims of nativism upon literary theory cast in sharp political relief an ongoing debate over the relation between literary theory and particular bodies of texts. We can take as a starting point a recent intervention on this issue, by Christopher Miller.

In his "Theories of Africans: The Question of Literary Anthropology," Miller addresses with subtlety and intelligence the problematic nature of the claim that Africa's literatures require their own particular kinds of reading. He proposes, as his title suggests, a kind of literary theory that is driven by the "anthropological" urge to question "the applicability of all our critical terms" and examine "traditional African cultures for terms they might offer."[24]

Miller's argument invites us to focus on two major issues. On the one hand—and this is the direction that his own inquiry takes—the invocation of anthropology as a model for theory is bound to pose questions, at the very least, of tact. As African critics have complained, anthropological reading often grows out of a view of the texts that regards African literature as a sociological datum simply because it does not deserve or require a literary reading. But that invites the more general question of the constitution of an African

22. See my "Alexander Crummell and the Invention of Africa," *Massachusetts Review* 30 (Autumn 1990): 385–406.

23. Fanon, *The Wretched of the Earth*, p. 212.

24. Christopher Miller, "Theories of Africans: The Question of Literary Anthropology," in Henry Louis Gates, Jr. ed., *"Race," Writing and Difference* (Chicago, 1986), pp. 281–300.

criticism, which will itself depend, finally, on facing the second problem posed by Miller's piece; namely, the question of the specificity of what is called literary theory to particular text-milieus. Miller's characterization of theory as "self-reflexivity" raises immediately the issue of the complex dependency of what is called literary theory on particular bodies of texts; if we are to begin to find a place for the term "theory" in African literary studies, this is a problem we shall have to address. And, as we shall see, central to this problematic is precisely the issue of what it is to carry out a literary reading.

Yet, to pose the question of theory's textual specificity is to presuppose a historically rather recent—though very powerful and very seductive—conception of what literary theory is or might be. Even as ambitious a study as Georg Lukács's *Die Theorie des Romans* is, finally, a historically conceived account of (some) novels; the work remains, from the viewpoint of this contemporary conception of theory, mere (but not, therefore, unmagnificent) *theoria*. What we have been introduced to, in the last two decades, is an epistemology of reading that is truly imperial: both more fine-grained and more general, more, as it were, "universal" in scope; a notion of theory that takes as its fundamental material language itself, rather than the formations of a particular genre. The object of study is now the nature of the linguistic act itself (or alternately, the nature of the "literary") rather than a particular literary formation that is thematically or formally delineated.

This conception of theory has found perhaps its most powerful exemplar in Paul de Man: when, for example, he announces that literariness—the property that emerges in a literary reading of any text—consists, at least in part, in "the use of language that foregrounds the rhetorical over the grammatical and the logical function."[25] Reading Proust so that "a vast thematic and semiotic network is revealed that structures the entire narrative and that remains invisible to a reader caught in naive metaphorical mystification," de Man remarks that

> The whole of literature would respond in similar fashion, although the techniques and the patterns would have to vary considerably, of course, from author to author. But there is absolutely no reason why

25. Paul de Man, "The Resistance to Theory," *Yale French Studies* 63 (1982): 14.

analyses of the kind here suggested for Proust would not be applicable, with proper modifications of technique, to Milton or to Dante or to Hölderlin. This will, in fact, be the task of literary criticism in the coming years.[26]

Yet this Euro-American conception of theory that de Man represents is riven precisely by these claims to a determined universality. On the one hand, we have this de Manian conception of literary theory as a discourse about literature-in-general; a discourse that attempts to characterize textuality itself, rather than to explore this sonnet or that novel. On the other, we see the equally familiar notion that "theories" should be in a certain sense text-specific—should address, that is, somehow particularly inter-related bodies of writing. We confront the question that Denis Kambouchner has posed so starkly: *"How is generality in literary theory possible?*—or even more simply, if we persist in recognizing generality as the fundamental condition of theoretical discourse: *how is a theory of literature possible?"* And to answer this question we must first distinguish two senses of the term "literary theory." As Kambouchner argues, "In its broader and more diluted sense this term, or title, would denote the totality of texts, theoretical in nature, devoted to literature, without discriminating as to their object, orientation, or validity. In its second stricter and stronger sense, it would designate only the general constitution of a coherent, unified theory."[27]

Consider, now, the tension between proposition and example—the sort of disruptive intertwining de Man himself finds everywhere—in de Man's grand passage cited earlier, in which the "whole of literature" mysteriously collapses into the high-canonical: Milton, Dante, Hölderlin. The fact is that despite this talk of the "whole of literature," there is, as Cynthia Chase argues, a complex interdependency between de Manian literary theory and a specific body of (largely Romantic) texts, which sits uneasily with the claim of epistemological universality that talk of "theory" inevitably implies. In short, anyone who accepts the relevance of poststructuralist thought for European texts from the Enlightenment on has reason to be uncomfortable with their extension to texts from outside this tradition—texts, as Christopher Miller puts it with, perhaps, a trace

26. Paul de Man, *Allegories of Reading* (New Haven, Conn., 1979), pp. 16–17.
27. Denis Kambouchner, "The Theory of Accidents," *Glyph* 7 (Baltimore, 1980), pp. 149, 150.

of a smile, "that might not be a rewriting of Hegel (or even of Kant)."[28]

It is hardly outrageous, I think, to suggest that literary theory in Kambouchner's stricter sense, taking for its subject the "text in general" is not, after all, something we need to be especially concerned with if our interest is in the peculiar characteristics of the African written text. It does not follow that we must think the project of literary theory, again in Kambouchner's strong sense, is uninteresting; far from it. To the extent that African textuality fails to conform to a literary theory in this strong sense, that is a problem for the theory, revealing it as yet another local principle masquerading as universal. This is a problem we can begin to address only and precisely by a serious analysis of African texts.

But since this theoretical task is motivated not at all by an interest in the particularities of individual genres and styles, it can take African texts as exemplars only at the cost of ignoring something that matters about them; namely, their specificity. And, in fact, one can distinguish here, in a way made familiar by methodological discussions of the relations between history and sociology, between two fundamental motivations for theoretical activity: the nomothetic and the idiographic. The positivists sought to apply their models of natural scientific explanation to the discipline of history, attempting to force historical explanation into the Procrustean mold of their "deductive-nomological" model; and it is a familiar objection that in so doing they ignored fundamentally different *urges* of historical and scientific explanation.

The deductive-nomological model, we recall, seeks explanation in terms of a reduction of some particular events to be explained to a general pattern: a derivation of this specific pattern of events from the wider pattern of laws of nature. And though there is, no doubt, truth in the claim that one way to understand a historical event is to see it as fitting into a general pattern—perhaps the aftermath of the French Revolution just *is* better understood as part of a pattern that is found also in the Russian Revolution—it is also true that the historian's concern remains often with the particular event. His-

28. It is important to be clear that Chase's claim for dependency is a complex one; de Man, she argues, is in part engaged in a critique of romantic ideology. See her "Translating Romanticism: Literary Theory as the Criticism of Aesthetics in the Work of Paul de Man," *Textual Practice* (forthcoming) for an elaboration of this point. Miller, "Theories of Africans," p. 281.

torians do not need to confirm or discover the pattern that nomothetic sociology seeks to discover; for they may use known patterns to
explore the minute particularity of some local configuration of fact.
If the nomothetic impulse is to seek general patterns, call them laws
or what-you-will, we might gloss the idiographic impulse—the
chronicler's impulse—as the desire to put our general knowledge to
the service of a particular narrative.

This issue is important in the present theoretical conjuncture
because we are in a poststructuralist age; and structuralism began,
at least on many accounts, with the application of Saussurean linguistics to the question of the literary text. But if one believes that
Saussurean linguistics works, it should work for African languages
as well as for the Indo-European ones that were its model. If one is
interested, however, by contrast, in acquainting oneself with the
particularities of Twi, surely something like Saussurean linguistics
is simply the wrong level, too high a level, of abstraction with which
to begin.[29]

What we *should* begin with is a firm contrast between a sense of
literary theory—the strict or nomothetic—in which it purports to
be a general theory of literature independent of particular text-
milieus, and the humbler aims of literary criticism—which is concerned with the specificity of particular texts and literatures and
may be concerned with what we value in reading as an encounter
with specific texts.

We shall not, of course, dissolve our problem with a definition.
On the one hand, there is no such thing as a "naive" reading innocent
of all theoretical presumptions; however carefully we distinguish
between theory and criticism we will not be able to eradicate theory
from our readings. And, on the other, there is something appealing
in the notion of African theories for African texts. Indeed one might
think that this possibility exerts an especially strong pull in light
of the fact that (as critics complain) contemporary theory has often
sponsored techniques of reading that yield somewhat homogeneous
results. Our modern theories are too powerful, prove too much. We
have learned to read Baudelaire so as to instantiate the disjunction
between rhetoric as trope and rhetoric as persuasion; but it is surely

29. See my "Strictures on Structures: On Structuralism and African Fiction," in
Henry Louis Gates, Jr., ed., *Black Literature and Literary Theory* (London, 1984),
pp. 127–50.

with a feeling of ennui that we greet the same outcome in reading
Rilke and Hölderlin and Proust and Wordsworth and Yeats and
Nietzsche and Locke and Hegel and Blanchot and—Lord bless us—
Fatal Attraction. Doubtless, then, the particularist's stance has been
strengthened by the fact that deconstruction—which, as it has been
institutionalized in this country, is widely identified with "theory"
itself—is a mode of reading that seems to share its motto with the
Holiday Inn: the best surprise is, apparently, no surprise.

At any rate, theory in the grand sense is surely yielding increasingly to a more particularized historical method. Today, as Marilyn
Butler, for example, has suggested, the question is: "How are we to
write historical criticism?"[30] And "history" here is, as it should be,
the occasion for a more political style of reading. Critics with these
sympathies may be more attuned to the distinctive circumstances
of composition of postcolonial literatures.

V

But what exactly, in the postcolonial context, is the content of
the nativist's injunction to read literature by means of a theory
drawn form the text's own cultural or intellectual inheritance? Initially it would seem that to accept this principle would have wide-
ranging consequences for the way we read all literature. For it seems
to accord to African literature a deference that we do not accord the
high-canonical works of Western literature. Most of us are inclined
to think that our insights into (say) the cultural production of genre
and gender are not to be kept for our own age and region; we do *not*
think that a feminist or Marxian reading of Milton is merely an
exercise in cultural imperialism (a temporal *imperium* corresponding to the geographical). The book that is widely regarded as having
revitalized modern Wordsworth criticism (I refer to Geoffrey Hart-
man's 1964 study) draws extensively on the categories of Jung and
of the German phenomenologists—not because anyone supposed
these were part of Wordsworth's intellectual climate, but because

30. Marilyn Butler, "Against Tradition: The Case for a Particularized Historical
Method," in *Historical Studies and Literary Criticism*, ed. Jerome J. McGann (Madison, 1985).

it was thought they might help explicate the nature of Wordsworth's poetic achievements.

Then again, we could indeed replace such a pluralism of critical perspectives with a criticism grounded on the text's (or its author's) own cultural or intellectual foundations; but there would be nothing recherché about that attempt either. J. R. Caldwell's classic *John Keats's Fancy* (the examples are taken almost entirely at random) reads Keats in terms of the categories of associationism, categories that loomed large in Keats's own literary and intellectual inheritance and were part of the general intellectual and literary legacy of the eighteenth century. Anthony Nuttall has read Wordsworth in terms of Lockean psychology—again, something indigenous to the poet's own intellectual climate; something, so to speak, from the inside.

One trouble with *this* rationale for nativism, though, is precisely that it ignores the multiplicity of the heritage of the modern African writer. To insist on nativism on these grounds would be to ignore plain facts: to ignore the undeniable datum that Soyinka's references to Euripides are as real as his appeal to Ogun (and also to Brazilian syncretisms of Yoruba and Christian religions); or the certainty that, whatever their ethical or legal relations, Yambo Ouologuem's *Le Devoir de Violence*, is intimately bound up with Graham Greene's *It's a Battlefield*; or Achebe's report, apropos of his reading as a child, that "the main things were the Bible and the Book of Common Prayer and the [English] Hymn Book."[31]

No one should contest the point that an adequate understanding of a work of literature will involve an understanding of its cultural presuppositions. Does it matter to *Madame Bovary* how adultery matters in the France of her day? Then it matters to Soyinka's *Death and the King's Horseman* that the death of the title is a death whose meaning the king's horseman accepts, a death he has chosen. But the history of the reception of African literature in the West suggests that awareness of cultural context has not been the problem: on the contrary, people have been all too eager to attend to the ethnographic dimension of African literature. (Significantly, when Cambridge University appointed Wole Soyinka as a lecturer, it was through the

31. For an illuminating discussion of the charges that Ouologuem was guilty of "plagiarism" of Greene's work, see Christopher Miller's *Blank Darkness: Africanist Discourse in French* (Chicago, 1985), pp. 219–28. See "Interview with Achebe" (Anthony Appiah, John Ryle, and D. A. N. Jones), *Times Literary Supplement*, February 26, 1982, p. 209. This is from my own transcription, which was edited for publication.

Department of Anthropology.) And, as I've suggested, it would be another thing altogether to hold that a critical perspective that simulates the authorial can vouchsafe a reading more adequate to the text. Dr. Johnson had undoubted advantage as a reader of his contemporaries, and we benefit from his insights, but that does not mean that we will—or that we should—afford him the last word on the subject.

There is, at all events, a fundamental reason why nativism in theory is unlikely to lead us away from where we already are. Time and time again, cultural nationalism has followed the route of alternate genealogizing. We end up always in the same place; the achievement is to have invented a different past for it. In the fervor of cultural reassertion, as Immanuel Wallerstein has observed, "the antecedents of scientificity were rediscovered under many different names"; today certain African intellectuals are doing the same for literary theory.[32] If we start with a conception of hermeneutics borrowed from the Western academy, we may well succeed in producing an "elegant variation," inserting the odd metaphor from indigenous oracle interpretation, say. But the whole exercise puts me in mind of a certain disreputable trading concern I once visited in Harare—a product of the frankly desultory attempts at sanctions against the Republic of South Africa. Their specialty was stamping "Made in Zimbabwe" onto merchandise imported, more or less legally, from the South. Perhaps a few are really fooled: but the overall effect of the procedure is only to provide a thin skein of legitimacy to stretch over existing practices.

For all our gestures of piety toward the household gods cannot disguise that fact that the "intellectual" is the product of a particular social formation—that, as Gayatri Spivak has taught me (and, no doubt, many others) to see, there is a sense in which the "Third World intellectual" is a contradiction in terms; precisely because, as I said at the start, intellectuals from the Third World are a product of the historical encounter with the West. And the problematic from which the theoretical discourse about literature arises is not a universal one—not, at least, until it is *made* universal. Literary theory is not only an intellectual project, it is also a genre; and genres have histories, which is to say times and places. Here again, the covert universalism within the rhetoric of particularism rears its head: for

32. Immanuel Wallerstein, *Historical Capitalism* (London, 1983), p. 88.

it is surely Eurocentric presumption to insist on a correspondence within African culture to the institutional discourses of the West.

VI

But there is another difficulty with this nativism in theory: namely, that (in keeping with the rhetoric of contemporary theory generally) it grounds a politics of reading on a spurious epistemology of reading. And the talk of theoretical adequacy—which is both the carrot and the stick—is seriously misleading.

In place of this, I think we shall be better off in our choice of theory if we give up the search for Mr. Right; and speak, more modestly, of *productive modes of reading*. Here, especially in approaching these texts for which we lack well-developed *traditions* of reading, we have the opportunity to rethink the whole activity of reflection on writing. Accordingly, before I turn, finally, to some of the particulars of African literary production, I want to say a little about an alternative to the epistemology of reading that informs much of our current rhetoric.

To focus on the issue of whether a reading is *correct* is to invite the question, "What is it that a reading is supposed to give a correct account *of?*" The quick answer—one that, as we shall immediately see, tells us less than it pretends to—is, of course, "the text." But the text exists as linguistic, as historical, as commercial, as political event; and while each of these ways of conceiving the very same object provides opportunities for pedagogy, each provides different opportunities: opportunities between which we must choose. We are inclined at the moment to talk about this choice as if the purposes by which it is guided were, in some sense, given. But were that true, we would have long agreed on the nature of a literary reading: and there is surely little doubt that the concept of a "literary reading," like the concept of "literature" is what W. B. Gallie used to call an "essentially contested concept." To understand what a reading is, is to understand that what counts as a reading is always up for grabs.

By what purposes, then, should we judge our readings? To offer an answer to this question is not to rise above the contest, but to engage in it: to take a stand and to argue for it. And I think it will be clear enough why the overwhelming differences between the sociopolitical situations of teachers of literature in Africa, on the one hand, and the West, on the other, may very well suggest different stands, different arguments, and, thus, different conceptions of reading.

Consider, then, these differences: the African teacher of literature teaches students who are, overwhelmingly, the products of an educational system that enforces a system of values that ensures that, in the realm of cultural production, the West in which they do not live is *the* term of value. The American teacher of literature, by contrast, has students for whom the very same West is the term of value, but for whom that West is, of course, fully conceived of as their own. While American students have largely internalized a system of values that prohibits them from seeing the cultures of Africa as sources of value for them—despite ritualized celebrations of the richness of the life of savages—they have also acquired a relativist rhetoric, in which this "for them," allows them, at least in theory, to grant that, "for the Other" his or her world is a source of value. American students would thus expect African students to value African cultural production, *because it is African;* while African students, raised without relativism, expect Americans to value their own cultural products because they are, by some objective standard, superior.

These sociological facts, reflexes of asymmetries of cultural power, have profound consequences for reading. If one believes that the kinds of cultural inferiority complexes represented in the attitudes of many African students need to be exorcised, then the teaching of literature in the Westernized academy in Africa will require an approach that does three crucial things. The first is to identify accurately the situation of the modern African text as a product of the colonial encounter (and neither as the simple continuation of an indigenous tradition nor as a mere intrusion from the metropole). The second is to stress that the continuities between precolonial forms of cultural production and contemporary ones are nevertheless genuine (and thus provide a modality through which students can value and incorporate the African past). Third, the approach must challenge directly the assumption of the cultural superiority of the West, both by undermining the aestheticized conceptions of value that it presupposes, and by distinguishing sharply between a domain of technological skill in which—once goals are granted—comparisons of efficiency are possible, and a domain of value, in which such comparisons are by no means so unproblematic. This final challenge—to the assumption of Western cultural superiority—requires us, in the last analysis, to expose the ways in which the systematic character of literary (and, more broadly, aesthetic) judgments of value is the product of certain institutional practices and not something that exists independently of those practices and institutions.

In the American academy, on the other hand, the reading of African writing seems to need to be directed by other purposes: by the urge to continue the repudiation of racism; by the need to extend the American imagination—an imagination that regulates much of the world system economically and politically—beyond the narrow scope of the United States; by the desire to develop views of the world elsewhere that respect more deeply the autonomy of the Other; views that are not generated by the local political needs of America's multiple diasporas.

To stress such purposes in reading is to argue that, from the standpoint of an analysis of the current cultural situation—an analysis that is frankly political—certain purposes are productively served by the literary institutions of the academy.

VII

Having made these distinctions, it may be as well to insist that some of our critical materials can be put to use on both sides of the Atlantic. Thus, for example, there are distinctive formal features that arise, as has often been pointed out, from the particular closeness of African readers and writers to living traditions of oral narration. Addressing the incorporation of orality in writing allows us both to meet the need to connect modern African students with their geographical situations, and the concern to expand the American students' imagination of the world.

And—to provide another less familiar example—African writing raises a set of difficulties that stem from one of the characteristics of the cultural situation of African writers in the colonial languages: namely, the fact that they conceive of themselves always as addressing a readership that encompasses communities wider than any "traditional" culture. To address these issues productively is to allow students to explore the space of cultural politics: to allow students both African and Western to learn to resist facile reductions of modern African cultural production.

The most often-discussed consequences of the situation I have just outlined appear at the thematic level. When authors write in English or French about lives in their own countries in all their specificity, they necessarily find themselves accounting for features of those lives which derive from that specificity. This entails the use of particular concepts of, for example, kinship and family, marriage and status. As we have seen, the presentation of such details has often been read, especially by people outside Africa, as anthropologizing. We are told that Achebe's *Arrow of God*, for example, fails, in part, because it cannot take its setting for granted; that Achebe is always telling us what we need to know, acknowledging the reader's distance from Igbo traditions, and thus, allegedly, identifying the intended reader as a foreigner. I have heard the same point made about Soyinka's dramas, and I confess to finding it difficult to accept. For there are reasons, reasons highly specific to the situation of black African writing in metropolitan languages, why this criticism is a mistake.

There is one trivial reason. Achebe and Soyinka are very consciously writing for Nigerian—and not just Igbo or Yoruba—audiences. The fact that a certain amount of detail is introduced in order to specify a thick description of the cultural milieu simply does not imply a foreign—if that means a non-African—reader. That is the first point.

But this reason *is*, essentially, trivial because of a second point. To make that point I should begin with a not-to-be-neglected fact: Achebe and Soyinka are popular writers at home. If the presence of these accumulations of allegedly ethnographic detail were indeed a way of identifying an alien reader, why do Nigerian (and more specifically Yoruba or Igbo) readers not find them alienating? The fact is that the accumulation of detail is a device not of alienation but of incorporation. The provision, in traditional narrations, of information already known to the hearer does not reflect a view of the hearer as alien. Otherwise oral narrations would not consist of twice-told tales. The function of a rehearsal of the familiar in narration often depends precisely on our pleasure in recognizing in a tale what we already know.

The centrality of the inscription of the social world out of which one writes is only an example, of course, of the sort of circumstance we need to be aware of it we are to write intelligently about modern African writing. And it depends essentially upon seeing the writer, the reader, and the work in a cultural—and thus a historical, a political and a social—setting.

Let me end with an observation that derives from just such a contextualizing grasp, one that identifies the dual sources of the situation of the modern African text. Chinua Achebe once remarked,

> I'm an Igbo writer, because this is my basic culture; Nigerian, African and a writer...no, black first, then a writer. Each of these identities does call for a certain kind of commitment on my part. I must see what it is to be black—and this means being sufficiently intelligent to know how the world is moving and how the black people fare in the world. This is what it means to be black. Or an African—the same: what does Africa mean to the world? When you see an African what does it mean to a white man?[33]

Notice the presupposition of Achebe's question—"When you see an African what does it mean to a white man?" Here is the recognition that a specifically African identity began as the product of a European gaze.

Anthropologizing modes of reading would stress the sources of Achebe's "social vision" in an African setting.[34] It seems to me, by contrast, essential to insist that the nationalist dimensions of public history that are central to so much modern African writing are not mere reflexes of the epic mode of oral history and myth; they grow out of the world situation of the African writer and not out of a purely local eccentricity. Achebe is a fine example of someone who draws on the reserves of his native "orature"; but we misunderstand those uses if we do not see them in their multiple contexts.

VIII

We need to transcend the banalities of nativism—its images of purgation, its declarations, in the face of international capital, of a

33. "Interview with Achebe."
34. Soyinka, of course, uses the expression "social vision" to other more complex purposes in Wole Soyinka, Myth, Literature and the African World (Cambridge, 1976). For further discussion of these issues see my "Soyinka and the Philosophy of Culture," in P. O. Bodunrin, ed., Philosophy in Africa: Trends and Perspectives (Ile-Ife, Nigeria, 1985), pp. 250–63.

specious "autonomy," its facile topologies. The language of empire, of center and periphery, identity and difference, the sovereign subject and her colonies, continues to structure the criticism and reception of African literature *in* Africa as elsewhere. And this makes the achievement of critical balance especially difficult to maintain. On the one hand, we find theorists who emphasize the processes of demonization and subjection, the ways in which the margin is produced by the cultural dominant; Europe defining her sovereignty by insisting on the otherness of her colonies. On the other (Other?) hand, talk about the production of marginality by the cultural dominant is wholly inadequate by itself. For it ignores the reciprocal nature of power relations; it neglects the multiform varieties of individual and collective agency available to the African subject; and it diminishes both the achievements and the possibilities of African writing.

The point to be borne in mind here is not that ideologies, like cultures, exist antagonistically, but that they *only* exist antagonistically. In the ferment of present-day African literary debate, it is important to remember that the very meaning of postcolonial discourse subsists on these conflictual relations. Indeed, those conflicts are *the* topos of contemporary African literature.

Yet I, at least, worry about our entrancement with the polarities of identity and difference; partly because the rhetoric of alterity has too often meant the evacuation of specificity; partly because too many African intellectuals, captivated by this Western thematic, seek to fashion themselves as the (image of the) Other. We run the risk of an ersatz exoticism, like the tourist trinkets in the Gifte Shoppes of Lagos and Nairobi.

Nativism invites us to conceive of the nation as an organic community, bound together by the *Sprachgeist*, by the shared norms that are the legacy of tradition, struggling to throw off the shackles of alien modes of life and thought. "Here I am," Leopold Senghor once wrote, "trying to forget Europe in the pastoral heart of Sine."[35] But for us to forget Europe is to suppress the agon of history. And surely that has always been the task of the organicist aesthetic: to conceal the startling violence that sustains the dominion of culture.

35. "Tout le long du jour," in Leopold Senghor, *Chants d'ombre* (Paris, 1964).

6

Autoethnography: The An-archic Style of *Dust Tracks on a Road*

FRANÇOISE LIONNET

The words do not count.... The tune is the unity of the thing.
> —Zora Neale Hurston, 1942

The greatness of a man is to be found not in his acts but in his style.
> —Frantz Fanon, 1952

Black women have written numerous autobiographies, among which *Dust Tracks on a Road* takes the prize for inscrutability." This is the statement with which Michele Wallace concludes her recent evaluation of Zora Neale Hurston's work and of the interest that revisionist critics of different stripes have taken in Hurston's corpus during the past decade.[1] Hurston's contributions as novelist, anthropologist, and folklorist are now widely recognized. Provocative questions remain, however, about the 1942 autobiography, which does not fit into any of the usual expectations about the genre. This is not terribly surprising in view of the fact that Hurston was not one to conform to any established narrative "models."

In fact, to glance at the table of contents of *Dust Tracks* is to

1. Michele Wallace, "Who Dat Say Who Dat When I Say Who Dat? Zora Neale Hurston Then and Now," *Voice Literary Supplement*, April 1988, pp. 18–21, quotation on p. 21.

notice that it presents itself as a set of interactive thematic topoi superimposed on a loosely chronological framework. The seemingly linear progression from "My Birthplace" to "Looking Things Over" is more deceptive in that regard than truly indicative of a narrator's psychological development, quest for recognition, or journey from innocence to experience as traditionally represented in confessional autobiographies. The chapter entitled "Seeing the World as It Is," which Hurston meant to be the final one in her first draft of the book, is a philosophical essay on power, politics and human relations on a planetary scale.[2] It is the radical testament of a writer who rejects bitterness and resentment and, refusing to align herself with any "party," explains that it is because she does "not have much of a herd instinct" (*DT*, pp. 344–45). Rather than recounting the events of her life, Hurston is more interested in showing us who she is— or to be more precise, how she has become what she is: an individual who ostensibly values her independence more than any kind of political commitment to a cause, especially the cause of "Race Solidarity" as she puts it (p. 327). Hers is a very controversial enterprise which has been much criticized because it leaves itself open to charges of accommodationism (p. xxxviii), and disappoints the expectations of "frankness" and "truthfulness" that are all too often unproblematically linked to this genre of self-writing. Openly critical of *Dust Tracks* in his Introduction to the second edition, her biographer Robert Hemenway puts it thus: "Style . . . becomes a kind of camouflage, an escape from articulating the paradoxes of her personality" (p. xxxviii).

An-archy and Community

"The stuff of my being is matter, ever changing," wrote Hurston. In light of the skepticism with which contemporary literary theory has taught us to view any effort of self-representation in language, I would like to propose a different approach to the issue of Hurston's presumed insincerity and untrustworthiness.[3] It may perhaps be

2. See Hemenway's comments in the "Appendix" to *Dust Tracks on a Road*, 2d ed., ed. Robert Hemenway (Urbana, Ill., 1984), p. 288. All page references to this work, abbreviated *DT*, are given in the text.

3. For an overview of contemporary theories of autobiography see Paul John Eakin, *Fictions in Autobiography* (Princeton, N.J., 1985), esp. chap. 4.

more useful to reconsider *Dust Tracks on a Road* not as "autobiography" but rather as "self-portrait," in the sense redefined by Michel Beaujour in his book *Miroirs d'encre:* "Des textes qui se tiennent par eux-mêmes, plutôt que la mimesis d'actions passées."[4] I hope to elaborate a conceptual framework that would not conflict with Hurston's own avowed methodology as essayist and anthropologist. Indeed, what I would like to suggest here is that *Dust Tracks* amounts to "autoethnography," that is, the process of defining one's subjective ethnicity as mediated through language, history, and ethnographical analysis. In short, I want to show that her book amounts to a kind of "figural anthropology" of the self.[5]

In an essay titled "On Ethnographic Allegory," James Clifford refers to the "allegory of salvage," which generally tended to dominate the representational practice of fieldworkers in the era of Boasian anthropology. For them, the preservation of disappearing cultures and vanishing lore was seen as the vital "redemption" of the "otherness" of primitive cultures from a global process of entropy: "The other is lost, in disintegrating time and place, but saved in the text." This textualization of the object of representation incorporated a move from the oral-discursive field experience of the collector of folklore to his or her written version of that initial intersubjective moment—a transcription that is also a way of speaking *for* the other culture, of adopting a ventriloquist's stance. Having been trained under Franz Boas, Hurston was supposed to be going in the field to do just that: salvage her own "vanishing" Negro culture. Her position of fundamental liminality—being at once a participant in, and an observer of, her culture—would bring home to her the distorting effects of that problematic shift from orality to fixed, rigid textuality, and thus reinforce her skepticism in the anthropological project, in her assigned role as detached, objective interpreter and translator. The fact that she had shared in that rural culture, during her childhood in Eatonville, Florida, prevented her from adopting the nostalgic pose so common to those Western eth-

---

4. Michel Beaujour, *Miroirs d'encre* (Paris, 1980), p. 348: "Texts which are self-contained rather than being the representation of past actions." All translations are mine.

5. This phrase is used by Michel Serres in *The Parasite*, trans. Lawrence R. Schehr (Baltimore, 1982), p. 6. The French phrase is "une anthropologie figurée." See Serres, *Le Parasite* (Paris, 1980), p. 13.

nographies that implicitly lament the loss of an Edenic and preindustrial past of humankind.[6]

This same skepticism about the writing of culture would permeate the writing of the self, the autobiography, turning it into the allegory of an ethnographic project that self-consciously moves from the general (the history of Eatonville) to the particular (Zora's life, her family and friends) and back to the general (religion, culture, and world politics in the 1940s). Unlike black spiritual autobiographies that exhibit a similar threefold pattern—death, conversion, and rebirth—as well as their author's strong sense of transcendent purpose, *Dust Tracks* does not seek to legitimate itself through appeal to what William L. Andrews has called a "powerful source of authorization" such as religion or other organized system of belief.[7] It is in that sense that *Dust Tracks* is a powerfully an-archic work, not anchored in any original and originating story of racial or sexual difference.

The tone of the work and its rhetorical strategy of exaggeration draw attention to its style and away from what it directly denotes. For example, the phrase "There were no discrete nuances of life on Joe Clarke's porch... all emotions were naked and nakedly arrived at" (*DT*, p. 62) is a statement that describes the men's reactions to instances of adultery (a folksy topic). But this statement also carries historical implications about the pioneer spirit in general, as the following passage makes clear: "This was the spirit of that whole new part of the state at the time, as it always is where men settle new lands" (p. 62). Similarly, when Zora talks about her unhappy love affair, it is through vivid images that convey, with some irony, the universality of pain rather than deep personal anguish: "I freely admit that everywhere I set my feet down, there were tracks of blood. Blood from the very middle of my heart" (p. 260). Regretting the loss of the "halcyon days" of childhood, she bemoans the spirit of gravity that pervades adulthood and makes us unable to "fly with the unseen things that soar" (p. 78). And when discussing race, her denial, "No, instead of Race Pride being a virtue, it is a sapping vice" (p. 325), implicates us directly into that seemingly volatile statement

6. James Clifford and George E. Marcus, eds., *Writing Culture: The Poetics and Politics of Ethnography* (Berkeley, Calif., 1986), pp. 112–15.

7. See William L. Andrews, ed., *Sisters of the Spirit* (Bloomington, Ind., 1986), p. 13. Hurston is not interested in *organized* resistance to patterns of social injustice, which does not imply that she is not strongly critical of injustice: see *DT*, pp. 336ff.

instead of pointing us to the obvious historical context of the moment, that is, the rise of Fascism, the Second World War, colonialism, the hypocrisy and self-satisfaction of "the blond brother" (p. 343), and the preponderance of "instances of human self-bias" (p. 281). Clearly, *Dust Tracks* does not gesture toward a coherent tradition of introspective self-examination with soul-baring displays of emotion.

Paradoxically, despite its rich cultural content, this work does not authorize unproblematic recourse to culturally grounded interpretations. It is an orphan-text that attempts to create its own genealogy by simultaneously appealing to, and debunking, the cultural traditions it helps to redefine. Hurston's chosen objects of study, for example, the folktales that come alive during the storytelling or "lying" sessions she observes are indeed never "fixed." Their content is not rigid and unchanging, but generally varies according to the tale-telling situation. It is the contextual frame of reference, the situation of the telling, that determines how a tale is reinterpreted by each new tale-teller; hence, for the anthropologist, there is no "essential" quality to be isolated in the content of those tales, but there is a formal structure that can and must be recognized if she is to make sense of, and do justice to, the data gathered. Hurston's chapter titled "Research" puts the matter quite clearly and succinctly:

> I enjoyed collecting folk-tales and I believed the people from whom I collected them enjoyed the telling of them, just as much as I did the hearing. Once they got started, the "lies" just rolled and story-tellers fought for a chance to talk. It was the same thing with the songs. *The one thing to be guarded against, in the interest of truth, was over-enthusiasm. For instance, if the song was going good, and the material ran out, the singer was apt to interpolate pieces of other songs into it.* The only way you can know when that happens, is to know your material so well that you can sense the violation. Even if you do not know the song that is being used for padding, you can tell the change in rhythm and tempo. *The words do not count. The subject matter in Negro folk-songs can be anything* and go from love to work, to travel, to food, to weather, to fight, to demanding the return of a wig by a woman who has turned unfaithful. *The tune is the unity of the thing.* And you have to know what you are doing when you begin to pass on that, because Negroes can fit in more words and leave out more and still keep the tune better than anyone I can think of. (*DT*, pp. 197–98; my emphasis)

The whole issue of form and content, style and message, is very astutely condensed here: "truth" is clearly a matter of degree, and can easily be distorted by the "over-enthusiasm" of the performer. If "over-enthusiasm" can be seen as another word for hyperbole, then Hurston the writer is hereby cautioning her own reader to defer judgment about the explicit referentiality of her text. Why come to it with preconceived notions of autobiographical truths when the tendency to make hyperbolic and overenthusiastic statements about her subject matter is part of Hurston's "style" as a writer? Could we see in this passage Hurston's own implicit theory of reading, and use it to derive our interpretive practice from the work itself, instead of subjecting the text to Procrustean notions of autobiographical form?

Indeed, Hurston is fully aware of the gaps and discrepancies that can exist between intention and execution, reality and representation, reason and imagination, in short between the "words" or "subject matter" and the "tune" that is the source of unity for the singers on the porch. For her too, the flow of creative energy is a process of imaginative transfiguration of literal truth/content through rhetorical procedures. The resulting text/performance thus transcends pedestrian notions of referentiality, for the staging of the event is part of the process of "passing on," of elaborating cultural forms that are not static and inviolable but dynamically involved in the creation of culture itself. It is thus not surprising that Hurston should view the self, and especially the "racial self," as a fluid and changing concept, as an arbitrary signifier with which she had better dispense if it is meant to inhibit (as any kind of reductive labeling might) the inherent plasticity of individuals.[8] Viewed from such an angle, we

8. This is not the place to engage in a detailed analysis of the methods and assumptions of Hurston's great teacher and mentor, "Papa" Franz Boas. Suffice it to say that as an anthropologist he was a firm believer in "the plasticity of human types": his research in *Changes in Bodily Forms of Descendants of Immigrants*, published in 1911, served to convinced him that physical and mental characteristics were not simply inherited but did undergo profound modifications over time and in new surroundings. Furthermore, his views in "The Race Problem in Modern Society," published in a work that was to be widely influential and of fundamental importance to the field of anthropology, *The Mind of Primitive Man*, could not fail to influence Hurston's own attitudes about the race problem in America, to reinforce her personal tendency toward individualism and to strengthen her belief that humans are infinitely variable and not classifiable into distinctive national or racial categories. As Boas puts it, "Our tendency to evaluate an individual according to the picture that we

might say that far from being a "camouflage" and an "escape," *Dust Tracks* does indeed *exemplify* the "paradoxes of her personality" by revealing a fluid and multidimensional self that refuses to allow itself to be framed and packaged for the benefit of those human, all too human mortals, "both black and white who [claim] special blessings on the basis of race" (*DT*, p. 235).

Indeed, in the case of the folkloric forms she studies, the plasticity of the subject matter of songs and tales is corroborated by Hurston's research experience in the field. If we can be justified in seeing the "subject" of the autobiography and the "subject matter" of folklore as homologous structures or topoi reflecting and mirroring each other, then the dialogue between these homologies shapes the autobiographical text while revealing the paradoxes of the genre. This dialogue serves to illuminate Hurston's combined identities as anthropologist and writer, as these simultaneously begin to emerge and to converge in *Dust Tracks:* in the process of articulating their differences, she actually establishes their inescapable similarities, prefiguring the practice of such theorists as Clifford Geertz or Victor Turner. As Hemenway rightly points out, "Zora never became a professional academic folklorist because such vocation was alien to her exuberant sense of self, to her admittedly artistic, sometimes erratic temperament, and to her awareness of the esthetic content of black folklore."[9] But such a psychologizing approach does not suffice to clarify the work and explain Hurston's liminal position, her confident straddling of high (academic) and low (folk) cultures, the ease with which she brings to the theoretical enterprise of the academic collector of lore the insights and perceptivity of the teller of tales. What makes the autobiography interesting is that it unfolds

---

form of the class to which we assign him, although he may not feel any inner connection with that class, is a survival of primitive forms of thought. The characteristics of the members of the class are highly variable and the type that we construct from the most frequent characteristics supposed to belong to the class is never more than an abstraction hardly ever realized in a single individual, often not even a result of observation, but an often heard tradition that determines our judgment." Boas, *The Mind of Primitive Man*, 1911, cited in Ashley Montagu, *Frontiers of Anthropology* (New York, 1974), pp. 332–44. Boas recognizes the role played by "tradition" and ideology in our construction of the world and his work paves the way for what might be called Hurston's dynamic and contextual approach to culture and to private forms of behavior.

9. Robert Hemenway, *Zora Neale Hurston: A Literary Biography* (Urbana, Ill., 1980), p. 213. Hereinafter cited as *H*.

the structures of meaning—the cultural "topics" that are discussed chapter by chapter (history, geography, mythology, kinship, education, work, travels, friendship, love, religion, politics, philosophy, and so on)—through which the creative artist gives shape to her personal experiences as seen through the "spy-glass" of anthropology.[10]

Moving away from what might be the sterile analyses of a fieldworker to the inspirational language of an artist, Hurston involves herself and her reader in a transformative process. She does not just record, describe, and represent, she transforms and is transformed in turn by her autobiographical performance. To look at life from an aesthetic point of view and to celebrate her ethnic heritage are thus two complementary projects for her. Life is an aesthetic experience, a staged performance, reflected in the autobiography as well as the fictional writings, and literature is a means of recording with "a studied antiscientific approach" (*H*, p. 213) the lives and subjective realities of a particular people, in a specific time and place. It is this apparently antagonistic movement between life and literature, reality and its representation, orality and literacy, that informs the structural coherence of *Dust Tracks*, rather than the simply linear progression through the lived life. What the text puts in motion is a strategy of displacement regarding the expectations governing two modes of discourse: the "objective" exteriority is that of the autobiographer whose "inside search" does not bear out its promise of introspection whereas the "intimate" tone is that of the anthropologist who implicates herself in her "research" by delving into Hoodoo, by performing initiation rites, and, in an ironic and clever reversal of the ventriloquism of ethnography, by letting her informants inform *us* about Zora's persona in the field. As Big Sweet puts it, "You ain't like me. You don't even sleep with no mens. . . . I think it's nice for you to be like that. You just keep on writing down them lies" (*DT*, p. 189).

So, if Hurston sometimes seems to be aspiring toward some kind of "raceless ideal" it is not because she is interested in the "universality" of human experiences; quite the contrary, she wants to

10. See Zora Neale Hurston, *Mules and Men* (Bloomington, Ind., 1978), p. 3 (hereinafter cited as *MM*); also Barbara Johnson, "Thresholds of Difference: Structures of Address in Zora Neale Hurston," in *"Race," Writing, and Difference*, Henry L. Gates, Jr., ed. (Chicago, 1985), pp. 317–28.

expose, as Hemenway explains, "the inadequacy of sterile reason to deal with the phenomena of living" (*H*, p. 213), and "race" in that context is but a reasonable, pseudoscientific category for dealing with a basically fluid, diverse, and multifarious reality: "The stuff of my being is matter, ever changing, ever moving, but never lost" (*DT*, p. 279). Her philosophical position in *Dust Tracks* is in fact echoed more than twenty years later by Frantz Fanon in *The Wretched of the Earth:* "This historical necessity in which the men of African culture find themselves, that is the necessity to racialize their claims and to speak more of African culture than of national culture will lead them up a blind alley."[11] Fanon's warning that the undefined and vague entity "African culture" was a creation of European colonialism led him to emphasize local, historically and geographically specific contingencies, rather than "race" as a general and abstract concept: "And it is also true that those who are most responsible for this racialization of thought—or at least of our patterns of thought—are and remain those Europeans who have never ceased to set up white culture over and against all other so-called non-cultures" (*WE*, p. 212; Fanon's original phrase reads, "d'opposer la culture blanche aux autres incultures").[12] Similarly, Hurston's interest in the various folk communities of Eatonville, Polk County, Mobile, New Orleans, Nassau, Jamaica, and Haiti stemmed from the belief that the universal can only be known through the specific, and that knowledge grounded in firsthand experience can yield more insights into the human condition, and into the processes of acculturation, differentiation, and historicization to which human beings are subjected. I would thus argue that her unstated aim is identical to Fanon's later formulation: to destroy the white stereotype of black *inculture* not by privileging "blackness" as an oppositional category to "whiteness" in culture, but by unequivocally showing the vitality and diversity of nonwhite cultures around the Caribbean and the coastal areas of the South, thereby dispensing completely with "white" as a concept and as a point of reference. Unlike the proponents of the Negritude movement whose initial thrust was to fight against white racism and prejudice, Hurston assumes the su-

11. Frantz Fanon, *The Wretched of the Earth*, trans. Constance Farrington (New York, 1968), p. 214. Hereinafter cited as *WE*. I have modified the translation in each of the citations used.

12. Frantz Fanon, *Les Damnés de la terre* (Paris, 1968), p. 146. The word "inculture" is practically untranslatable into English.

premely confident posture of the anthropologist who need not *justify* the validity of her enterprise, but can simply *affirm* by her study the existence of richly varied black cultures, thus delineating the semiotics of spaces where, in Houston A. Baker's words, "white culture's representations are squeezed to zero volume, producing a new expressive order."[13]

What must not be overlooked, therefore, in the quoted passage from "Research" is the emphasis Hurston puts on contextual considerations and the implicit distinctions that she then draws between her own position as anthropologist observing the event and the role of the singers who are directly involved in the performance. For example, it is important for the anthropologist—and for the literary critic attempting to model her approach on Hurston's—to know the "material," that is, to be steeped in the historical, geographical, and vernacular contexts of the "songs" in order to be able to determine where "pieces of other songs" are "interpolated" and used as "padding" when the original material "ran out." Does this imply that for Hurston there is a certain autonomy of the original text which is "violated" by the "interpolation" of fragments of other songs? It would seem rather that as an anthropologist she feels that it is important to make those kinds of distinctions, yet she recognizes that for the singers this is a very unimportant question: the song goes on, the participants collectively "keep the tune" and do not worry about the singularity or inviolability of a given text or song. In other words, the question of intertextuality or of hybridization of content is not a significant one for the artists (they do not see it as a transgression of rules of identity), however important it may be for the observer who wants to be able to determine where one particular song ends and where the next one starts. The question of establishing boundaries is thus raised and examined by the anthropologist while the artist in her recognizes both the futility of making such conceptual distinctions and the severely limiting project of establishing the "true" identity and originality of the subject matter—or of authorial subjectivity, permeated as it is by the polyphonic voices of the community that resonate throughout the text and thereby reflect different narrative stances, different points of

13. Houston A. Baker, Jr., *Blues, Ideology, and Afro-American Literature: A Vernacular Theory* (Chicago, 1984), p. 152.

view on life and on Zora herself.[14] Indeed, since "no two moments are any more alike than two snowflakes" (*DT*, p. 264), there is no inconsistency in presenting a multitude of personas and being nonetheless sincere. As a well-known folk aphorism puts it, "Li'l flakes make de deepest snow": what appears to be homogeneous is in fact a complicated layering of vastly disparate elements.

The chapter "Seeing the World as It Is" emphasizes Hurston's intentions and method: "I do not wish to close the frontiers of life upon my own self. I do not wish to deny myself the expansion of seeking into individual capabilities and depths by living in a space whose boundaries are race and nation" (*DT*, p. 330). Clearly here, race and nation are singled out as colonizing signs produced by an essentializing and controlling power ("Race Pride," *DT*, pp. 324ff) external to the inner self and bent on denying her access to "spaces" other than the ones to which she ostensibly belongs by virtue of her concrete situation. Her free-spirited call for "less race consciousness" (p. 326) is to be understood in the context of her unabashed denunciation of "democracy" as just another name for selfish profiteering by the West at the expense of those "others" who live far away from the so-called democratic nations of Europe and America (pp. 338ff). These subversive and politically anarchic statements—which provoked the Procrustean editing of the autobiography—are the logical consequence of the ethnographer's skepticism. Because she remains radically *critical* without proposing positive and totalizing alternatives, she exemplifies a truly philosophical turn of mind.[15] She invites and provokes her readers to think beyond the

14. See Claudine Raynaud, "*Dust Tracks on a Road*: Autobiography as a 'Lying' Session," in *Studies in Black American Literature*, vol. 3, "Black Feminist Criticism and Critical Theory," ed. Joe Weixlmann and Houston A. Baker, Jr. (Greenwood, Fla., 1988). Whereas Raynaud would tend to see the autobiography as founding the self in a gesture of appropriation of the perennial proverbs and sayings of the community, I prefer to see in the text a continuing tension between philosophical skepticism about communal values and visionary creation.

15. It might be appropriate to add that Hurston shows a truly "metaphysical" turn of mind besides her properly "exegetical" talents. See a reference to the Robert Penn Warren and Sterling Brown debate in Henry L. Gates, Jr., *Figures in Black: Words, Signs and the "Racial" Self* (New York, 1987), p. xix. And indeed, Fanon takes up the same relay: the last words of *Black Skin, White Masks* are "O my body, make me always a man who questions!" (trans. Charles Lam Markmann [London, 1986], p. 232; hereinafter cited as *BSWM*). It is not likely that Fanon either knew or read Hurston, although he was familiar with the work of Langston Hughes, but Hurston's and Fanon's accomplishments in *Dust Tracks on a Road* and *Black Skin, White*

commonplaces and received ideas of our cultures, beyond those pro-
verbial voices of the community, *vox populi, ouï-dire*—always rendered in free indirect speech—which enunciate the webs of beliefs
that structure local consciousness of self.[16] Reporting those quotidian voices, she establishes cultural context, but by her skeptical
detachment, she proceeds to undermine the gregarious values of the
group, be it those of the folk community (involved in "specifying"
[*DT*, pp. 186; 304], in "adult double talk" [p. 62], and whose verbal
creativity is however celebrated) or the social consensus that articulates interdictions and contradictions of all sorts ("This book-
reading business was a hold-back and an unrelieved evil" [p. 117];
"If it was so honorable and glorious to be black, why was it the
yellow-skinned people among us had so much prestige?" [p. 226];
"Not only is the scholastic rating at Howard high, but tea is poured
in the manner!" [p. 156]). These "common" values are now made
available for parody. She thus opens up a space of resistance between
the individual (*auto-*) and the collective (*-ethno-*) where the writing
(*-graphy*) of singularity cannot be foreclosed.

Yet, a nagging question remains: how can Hurston's historical,
embodied self, subject to the determinants of time and place—an
African-American woman confronting racism and a world war—
represent the site of a privileged resistance to those webs of belief
that might encourage resentment and fixation on an unjust and
painful past? As she puts it: "To me, bitterness is the under-arm
odor of wishful weakness. It is the graceless acknowledgment of
defeat" (*DT*, p. 280). Since both the perpetrators and the immediate
victims of slavery are long dead, and since she has "no personal
memory of those times, and no responsibility for them" (p. 282),
she affirms that she would rather "turn all [her] thoughts and energies on the present" (p. 284). This affirmation of life against "the

---

Masks derive from a parallel need to shake off the totalizing traps of historical
determinism, and to do so in a style that is its own message: narrative and aphoristic
in order to subvert the cultural commonplaces they both abhor. See also Chester J.
Fontenot's study of Fanon and his useful discussion of form and content in *Black
Skin, White Masks:* "Visionaries, Mystics and Revolutionaries: Narrative Postures
in Black Fiction," in *Studies in Black American Literature,* vol. 1, ed. Joe Weixlmann
and Chester J. Fontenot (Greenwood, Fla., 1983).

16. For a detailed discussion of the philosophical and linguistic implications of
the "discours indirect libre," see Gilles Deleuze and Félix Guattari, *Mille Plateaux*
(Paris, 1980), pp. 95–109.

clutching hand of Time" (p. 284) is a creative release from the imposition of origin and the prison of history. Zora becomes like a
joyful Zarathustra whose world is no longer limited and bound by
the reality principle, and who advocates deliverance from the spirit
of revenge. But can this visionary posture of the self-portraitist allow
for a positive involvement in the shaping of reality, present and
future? How can it be reconciled with the anthropological claim to
locally specific knowledge? And with the historical novelist's success in drawing the suggestive allegorical fresco of a mythic Afro-
Mediterranean past in *Moses, Man of the Mountain?*

Since Fanon too denounced revenge and fixation on the past as "a
crystallization of guilt" (*BSWM*, p. 228), perhaps he can provide some
form of answer to the questions we ask of Hurston. If resentment
is the essence of negative potentiality for the self, it is clear why
Hurston rejects it outright. She wants the utmost freedom in "seeking into individual capabilities." Fanon was well aware of the peculiarly *racial* dilemma facing the children of the colonialist
diaspora: their marginality could not simply be articulated in terms
of binary categories of black versus white. Fanon's plea against racialist attitudes thus echoes Hurston's reformulation of freedom and
responsibility on a planetary scale:

> I as a man of color do not have the right to hope that in the white
> man there will be a crystallization of guilt toward the past of my race.
> (*BSWM*, p. 228)
>
> I find myself—I, a man—in a world where words wrap themselves in
> silence; in a world where the other endlessly hardens himself.... I am
> not a prisoner of history. I should not seek there for the meaning of
> my destiny. I should constantly remind myself that the real *leap*
> consists in introducing invention into existence. (P. 229)
>
> It is through the effort *to recapture the self and to scrutinize the self,*
> it is through the lasting tension of their freedom that men will be
> able to create the ideal conditions of existence for a human world. (P.
> 231, my emphasis)

The wish to "create...ideal conditions of existence" is synonymous here with the fight against all petit bourgeois mental habits
that tend to favor manifestations of closure. Fanon wants to de-
mythologize history and prevent it from being used as the source of
"reactional" behavior because, as "Nietzsche had already pointed
out," and as he himself elaborates, "there is always resentment in

a *reaction"* (*BSWM*, p. 222). While severely criticizing his fellow colonized intellectuals for simply reproducing the values of the colonizer and adopting racialist thinking, Fanon did not hesitate to state that the quest for disalienation must be mediated by the refusal to blindly accept the "Tower of the Past" (p. 226) and the problems of the present as definitive, in other words, by the belief that only the poetry of the future can move and inspire humans to action and to revolution. Unlike Fanon, Hurston did not develop the visionary perspective into a revolutionary one, but her mystical desire to be one with the universe stems from a similar utopian need for a "waking dream" of the possible which might inspire us to see beyond the constraints of the here and now to the idealized vision of a perfect future—albeit, in *Dust Tracks*, a life after death in which the substance of her being is again "part and parcel of the world" and "one with the infinite" (*DT*, p. 279).[17] Both Fanon and Hurston thus suggest that we urgently need to retrieve those past traditions that can become the source of reconciliation and wholeness, for it is more important to learn from those traditions than to dwell on pain and injustice.

For Hurston, however, the tensions involved in "the effort to recapture . . . and to scrutinize the self" is inseparable from what Beaujour has called "a type of memory, both very archaic and very modern, by which the events of an individual life are eclipsed by the recollection of an entire culture." As anthropologist Michael M. J. Fischer has stressed, ethnic memory is not only past-, but future-, oriented.[18] In *Dust Tracks*, it seems quite clear that the dynamics of interpersonal knowledge within the intercultural strands of memory are inseparable from Hurston's project of self-portraiture, since to recapture the past is quite literally to create a new field of knowledge within her academic discipline: "If science ever gets to the bottom of Voodoo in Haiti and Africa," wrote Hurston, "it will be found that some important medical secrets, still unknown to medical science, give it its power, rather than the ges-

---

17. The phrase "waking dream" is Ernst Bloch's. See Anson Rabinbach, "Unclaimed Heritage: Ernst Bloch's *Heritage of Our Times* and the Theory of Fascism," *New German Critique* 11 (Spring 1977): 7. Hurston was familiar with the German philosophical tradition of utopian thinking. In particular, she mentions Spinoza (*DT*, p. 285). See also my comments in note 23.

18. Beaujour, *Miroirs d'encre*, p. 26. Michael M. J. Fischer, "Ethnicity and the Post-Modern Arts of Memory" in Clifford and Marcus, *Writing Culture*, p. 201.

tures of ceremony" (*DT*, p. 205). By suggesting historically valid
mythological connections between ancient deities and prophets
such as Isis and Persephone on the one hand, and Damballah, Thoth,
and Moses on the other, and between those figures and the "two-
headed" magicians of Hoodoo (p. 191) who know the creative power
of words, Hurston leaves the door open for a historical revision, both
of Hoodoo religion and of antiquity, implying "two-headed" origins
in Egyptian and Greek contexts for both Euro-Americans and African-Americans. Because such a thesis would have been rejected by
contemporary scholars who then followed the "Aryan model" of
antiquity, Hurston can only allude to it through literature.[19]

A comparison of the thematic similarities in her work does show
that she was quite consciously using those ancient "personas" as
multiple facets of her own self and of her own Afro-Mediterranean
genealogy. One of her first published stories, "Drenched in Light,"
is the story of "Isis Watts," a protagonist who is clearly autobiographical, as is "Isis Potts" of *Jonah's Gourd Vine*.[20] This same
persona is reintroduced in *Dust Tracks* under the name of "Persephone." The similarity of the protagonists suggests that the three
narratives form a triptych: it is only when taking into consideration
the mythological background of those names that we can accurately
understand the process of self-discovery through self-invention that
characterizes Hurston's method. Tellingly, this process is a search
for familial and maternal connections, for "mirrors" that can reflect
positive aspects of the past instead of being the alienating images
of subaltern faces.

History and Memory:
The Shuttle of Persephone

It is significant that the only events of her "private" life on which
Hurston dwells in *Dust Tracks* are those that acquire deep symbolic

19. See Martin Bernal's revision of that model in *Black Athena* (London, 1987). For
Hurston's use of Damballah, Moses, and Thoth as facets of the same mythological per-
sona see her *Moses, Man of the Mountain* (Urbana, Ill., 1984), and Karla F. C. Holloway,
The Character of the Word (New York, 1987), chap. 3, hereinafter cited as KH.

20. "Drenched in Light" is reprinted under the title "Isis" in *Spunk: The Selected
Stories of Zora Neale Hurston* (Berkeley, Calif., 1985), pp. 9–18. For the passages of
Jonah's Gourd Vine used here, I quote from *I Love Myself When I Am Laughing: A
Zora Neale Hurston Reader*, ed. Alice Walker (New York, 1979). Hereinafter cited
as *ILM*.

and cultural value. The death of the mother and subsequent dispersion of the siblings echo the collective memory of her people's separation from Africa-as-mother and their ineluctable diaspora. That is why Kossola/Cudjo Lewis's story emblematizes Hurston's own sense of bereavement and deprivation: "After seventy-five years, he still had that tragic sense of loss. That yearning for blood and cultural ties. That sense of mutilation. It gave me something to think about" (*DT*, p. 204). Narrated at the end of the "Research" chapter, the embedded narrative of Kossola's life serves as a powerful counterpoint to Zora's own story of strife and reconciliation with her brothers (pp. 172–73). It is thanks to her research and professional travels that she becomes, like the legendary Isis of Egyptian mythology, the link that reunites, reconnects the dispersed siblings who can now "touch each other in the spirit if not in the flesh." The imagery that describes the disintegration of the family unit is a clear reminder of the historic conditions of the Middle Passage:

> I felt the warm embrace of kin and kind for the first time since the night after my mother's funeral, when we had huddled about the organ all sodden and bewildered, with the walls of our home suddenly blown down. On September 18th, that house had been a hovering home. September 19th, it had turned into a bleak place of desolation with unknown dangers creeping upon us from unseen quarters that made of us a whimpering huddle, though then we could not see why. But now that was all over. (Pp. 173)

As private experiences echo collective ones and punctuate the deployment of the self-portrait, a picture of the fieldworker as keeper of important knowledge, as go-between whose role is to facilitate the articulation of collective memory, emerges. By foregrounding the fact that the field research is the causal link to an empowering reunion with her scattered siblings, Hurston makes a narrative move with much broader implications for the social lives of Afro-Americans. She implies that connections to the past must not be severed if we are to regain a sense of what "touch[ing] each other in the spirit" can be like, but also that a sense of history must not simply be allowed to degenerate into the remembrance of paralyzing images. That is why she also remarks that "any religion that satisfies the individual urge is valid for that person" (*DT*, p. 205), since ancient traditions such as Voodoo contain "the old, old mysticism of the world in African terms" (*H*, p. 249), are useful to a "thick de-

scription" of cultural nuances, and to help demarcate the historical
context relevant to the study of folklore.[21]

Hurston's aim is to maintain the integrity of black culture without
diluting it, and to celebrate its values while remaining critical of
those pressures from within the "family" which can mutilate individual aspirations—as her oldest brother Bob had been guilty of
doing to her when she went to live with him hoping that he would
help put her through school, only to find herself playing the role of
maid to his wife. It is this de facto lack of solidarity among "brothers" that Hurston observes and which forms the basis for her critique
of a blanket endorsement of simple-minded, universal "Race
Solidarity" (DT, p. 327), or of a form of Pan-Africanism which
in the 1930s and 1940s must have sounded disturbingly like Pan-
Germanism whose evil historical consequences were well understood. The text of Dust Tracks thus shuttles between appreciation
and opprobrium, finding its impetus in the joyful affirmation of its
contradictions. To recall the past in order to transcend it, Fanon
would also point out, is the only emancipatory stance we can confidently adopt without risk of falling prey to reactionary forces.

Thus, the chapter titled "Religion," reveals Hurston's total indif-
ference to the "consolation" traditional religion affords: "I am one
with the infinite and need no other assurance"(DT, p. 279). Her style
subverts the need for such "organized creeds" which are but "collections of words around a wish" (p. 278), and which Fanon would
denounce as the motor of a closed society... in which ideas and
people are in a state of decay."[22] Comfortable in the knowledge that
the whole world is in a Heraclitean flux of becoming, Hurston affirms a principle of eternal change based in her observation of the
radical fluidity of inorganic, organic, social, and cultural forces:

> I have achieved a certain peace within myself, but perhaps the seeking
> after the inner heart of truth will never cease in me.... So, having
> looked at the subject from many sides, studied beliefs by word of
> mouth and then *as they fit into great rigid forms, I find I know a
> great deal about form, but little or nothing about the mysteries I
> sought as a child.*... But certain things have seemed to me to be true
> as I heard the tongues of those who had speech, and listened at the

21. "Thick description" in the sense used by Clifford Geertz in *The Interpretation
of Cultures* (New York, 1973), chap. 1.
22. Fanon, *BSWM*, p. 224. Translation modified here. See also Fontenot, "Visionaries," p. 84, for a discussion of "open" and "closed" society as defined by Fanon.

lips of books.... The springing of the yellow line of morning out of
the misty deep of dawn, is glory enough for me. I know that nothing
is destructible; things merely change forms.[23]

Poetic speech has now replaced the folk idiom, the artist, the
anthropologist. The distinction between form and content ("mysteries") is again made, but then put under erasure: "things merely
change forms" and content is never lost. Yet knowledge of content
is determined by the "great rigid forms" that structure the universe
while veiling the motley appearance of "matter." These allegories
of death and rebirth, change and permanence, temporality and eternity, map retroactively the territory of the autobiographical text and
the life it attempts to represent. By retracing those ephemeral "dust
tracks" that the trajectory of the table of contents surveys, Hurston
seems to spiral out into infinity and the cosmos: "The cosmic Zora
emerges."[24] Her journey, like that of the storytellers who never leave
the porch, is an itinerary through language, "a journeying by way
of narrating." That is why it is impossible to make, on a theoretical
level, "any clear-cut division between theme and form, between
journey as geography and journey as narrative."[25] The "curve in the
road" at which Hurston sees her first "vision" (*DT*, p. 93) is a mythical point of departure for the global adventure during which she
will learn to take distance from the "tight chemise" and the "crib
of negroism" (*MM*, p. 3) which have shaped her. Distance alone can
enable her to recognize and assemble the fragments of her changing
folk culture in the New World, and because she is dealing with
familiar territory, she does not run the risk of subjugating the
"other" to her self, of making them into marionettes for the benefit
of those patrons who are only interested in the static "primitive"
aspects of her research. Being engaged in a truly dialogical enterprise,
and not in the delusions of Boasian "pure objectivity" to which she
alludes ironically (*DT*, p. 174), she can negotiate the terms of her
insertion within and without the ethnographic field, and even parody

23. *DT*, p. 279, my emphasis. Hurston's Spinozist philosophy is evident here. See
B. Spinoza, *Ethics* (n.p., 1981), part I, proposition VIII: "Every substance is necessarily
infinite" (p. 32). As S. P. R. Charter puts it in the introduction to this edition of
Ethics, "Spinoza attempted to unite the mind/body complexity and the realities of
existence with the all-embracing actuality of Nature, and to do so organically—that
is, without the imposition of man-made religious structures" (p. 3).
24. Hurston, "How It Feels to Be Colored Me," in *ILM*, p. 155.
25. See Alexander Gelley, *Narrative Crossings* (Baltimore, 1987), p. 31.

popular beliefs with impunity: the jokes come naturally with the territory of storytelling.

Similarly, the discursive enterprise of self-portraiture is a process of collecting and gathering, of assembling images and metaphors to portray a figural self, always already caught in entropy and in permanent danger of returning to "dust," of becoming again "part and parcel" of the universe. In what follows, then, I would like to examine briefly the textual mechanism that generates the journey of ethnic self-scrutiny, the slippage between particular and universal, individual and collective, daughter and mother(s), the self and its mythologies. In describing these displacements, I want to show how the collective functions as a silverless mirror, capable of absorbing the self into a duplicitous game where one code, singularity, is set aslant by another, syncretic unity with the universe, thus preventing narrative closure.[26] The tensions at work in *Dust Tracks* between these two sets of expectations (local versus universal knowledge) are not simply resolvable through (ethnographic) narrative moves. They constitute what Stephen Tyler has called the proper domain of "post-modern ethnography," neither "the upward spiral into the Platonic... realm of conscious thought and faceless abstraction...," nor the "descent 'beneath the surface' into the Plutonic 'other of separation.' " Hurston's approach to the study of culture indeed prefigures the future trend of the discipline as outlined by Tyler: "The ethnographic text will thus achieve its purposes not by revealing them, but by making purposes possible. It will be a text of the physical, the spoken, and the performed, an evocation of quotidian experience, a palpable reality that uses everyday speech to suggest what is ineffable, not through abstraction, but by means of the concrete. It will be a text to read not with the eyes alone, but with the ears in order to hear 'the voices of the pages.' "[27]

Hurston too captures the voices of the people and relays them through the "lips of books," which do not "announce" their purpose but braid "palpable reality" with the incommensurable, the quotidian with the ineffable. She makes it possible to envisage purposive,

26. What I call the silverless mirror here is to some extent assimilable to what Houston A. Baker, Jr., associates with the term "black (w)hole": "a *singularly* black route of escape." See Baker, *Blues*, p. 155. By analogy, it refers also to the covered looking glass in the room of the dying mother (p. 88): I return to this later.

27. Stephen Tyler, "Post-Modern Ethnography: From Document of the Occult to Occult Document," in Clifford and Marcus, *Writing Culture*, pp. 133, 136.

enabling, and empowering structures of meaning that do not coerce the subject into historically and Eurocentrically determined racial metaphors of the self. She succeeds in tracing a map of her territory—a symbolic geography—by using the same accommodating principles that governed the expedient building of roads over the winding path of the foot trail between Orlando and Maitland. The metaphor of the road which curves effortlessly around "the numerous big pine trees and oaks" (*DT*, p. 7) reinforces a principle of flexibility, a respect for nature rather than the need to dominate it, a pliability that connotes the plasticity of human forms, the capacity to undergo mutations, to endure and survive hardships in that middle passage from birth to death, from mud to dust.

The allegory of the voyage which is only a return to one's point of departure is already present in the first chapter, "My Birthplace." The "three frontier-seekers" who embark for Brazil only to return to the United States prefigure Hurston's journeying through black folklore in order to rediscover the "geography...within" (*DT*, p. 115), the lost community of her childhood in "a pure Negro town!" (p. 9). Her search for an originary plenitude is the universal biblical "return to dust" at the end of the road of life—not the romantic nostalgia for a prelapsarian time of innocence. In that respect, the death of her mother represents the first moment in a chain of de-stabilizing experiences that undermine forever her sense of belonging to a specific place:

> That hour began my wanderings. Not so much in geography, but in time. Then not so much in time as in spirit.
> Mama died at sundown and changed a world. That is, the world which had been built out of her body and her heart. Even the physical aspects fell apart with a suddenness that was startling. (P. 89)

The death scene of the speechless mother becomes the motivating factor for writing, for the effort of self-fashioning that is also an effort to stave off death. Hurston's wandering phase will be the result of this experience of absence and loss which is repeated on different levels throughout the next chapters. The narrator attempts to fill the void of death by journeying *and* by narrating.

That is why it is interesting to note that the description of the mother's death in *Dust Tracks* closely parallels the fictional rendering of that scene in *Jonah's Gourd Vine*. Telling details are repeated almost word for word: "I could see the huge drop of sweat collected in the hollow at Mama's elbow and it hurt me so" (DT, p. 88) and "Isis saw a pool of sweat standing in a hollow at the elbow" (ILM, p. 195); "I thought that she looked to me. . . . I think she was trying to say something, and I think she was trying to speak to me" (DT, p. 88) and "Isis thought her mother's eyes followed her and she strained her ears to catch her words" (ILM, p. 195). "Isis" is indeed the fictional alter ego that Hurston chooses for herself, the name of an ancient Egyptian goddess who wandered the world in search of her dismembered brother, a mythical representation of interiority as experience of death. In Egyptian mythology, Isis's brother Osiris is both the god of fertility (like Demeter/Ceres in the Greco-Roman myth) and the king and judge of the dead. He is also the companion of Thoth, god of death and of writing, who helps him preside in the Underworld. Hurston thus makes an implicit connection between the Osirian mysteries tied to the cult of the dead and of which Isis was the high priestess, and the occult practices of Hoodoo of which Hurston herself became an initiate. Having flippantly named herself the "queen of the niggerati" (KH, p. 24) in one of her histrionic moments among her New York friends, Hurston then proceeded to develop (in the autobiographical triptych) the theme of a life lived in the shadow of Isis/Persephone, queens of the Underworld, of the "dark realm" of otherness, and she did so in a mythically accurate and artistically sensible manner. The persona "Isis"—both the goddess and the fictional daughter of Lucy Potts—is like the mirror that figures prominently in the mother's death scene. She is an image of memory and interiority, an "other" who focuses, crystallizes, and gives sharp contours to the project of self-invention. She is an important thread in the process of "re-membering" one's past and one's own mortality as one pays homage to the dead and departed. Here, the folk custom of veiling the mirror (so that the dead may rest in peace and not trouble the living) is implicity criticized. The dying mother suggests that the mirror should not be veiled if the past, and the faces of our mothers in it, are to leave their imprint on the memory of the living so that we may live in peace with history, and be thus able to "think back through our mothers," as Virginia Woolf believed it was important for women to be able to do.[28]

What the death scene allegorizes then is Hurston's subtle and

28. See Jane Marcus, "Thinking Back Through Our Mothers," in New Feminist Essays on Virginia Woolf (Lincoln, Neb., 1981), pp. 1–30.

complex view of the relationship of individuals to culture and history. Some elements of culture, because they are unexamined traditions, "village customs" (*DT*, p. 86), "mores" (89), upheld by the voices of patriarchy (the "village dames" or phallic women, and the father, who together prevent her from fulfilling her mother's wishes), are destructive and stultifying. The child's (Isis's and Zora's) experience of anxiety and guilt is the result of those unexamined cultural myths that thwart the mother's desire to remain imprinted on the daughter's memory. As Adrienne Rich has put it: "The loss of the daughter to the mother, the mother to the daughter, is the essential female tragedy."[29] The loss entailed because of the patriarchal customs of the "village" is a painful enactment of separation and fragmentation, of lost connections to the mother as symbol for a veiled and occulted historical past. Both Albert Memmi and Frantz Fanon would later point out that our problem as colonized people (or gender) is that we all suffer from collective amnesia. The self-portrait Hurston draws in *Dust Tracks* is the performance of an anamnesis: not self-contemplation but a painstaking effort to be the voice of that occluded past, to fill the void of collective memory.

Indeed, Zora feels that her mother "depended on [her] for a voice" (*DT*, p. 87), and in *Dust Tracks* she chooses the mythical Persephone as alter ego. The Greek word for voice is *phone* and the scene of the mother's death is symbolic of the daughter's responsibility to articulate her story, to exhume it from the rubble of patriarchal obfuscation. Martin Bernal has pointed out that the Eleusinian story of Demeter searching for Persephone has its roots in the Egyptian myth of Isis and Osiris.[30] By identifying with Persephone in *Dust Tracks*, Hurston makes a brilliant and sophisticated rapprochement between the two myths—a connection, says Bernal, that classicists who follow the "Aryan model" of antiquity have studiously avoided to make. Hurston approaches Afro-Mediterranean antiquity with the intuitions of the anthropologist who sees connections where traditional classical scholarship had not.

The displacement from Isis to Persephone as choice of objective

29. Adrienne Rich, *Of Woman Born* (New York, 1976), p. 237. As Sandra M. Gilbert and Susan Gubar have amply demonstrated, the lack of a female tradition in which to insert herself is a source of great "anxiety of authorship" for the woman writer. See their *The Madwoman in the Attic: the Woman Writer and the Nineteenth-Century Literary Imagination* (New Haven, Conn., 1979), esp. pp. 45–92.

30. Bernal, *Black Athena*, pp. 69–73.

persona is significant in helping us understand Hurston's feeling of
being an orphan, of being cut off from her origins or *arche*. "Isis" is
the wanderer who conducts her research, establishes spatiotemporal
connection among the children of the diaspora, and "re-members"
the scattered body of folk material so that siblings can again "touch
each other." "Persephone," on the other hand, is not a rescuer, but
rather a lost daughter whose mother searches for her with passion.
She is an ambiguous figure "with her loving and hellish aspects."[31]
Ironically, it is Zora's reading of the Greco-Roman myth ("one of
my favorites," *DT*, p. 48) during the visit of two white women at
her school that attracts attention to her brilliance and configures
her later "rescue" by other white mentors, friends who become
surrogate mothers (as is Helen in "Drenched in Light"). If, as Ronnie
Scharfman has noted, "mirroring" and "mothering" are twin terms
for defining the reciprocal nurturing bonds that a female subject
needs in order to feel anchored in the tradition linking her to her
mother(s), then Hurston's vain efforts to prevent the veiling of the
mirror in the mother's room must be understood as an allegorical
attempt to look into the mirror of her mother's soul, to retain severed
connections, to recapture and to "read" the dark face of the mother
in the silverless mirror of the past, and to become the voice that
bridges generations.[32] Those efforts also prefigure her professional
predicament as an adult. Persephone was the queen of Pluto's dark
realm of the dead, but she also traveled back and forth between the
Underworld and "the sunlit earth" (*DT*, p. 49), like Hurston who
retrieves the voices of her black culture in order to call her readers
"back to primal ground" (KH, p. 113). Caught between the upper
and the lower realms, the black and the white world, life and death,
she bridges the tragic gap of separation by writing. As Beaujour has
explained, "The self-portrait tries to reunite two separate worlds,
that of the living and that of the dead."[33]

Hurston's description of a ceremony in which she participates in
New Orleans draws the obvious parallel: "I had to sit at the cross-
roads at midnight in complete darkness and meet the devil, and
make a compact. There was a long, long hour as I sat flat on the

31. Ibid., p. 70.
32. Ronnie Scharfman, "Mirroring and Mothering in Simone Schwarz-Bart's *Pluie
et vent sur Télumée Miracle* and Jean Rhys's *Wide Sargasso Sea*," *Yale French Studies*
62 (1981): 88–106.
33. Beaujour, *Miroirs d'encre*, p. 161.

ground there alone and invited the King of Hell" (*DT*, p. 192). Since we also know that fasting was an essential part of her initiation, the parallel with Persephone is even more convincing, as Persephone's fate was to be Pluto's queen for three months of each year because "she had bitten the pomegranate" (p. 49). Cleansing by fasting is of course a common part of initiatory practices in numerous religions and underscores Hurston's philosophy of the universal oneness of religious symbolisms.

When the child's experience of absence, in *Dust Tracks*, becomes specifically racial, we have a new and negative dimension to the metaphor of the mirror. As she puts it, "Jacksonville made me know that I was a little colored girl" (p. 94). This discovery of the ethnic self as mirrored by the other, the white culture of Jacksonville, functions in the text as another moment of an-archic self-discovery. The image reflected in the mirror of white culture is like the photograph in which Janie, in *Their Eyes Were Watching God,* cannot recognize herself because she does not yet know that she is colored, that for the white family who calls her "Alphabet," she is different because she symbolizes namelessness, darkness, absence, and lack.[34] This is Janie's first experience of difference: that of her face as a bad photograph, as a "negative" and a flaw in the developed picture she holds in her hand. This scene of nonrecognition, like the deathbed scene, is the primal motivation for the journey of self-discovery through language. Isis, Persephone, Thoth, and Osiris are thus the four poles that mark the perimeter of Hurston's cultural mythology of the self. Thoth's gift links writing to death and to immortality; here the thread of memory allows Janie/Zora to "[pull] in her horizon like a great fish-net" (*TE*, p. 286) in which the fragments of a faceless past are reassembled and given new names, new origins.

When we look at the allegory of the veiling of the mirror in *Dust Tracks* in the context of those similar scenes in the novels, a very strong statement about the self and its enabling and distorting mirrors emerges. The idea that a mirror can be the vehicle of a negative self-image (depersonalization and loss) seems to be tied to two cultural myths, perceived as destructive and debilitating by the child. One is the patriarchal folk belief about mirrors and death; and the other arises from the white culture's myths about blackness as rad-

<hr>

34. Zora Neale Hurston, *Their Eyes Were Watching God* (Urbana, Ill., 1978), p. 21. Hereinafter cited as *TE*.

ical otherness and absence. In both cases, reflections are void, absent, or distorted because they emanate from a reductionist context. The realities of a culture's myths about death and otherness become a burden and a distortion of the historical metaphors by which women must learn to live if we are to recapture the faces of our mothers in the mirrors of the past, and reconstruct their voices from the pieces of that past. It is by uncovering those mirrors that we can begin to articulate connections to ancient and empowering symbols of femaleness. Hence the anguish of the child at not being able to fend off the voices of white and black patriarchy that rob her forever of the peace that comes from seeing the face(s)—and knowing the mythical name(s)—that connect her to a cultural tradition not grounded only in darkness and silence. Again Beaujour's formulation is valid here: "The self-portrait is constructed around an empty center: vanished places and disturbed harmonies."[35] The experience of death generates the writing of a self-portrait through which appears, pentimento, the mother's lost face.

The child who leaves Eatonville after her mother's death experiences alterity and dislocation, distances herself forever from the illusory possibility of an unexamined and unmediated participation in the network of relations that constitute culture. In effect, her avocation as anthropologist starts right then and there. Her exile from Eatonville is the first step on the nomadic road of lore collecting, a road along which "the subject looks for soul-mates while simultaneously affirming [her] absolute difference from all others" (Beaujour, *Miroirs*, p. 15). That is why the collective voice is so often relayed with irony and pathos: the self-portrait is the medium of subversion par excellence that relativizes the fetishistic recourse to a foundational world beyond its discourse. It evokes the ethnic reality of which it partakes, but in so doing puts into question the mimetic principles of description and classification that inform its writing. It thus simultaneously demystifies the writing of both the self (auto) and the culture (ethno) because it involves both the individual and her cultural contexts in a dialogue that transcends all possibility of reducing one to the other: "Mirror of the subject and mirror of the world, mirror of the 'I' searching for a reflection of its self through the mirror of the universe: what might first appear as

35. Beaujour, *Miroirs d'encre*, p. 22. Subsequent page numbers are cited in the text.

a simple correspondence, or a convenient analogy, proves under close scrutiny to be a homologous relation warranted by the rhetorical tradition and the history of literature" (*Miroirs*, p. 31). Beaujour's formulation can be applied to *Dust Tracks* with an important modification: it is not the medieval rhetorical tradition that furnishes the topics of mimesis, but the anthropological essay with its system of categories which locate culture at the nexus of history and geography, religion and myth, as mentioned earlier. What this means for the "self-portrait" according to Beaujour is that writing is engendered primarily by the *impossibility* of self-presence, by the realization that realist narratives are functionally distorting and that myths are more appropriately evocative and suggestive of a subject's liminal position in the world of discursive representation.

Here, a myth of ancient Afro-Mediterranean folklore establishes the parameters according to which Hurston will go on performing the role of daughter after her mother's death and until they can both be syncretically reunited. The faceless woman encountered on a porch in Jacksonville during a school walk, and "who looked at a distance like Mama" (*DT*, p. 96) prefigures the last of her twelve "visions": the two women, one young (herself?), one old (the mother?), whose faces are averted as they are "arranging some queer-shaped flowers such as [she] had never seen" (p. 58). This indirect allusion to the funeral flower—the white narcissus—is also the figure of the self reflected in the pool of language, the dark ("miroirs d'encre") medium of self-knowledge, the white symbol of death's attraction. It is an unformulated, unnamed, but richly suggestive allusion to the desire for the absent mother, which will be reenacted both in the bonds of female friendships (the visitors at the school, Big Sweet, Fannie Hurst, Ethel Waters, the Dahoman Amazons, and so on) and in those of hatred or rivalry with other women (her stepmother, and knife-toting "Lucy").[36] At once Persephone and Narcissus, the autobiographical narrator attempts to recapture the (m)other in the self and the self through the (m)other:

> Once or twice I saw the old faceless woman standing outdoors beside
> a tall plant with that same off-shape white flower. She turned suddenly

---

36. For an analysis of the "thematic consistency . . . found in these echoing episodes of female strength," see Raynaud, *"Dust Tracks on a Road:* Autobiography." On this aspect of the text, I am in complete agreement with Raynaud.

from it to welcome me. I knew what was going on in the house without going in, it was all so familiar to me.

I never told anyone around me about these strange things. It was too different. They would laugh me off as a story-teller. Besides, I had a feeling of difference from my fellow men, and I did not want it to be found out.[37]

Hurston's experiences of singularity and difference are intimately connected to her visions of death. Not surprisingly, the reference to "Pluto's dark realm" (*DT*, p. 48) and to the temporary reunification of Persephone with her mother turns upside down the circumstances of her life, and transforms the past by reorienting it toward an un-lived future where the lost potentialities of love and daughterhood are given a second chance, and an elusive possibility of peace and transfiguration:

> I stood in a world of vanished communion with my kind, which is worse than if it had never been. Nothing is so desolate as a place where life has been and gone. I stood on a soundless island in a tideless sea.
>
> Time was to prove the truth of my visions...bringing me nearer to the big house, with the kind women and the strange white flowers. (P. 59)

If the mother is a figure for the "lost" potentialities of history and for the "dark" continent of Africa, it is not surprising that images of death and decay begin to pervade her self-recollection during those years of loneliness and wandering in which she feels "haunted" (*DT*, p. 116). Just like "Lazarus after his resurrection," she cannot expe-rience her own self in a unified way, since past and present, mind

---

37. *DT*, pp. 58–59. See Beaujour's discussion in *Miroirs d'encre* of the associations among Demeter, Persephone, and Narcissus in Greek mythology, and the connections between these divinities and death. His argument is that narcissism as commonly understood in psychoanalytic terminology is a distorted and reductive interpretation of the myth and that far from being "narcissistic" in that sense, "l'autoportrait tente de réunir les deux mondes séparés de la vie et de la mort....Narcisse accède par l'anamnèse à...l'invention poétique des souvenirs d'enfance, qui restitue un paradis intemporel: à la fois trésor individuel et topique culturelle" ("the self-portrait tries to reunite two separate worlds, that of the living and that of the dead....Through anamnesis, Narcissus...performs a poetic invention of 'childhood memories' which recreates a timeless paradise, at once personal treasure trove and cultural topic"), p. 161. See esp. 156–62.

and body, can never coincide completely: "I walked by my corpse. I smelt it and felt it. I smelt the corpses of those among whom I must live, though they did not. They were as much at home with theirs as death in a tomb" (p. 117). Like the Zombies she will later study, she is a living-dead whose childhood memories of that time— between ten and fourteen years of age—are the undeveloped photographic negative of the images of singular blankness that will keep recurring in later chapters. For instance, her first love affair, although it provides the closeness and warmth she had sorely missed ever since her mother's death, turns into an oppressive relationship that imprisons her inside feelings of doubt and unreality that cannot be shared with the husband: "Somebody had turned a hose on the sun. What I had taken for eternity turned out to be a moment walking in its sleep. . . . A wind full of memories blew out of the past and brought a chilling fog" (p. 251).

Numbed by the impossibility to communicate, life is drained out of her, and she buries herself in her work. The next time she falls in love, the pattern seems to repeat itself. She is thwarted by the conflicts caused by her career, the man's possessiveness, and his complaints that her "real self had escaped him." She is not permitted to have a life of her own, is restrained by limiting circumstances, "caught in a fiendish trap" (*DT*, p. 259). Love is never experienced as an empowering force—unlike friendship, this "mysterious and ocean-bottom thing" (p. 321) without which life is not worth much: "To live without friends is like milking a bear to get cream for your morning coffee. It is a whole lot of trouble, and then not worth much after you get it" (p. 248). In contrast to the flatness of her lovelife, her affective landscape is peopled with many picturesque and vivid portrayals of friends. The topic of "friendship" is a much richer and more satisfying one than "love," and the treatment it receives in *Dust Tracks* bears testimony to the importance that self-portraitists have accorded to the interface with an "other" whose ambivalent companionship may be the spur that compels a writer to articulate the potentialities of his or her vision.[38] "Conversation is the ceremony of companionship" (p. 248), Ethel Waters says to Zora, and

---

38. Augustine, Montaigne (O un amy!), Gertrude Stein, Christopher Isherwood, Roland Barthes are but a few. See Réda Bensmaïa, *The Barthes Effect: The Essay as Reflective Text* (Minneapolis, 1987), esp. pp. 62–89.

Zora's self-portrait is this conversation with the past, a ceremony for the dead mother(s), but one which simultaneously empowers the living.

The narrator also experiences singularity as separation from the realm of nature. After her departure to Jacksonville, her introduction to formal education goes together with another deprivation that adds to her grief and mourning: "The loving pine, the lakes, the wild violets in the woods and the animals [she] used to know" (*DT*, p.95) are no longer part of her daily life. Orphaned for a second time when her father asks the school to "adopt" her, she is nonetheless sent home on the riverboat, and she experiences a thrilling form of rebirth because she is again part and parcel of nature: "The water life, the smothering foliage that draped the river banks, the miles of purple hyacinths, all thrilled me anew. The wild thing was back in the jungle. The curtain of trees along the river shut out the world so that it seemed that the river and the chugging boat was all that there was, and that pleased me a lot" (p.109). The floating boat and the trees that "shut out the world" are like the protective layers of a womb; the boat's chugging motor connotes a maternal heartbeat, a reassuring companion that spells the return to an earlier form of peace and harmony. These layered allusions to the archaic times of a prenatal life and the historical moments of preslavery days in Africa again configurate the mother as the sheltering presence. Her disappearance generates the nomadic search for collective meanings that will establish a system of resonance between seemingly heterogeneous entities or "topics," such as daughterhood, friendship, nature, and antiquity. All of these topics can be seen as so many inaugurating moments of similarity within difference, of self-absorption in an enigmatic mirror.

Later on, when working as a maid for the soprano of the traveling opera company, Zora becomes a kind of mascot for the whole company and her writing career gets started: "I got a scrapbook . . . and wrote comments under each picture. . . . Then I got another idea. I would comment on daily doings and post the sheets on the callboard. . . . The results stayed strictly mine less than a week because members of the cast began to call me aside and tell me things to put in about others . . . It was just my handwriting, mostly" (*DT*, pp.138–39). She becomes the repository of other people's words, a kind of transparent mind or ghostwriter. She experiences another form of Zombiehood, mediated by the acquisition of language, by the absorption of other voices, just like all that "early reading" which had given her "great anguish through all [her] childhood and adolescence" because as she puts it, "My soul was with the gods and my body in the village. People just would not act like gods" (p. 56). Her experiences at school, in Baltimore, follow the same pattern: "And here I was, with my face looking like it had been chopped out of a knot of pine wood with a hatchet on somebody's off day, sitting up in the middle of all this pretty" (p. 151). Undefined features, "a woman half in shadow," the self-portraitist draws a picture of herself that remains "a figure in bas relief," an intaglio, "the weaving of anthropology with thanatography."[39]

These echoing patterns of disfiguration and death provide an improvisational rhythm to the text, giving it the ebb and flow of musical counterpoint, and suspending meaning between suggestive similarities that the reader is free to associate or not. One subtle parallel that the text thus draws is between two gruesome events: the decapitation of Cousin Jimmie, "mother's favorite nephew" (*DT*, p. 85) who had been assassinated before Zora's birth and whose unintentional shooting by a white man had been covered up to look as though a train had killed him; and the similar fate which had befallen the son of Kossola/Cudjo, David, who was actually beheaded in a train accident. In both cases, it is the grief of the parental figures that resonates in the text, rather than a hypothetical repetition of real-life events. Indeed, framing as they do Hurston's vision of the two faceless women and Kossola's stories of famed Dahoman Amazons who sack cities and carry "clusters of human heads at their belts," the stories underscore a pattern of singular repetition which would seem to point not to referents beyond the text, but to the allegorical disfiguring of generation upon generation of black individuals whose plight is ignored or covered up, except in the memory of those who grieve for them (as Cudjo's Takkoi King beheaded by the Amazons is also mourned by his people—cf. *DT*, p. 201).

The ephemeral quality of collective memory itself is reflected in the transient nature of Hurston's "first publication." "On the black-

---

39. "A woman half in shadow" and "figure in bas relief" are from Fannie Hurst, "A Personality Sketch," reprinted in *Zora Neale Hurston*, ed. Harold Bloom (New York, 1986), pp. 24 and 23, respectively. The first phrase is also the title of Mary Helen Washington's introduction to *ILM*. The last quotation is from Beaujour, *Miroirs d'encre*, p. 13.

board...I decided to write an allegory using the faculty members as characters" (*DT*, p. 153). The "allegory" is the source of much entertainment and laughter for her schoolmates, a successful rehearsal for her future tale-telling and an important metaphoric hyphen between the immediacy of oral performance and the permanence of the written words. Like these allegorical portraits that will be erased once they have served their purpose, her twelve visions which were initially meant to structure the deployment of the autobiography are soon forgotten because they do not need to be used. The tale-teller dynamically reshapes her material as she goes along, the content of the visions becoming irrelevant since the essay form of the latter chapters ("My People! My People!" "Looking Things Over," "The Inside Light," and so on) spontaneously generate a framework through which to communicate her philosophy.

As she ironically suggests when referring to the religious congregation's telling of their experiences, "These visions are traditional. I knew them by heart as did the rest of the congregation, but still it was exciting to see *how the converts would handle them. Some of them made up new details. Some of them would forget a part and improvise clumsily or fill up the gap with shouting.* The audience knew, but everybody acted as if every word of it was new" (*DT*, p. 272, my emphasis). Inconsistencies are inherent to the performance of traditional cultural forms. It is precisely in the way they individually diverge from the set norms that the "converts" excite interest in the "audience." The "origin" of the tradition must be acknowledged but this does not give sanction to simple repetition of form. Each new performer signifies upon that origin by transforming it, thus allowing for infinite possibilities of permutations. To approach a form genealogically, then, is to attempt to retrace its transformations back to an origin—*arche*—which will always prove elusive since every discrete manifestation is the interpellation of a previous one that sets the stage for the next one, and so on ad infinitum. Whether Hurston's twelve visions signify upon the religious tradition or upon the vernacular ritual of the "dozens" (cf. pp. 187, 217) or both, is of no importance. In either case she can make vicarious use of the clichés, parody some of them, ignore the rest and "tell a story the way [she] wanted, or rather the way the story told itself to [her]" (p. 206). Since "playing the dozens" or "specifying" is a form of invective and name calling that points genealogically to a fictitious origin—"they proceed to 'specify' until the tip-top branch of your family tree has been given a reading" (p. 217)—we can readily infer that this "self-affirming form of discourse" does not require foundational support in reality.[40] It is by virtue of its perlocutionary function that it affirms the underlying gutsiness and creativity of the agent of discourse, drawing a portrait of the self as capable of enduring, diverging, and surviving because of adhesion to the formal aspects of a cultural tradition that is dynamic and improvisational and allows the storyteller to "keep the tune" for the benefit of the collectivity, to lift the veil on the mirror of a different history, to be a "keeper of memories."[41]

In *Dust Tracks*, we have a powerful example of the braiding (or *métissage*) of cultural forms, since Persephone figures both as the voice of the dead mother and as the boundary crosser who links up two different worlds. Turning upside down the mythical relation between Ceres and her daughter, Hurston invents her own reading of the tradition, signifying upon that tradition in a specifically "black" way, diverging from the Greco-Roman text in the only possible way for the African-American self-portraitist: to rejoin her mother, Zora/Persephone must travel back to the Underworld, to the "dark realm" of her own people, to the friendship with Big Sweet, in order to learn to say what her dying mother could not, in order to name the chain of legendary female figures who can teach her to "re-member" and to speak the past.[42]

40. See Susan Willis, *Specifying* (Madison, 1987), p. 31.
41. Hurston, *Moses, Man of the Mountain*, p. 350.
42. For a detailed discussion of the concept of *métissage* as used here and as formulated by Caribbean writer and theorist Edouard Glissant, see the introduction to my *Autobiographical Voices: Race, Gender, Self-Portraiture* (Ithaca, N. Y., 1989).

7

"The Very House of Difference": Race, Gender, and the Politics of South African Women's Narrative in *Poppie Nongena*

ANNE McCLINTOCK

> Advocating the mere tolerance of difference between women is the grossest reformism. It is a total denial of the creative function of difference in our lives. Difference must be not merely tolerated, but seen as a fund of necessary polarities between which our creativity can spark like a dialectic. Only then does the necessity for interdependency become unthreatening. Only within that interdependency of different strengths, acknowledged and equal, can the power to seek new ways of being in the world generate, as well as the courage and sustenance to act where there are no charters.
> —Audre Lorde, *Sister Outsider*

The day after Christmas during South Africa's "year of fire," when the Soweto uprising of 1976 was still shaking the country, a black woman whom we have to call "Poppie Nongena," though that is not her real name, arrived at the door of Elsa Joubert, a white Afrikaans writer and mother. Nongena was in great distress. The township from which she had fled was in turmoil. Conservative vigilantes armed by the police were on the rampage, and thousands of people had taken flight into the bush and surrounding townships. The police were searching for Nongena's brother on charges of "murder," and she had spent the night huddled with her children in the wind-torn bushes of the Cape Flats.

While the black townships burned, Joubert herself was about to go on holiday with her family. For some time previously, she had been casting about for the topic of a new book. During the unsettling days of the rebellion, the idea of writing something about the "bantustans" had taken her to pass offices, hospital clinics, schools and churches; she interviewed and observed, but nothing had struck her with quite the force of Nongena's story. So the two women came to an agreement. Joubert would transcribe and edit Nongena's life story, and, should the book sell, the proceeds would be divided equally between them. Nongena needed money for a house, and Joubert's cautious estimate of a couple of thousand rands was an undreamed-of windfall. Over a period of six months, Nongena returned three times a week to tell her story in a series of taped interviews. The story emerged in fragments and patches, pieced together by Nongena's unflagging and extraordinary memory. Two years later, it was published in Afrikaans under the title *Die Swerfjare van Poppie Nongena* (*The Long Journey of Poppie Nongena*). The book reappeared in English in 1980, translated by Joubert herself, and became an overnight sensation.[1]

In many respects, it is a scandalous book. Nothing like it had ever appeared in South Africa. First, it is a political scandal, for it speaks of the life of a very poor black woman, recounting her childhood shuttling from shantytown to shantytown, child labor in a white-owned fish factory, a reluctant marriage, the miscarriages and the births of her children in wind and sand, the bad infinity of work for white families, her husband's health broken by poverty and fatigue, the domestic violence of despairing men wedded to drink, the tightening of the influx and pass laws for women, the police raids and evictions, the refusals to leave, the ignominies and ordeals at the pass offices, forced removal to the desolation of the Ciskei bantustan, the forbidden returns, the dogged perserverance, the family loyalties and survivals—and then finally the nationwide rebellion of 1976, "the revolt of the children."

If the book is a political scandal, it is also a literary scandal. All

1. Elsa Joubert, *Poppie Nongena*, 2d. ed (London, 1981). Further page references are given in the text.

stories of genesis are stories of political power and all publication
involves a delegation of authority. Edward Said points out that the
word *author* itself springs from the same etymological roots as *authority* and is attended by potent notions of engendering, mastery,
and property. The entry into autobiography, particularly, is seen to
be the entry into the political authority of self-representation. The
narrative of an impoverished black woman taking possession of her
history in the privileged male sanctum of the South African publishing world was a scandal in itself. At the same time, the book
tramples underfoot any number of aesthetic expectations. At once
autobiography, biography, novel, and oral history, the narrative is
also none of these; it is a generic anomaly. Moreover, as the doubled-
tongued collaboration of two women, it flouts the Western notion
of the individual engendering of narrative. Finally, it is a female
collaboration across the forbidden boundary of race, if a decidedly
problematic one. So the book's unruly political substance, its birth
in the violent crucible of the Soweto uprising, its doubled and contradictory female authorship, its violation of racial, gender, class,
and aesthetic boundaries, all amounted to a flagrant challenge to a
number of white male certainties.

Yet the book was met by a standing ovation in the white community. Within a week it won three major literary awards, was
reprinted three times in six months, and was rapidly translated into
English, French, Spanish, and German—an astonishing welcome for
any book in Afrikaans, let alone a book by two women. *Rapport*, an
Afrikaans Sunday paper, serialized the entire narrative, as did some
white English women's magazines. Conservative cabinet ministers
read it, business leaders read it, housewives and schoolteachers read
it. Well over a hundred reviews, articles, letters, and reports debated,
discussed, and analyzed it. It has never been banned. Most black
readers and critics have applauded it. Yet for the most part the white
Left has ignored it. What is the meaning of this paradox?

The most striking feature of the articles and reviews that flooded
the newspapers and magazines was the unanimous stridency with
which the book was declared to be *apolitical*. In an important paper
David Schalkwyk garnered a sample of the reviews which urgently
blare the book's "lack" of politics.[2] I offer a summary handful: "Elsa

2. David Schalkwyk, "The Flight from Politics: An Analysis of the Reception of
'Poppie Nongena,' " *Journal of Southern African Studies* 12 (April 1986): 183–95.

Joubert's book is never political," declared Maureen Pithey of the *Cape Times*. "Its honesty is apolitical," approved Lynne Burger of the *Eastern Province Herald*. "The book is furthermore no political accusation," Audrey Blignaut hastened to assure his readers. "Politics do not enter in," agreed Colin Melville of *The Star*.[3] Other examples abound.

Yet the unanimity of these reviews is riven with inconsistency. On the one hand, Audrey Blignaut could offer the book's *literariness* as evidence that it is "no political accusation." As he put it in *The Star*, the book is "not a sociological report. It is a work of literature." Yet a letter to *Die Burger* could offer as its evidence for the book's lack of politics precisely the opposite view. The book is apolitical, not because it is literary, but because it is not. It is "a fairly objective report rather than a novel." In what follows, I wish to refuse the national whitewash of the narrative as apolitical by exploring the contradictory politics of the book's reception and the ambiguous politics of female collaboration across the boundaries of race and class difference.[4]

The Politics of Reception

The public reception of *Poppie Nongena* as apolitical had its own political logic. The separation of politics and literature is a political separation with a real social history. Raymond Williams has pointed out that the flight into aestheticism is "above all related to a version of society: not an artistic consciousness but a disguised social consciousness in which the real connections and involvements with others could be plausibly overlooked and then in effect ratified."[5] In South Africa the cleavage of politics and literature has taken a peculiarly paradoxical form, and it is out of these paradoxes that the anomalous reception of *Poppie Nongena* arose.

What South African novelist Andre Brink has called *Poppie Nongena*'s "unique topicality," arose in part from the fact that the "group of people in the center of the story are not only Afrikaans-speaking

3. *The Cape Times*, August 7, 1980; *Eastern Province Herald*, April 17, 1979; *Beeld*, November 20, 1978 (trans. Schalkwyk); *The Star*, October 1, 1980.

4. *The Star*, October 1, 1980; *Die Burger*, January 16, 1979. In an unpublished study, I examine in detail the politics of the family and women's resistance to forced removals in South Africa as embodied in the narrative.

5. Raymond Williams, *George Orwell* (New York, 1971), p. 56.

Xhosas, but in actual fact refer to themselves as *Afrikaners*."[6] Ampie
Coetzee, an Afrikaner himself, noted that most of the Afrikaans
reviewers gave the book prominence first and foremost because it
was written, not in English, or in an African language, but in Afrikaans. The *Cape Times* agreed: "In this book black Afrikaners speak
with their own authentic voices ... Poppie Nongena ... was born Afrikaans."[7] Indeed, for Joubert, who did not know any African languages, the fact that she and Nongena shared Afrikaans as their first
language was the enabling condition of the book. "Elsa Joubert em-
phasises that Poppie is Afrikaans-speaking, and how through her she
became acquainted with the Afrikaans of Afrikaans-speaking
blacks."[8] Yet as a collaboration in Afrikaans between a black woman
and a white woman the book straddles some of the deepest fault
lines of Afrikaner nationalism.

It has never been easy to ban or dismiss an Afrikaans book, however irksome. The Afrikaans language carries an almost mystical
potency in the Afrikaans mind. After the Anglo-Boer War (1899–
1902), the tattered remnants of the bloodied Boer communities had
to be forged into a national counterculture if they were to survive
in the new British capitalist state. Ernest Gellner has made the point
that "nationalism is not the awakening of nations to self-consciousness: it invents nations where they do not exist."[9] Nations are not
organic, natural givens, flowering spontaneously into history as the
teleological unfolding of a national spirit, but are, as Benedict Anderson puts it, "imagined communities." This does not mean that
nations are allegorical phantasmagoria of the mind, but that they
are intricate social fabrications invented through daily contest—in
newspapers, schools, churches, presses and popular culture. In the
early decades of the twentieth century a revamped Afrikaans became
the unifying "national" language for a white brotherhood of embit-

6. *Rapport*, December 3, 1978.
7. *The Cape Times*, December 6, 1978.
8. *Rapport*, December 3, 1978.
9. The creation of this Afrikaans constituency demanded the conscious invention
of a single print-language, a popular press, a literate populace, and an active intellectual class. As Isabel Hofmeyr has shown, the *taalbeweging* (language movement)
of the early twentieth century represented just such an invention, refashioning the
myriad Boer vernaculars into a single, identifiable Afrikaans language, while purging
it of its working-class, rural associations. See Ernest Gellner, *Thought and Change*
(London, 1964), p. 169.

tered farmers and workers, a frustrated petite bourgeoisie, and a small, ambitious clique of capitalists.[10]

In this society the Afrikaans writer stands in an ambiguous position. Afrikaans writers such as Joubert are seen as the midwives of the "national soul," and are accorded unusual power. Both revered and feared, the Afrikaans writer is granted a great deal of social importance and a certain political immunity. One of the most famous of Afrikaans writers, Brink, could comment in the 1960s, at the end of a decade of bannings, detentions, censoring, murders, and suicides of black writers: "The Afrikaans writer . . . still has the uneasy knowledge that although the authorities loathe his guts, no official action has been taken against an Afrikaans book (yet)."[11]

There is a second dimension. The fact that Afrikaans was also the first language of a couple of million so-called "coloureds" would remain a stubborn thorn in the flesh of Afrikaner nationalism. In 1976 the black community rejected with unmistakable vehemence a state decree that math and social science be taught in Afrikaans. A few years later, the Nationalists would attempt their most ambitious, and fatal, attempt to draw into the laager a brethren of the Afrikaans-speaking so-called "coloureds." Thus a book in which a black Xhosa woman and her fragmented family speak Afrikaans as their first language could not simply be tossed into the flames. Rather, a far more difficult task of political disinfection had to be performed.

A countrywide effort of white nationalist hygiene began. The few voices that attempted to investigate the book's complex and ambiguous politics were drowned out in the unanimous hubbub that the book had no politics at all, that it was universal, that it dealt with "family issues" and therefore lay beyond the provenance of politics and history proper. At the same time, a well-established critical discourse that defined great literature as apolitical lay ready to hand. In terms of the prevailing white South African liberal aesthetic based in the universities and white literary journals, politics was seen as a squalid activity made up of venal party polemics and pamphleteering, rife with prejudice, self-interest, cliché, and mun-

10. Benedict Anderson, *Imagined Communities: Reflections on the Origin and Spread of Nationalism* (London, 1983). During the 1960s, with power confidently clenched in Afrikaans fists, an unabashedly phallic monument to Afrikaans was erected as testimony to the engendering potency of the language.

11. Andre Brink, *Writing in a State of Siege* (New York, 1983), p. 36.

danity. Great literature, on the other hand, was seen to transcend the mediocre noon of everyday, inhabiting an inscrutable, hermetic realm of essential and timeless truths. Works of art that embody these truths are the gifts of individual genius, exemplifying a unity of vision, wholeness of experience, immanent and universal value, irony of tone, complexity of form, cultivated sensibility, and a moral discrimination untainted by the platitudes of political dogma—the familiar liberal aesthetic inherited by white academics trained in the Leavisite school.[12]

Most important for my purposes, however, was the argument that *Poppie Nongena* is apolitical because it is primarily concerned with a woman's attempt to keep her family together. If politics has been separated from art, it has also been separated from the family. As one newspaper put it, the book is apolitical because people in it are intent only "on obtaining a pass, keeping the family together somehow."[13] On this view, the family is seen to inhabit a sphere set apart from organized politics and history. Thus women's resistance to the bantustan policy, the pass system, the domestic violence, and the plunder of their labor, could be dismissed as beyond the proper provenance of organized politics and beyond the realm of history. In what must be one of the most risible comments on the book to date, *Die Burger* announced that the book was apolitical because "Poppie's problems are generally human ones, they are universal."[14] But being a perpetual minor in the eyes of the law and under the permanent tutelage of a male relative, being "endorsed out" of one's home on marriage and forced to depart for a husband's "bantustan" often hundreds of miles away, being ineligible for residence rights without the signature of a male relative, pregnancy, birth, and child raising

---

12. It should also not be forgotten that the historical separation of literature and politics began at that moment in Western history when women began to read and write in large numbers. As the "damned mob of scribbling women," in Nathaniel Hawthorne's dyspeptic phrase, entered the public literary domain, literature was defined as separate from politics. Similarly, as colonized countries wrestled their way into independence after the Second World War, and as women and men of color entered the universities in significant numbers, insisting on defining an alternative subjectivity to the enshrined white male subjectivity, at just that moment, the requiem was rung on "the subject." At just that moment when disenfranchised voices forcibly clamored for the privilege of defining their own identity and authority, "the author" was declared dead.

13. *The Cape Times*, December 6, 1978.

14. Letter to *Die Burger*, January 16, 1979. Trans. Schalkwyk.

under the most perilous of circumstances: these are not problems
that are faced by white men or white women. These problems are
not even faced by black men. Far from being universal problems,
they are problems that confront black women alone, and they were
written into South African statute books at identifiable historical
moments. Only by the most contorted efforts can they be whitewashed as the universal dilemmas of "Greek tragedy."[15]

Arguably, the most disturbing act of complicity with the book's
reception was Joubert's own insistence that the book is apolitical.
She has been widely ventriloquized as calling it nothing more than
"a pure human interest story." "The point is," she avows, "it is not
a political book. I wrote it because the theme was one that interested
me. I wanted to bring across the person as a human being. And that
is as far as my interest goes."[16] A headline in *Die Oosterlig* happily
assured its readers: "Politics Not Her Motive," as if clearing Joubert
of some sordid misdemeanor.[17] Again and again, major papers trum-
peted the evidence of "authorial" intention (what, one wonders, did
Nongena think?). One cannot wish Joubert's prevarications away as
the tongue-in-cheek caution of a writer in fear for her life or craft.
Unlike Nongena she was in no imaginable danger. Rather, her life
as a woman and mother lent her a gender affinity and a very genuine
empathy for Nongena; but her racial privilege and her recently won
place in the world of the white male intelligentsia underscored her
loyalty to an ideology of aesthetic detachment from politics. She
was willing to go so far and no further. Moreover, Joubert's contradictory position was shaped by a general crisis in the liberal intelligentsia. During the 1970s one witnessed for the first time a
courting of black writers by white writers and critics, who attempted
to borrow on the authenticity of black writers to compensate for
their own dwindling legitimacy.[18] The privilege of education can
breed isolation and a sense of unrepresentativeness—sharpened into
urgency by the Soweto rebellion. Speaking through the voice of the
disempowered becomes, in part, a way of lessening the marginalization of privilege.

15. Letter to *The Argus*, March 14, 1978.
16. *Rand Daily Mail*, January 4, 1979.
17. *Die Oosterlig*, March 9, 1979.
18. See my article *"Azikwelwa* (We Will Not Ride): The Politics of Value in Black
South African Poetry," in *Politics and Poetry*, ed. Robert van Hallberg (Chicago,
1987), pp. 597–623.

The public whitewash of *Poppie Nongena* as "apolitical" arose, then, from the ways in which the contradictions of the moment fused and shaped each other: Joubert's conflicting gender, race and class loyalties, the peculiar immunity of the Afrikaans writer, the contradictions within Afrikaner nationalism, the black rejection of Afrikaans, the ambiguous position of the liberal intellectual, the historical separation of the political realm from the aesthetic realm, and the historical definition of "the family" and the female as out-side politics proper.

Marnea Lazreg, an Algerian feminist writing about the power of interpretation, has said, "A feminist engaged in the act of repre-senting women who belong to a different culture, ethnic group, race, or social class wields a certain power over them; a power of inter-pretation. However, this power is a peculiar one. It is borrowed from the society at large which is male centered."[19] In what follows, I wish to consider the relations of interpretive and narrative power that hold between Joubert and Nongena, by exploring the vexed politics of autobiography and oral history. What are the relations of power between a black and white South African woman, when an oral narrative is transcribed, selectively edited, and published? In broaching this question, I am aware that I, too, am inevitably and problematically implicated in the politics of interpretation. In the pages that follow I point out the implications for feminism of this contradiction, a contradiction that enters the book initially as a generic riddle.

Narrative Production and Social Identity

The reception of *Poppie Nongena* is eloquent of the degree to which text is an event under contest. Reading is a dynamic practice that occurs across time, and takes the form of a relation between the text and different readers' class, race, and gender loyalties; ed-ucational, cultural, and personal histories; and different expectations and habits of thought. Literary texts are historical events, which differ from other events in that they are organized according to

19. Marnea Lazreg, "Feminism and Difference: The Perils of Writing as a Woman on Women in Algeria," *Feminist Studies* 14 (Spring 1988): 81–107.

aesthetic as well as other criteria. Every text is in this way a situation in progress.

Despite their unanimity in applauding *Poppie Nongena*'s lack of politics, critics have been vexed by their inability to tuck the book into the Procrustean bed of male tradition. Soon after the narrative's publication, a small squabble broke out in an Afrikaans literary journal over its style. The Afrikaans critic Gerrit Olivier lambasted Joubert for "her" muddled narrative mode, her slipshod, uneven, and fragmented style. Richard Rive, a black critic, countered by accusing Olivier of being petty, of trafficking in trivia, of dwelling on niceties of form when what mattered was the political power of the book.[20] Olivier's charges of formal impropriety are charges that have been thrown at women's heads for some time: the absence of a centered narrative voice, the lack of closure, the failure of formal finesse and finish. Rive's defense, on the other hand, dismisses the book's narrative form as an aesthetic irrelevancy, and rehearses thereby the cleavage of politics and aesthetics. I wish to refute both positions, and argue that the book's narrative mode is inseparable from its social and political concerns.

What, then, are we to call this text? Is it a novel? an autobiography? a biography? an oral history? an oral autobiography? Its chameleon quality has perplexed its readers. It has been claimed for fiction, and has been dubbed "a human novel," "a religious novel," a "novel" with "a revolutionary perspective," and "*literature* proper."[21] It has also been claimed for nonfiction: defined as "a sober report," "good reportage," "based solely on facts."[22] Andre Brink offered a compromise, and borrowed Norman Mailer's term "faction"—a label summarily rejected by Jean Marquard on the grounds that it insinuated inauthenticity: "Faction," Marquard writes, is "a mixture (as the name suggests) of 'fact' and 'fiction,' whereas Poppie does not depart from 'truth' (as defined by Poppie's rendition) at any stage.... The novel therefore is of a documentary kind."[23]

The contradictions in the book's status are most visible where they are most vigorously repressed: on the title page and the copy-

20. Jean Marquard, "Poppie," *English Studies in Africa* 28 (1985): 135–41.

21. *The Sowetan*, July 18, 1981; *Die Beeld*, March 22, 1979; *Die Oggenblad*, February 28, 1979; *Rapport*, December 3, 1978.

22. Dust jacket to 1980 edition of *Poppie Nongena*; *Sunday Times*, December 3, 1978; *Rapport*, February 14, 1979.

23. Marquard, "Poppie," p. 137.

right page. As if the spectacle of a black and a white woman col-
laborating across race and class were too unseemly, not one publisher
has published the book as a collective narrative or given Nongena
coauthorial status. The story has been marketed as a novel *by* Joubert
about Nongena. Except for a woefully inadequate and easily missed
prefatory note, Nongena's crucial engendering role is entirely erased
and she is contained in the title page as nothing more than Joubert's
fictive creature. Readers might be forgiven for assuming (as many
do) that Nongena is no more than Joubert's novelistic invention.
Indeed, this has often been given as a reason on the white male Left
for dismissing the book as a suspect, if well-intentioned, fabrication
by a white woman.

Yet the narrative is beset by contradiction. Paradoxically, Joubert's
claim to the authenticity of "her novel" entails erasing her own role
as novelist. Her "novel," she claims, is authentic since it is no more
than a factually accurate record of Nongena's own life history: "I
kept myself out of the story, held it up as a kind of mirror to reality."
Joubert also states, "I knew at once: no travelogue, no allegory, but
the stark truth, the story of this woman's life. This was where my
study, my research, my travels in my own country had been leading
to."[24] If the book is "no allegory, but the stark truth," on what
grounds can Joubert call the book a "novel" and claim the status of
single author?

Joubert's use of the Aristotelian metaphor of art as mimetic surface
to life's truth, and her image of herself as merely holding the "mirror" to the "reality" of Nongena's life, evades the political and aesthetic questions raised by her own editorial interventions, and
obscures thereby the ambiguous politics of female collaboration
with which the narrative is inscribed and visibly marked.

Moreover, Joubert's claims are contradictory. She insists she is
nothing more than a mimetic reflector, delivering the stark truth of
Nongena's authentic speaking voice without mediation or intrusion.
Yet when she wishes to argue the book's lack of politics, she arro-
gates to herself the privilege of authorial intention. This contradiction appears most strikingly on the copyright page. There Joubert's
prefatory note reads as follows: "This novel is based on the actual
life story of a black woman living in South Africa today. Only her

24. Ibid, p. 137. Elsa Joubert in *Momentum: On Recent South African Writing*,
ed. M. J. Daymond, J. U. Jacobs, and Margaret Lenta (Pietermaritzburg, 1984), p. 60.

name, Poppie Rachel Nongena, born Matati, is invented. The facts were related to me not only by Poppie herself, but by members of her immediate family." The prefatory note and the copyright on the same page are thus entirely at odds. The prefatory note testifies to Joubert's absence of invention. The copyright, however, grants her legal entitlement to the narrative as sole creator. To call a narrative a novel is to raise expectations of a fictional or inventive treatment of events. Yet Joubert claims that her "novel" is based only on the "facts" of an actual life story. "Only her name, Poppie Rachel Nongena, born Matati, is invented." Can the invention of one name turn a life history into a work of fiction? By the same token, what fiat of white arrogance allows Joubert to claim the engendering status of author for herself? What legal concept of narrative ownership entitles her to sole possessive power of copyright, when the narrative is manifestly and in every way the collective production of two women? Indeed, the incoherence threatening the concept of individual possession of a text (a concept of individual textual property that emerged in the eighteenth century as writers for the first time found themselves able to earn a livelihood from the sale of their books to the public) marks a general historical contradiction within South African culture between a decidedly imperialist notion of individual textual authority and indigenous notions of communal and performative culture, which entail a dispersed sense of narrative creativity.

Nongena did indeed insist on a pseudonym, presumably out of fear for herself and her family. And Joubert has kept Nongena's real name and identity secret, despite being hounded by international interviewers and journalists to divulge her identity. Yet it would have been perfectly feasible to publish the narrative as a collaboration. Instead, the erasure of Nongena's identity and name, in contrast to Joubert's instant access to an international literary name, bears eloquent witness to the imbalances in racial and class power between the two women and their different relations to the state. In publishing this troublesome narrative as a white woman's novel *about* a black woman, the scandal of a black woman's engendering of narrative, and the scandal of female collaboration across race is hushed, the hierarchy restored, the boundaries redrawn. The title page and the copyright page are thus fully expressive of the politics of excision and amnesia that has marked the extraordinary reception of the book as a whole.

To dismiss the narrative as a white woman's "apolitical novel" is, therefore, to be complicit in the conservative politics that shaped the publication and reception of the book, and to acquiesce in the erasure of Nongena's engendering role. Such an erasure of what Abena Busia has called "the endangered body" of the black woman, preempts any serious discussion of the deeply problematic theoretical, political, and cultural issues the book raises.

The marketing of the book as a novel is directly contradicted by the narrative itself, which is deeply scored by its collective engendering, as well as by textual signs of the imbalances of racial and class power that govern the collaboration. What then are we to call this text? Since *Poppie Nongena* appears to be the life history of a woman as told by herself, it is in many important respects an oral autobiography transcribed to print. Yet the narrative does not observe Philippe Lejeune's "autobiographical pact" between the identity of the speaking "I," the main character and the author.[25] It retains the personal texture and idioms of Nongena's first-person voice, but is also a thing of print, mediated by Joubert's editorial interventions and a second narrative voice. Nor can it simply be subsumed under the category of biography. As a biographer might, Joubert checked and rechecked every detail of Nongena's life story; she traveled to every place mentioned in the story, interviewing wherever possible everyone who is mentioned in the story, and speaking when possible to Nongena's family members. But, unlike most biographers, she constantly read the narrative back to Nongena, who corrected her and advised changes and revisions. Moreover, unlike most biographies, at least a third of the narrative is in the first person. What then are we to make of this paradoxical text? What are the politics of female authorship, and what are the politics of race and class when women collaborate from positions of unequal power? If the paradoxes of the book's ambiguous politics are to be examined, the text's status as a collaborative narrative needs to be explored.

The Politics of Gender and Social Identity

The first word of *Poppie Nongena* is "we." To open the book is immediately to notice an absence—the centered, univocal speaking

25. Philippe Lejeune, *L'Autobiographie en France* (Paris, 1971), subsequently modified in *Pacte autobiographique* (Paris, 1976).

"I" of canonized male autobiography has vanished. This is how the book begins:

> We are Xhosa people from Gordonia, says Poppie. My mama used to tell us about our great-grandma Kappie, a rich old woman who grazed her goats on the koppies this side of Carnarvon. . . . She told our mama about the old days. . . . We saw the Boers coming on horseback, she said. . . . And then Jaantjie rode away with them . . . Jaantjie, take the horses and flee, the Boer shouted when he saw the English soldiers . . . but by then, old woman—so he came and told our great-grandma Kappie—your child was dead. (P. 11)

From the outset, the book denies the reader a privileged point of observation, a center such as the voluble "I" of autobiography once afforded. Opening the book, one hears a polyphony of female voices, the ancestral reverberations of great-grandmothers, grandmothers, and mothers, mingling, redoubling, and echoing almost indistinguishably within each other. The story-recorder's voice encloses Nongena's voice; Nongena, speaking in the narrative "present" remembers her mother's voice, who remembered in turn the voice of great-grandma Kappie who remembered the words of the Boers, and the man who came to tell her her son had died, long ago in the old days during the upheavals of the white people's wars. *Poppie Nongena* differs in this respect from the black male mission-school autobiographies of the 1960s, which generally open with the "I" of individual, if embattled, male identity.[26] In *Poppie Nongena* the life history does not flow from an originary moment in the birth of the individual. Rather, Nongena's birth is announced obliquely, in the third person, only after the larger community of women shaping her identity has been identified: "Lena's fourth child was brought to ouma Hannie who called her Poppie" (p. 13).

The opening pages of Nongena's narrative are eloquent of the *unnaturalness* of individual identity. From the outset, the construction of identity as collective enters the reader's experience of the

26. Both Ezekiel Mphahlele and Bloke Modisane's autobiographies attempt, in different ways, to reinvent a trajectory of selfhood compatible with the liberal notion of the (white, male) individual self. Both fail; both their autobiographies end with the abandonment of their familes, and flight into exile. By no means was this necessarily an easier choice; but it was a choice shaped in part by their mission school inheritance, their class positions as educated men, and the traitorous heritage of Western liberalism that did not fulfill its promise to them. See Ezekiel Mphahlele, *Down Second Avenue* (London, 1959); Bloke Modisane, *Blame Me on History* (Cape Town, 1986).

narrative as *form*. Poppie Nongena's oral memory, bequeathed
through the mother's line, recalls what the state would erase: the
stubborn collective memory of precolonial plenty as rich great-
grandma Kappie grazed her goats in the hills of the Karoo. But after
the turn of the century, Nongena's family, like millions of other
black South Africans, were forced off the land by the ruinous land
and hut taxes. Buffeted by the Anglo-Boer War, losing their livestock
to disease and their men to the white people's wars, they were
reduced to migrant laborers, landless and rightless, shuttling from
shantytown to shantytown, selling their labor for pittances on the
white farms and in fishing ports.

Ouma Hannie's children scattered—one to the farms, one to the
white people's war—the broken trajectory of the remainder of the
family following the inexorable economic logic of the railway loop-
ing together the fishing ports on the Atlantic, the merchant port at
Cape Town, and the mines in the interior. It was a family in transition, suspended between the remembered bounty of pastoral autonomy and the immiseration of wage labor. In the contradictions
of this transition different social forms of identity emerged.

The opening pages are a bewildering welter of family names, places
and kin relations. Voices merge, separate and merge again with other
voices. The difficulty of the reading comes to mirror the singular
ordeal of keeping the family together. One struggles to remember
who everyone is, to identify who is speaking, to remember in which
place they are now living. One is constantly obliged to turn to the
female genealogy at the opening of the book for guidance, and is
thus at every moment reminded that familial and social identity are
laborious constructions. What holds the community of identity together is the labor of oral memory, borne through the women's
tenacious will to remember and to speak. Oral memory is thereby
a denial of the dismemberment of history, an arduous life-giver.
Memory, in Don Mattera's words, is a weapon.[27] It is a device against
oblivion, a strategy for survival.

The permeable, collective construction of identity in *Poppie Nongena* is most visibly marked by the absence of any quotation marks
to distinguish one voice from the other. As the narrative progresses,
the reader is obliged to adjust rapidly to a welter of voices and
narrative identities. Identity comes to be experienced as a constant

27. Don Mattera, *Memory Is the Weapon* (New York, 1988).

reshaping of the boundaries of selfhood; indeed, it comes to be seen as the shifting outcome of community experience rather than any singularity of being (This differs from the "frame narratives" of Joseph Conrad, where speaking voices remain distinct). To continue reading, one is obliged to abandon the liberal nostalgia for a centered, sovereign perspective and a single, presiding consciousness. Rather one is invited to yield to an alternative notion of reciprocal, relational, and unstable identity. This unsteady metamorphosis of boundaries is quite different from the fractured, dismantled identity of Western postmodernism. Rather than the static, postmodern dissolution of the self (which has as its silhouette a tragic nostalgia for the centered, humanist individual), identity is experienced as communal, dynamic, and shifting, rather than as fractured, immobile, and solitary. The boundaries of the self are permeable and constantly open to historical change. In this way the narrative offers a number of challenges to hegemonic theories of autobioraphical narrative and identity.

From the beginning, Nongena's narrative renders untenable any notion that identity is a natural category. Obedient to tradition, all Ouma Hannie's daughters were married by force, including Nongena's mother, Lena: "That was the way the parents used to do it in those days. My mama didn't want my pa" (p. 12). Machine Matati paid *lobola* (bride-price) to Ouma Hannie, fathered four children, abandoned the family, went to war, and was never seen again. "He never looked after my children like a father should, [Lena] told ouma Hannie. I have no tears to weep for Machine Matati" (p. 33). Machine Matati was not exceptional. It is estimated that during the early decades of the twentieth century three-quarters of all black men lived apart from their families for over half the year, driven by land hunger, poverty, taxes, and desperation to the towns and cities. Yet the consequences for women of this massive dismembering of their families were contradictory.

On the one hand, the structure of labor within the black homestead enabled women to resist proletarianization longer than men. Since they were the traditional agriculturists, they could stubbornly remain to work the land and fend for their communities, while the men scattered to sell their labor on the wage markets. Women remained independent of the axis of capitalist formation for longer periods, and so were capable of greater militancy and refusal. Thus it happened that women and not men successfully refused the passes in 1913.[28] At the same time, however, black women bore the brunt of their families' efforts to survive, and suffered most intimately the cruelties of poverty, starvation, and disease, the unemployment, malnutrition, and infant deaths of the countryside. Men might appear once a year at the most, briefly and transiently for a couple of weeks, then vanish, perhaps for years, perhaps forever. Yet in the absence of men, women became more autonomous and self-sufficient. This is how it was in Poppie Nongena's family.

In the narrative Ouma Hannie presides as a ragged matriarch over the marriages and births of her children and grandchildren, taking in her grandchildren and rearing them as she had reared her own. Lena, Nongena's mother, is forced to work for a white family in a town more than a hundred miles away, so Nongena and her brothers live with their grandmother among the chicken coops and sandy streets of the shantytowns, selling rags and bones or doing laundry for whites. Ouma Hannie is "very strict with her children" (p. 14); it is she who wields authority in the family. She decides the marriages, she controls the ceremonies of *lobolo*, and she takes the *lobolo* money for her daughter's marriage.

Nongena's family becomes a constantly changing locus of struggle and division both within the family over women's domestic work, and between the family and the state. The boundaries of the family shift ceaselessly; kinship relations are fluid. It is a family without fathers and there is no "natural" mother: "We loved ouma more, more than our own mama," says Nongena (p. 17). The identity of "motherhood" is multiple and shifting—as is the case for most South Africans. As Johanna Masilela, childminder, says of the children in her charge: "They took me as their real, real mother. Because they don't know their mothers. They used to see their mothers late in the afternoon. I was their mother."[29] When Ouma Hannie takes sleep-in domestic work with a white family, Nongena and her brothers are farmed out among relatives in different towns. When Nongena's mother eventually returns to try to reassemble the family, her son, Mosie, "called kleinma Hessie mama because he had lived with her so long" (p. 36). Lena scolds Poppie: "Ag now, don't you

28. See Julia Wells, "Why Women Rebel: A Comparative Study of South African Women's Resistance in Bloemfontein (1913) and Johannesburg (1958)," *Journal of Southern African Studies* 10 (1984): 55–70.

29. " 'Let Me Make History Please': The Story of Johanna Masilela, Childminder," in *Class, Community and Conflict*, ed. Belinda Bazzoli (Johannesburg, 1987), p. 472.

know your brother, that's Mosie, over there" (p. 35). The idea of the natural nuclear family, presided over by a single male, loses all cohesion and splinters out into the world. Grandmothers are mothers, cousins are sisters, brothers are forgotten, there is no father, mothers are strangers, then they are mothers again. Together and apart, Nongena's loose family goes from town to town—then settles briefly at Lambert's Bay on the icy Atlantic, where they sell their labor in the white-owned fish factory.

The fluidity or multiplicity of identity born of this situation does not represent a mutilation or deformity of identity. Rather it demonstrates a resilient and flexible capacity to cross the uncertain boundaries of self and community. The fluidity and reciprocity of narrative identity in the story, the merging and division of voices, arises therefore neither from formal ineptitude, nor from some organic *jouissance* of the female body, but rather from a social situation where identity is experienced as reciprocal, constructed, and collective. Identity emerges from a community of experience, rather than from a transcendent unity of being. The narrative shifts and slippages manifest this reciprocity and fluidity of collective identity.

Here one might invoke the work of Nancy Chodorow, who argues that cultural patterns of childrearing give rise to different boundary experiences in males and females. In households where women are the primary caretakers, girls "come to define themselves as continuous with others; their experience of self contains more flexible or permeable ego boundaries. Boys come to define themselves as more separate and distinct, with a greater sense of rigid ego boundaries and differentiation." For Chodorow the young girl comes to experience a sense of "self in relationship."[30] While Chodorow does not pay sufficient attention to cultural variations in family relations, she makes a crucial departure from theories of archetypal gender difference by locating different boundary experiences in the historical, and hence mutable, social structures of childrearing and domestic divisions of labor.

Nevertheless, the narrative's polyphony of identities does not reveal a utopian democracy of storytelling. The story does not express the disappearance of power, but rather its redistribution under contest. Identity does not transcend power; it comes into being through

---

30. Nancy Chodorow, *Psychoanalysis and the Sociology of Gender* (Berkeley, Calif., 1978), p. 169.

ceaseless contest, and results in a dispersal and realignment of power rather than a vanishing of power.

This realignment of power is visibly expressed in the matrilineal genealogy that appears on the frontispiece, a reinvented family tree that bears at its head a single matriarch, and reckons descent through the female line. Genealogies are less accurate records of family relations than they are records of political power. Generally it is the victors who record history; it is they who inscribe their genealogies; generally these genealogies are male. The opening pages of *Poppie Nongena*, however, reckon history through the female line of grandmothers and mothers, dispersing authority through a female community, and figuring thereby a different engendering of hierarchy and a different notion of who authors history. The reinvention of genealogy is summed up in Nongena's Xhosa name: "Ntombizodumo, which means girl born from a line of great women" (p. 13). The reckoning of family genealogy through the mother's line marks in this way the beginning of a new contest for familial and historical power.

The dispersal and realignment of female power is most vividly manifested in the dispersal and realignment of the authority of narrative voice. Much of the interest of the narrative lies in its blurring of all distinctions between "truth" and "fiction," "autobiography" and "biography," "novel" and "oral history." An autobiography, conventionally, raises expectations that the self who recounts the tale and the author of the autobiography are at least referentially the same. Yet, as we have seen, the "I" of Nongena's tale and the "Joubert" of authorial copyright are not identical. Moreover, there are at least three narrators in what is essentially a heteroglossic and collective tale. Nongena speaks in the first person with the immediacy of oral storytelling as if recorded verbatim during the interview: "Auk! when it rained, we had to take off our shoes. . . . Ag, but it was so sad to be back in my house again." (pp. 80, 168). On a number of occasions, her speaking voice explicitly evokes Joubert's presence as interviewer and listener, explaining Xhosa or Afrikaans words or customs that she knows are unfamiliar to Joubert: "*Grootma* means a sister of your ma that's older than she is, and *kleinma* is her younger sister" (p. 12). Sometimes her comments bear vestigial traces of Joubert's questions: "At what time we started work? Now that was just when the boats came in" (p. 50). Thus Joubert's cultural ignorance, and the dialogic and public context of the narrative beginnings are inscribed in the text. The second narrator is not identical with Joubert's interviewing voice, but functions in some sense as an omniscient narrator: "Those years, 1966, 1967, the police were very hot, says Poppie."

Nevertheless, this intermediary narrator is not strictly speaking always an omniscient narrator, for it functions, on occasion, as an echo of, without being identical to, Joubert's interview voice: "The three sons of Lena had English names as well. Philip. Stanley and Wilson. Perhaps it was Machine Matati from Mafeking, who went to war for the English, who chose these new names. No, says Poppie, it was not just our pa who was educated, our ma had some learning too." The first three sentences could be either Nongena's testifying voice, or the intermediary narrator, but because of the unusual syntax, they lean toward Nongena's voice. The fourth sentence ("Perhaps it was Machine Matati...") is an oblique narrative echo of a question by Joubert, but is not recorded verbatim as her direct speech. At other moments the intermediary narrator frames the voices of other members of Nongena's family, taken from Joubert's interviews, and not from Nongena: "It's too much for Poppie, says Lena, to work in the factory and to look after her brothers and nurse her grandmother. She's not even fifteen years old" (p. 60). "I wasted my time at the Catholic school, Mosie says later" (p. 40).

In the narrative these voices merge and alternate rapidly, sometimes blending indistinguishably, sometimes separating and becoming relatively distinct, without being distinguished by quotation marks. Sometimes voices merge within a single sentence, sometimes they vacillate rapidly from sentence to sentence or paragraph to paragraph. Sometimes the narrator switches without warning from first to third person within a single paragraph: "I left the job at Mr Pullens because of the baby and so I had to stay at home to look after it. The child was breast fed and it's hard to give a suckling child to someone else to look after. This child was only four months younger than my ma's last child, her girlchild called Georgina, whom we still call Baby. Poppie's child was born in the house. A Xhosa district nurse, nurse Bam, helped her. It was a girl and they christened her Rose in the Holy Cross church. Her Xhosa name was Nomvula, meaning child born on the day it rained" (p. 112). Here the first three sentences are obviously first person, the fourth changes abruptly to third person, as does the fifth, but the last two sentences could be either.

Often the narrative switches person without warning from paragraph to paragraph. A paragraph in the third person begins: "When Poppie grew too big... " (p. 15), and is followed without announcement or identification by a paragraph in Nongena's first person voice: "Our house was built partly of reeds and clay" (p. 15). At certain critical moments the narrative switches to second person: "You have to weep. You take it so much to heart" (p. 73). More infrequently, an intermediate narrator emerges that has been alternately dubbed "free indirect speech," "*erlebte Rede,*" and "narrated monologue," a transitional narrative form that hovers between first and third person: "She did not trust this earth; it looked dark and wet" (p. 198). "Poppie was a big girl now" (p. 26). Here the present tense deictics ("this," "now,") mark the narrator as not identical with an omniscient narrator, but rather tinged and colored by the point of view of the first person voice.[31]

Moreover, tenses slide constantly and unpredictably throughout the narrative. Sometimes the first person is in the past tense: "I was scared of the strange people and didn't look around too much" (p. 78). Sometimes the first person is in the present tense: "I cannot move, my feet are stone. I can see his blood on the road, but I cannot do anything" (p. 128). Sometimes tenses switch in mid-sentence: "It was a horrible place, I'm not used to such houses" (p. 78).

The lack of quotation marks throughout the narrative places a great responsibility upon the reader to make rapid adjustments in identity and time. Quotation marks testify to an ideology of language as individual property. As textual markers they enclose and fence certain arrangements of words as the property of a single speaker. Language enters the provenance of possessive individualism and distinct identity. In contrast, *Poppie Nongena*, rather than embodying isolated and separate identities, invites one to experience narration along a dynamic, collective continuum of voices and identities, at moments distinct and at moments inseparable. More than anything, the narrative is deeply inscribed by its oral and dialogic conditions of production and by the fluctuations of person and

31. See Ann Banfield, "The Formal Coherence of Represented Speech and Thought," in *PTL: A Journal for Descriptive Poetics and Theory of Literature* 3 (1978): 289–314; Dorrit Cohn, "Narrated Monologue: Definition of a Functional Style," *Comparative Literature* 14 (1966): 97–112.

time that characterizes oral memory: instead of a single, individual style, it establishes a collective or interpersonal rhetoric.

The narrative began as an oral narrative, and oral memory is from the outset collaborative and multitongued. In addition, the conditions under which Nongena's story came into being were public, performative, and dialogic. The narrative form is, therefore, neither the expression of a damaged consciousness nor the mark of female aesthetic ineptitude. If, therefore, one is to understand the confusion and reinvention of narrative and identity boundaries in *Poppie Nongena*, one must situate the narrative in the social conditions under which it emerged, particularly the ruptured shapes of family and community life. The narrative unsteadiness bears witness to the onslaught on black communities by the state, and is neither the sign of formal ineptitude, as Olivier argued, nor of formal irrelevance, as Rive argued. Nor can the narrative ruptures be seen as simply an archetypal, pre-Oedipal *jouissance* of the word, as figured in some Western feminist literary theories. Rather, the ruptures and reinventions of narrative boundaries coincide with the ruptures and reinventions of the black community, emerging out of the social conditions of the time. The narrative's originality reveals a resistant, dynamic, protean, and collective identity, expressing in its stubborn reinvention of collective identity a tenacious refusal to break.

The Politics of Women's Narrative and Difference

Audre Lorde has written: "It was a while before we came to realize that our place was the very house of difference rather than the security of any one particular difference." In South Africa very little is known about how ordinary women like Nongena live out the contradictions in apartheid, and even less is known about how women resist these changes, and engage in contests for power.[32]

32. Audre Lorde, *Zami: A New Spelling of My Name* (Freedom, Calif., 1982), p. 226. A brilliant exception to the lack of information about South African women is Cheryl Walker, *Women and Resistance in South Africa* (London, 1982). See also Jo Beall, Shireen Hassim, and Alison Todes, "A Bit on the Side?: Gender Struggles in the Politics of Transformation in South Africa," *Feminist Review* 33 (Autumn 1989): 30–56. Frene Ginwala, "ANC Women: Their Strength in the Struggle," *Work in*

Oral narratives such as Nongena's are thus of great importance in expressing, in however oblique or mediated a form, some insight into the myriad, hidden experiences of women. At the same time, such narratives offer deep-reaching challenges to a number of Western theories about the formation of selfhood, narrative authority, and social identity.

In the history of the West, autobiography is the genre most closely associated with the idea of the potency of self-identity—metonymically expressed in the signature: the emblem of a unique, unrepeatable, and autonomous identity, created at a stroke of the metaphorical pen.[33] Typically, the Western male autobiography, in its dominant form, has been seen as the unfolding heroics of a single mind. As James Olney puts it: "Separate selfhood is the very motive of creation."[34]

It is commonly argued that autobiography's rise had to do with the historical evolution of the self-conscious (Western, male) individual during the Renaissance. George Gusdorf, for one, takes the flowering of wonder at the (male) self's individual destiny after the Copernican revolution as evidence of the evolutionary flowering into self-consciousness of the European race. As he sees it, all other cultures that have not awakened to autobiography have not awakened to history proper. His claim is explicitly masculine and explicitly imperialist: "It would seem that autobiography is not to be found outside our cultural area; one would say that it expresses a concern peculiar to Western man, a concern that has been of good

Progress 45 (November/December 1986): 11–14. Cock Jacklyn, *Maids and Madams* (Johannesburg, 1980). Mamphela Ramphele and Emile Boonzaaier, "The Position of African Women: Race and Gender in South Africa," in *South African Keywords*, ed. E. Boonzaaier and J. Sharp (Cape Town, 1988), pp. 153–66.

33. See Sandra Gilbert and Susan Gubar, *The Madwoman in the Attic: The Woman Writer and the Nineteenth-Century Literary Imagination* (New Haven, Conn., 1979), chap. 1, for the metaphor of writing as phallic power.

34. George Gusdorf, often regarded as the premier don of autobiographical theory, calls autobiography an "apologetics or theodicy of the individual being," and speaks of autobiography's affinity with the silver-backed Venetian mirrors: henceforth the mirror-text would reflect back the narcissistic image of the master self. See Gusdorf, "Conditions and Limits of Autobiography," in *Autobiography: Essays Theoretical and Critical*, ed. James Olney (Princeton, N.J., 1980), pp. 39, 32. Olney defines the autobiographer in terms of a separate and unique (male) selfhood. The autobiographer is "surrounded and isolated by his own consciousness, an awareness grown out of a unique heredity and unique experience." James Olney, *Metaphors of Self: The Meaning of Autobiography* (Princeton, N.J., 1972), pp. 22–23.

use in his systematic conquest of the universe."[35] Yet, as Leila Ahmed points out, "Autobiography is an anciently known form in Islamic-Arabic letters" (examples predating Western ones as early as 1111). Gusdorf's claim is therefore "at least with respect to Islamic and Arabic civilization, quite simply incorrect."[36] Indeed, what Gusdorf portrays as a grand racial awakening to the individual's "autonomous adventure" of selfhood, may, more properly speaking, be seen as the historical emergence of the ideology of possessive individualism as a rhetoric at the service of a new merchant and trading class eager to challenge traditional modes of legitimacy invested in the medieval papacy, the monarchy, and the landed aristocracy. The ideology of individualism was a rhetoric of selfhood invented by certain elected males and defined at the expense of the autonomy and freedom of other disempowered groups, most notably women, but also certainly including men.

Women have seldom been allowed to share the delights of Gusdorf's "autonomous adventure" of individual selfhood, female inventions of the self being typically subject to the careful and violent amnesias of male tradition.[37] Moreover, a number of feminists have argued recently that the many autobiographies written by women over the centuries are different from those written by men.[38] Wom-

35. Falling under the racist spell of the nineteenth-century idea of progress, Gusdorf claims that "primitives" (lacking autobiography and fearful of their image in the mirror) lag behind the Western "child of civilization" and reveal thereby that they have not yet emerged from "the mythic framework of traditional teachings . . . into the perilous domain of history." See Gusdorf, "Conditions," pp. 30, 33, 29.

36. Leila Ahmed, "Between Two Worlds: The Formation of a Turn-of-the-Century Egyptian Feminist," in *Life/Lines: Theorizing Women's Autobiography*, ed. Bella Brodski and Celeste Schenck (Ithaca, N.Y., 1988), p. 54.

37. In America, as Carolyn Heilbrun observes, it has only been since 1980 that male critics have even bothered to speak of the innumerable women's autobiographies that do exist. Carolyn G. Heilbrun, "Women's Autobiographical Writings: New Forms," in *Prose Studies* 8 (September 1985): 14. James Olney's 1980 collection, for example, devotes one solitary essay to women's autobiographies, while fifteen essays were devoted to male autobiographies. Paul Fussel's account of First World War autobiographies neglects to mention a single female autobiography, though by one estimate there were at least thirty substantial female accounts of the war. See Lidwien Heerkens, "Becoming Lives: English Women's Autobiographies of the 1930's," M.A. thesis, University of Leicester, 1984.

38. Mary Mason, for one, claims, "Nowhere in women's autobiographies do we find the patterns established by the two prototypical male autobiographers, Augustine and Rousseau; and conversely male writers never take up the archetypal models of

en's autobiographies, it is argued, do not as a rule genuflect to the
theodicy of the centered individual or to the idea of a chronological
whole, tending rather to be irregular, anecdotal, fissured, and po-
lyphonous.[39] Mary Mason has shown how in many female autobiographies, the single identity of the speaking self splinters into a
multiple fluidity of identification. Despite their myriad variations,
she argues, female autobiographies typically present the self as identity through relation. This identity through relation is not a relation
of dependency or mastery, but rather of recognition, whereby dis-
closure of the self emerges through identification with some other,
who may be a person, family, or community.[40] Identity is thereby
represented as coming to being through community, rather than as
the individual heroics of the self unfolding in solitude.

Yet I would argue that the fluidity, unsteadiness, achronology,
and obliqueness that do indeed characterize such texts as *Poppie
Nongena* cannot be understood in terms of a theory of an *écriture
féminine* arising from a poetics of the flesh, nor as eloquent of a pre-
Oedipal, libidinal insurgency and unbounded female selfhood as
argued by a certain tendency of Western feminism.[41] Rather, the
narrative offers a number of challenges to the Eurocentric assumptions of this particular theory.

Some feminists have been justly skeptical of the idea of a universal, female "gynesis," fearful that it runs the risk of being fatally

---

Julian, Margerey Kemp, Margaret Cavendish, and Anne Bradstreet." "The Other
Voice: Autobiographies of Women Writers," in Olney, *Autobiography*, p. 210.

39. Estelle C. Jelinek, ed., *Women's Autobiography: Essays in Criticism* (Bloomington, Ind., 1980), p. 17. Neither, it is argued, do women's autobiographies flourish
at the high points of male history—revolutions, battles, and national upheavals, but
wax according to the climactic changes of other histories. Typically, male autobiographies reinvent the lives of military leaders, statesmen, and public figures, while,
as Conway points out, there are no models for women recounting successful political
lives, no models for the public admission of ambition, no models for the "proper"
stages of a career.

40. Mason, "The Other Voice," p. 210.

41. French feminist critics such as Julia Kristeva, Luce Irigaray, and Hélène Cixous
have, in different ways, discerned in women's writing a female bodily residue of
insurgent pleasures and rebellions, which evade cultural edicts and erupt mutinously
in semiotic discourse: unruly, gestural, rhythmic, repetitive, oral, pre-Oedipal and
unbounded. See Julia Kristeva, "Oscillations," *Tel Quel* 59 (Fall 1974); Luce Irigaray,
"Ce Sexe qui n'en est pas un"; and Hélène Cixous, "Sorties," *La Jeune Née*; all three
are trans. in *New French Feminisms: An Anthology*, ed. Elaine Marks and Isabelle
de Courtivron (Amherst, Mass., 1980).

essentialist, formalist, and utopian.[42] There is a very real danger in baptizing certain texts with the holy water of a new female privilege, erasing historical and cultural variations, and subsuming the multiplicity of women's lives into a single, privileged, and, as it happens, white, middle-class vision. The category of "woman" is a social construction, and the ruptures in women's narratives are expressive of ruptures in social experience. Narrative differences speak not of anatomical destiny and design, but of the daily difficulties women experience in negotiating their lives past the magisterial forms of male selfhood.[43]

It is essential to note, therefore, that many of the characteristics of autobiographies that have been defined as "female," are shared by autobiographies written by people of color, female and male, and by working-class men. Thus Mason's claim that nowhere do we find men's autobiographies exhibiting the features of female texts, is true only of the privileged tradition of empowered European males. Susan Stanford Friedman has pointed out that community identity frequently marks both women's and minorities' autobiographies.[44] It becomes important, therefore, not to speak of autobiographies in terms of essences or experience: "women's autobiography," "lesbian autobiography," "black autobiography." Identity is not an essence that can be distilled and revealed in a single genre or category. Such terms make it very difficult to articulate differences among members of different communities or within communities themselves. Iden-

42. Ann Rosalind Jones, "Writing the Body: Toward an Understanding of l'écriture féminine," in The New Feminist Criticism: Essays on Women, Literature, Theory, ed. Elaine Showalter (New York, 1985). The notion of an unbounded écriture féminine is entrammeled in the selfsame binary opposites it claims to be opposing—preserving the dualism of the male as rational, solipsistic and centered, the female as organic, cosmic, rhythmic, and unbounded, but only reversing the values. Paeans to a female language of anatomy are eerily akin to ancestral male dogmas that idolize woman as body, nature, unreason, empathy, selflessness.

43. Ann Jones asks, for example, whether women of color, who have been marginalized in very different ways from white women, experience body and language as white women do. Which women will be allowed to write the new body? What would the idea of refashioning the world through a semiotic jouissance of the written word mean to women from oral cultures, to women going blind over microchips, to women without access to abortion or contraception, to the millions of genitally mutilated women in the world? See Jones, "Writing the Body," p. 371.

44. Susan Stanford Friedman, "Woman's Autobiographical Selves: Theory and Practice," in The Private Self: Theory and Practice in Women's Autobiographical Writings, ed. Shari Benstock (Chapel Hill, N.C., 1988), p. 38.

tity is socially constructed, and men of color, for example, sharing many of the conditions of deprivation and dismissal faced by white women, evince comparable difficulties negotiating their way around the privileged conventions of sanctioned selfhood.

Nellie McKay points out, "In all aspects of its creation, early black autobiography altered the terms of the production of Western autobiography as they had been defined by the dominant culture."[45] Audre Lorde, the Afro-Caribbean lesbian writer and poet, suggests in the title of her book *Zami: A New Spelling of My Name* the fundamental inadequacy of the term "autobiography" and of Western conventions of selfhood for rendering the lives of women of color. She calls *Zami* a "biomythography," and thereby invites the reader into a new relation to the idea of a life story. The neologism "biomythography" yields a rich number of glosses. "Mythography" dispels at a stroke any nostalgia for autobiographical exactitude.[46] At the same time, the term suggests life through mythography, the life of the future born from the collective refashioning of the past. Moreover, as significant as what the term biomythography includes, is what the term leaves out. Lorde's refusal to employ the prefix "auto" as the single, imperious sign of the self, expresses a refusal to posit herself as the single, authoritative, engendering voice in the text. Rather, her life story is the collective, transcribed life of a community of women—not so much a perfect record of the past, as a fabulated strategy for community survival.[47]

Poppie Nongena's narrative can perhaps be seen as most closely akin to the Latin American *testimonios*. In an important article

45. Nellie McKay, "Race, Gender and Cultural Context in Zora Neale Hurston's *Dust Tracks on a Road*," in Brodski and Schenck, *Life/Lines*, p. 176.

46. Lorde, *Zami: A New Spelling of My Name*. All autobiographies are, in Simone de Beauvoir's term, "fictions of selfhood." Any life story is, as Colette knew, a fabulation of arranged fragments, involving a welter of caprice, whimsical omissions, and crafted inventions, governed overall by the contrivances and transformations of genre.

47. Similarly, Bernice Johnson Reagon has called black women's writing "cultural autobiography" in the sense that a black women's identity is inseparable from her relations to her community. Bernice Johnson Reagon, "My Black Mothers and Sisters or On Beginning a Cultural Autobiography," *Feminist Studies* 8 (Spring 1982): 81. Stephen Butterfield writes: "The "self" of black autobiography...is conceived as a member of an oppressed social group, with ties and responsibilites to the other members. It is a conscious political identity, drawing sustenance from the past experience of the group." Butterfield, *Black Autobiography in America* (Amherst, Mass., 1974), pp. 2–3.

Doris Sommer argues that the "testimonial," a life told to a journalist or anthropologist for political reasons, cannot simply be subsumed under the autobiography, and she has identified a number of
distinctive features that closely resemble *Poppie Nongena*. The testimonial's most salient feature, she notes, is "an implied and often
explicit 'plural subject,' rather than the singular subject we associate
with traditional autobiography." As is the case with *Poppie Nongena*, the narrator's "singularity achieves its identity as an extension
of the collective." Yet the plural voice is plural not in the sense of
speaking for, or being representative of the whole, but in the sense
that it cannot be seen out of relation to communities (as in Nongena's case, the family, church, and finally the national revolution).
The reader is thus invited to participate in a branching network of
relationships that spread away from all centers, and across many
dimensions of time. The testimonial is always dialogic and public,
with a collective rather than individual self. As in Nongena's narrative, testimonials visibly present a staging of social difference in
which a privileged scribe records the unprivileged oral testament.
Testimonials thus have an oral and performative quality that other
autobiographies do not, bearing the imprint of both speakers' voices,
the doubled nature of the writing and the dispersed authority of
voice. "For unlike the private and even lonely moment of autobiographical writing, testimonials are public events." By the same token, "testimonials are related to the general text of struggle . . . [and]
are written from interpersonal class and ethnic positions."[48]

Because of the collective and public nature of the testimonial
narrative, the reader's identification with the narrative persona is
always deferred. In *Poppie Nongena* the rapid vacillation of person
and voice prevents any easy identification with one single perspective. Nongena's relation to her probable readers is inevitably problematic, involving as it does transgressions of class, racial, and
gender affinities, not to mention language and country. No simple
unanimity of readership is remotely imaginable and the narrative
acknowledges this historical imbalance in its refusal to yield a single
consoling point of identity. What this effectively does is call on the
reader to enter into collaboration with the collective history. The
reader is invited to extend the historical community, and that ex-

---

48. Doris Sommer, "Not Just a Personal Story: Women's *Testimonios* and the
Plural Self," in Brodski and Schenck, *Life/Lines*, pp. 107, 118, 129.

tension is not simply the embrace of a given community, but involves active participation, the labor of identification, and, above all, hard choices about the politics of social transformation.

Had Joubert dispensed with the intermediary narrator and rendered the narrative entirely in the first person, she would effectively have erased a crucial dimension of the narrative's condition of production, concealing her own interventions and selections, and masquerading as a far more innocent and passive amanuensis than she really was—although she does do this in the self-contradictory prefatory note. As it is, the narrative reveals itself to be profoundly paradoxical in its beginnings, production, and reception. It preserves its doubled production and heteroglossic nature far more visibly than many other oral histories that seek to diminish or erase entirely the interventions and selections of the oral historian. The relation between the two women is undeniably one of racial, class and imperial power, crosshatched and contradicted by empathy and identification based on gender, shared language, and motherhood. Indeed, the narrative relations between the two women mirror the social relations between many black South African domestic workers and their female employers: relations of strained, ambiguous, and uneven intimacy in the context of massive social inequity. Such a context renders problematic any easy notions of global sisterhood. Yet to will away Joubert's voice and yearn for Nongena's unmediated voice is to hanker after an anachronistic Western notion of individual purity and creative singularity. We may balk at being refused identification with a single self, but through this refusal we are invited into an altogether different notion of identity, community, narrative power, and political change.

Jean Marquard has pointed out that *Poppie Nongena* predated by a number of years the emergence in South Africa of what has been dubbed "history from below," "people's history," and "oral history."[49] Yet, largely because of the politics of the book's marketing and reception, the narrative has not received the serious attention as an oral testimony that other later forms of oral history have received.

In South Africa the "new history" emerged largely in response to the massive growth of extraparliamentary activism in the indepen-

49. Marquard, "Poppie," p. 137. I am grateful for David Goldberg's discussion of this point with me.

dent unions and in community organizations that have been mobilized irrepressibly around the country over the issues of rent, transport, housing, and education. The new history has taken at least three directions. Largely empirical, politically radical academic histories have explored, for example, the rise and fall of the African peasantry, the making of the black proletariat, the different histories of the Zulu, Xhosa, Pedi, and so on. These are written by highly trained white academics for a specialized academic readership. On the other hand, histories such as those produced by the Labor History Group; illustrated booklets in English, Zulu and Xhosa; and Learn and Teach are written for a popular mass readership by intellectuals or community activists committed to placing their training and expertise at the service of the communities. Third, histories are produced by nonacademics, workers and students for worker publications and community broadsheets such as Fosatu Worker News, and Izwi Lase Township, as well as popular comic-book representations of history, which attempt to put the writing and reading of history in the hands of the communities themselves. Crucial to the development of these latter forms of social history has been the emergence of oral history.

Oral history, both in South Africa and elsewhere, offered the delirious promise of brushing history against the grain, in Walter Benjamin's justifiably famous phrase. It promised to restore the vivid, ordinary lives of those who saddled the colonial's horses, hammered out the railways and dug up the diamonds, washed the settlers' babies, and cooked the evening meals. Oral history promised a more democratic history. Paul Thompson argues: "It gives back to the people who made and experienced history, through their own words, a central place."[50] New areas of social life, particularly family histories and domestic power relations, the myriad forms of popular culture, the dynamics of informal social groupings such as squatter communities and shebeens, hitherto secret, taboo, or neglected were opened to public history.

Oral history is not simply a new technique for recovering the past in its purity. Rather, it invites a new theory of the representation of history. Not only is history produced by miners, prostitutes, moth-

---

50. Paul Thompson, "History and Community," in *Oral History: An Interdisciplinary Anthology*, ed. David K. Dunaway and Willa K. Baum (Nashville, Tenn., 1984), p. 39.

ers, and farmworkers, but the recording of history is itself both the outcome of struggle and the locus of struggle itself. Without doubt, oral history is potentially a technology for reproducing political memory, accessible for the first time to the silenced, the inaudible, the disenfranchised, women, the working-class, ordinary people. But oral histories themselves are not necessarily progressive, nor are all the uses to which oral narratives may be put, as the reception of *Poppie Nongena* exemplifies. The representation of history, including oral history, is itself a contested historical event. The collection and preservation of human memory is less a technique for increased historical "accuracy" than it is a new, contested technology for historial power.

"Accuracy" in history is a genre. Empiricism is a mode of ordering past experience according to certain rhetorical and disciplinary conventions. The quest for the "real" past is as utopian as Alice's quest for the white rabbit, which glances anxiously at its watch before vanishing. History is always late. Empirical oral history, if defined as the effort "simply to preserve and collect human memories," is a mode of historical taxidermy, a technology of reproduction for rendering past events in a permanent stasis of lifelikeness.[51] Empiricism privileges the idea of history as a series of pure, recoverable events, a notion that can be upheld only by radically depoliticizing the dynamics of power that underlie the activities of history making. As Frantz Fanon put it, "For the native, objectivity is always directed against him."[52] Oral history may for this reason also conceal a poetics of nostalgia. In its empirical guise, oral history fulfills the nostalgic desire to represent history whole, to preserve, to embalm: it is a politics of reproduction. It represents the aggressive desire for historical completion and coherence that characterizes all archives. The oral archive can thus become a political instrument for the bureaucratization of working lives, serving as a visible monument to the power of the bureaucracy as a system of ordering knowledge and delegating authority.

The production of oral history is a technology of power under contest, which cannot be seen in isolation from the contexts of power from which it emerges. Oral history involves the technolog-

51. Samuel Hand, "Some Words on Oral Histories," in Dunaway and Baum, *Oral History*, p. 52.

52. Frantz Fanon, *The Wretched of the Earth* (New York, 1963), p. 77.

ical reproduction of people's memories, the unstable life of the unconscious, the deformations, evasions, and repressions of memory, desire, projection, trauma, envy, anger, pleasure. These obscure logics cannot be wished away as the irksome impurities of oral history, but should be integrated into oral history as a central part of the process. No oral history is innocent of selection, bias, evasion, and interpretation. Very real imbalances of power remain in current contexts. Frequently, oral histories, as with *Poppie Nongena*, perpetuate the hierarchy of mental and manual labor of the societies from which they emerge: the hierarchy of those who work and speak, and those who think and write. In many oral histories, as with *Poppie Nongena*, the multiple authorship of the narrative is submerged in the executive, choreographing authority of the "historian." The oral narrator becomes a Svengali's Trilby, at the beck and call of the master or mistress of ceremonies, bestowing prestige and glamor on the historian's professional name, without herself benefiting one whit.

In the dust jacket, title page, packaging, and presentation of *Poppie Nongena*, Nongena is undoubtedly Trilby to Joubert's Svengali. Nongena is presented as Joubert's fictional creature, and most people who are unaware of the circumstances of the book's production, read it as a white woman's novel, and dismiss it on those grounds as deeply suspect. Nevertheless, to accept the dismissal of the narrative at face value is to accept the woeful whitewashing politics of the book's publication, and to acquiesce in the erasure of Nongena's creative authority. Indeed, the narrative itself expresses a far more complex hierarchy of relations, and much of the great value and interest of the book lies in the way in which these shifting imbalances of power, the paradoxes and ambiguities arising from its doubled authorship, the contradictions between the two women's relation to apartheid, are integrated into the texture of the narrative itself.

While it seems that Nongena does most of the "talking," in fact only 30 percent is her own voice; the rest comprises Nongena's ventriloquizing of her family's voices, and Joubert's record of her oral interviews with these family members, all orchestrated by Joubert's narration. At a few moments, the inequity of Joubert's orchestration of a virtuoso performance of Nongena's story is offset by the textual record of Joubert's own questions, her queries, her ignorance. There are also moments inscribed in the narrative when

Nongena corrects Joubert for incorrect assumptions or questions: these moments are not elided from the narrative as they so often are in oral history. The constant shifting of voices in the narrative denies us identification with one voice. At no point can empowered readers assume an easy identification with Nongena, and thus forget their own privilege in a cathartic identification with the voice of the disempowered. The imbalances in power between the two women score the narrative, and the reader is obliged as a result to experience the discomfort of these imbalances as a central experience of the reading itself, and to be conscious at every moment of the contradictions underlying the process of narrative collaboration. No one, not even Joubert, is allowed a finally privileged perspective. The reader is thus equally denied a consoling organizing perspective, and is forced to yield to a sense that all narrative and all history arise from a community of effort and a community of social construction, which are shaped by uneven social relations of power. Most oral histories do not record these contradictions, erasing the historian's editorial interventions and preserving the "voice" of the narrator in artifical purity, while giving executive authority to the invisible historian. Unlike most oral histories, the imbalances between Nongena and Joubert are inscribed in the narrative itself, becoming an integral part of the reading experience, and hence they avoid the politics of concealment that generally operate in "empirical" oral histories. The imbalances are flagrantly there, unavoidable and vexing, contradictory and irresoluble, insisting on interpretative contest and political analysis. Most importantly, the narrative resists any effort to imagine that the imbalances between the two women could be resolved by a more equitable redistribution of purely narrative identity. Rather, the uncertainty of its ending acknowledges finally that narrative transformation has to be attended by full social transformation.

As Teresa de Lauretis argues, to pose the question of gender as arising from a fundamental sexual difference between men and women, or as arising more abstractly from signification and discursive effects, from *différance,* where "woman" comes to figure *différence tout court*—to pose the question of gender in such a way has the effect of universalizing gender opposition and making it impossible to articulate differences among and within women. She calls rather for a "subject constituted in gender, to be sure, though not by sexual difference alone, but rather across languages and cultural representations; as subjects en-gendered in the experience of race and class, as well as sexual relations; a subject, therefore, not unified but rather multiple, and not so much divided as contradicted." Gender is thus the representation of changing social relations: "it presents an individual for a class." The "subject of feminism" is therefore "one whose definition or conception is in progress," and which cannot be found in identities alone—but rather in the politics of alternative social, political, and communicative forms, in political practices of self-representation that illuminate the "contradictory, multiple construction of subjectivity."[53] Similarly, Biddy Martin writes of "recent autobiographical writings that work against self-evidently homogenous conceptions of identity," writings in which lesbianism, for one, comes to figure as something other than a totalizing self-identification and something other than exclusively psychological.[54] Here the appeal is to institutional analyses of social and cultural power, rather than a focus on identity alone. The importance of these points is that they allow us to examine women's narratives in the context of theories and politics of social transformation, rather than an ahistorical psychology, or poetics of identity.

The identity of gender, race, class, or sexual preference cannot guarantee political correctness. Feminist agency should be sought not in a homogenous psychology of identity alone (the lesbian, woman of color, working-class female life), but through a politics of organization and strategy that takes into account the myriad differences and loyalties that crisscross women's lives with conflicting passions. Audre Lorde has remarked: "As a Black lesbian feminist comfortable with the many different ingredients of my identity, and a woman committed to racial and sexual freedom from oppression, I find that I am constantly being encouraged to pluck out some one aspect of myself and present this as a meaningful whole, eclipsing or denying the other parts of self. But this is a destructive and fragmenting way to live."[55] Feminism should be enacted where these

53. Teresa de Lauretis, *Technologies of Gender: Essays on Theory, Film and Fiction* (Bloomington, Ind., 1987), pp. 1–2, 5, 9–10.

54. Biddy Martin, "Lesbian Identity and Autobiographical Difference[s]," in Brodski and Schenck, *Life/Lines*, p. 82.

55. Audre Lorde, "Age, Race, Class, and Sex: Woman Redefining Difference," in *Sister Outsider: Essays and Speeches* (Trumansburg, N.Y., 1984), pp. 120–21.

conflicting loyalties emerge and intersect under specific historical circumstances. In this way we can avoid the reduction of politics to a poetics of the flesh, an erotics of power mysteriously transcending historical difference, which itself masks differences of power among women as well as similarities of power and disempowerment between women and men (of race, class, nation).

This means that narrative itself cannot be the only tool for transforming the master's house. Rather the social and political context of the engendering of narrative has to be massively transformed: and this involves a radical, active, political transformation. The politics of memory and authorship are inextricably entangled with the politics of institutional power in all its forms: the politics of family households, domestic labor, education, and publishing and reception. History is a series of social fabulations which we cannot do without. It is an inventive practice, but not just any invention will do. For it is the future, not the past, that is at stake in the contest over which memories survive.

8

Beyond the Limit:
The Social Relations of Madness in
Southern African Fiction

STEPHEN CLINGMAN

A person who thinks that he is empowered to separate his
inner world from the outer one has no inner world from
which something might be separable.

     —Elias Canetti, commenting on Kafka

I

It turns out that the darkness at the heart of the colonial experience
may be a certain history of madness.[1] Other features of colonial
history are more familiar: its origins in an age of European expansion,
its forms of economic exploitation and political subjugation, the
social history of communities in transition, modes of cultural imperialism and cultural resistance. These aspects engage the labors
and thoughts of historians, anthropologists, and other investigators
of the past. Yet, half-buried, half-revealed—as phenomena relating
to the unconscious usually are—the theme of madness emerges as
adjunct to, and part of, these other histories.

1. The epigraph is from John Bayley, "Canetti and Power," *London Review of
Books* (December 1981–January 1982): 6.

It is there, for example, in two founding texts of the colonial era. At the center of Joseph Conrad's *Heart of Darkness* is the vision—and specter—of madness. Here are the supposedly "unspeakable" practices of the indigenous inhabitants (the representation of which, among other things in the novel, so outraged Chinua Achebe).[2] What happens to Kurtz as he "goes native" is that, it seems, he simultaneously goes mad. The accountant Marlowe meets at the river station retains his sanity, but he does so, significantly, by clinging religiously to the rules and regulations of his European framework, including the starched white shirts he insists on wearing daily. Yet it seems safe to surmise that he would not have to do this if he did not feel under constant threat. Even the narrative framing of the novel mimes this sense of danger, as the text proceeds (analogically) to deeper and deeper levels and more interior modes, where fact and fantasy mingle licentiously. There are ways of universalising these issues—a standard critical procedure—but why ignore the fact that they emerge so strongly from the colonial setting?

E. M. Forster's *A Passage to India* evokes this same feeling of threat. From the first page of the novel there is a carefully articulated sense of the tumult and riot of the Indian continent, overburdening the linear, sparse lines of the European mental framework. At the heart of this book, too, there is a moment of madness. For this is what happens to Adela Quested ("addled quest": her name sounds sufficiently like a summary of the whole colonial undertaking) in the Marabar Caves—that interior setting without an exterior, where all normal shapes and points of coherence become void. This setting is also one of projection, where Adela's own sense of threat rebounds upon her; yet in her mind it is displaced onto Aziz, and the accusation of a sexual attack formulates. In a novel where "nothing" means "everything" and "everything" comes to "nothing" we have a world turned upside down and inside out—which is one, albeit literary, definition of madness.

One should distinguish between instances in which madness appears as a theme, and is perhaps categorized as such, and those in which it in a sense takes control of the text. Labels of madness are notoriously imprecise, and may be stylized or misleading; they are easily prone to rhetorical manipulation for other purposes. Shoshana

2. Chinua Achebe, "An Image of Africa," *The Massachusetts Review* 18 (Winter 1977): 782–94.

Felman remarks that *"to talk about madness* is always, in fact, *to deny it."*[3] From this point of view cases in which madness seems to take control of the text may be more reliable as an index of a real threat of mental destabilization. Yet even of instances that are plainly thematic and under the apparent control of the writer, we should ask a simple question: are writers entirely at large to choose whatever themes they wish? Is it not also true, as Nadine Gordimer has remarked, that "themes choose writers," and that writers are "selected" by the "consciousness of [their] era"?[4] If so, we emerge with a minimal observation at least: that the theme of madness does seem to be connected with colonial history and is revealed as such in fiction.

It is one thing to say this, quite another to establish with any reliability the shape, trajectory, and transformations of this theme in its successive appearances in colonial and—now I might add—postcolonial fiction. What are its patterns of cause and effect within the broader history of which it is a part? What are its structural relationships within this setting, which might also account for the inevitability of its appearance? Why is fiction the privileged site where this theme is set into motion? These of course are large questions and cannot be answered in full here. Instead I will limit myself to the southern African setting at certain moments over the past hundred years, and make a preliminary approach to some of these issues. For within southern African fiction it is a remarkable—but not accidental—fact that the theme of madness has arisen again and again, though in different forms, over the past century. It is my suggestion that the theme of madness is itself something that has a history within this setting, although that history is not linear, or even necessarily progressive. All I want to do is dip into and out of this history, raising certain hypotheses that might offer bases for further exploration.

In highlighting various aspects of, and within, this theme, I should

3. Shoshana Felman, *Writing and Madness* (*Literature/Philosophy/Psychoanalysis*) (Ithaca, N.Y., 1985), p. 252.

4. For the first statement see Nadine Gordimer, "What Shall I Write About?" (unpublished typescript in possession of the author, ca. 1961), p. 15: "We do not choose themes because they are topical or timely, they choose *us* because they are the very stuff of our lives." For the second, see "Selecting My Stories," in Nadine Gordimer, *The Essential Gesture: Writing, Politics and Places*, ed. Stephen Clingman (New York, 1988), p. 116.

make my position clear. It does not seem to me to be finally helpful to essentialize either the condition of madness or the work of literature, or—most especially—the relationship between the two, as, for example, Shoshana Felman does in her book *Writing and Madness*. For Felman "writing" and "madness" are nothing other than mutually referential: "if something like literature exists," she remarks, "only madness can explain it"; similarly she maintains that "madness . . . can be defined as nothing other than an irreducible resistance to interpretation"—which is what she assumes literariness to be also.[5] But is it true that madness cannot be interpreted—perhaps not as a thing in itself, but in terms of the *conditions* that promote its appearance and the *context* in which it gains its significance? Why should *all* literary works be "mad"? Are they all *equally* mad, mad in the same way, or products of the same *kind* of madness? If one does not grant these questions one loses all sense of distinction, of historicity, of politics, and ultimately—I would suggest—of significance itself. The position here, then, is very different. It is that madness, at least in the literature we are considering, is the product of *social* relations, albeit varying and shifting ones. Moreover, the works under discussion are themselves "social" *relations*—narratives deeply embedded in the history of their societies, and fashioned to grapple at both conscious and unconscious levels with issues emerging from substantial social perturbations.

II

Olive Schreiner is widely credited as being the writer who originates modern white South African literature: her novel, *The Story of an African Farm*, published in 1883 when the author was in her early twenties, is sometimes seen as a kind of genetic blueprint, containing within it the basic patterns of all later developments in white fiction. Yet, in both Schreiner's life and work, the issue of mental instability arises immediately. She herself suffered from a form of psychosomatic illness all her adult life. Her biographers, Ruth First and Ann Scott, point out that this had a sexual dimension, insofar as she was compelled to play a male role in a man's world

5. Felman, *Writing and Madness*, p. 254.

as a female. Also, there was a deep ambiguity of belonging: in England, where she was lionized upon publication of her novel, she longed for South Africa; in South Africa, for England. Ultimately she came to feel that she was in no real relationship with life or thought "in England or Africa or anywhere else."[6] Committed intellectually to ideas of freedom—Schreiner was friendly with Havelock Ellis, Edward Carpenter, Eleanor Marx; she wrote *Woman and Labour*, one of the founding texts of modern feminism; she grew ever more fervent in her anti-imperialism—nonetheless the presiding feeling of her life is one of *constriction*. In that very early novel of hers this is represented with great power. Here we see her main female character, Lyndall—a woman of the utmost intelligence— offer an entirely damning attack on the nature and effects of sexual oppression; but she dies as its victim, oscillating on the edge of mental breakdown, a life of the greatest promise snuffed out by the stifling environs of the colony.

This is essentially a feminist anguish, within the colonial setting. Inseparably surrounding this theme is a larger and encompassing topic, however. The novel is presented as "the story of an *African farm*"; as Schreiner herself pointed out, it was a novel of belonging to Africa, of "settlement," as it were. But how deep does its belonging go? Colonial history tells the story of a different kind of belonging, in which foreign land is appropriated and is said to belong to the colonizing power; at the same time the land and its indigenous inhabitants alike become "subject" to the colonizing authority, part of its own subjectivity. But—to adapt Robert Frost's comment on a different colonial history—can the land belong to one if one does not belong to the land?[7] This is essentially the problem raised by *The Story of an African Farm*. For, despite its claims to "settlement," the tale the novel tells is more properly one of *alienation:* surrounded by a hostile—or, at best, indifferent—universe, there is no

6. Olive Schreiner, *The Story of an African Farm* (1883); intro. Dan Jacobson (Harmondsworth, 1971). For the "anticipatory" nature of this novel see Stephen Gray, *Southern African Literature: An Introduction* (Cape Town, London, 1979), chap. 6, "Schreiner and the Novel Tradition." Olive Schreiner to S. C. Cronwright-Schreiner, London, November 30, 1914, quoted in Ruth First and Ann Scott, *Olive Schreiner* (London, 1980), p. 335.

7. "The land was ours before we were the land's": Robert Frost, "For John F. Kennedy His Inauguration," *In the Clearing* (London, 1962), p. 31.

sense in which the novel or its characters feel really at home in their setting.[8] We watch the spiritual trajectory of the characters, from the rough and ready comedies and brutalities of their childhood on the Karroo farmstead where the novel is set, to the kind of "transcendental homelessness" of which Lukács speaks in his *The Theory of the Novel*.[9] The "subjectivity" of the novel—far from being proud or self-confident—becomes a deeply ambiguous one, unsure of its past, its present, or its future. Yet the novel still remains the story of an "African" farm: this is the informing ethos of the work, the containing setting for its themes of mental anguish.[10]

What emerges from this for a broader history of the theme of madness in colonial fiction as a whole? Simply this: that insofar as alienation—from the foreign land, the continent, and its peoples— is the *reality* of the colonial enterprise, what takes the place of any real relationship for the colonizers is *projection*, the projection of subjective feelings onto that alien setting, or people. Thus, whereas it is the colonizers themselves who are alien, they present as alien the foreign continent or its people; where the colonizers themselves present the real threat in that situation, it is the continent and its people that are felt as threatening. Indeed, the less *real and equitable* contact there is with the colonized, the more scope there is for various mythic imaginings and projections about them. And it is here that the space is created for forms of mental instability—either by way of projection, or else because of a sense of threat. Conrad's *Heart of Darkness*, incidentally, reveals both. Thus we see how the theme of madness is linked to an ambiguity at the core of colonial history.

Let us consider the theme in a different form, as it appears in two South African novels written in the 1920s: here I want to explore certain connections between race, sexuality, and madness. It is no accident that these issues appeared in South African fiction at this time, for the 1920s was a decade in which questions of race assumed

8. See Nadine Gordimer, "English-Language Literature and Politics in South Africa," in Christopher Heywood, ed., *Aspects of South African Literature* (London, 1976), p. 103.

9. Georg Lukács, *The Theory of the Novel*, trans. Anna Bostock (London, 1971), p. 41.

10. For further discussion see Stephen Clingman, *The Novels of Nadine Gordimer: History from the Inside* (London, 1986), pp. 135–36.

an unprecedented importance. After the First World War, as South Africa settled into its patterns of modern development, racial legislation proliferated, dealing with labor relations on the mines and in industry, regulating living areas, and even sexual relations.[11] Race, we might say, was becoming the major ideological instrument of organizing class structures. South Africa was no longer a colony— it was becoming a modern industrial state, and was indigenously governed—and its focal issues were, equally, transforming.

In this setting Sarah Gertrude Millin's God's Stepchildren was written as an experimental novel, that is, a novel that quite literally sets up a social "experiment" to see what happens when the races mix.[12] Like many such experiments, its findings are included in the form in which it conceptualizes the problem. The tone is fixed from early on. Set (to begin with) in the first half of the nineteenth century, it shows the Reverend Andrew Flood (the name is significant) who has come out to South Africa as a missionary. From the start he is presented as degenerate, physically, morally, mentally, and when he finds that even the local Hottentots, whom he wishes to convert, deride him, he decides he can only achieve his objective by converting to their condition. He marries a Hottentot wife, who bears him a (racially mixed) child. This by no means helps Flood make any more converts, and he soon realizes the futility of his ways. He ends literally mad, rambling and bumbling, mumbling to himself in his decrepitude. As for his "sin," however—for that is partly the framework within which Millin considers his history—it continues. "Aprés moi le Flood," we might say: Millin then explores the effect of this original act of miscegenation through four generations, and as might be expected, it is wholly decisive. Whereas in the fourth generation the last character she creates is 15/16 white, the truth of the matter is that "blood will out": this character, who suffers from shell shock in the First World War, derides himself miserably because, he feels, it is his black blood that has let him down (the fact that huge numbers of white men suffered the same fate appears to have escaped Millin's attention). He decides to terminate the

11. Legislated variously by the Mines and Works Amendment Act (1926), the Natives (Urban Areas) Act (1923), and the Immorality Act (1927).

12. Sarah Gertrude Millin, God's Stepchildren (1924); rpr. with intro. by Tony Voss (Johannesburg, 1986).

degeneracy he carries, and expiate the sin of his fathers, by having
no more children; instead he returns as a missionary to those selfsame people whom Andrew Flood first fell among.

There is an obvious lunacy in all of this. Here we see the linkage
between racism and sexual projection, between miscegenation and
the labeling of "madness," which in themselves appear obsessive,
compulsive, and rather pathological. Indeed, the imagery Millin uses
to describe her "coloured" characters is quite remarkable if we take
it as an index of projection. Much of it seems to derive from standard
nineteenth-century notions or icons, such as the Hottentot Venus,
which, as Sander Gilman has shown, was a primary marker, as an
image, of a supposed black sexual degeneracy and biological inferiority.[13] But this in turn suggests that it would be a serious mistake
to take Millin's projections as a sign of an "individual" madness,
that is, her own. For when the book was first published it was
received with substantial acclaim in both Britain and the United
States (where, as a bestseller, it was lauded as "beautiful and mem-
orable" and "an absolutely first-rate contribution to the sum of human knowledge") and then later, predictably, in Germany where a
pirated edition was hailed (heiled?) as a Rassenroman by the Nazis.[14]
Following Sander Gilman's analytical models here we might see a
further subtle interplay of paradoxes and dynamics, for Millin herself
was Jewish. Given that the same intellectual tradition she was drawing on had seen Jews as associated with blackness and sexual degeneracy—as Gilman shows in his Difference and Pathology—
perhaps this was Millin's way, in the African setting, of displacing
those attributions. Or perhaps the starker identifications of color in
South Africa meant that Millin simply could not credit the logic of
wider associations: certainly it was a matter of absolute mortifica-
tion to her that the Nazis liked her novel. But the fact nonetheless
remains that her work was taken up, internationally, within a dominant framework of racial conceptualization. The simple, though
significant point, then, is that in following this theme we are not
dealing with individual conditions alone, but with larger mental

13. Sander L. Gilman, Difference and Pathology: Stereotypes of Sexuality, Race
and Madness (Ithaca, N.Y., 1985), chap. 3.

14. The second comment appeared in a letter from H. L. Mencken to Sarah Gertrude Millin. In England H. G. Wells compared the novel to A Passage to India. See
Martin Rubin, Sarah Gertrude Millin: A South African Life (Johannesburg, 1977), pp.
83–85, 174.

frameworks of which they are a part. What is seen as normal within such a framework can appear highly abnormal from without, and vice versa. In Millin's case we see the inner "madness" of the South African racial framework at a particularly expressive—but because of that also particularly vulnerable—moment.

Millin's novel is implicitly concerned with science, the pseudo-science of race.[15] William Plomer, whose *Turbott Wolfe* is the second major novel dealing with race in the 1920s, presents another view: "The chief tendency of modern science has been to produce noise."[16] In other ways, too, his novel seems diametrically opposed to Millin's: iconoclastically thumbing its nose at the sacred beliefs of white South African culture, it presents miscegenation not as a problem to be solved, but as the *solution* to South Africa's problems. An organization in the book called the Society for Young Africa puts this forward in fairly enthusiastic terms.

This does not mean that the novel has thereby emerged into the clear light of day in mental or political terms. On the contrary, its vision is fraught with dreams, nerves, visions, and deep-seated fears, mixed in equal proportions. The character, Friston, who is most deeply affected by all of this, remarks:

> I am obsessed . . . with dreams and visions, mostly of the future Africa. I do not tell you what I think: I tell you what I feel, which is what I dream, which is what I know. I have reached the pitch of understanding with the nerves. I look forward to the great compromise between white and black; between civilisation and barbarism; between the past and future; between brains and bodies; and, as I like to say, between habit and instinct. (P. 102)

Whites, it appears, have habit, and blacks have instinct. But when Friston sees his vision become reality—that is, when two of the (racially distinct) characters do fall in love—he cannot take it: he goes mad (and incidentally becomes a Bolshevik agent) before being killed. So the theme of madness enters once again, and the book ends in a state of formal disruption, with no clear logic to its denouement. There is some sense that the work's incoherence at the end has to do with a different dynamic, relating to Plomer's own

15. See Nancy Stepan, *The Idea of Race in Science: Great Britain 1800–1960* (London, 1982).

16. William Plomer, *Turbott Wolfe* (1925), ed. Stephen Gray (Johannesburg, 1980), p. 31; further page references are given in the text.

homosexuality, which could not be expressed straightforwardly, but which may have been exercised in the novel partly as an allegory of "miscegenation"—mixing what should not be mixed.[17]

With or without this dimension, however, there is only one explanation for what we see in the novel: that we are dealing in the widest sense with a framework of reality and what is permissible and impermissible within it. Notions of miscegenation, normally repressed, are deeply subversive in relation to this framework. Fantasy can be tolerated, but as soon as it is translated into reality it appears fatal to the framework itself. Friston's madness, and the novel's incoherence, are due to the force of the "return of the repressed." Strange as it may seem now, we get some sense of the presiding power of the South African racial framework (and, for Plomer, sexual framework) at the time when the novel was written— even for those who rejected it. And I think we learn that Fredric Jameson's notion of the "political unconscious" is an actual, psychological reality in South Africa, not only for individuals, but within wider mental frameworks at large.[18]

What happens, however, when you are on the other side of this line of repression, when you are condemned, so to speak, to the "unconscious" of a dominant society? Peter Abrahams's novel, *The Path of Thunder*, published in 1948, provides something of an answer.[19] Abrahams was himself, in South African terms, a "coloured"—a person of mixed race. As far as official white consciousness is concerned, the "coloureds" themselves are the objects of a repressed sexual history. This was especially true at the time the novel was written: as the Afrikaner nationalists were coming to power with their doctrine of apartheid, enjoining white supremacy and the purity of the white race, the existence of the "coloureds"—in part the historical offspring of encounters between (in the main) white Afrikaner men and black women—was an official embarrassment. The idea of a "return of the repressed" in this context would have had a political as well as psychological import. *The Path of Thunder* deals with that threat, as well as what it means

17. On the concealed topic of homosexuality in Plomer's novel, see Peter Wilhelm, "Mask and Reality in *Turbott Wolfe*," in ibid., pp. 180–85.

18. Fredric Jameson, *The Political Unconscious: Narrative as a Socially Symbolic Act* (Ithaca, N.Y., 1981).

19. Peter Abrahams, *The Path of Thunder* (1948; Cape Town, 1984).

for those who have to struggle back from the netherworld of an unacknowledged identity.

Perhaps unsurprisingly, the possibility of madness again lies at the center. The novel is set in a rural area of South Africa. Once again, as we find so often in these novels, we are in a symbolic heartland, where a wealthy white farm is juxtaposed with a poverty-stricken "coloured" village nearby. Here, madness has actually occurred: one of the characters is called Mad Sam, and through the course of the book we discover why. In an earlier time—almost a previous life, it seems—he had loved a white woman from the farm. One of the sons from the farm had discovered this, and literally beaten Sam into madness. The logic of this is clear: for a "coloured" person to claim his identity in relation to whites is a form of madness, and he must actually *be* mad if he is to survive in this alien framework at all. Also, Sam remembers the past: another form of madness in this context.

In the second generation the tragedy seems to be reworking itself. A young man, Lanny Swartz, born of the village, but educated in Cape Town, also falls in love with a young white woman associated with the farm, and she with him. Their love affair is discovered, and in the gathering crisis of the novel's ending Lanny finds out a secret relating to his own identity: that his own father was white, indeed that he was the old farmowner himself. Symbolically the model of a fractured family distills a whole racial history in South Africa: the white father refuses to recognize the identity or existence of his own "coloured" offspring; the typology of disinheritance takes on a deeply intimate, color-coded form. One may take it further: the new white "father" (the legitimate son of the old, and inheritor of the farm), representing the political as well as familial "law," "castrates" the "coloured" son in refusing to allow him to marry a white daughter from the household. In these ways, it is clear, a crucial gap is embedded in Lanny's identity that cannot be healed within existing reality. This might in itself produce madness, but Lanny's end is a different one: he and the woman he loves die in a gun battle with marauding white avengers from the farmhouse who cannot tolerate the fact of their cross-racial relationship. They transgress the law of this father, but are not able to overcome it.

The plot is a complex one and—again—fraught with deep emotion. Yet a number of points seem to emerge. The first is that where a dominant framework of reality allows no existence to any alternative, those whose reality *is* that alternative face a kind of madness or (symbolically) death; that is, an annihilation or disabling in some form. The shambling figure of Mad Sam, physically as well as mentally crippled, is a central symbol in this regard. By contrast, Lanny and his white lover attempt to claim their identity and humanity through physical (ultimately violent) resistance—something which Frantz Fanon later recommended as the solution to exactly the same problem.[20] But in *The Path of Thunder* we see what the South African half-life does to the personality and identity; also, that no full redemption of humanity seemed possible to Abrahams at the time when he wrote the novel. Incidentally, something else is revealed. At key points, as secrets from the past or present are being uncovered, the mode in which the novel is written becomes Gothic, which is after all the genre of mental edginess, hidden secrets, repressed desires, and deep-seated fears. This explains for me why much of South Africa in general—with its own secrets, forbidden realities, skeletons in the cupboard or in the jails—seems to exist in a Gothic mode.

It is all very well to talk of racism and madness, and of their interconnection, but how do these syndromes originate? We may grant that racial prejudice existed before the colonial era and that colonizers arrived in Africa with a repertoire of images and expectations that they may have been only too eager to see fulfilled. But can racism by itself explain *everything* that happened in the colonial context? Do we not also have to explain the *endurance* of racism in this setting?[21] On this theoretical and methodological issue Marx points out that a simple appeal to an "original" state of affairs is often futile: "Let us not be like the political economist who, when he wishes to explain something, puts himself in an imaginary original state of affairs. Such an original stage of affairs explains nothing. He simply pushes the question back into a grey and nebulous distance. He presupposes as a fact and an event what he ought to be deducing, namely the necessary connection between...two

20. "The colonized man finds his freedom in and through violence": Frantz Fanon, *The Wretched of the Earth* (1961; Harmondsworth, 1967), p. 68; and chap. 1, "Concerning Violence." Yet in this context we might also wonder how far Fanon's formulation might be a form of romanticization.

21. A question asked in a different context by Stanley Trapido, "South Africa in a Comparative Study of Industrialisation," *Journal of Development Studies* 7. 3 (1971): 313.

things."[22] If we are taking the topic of madness seriously, it seems to me that we must try to determine the precise points at which it intervenes, and why, and how, rather than simply ascribe everything rhetorically to the "obvious" madness of racism. Racism, like madness, should also be seen as an *effect* of the colonial or apartheid situation, and not simply as an all-encompassing cause.

It is the great virtue of Doris Lessing's The Grass Is Singing (first published in 1950) that it provides the basis for an explanation in these terms.[23] Like Schreiner and Plomer, Lessing was very young when she wrote her novel—and this is important, because it means that all three writers were open to the symbolic dimensions of their immediate worlds, which in a sense were expressed through their writing, and which they had not fully controlled or distanced in their own lives. At the same time Lessing's novel provides a *material* setting, and a set of material explanations, for the growth, presence, and force of that symbolic dimension in her world.

My account here can by no means be exhaustive; as the novel is reasonably well known, all I shall do is point out a number of patterns. The story concerns a young white woman, not very talented, not well educated, who marries a young farmer in one of the rural districts of Southern Rhodesia (Zimbabwe) some time before the Second World War. The farmer has bad luck; he has bad vision economically; he falls prey to illness. The wife, largely confined to her run-down household, has a series of servants come to work for her; most leave because of her ill treatment of them. Once, on one of her rare forays out into the fields when her husband was ill, she had whipped a male fieldworker. When he later arrives to work in the house, the air becomes charged with sexual and psychological threat and promise. The woman falls into bouts of projection and fantasy; she sleeps longer and longer hours; the servant has to take care of her physically. Ultimately she descends into madness, and when the servant finally kills her it comes as the climax to which her whole life has led, but also as a release.

Recounted so plainly the story may appear melodramatic, but this does no justice to the intensity with which substantial themes are treated in the book. First, the novel reestablishes and then elaborates

22. *Economic and Philosophical Manuscripts*, in *Karl Marx: Selected Writings*, ed. David McLellan (Oxford, 1977), p. 78.
23. Doris Lessing, *The Grass Is Singing* (1950; Harmondsworth, 1961).

the colonial problematic identified earlier. Mary Turner, the white
woman, is profoundly alienated from the African continent. She
hates it, she fears it, she avoids any real contact with it. In place of
contact then comes projection: she feels the bush creeping in towards *her* (the significance of the title of the novel). At the same
time—and this is crucial for a history of colonial consciousness—
there is a symbolic displacement in her mind: the continent and its
indigenous inhabitants become identified, so that the idea of the
bush creeping in to get her is associated with the threat of the
Africans doing the same, and vice versa. Colonial consciousness feels
an overwhelming need to *tame* the foreign environment—Mary
Turner had whipped the fieldworker in the fields—but when *he*
comes *inside* her household—*untamed*, she fears—this symbolic
hierarchy is overturned: another definition of madness.

Economically, the novel is astute. It is set in a context of agricultural recession for the small, undercapitalized farmer in Rhodesia, when feelings of depression or despair would have been likely
to be at their height; this is a significant aspect of the processes we
are describing.[24] The question of *labor* then also becomes central.
A white political economy allows no equitable working relationship
with the local people. Therefore no common culture can develop:
one of Mary Turner's greatest fears is that her husband will become
just like the blacks who work for him. In the space that then opens
up between employer and worker all kinds of racist imaginings and
projections proliferate, especially in a period of "primitive accumulation," which is what we see on the farm. In addition, as discursive counterpart to the lack of equitable working relationships
there is in no sense any real dialogue on the farm. Colonial consciousness indulges in an obsessive, echoing monologue which, in
its vertiginous anxiety, reinforces the patterns of oppression and
exploitation from which it derives.

In Mary's case these issues are conjoined with that of her gender.
For in the colony white women are the most fetishized of objects,
but this, equally, cuts them off from any real contact with local
environment or people. In her own *household* Mary does no work:

24. For the overall impression of perennial crisis for small farmers in Zimbabwe
from the 1920s to the 1940s (particularly for those who did not participate in the
irregular tobacco booms of the period), see Ian Phimister, *An Economic and Social
History of Zimbabwe: Capital Accumulation and Class Struggle* (London, 1988),
chaps. 3–5.

she stands and watches her servant as he does it all, again a situation of potentially very great tension. What takes the place of work is fantasy, projection, displacement, repression—all of which are deeply embedded in Mary's framework of reality, which is itself embedded in the economic and social relationships of her situation. In this setting we see an *etiology* of racism and madness—an extraordinary achievement on Lessing's part. In itself her book is like a symbol—something that concentrates and distills what is going on beneath the surface in a wider context at large. Here we see again that the "return of the repressed" can signify on political and psychological levels at once. And we realize that for an oppressive colonial society what lies beyond the edge of its framework of reality is quite literally the threat of the "unknown," or madness.

Let me clarify this threat: obviously I do not think it is a *real* one, that is, when liberation or the revolution comes that all the oppressors will suddenly go mad. But it is their *perception or projection* of that threat at whatever buried levels that matters, that *produces* the theme of madness in the present. Similarly, not all colonial women explicitly suffer from Mary Turner's syndrome; but here we see the power of fiction to present in condensed form a contemplation of patterns more broadly or weakly dispersed through society, which may be activated under certain conditions, or else subliminally present all the time.

No account of this theme in the southern African setting would be complete without mention of Bessie Head's *A Question of Power*, a novel that offers one of the most stunning depictions of madness in African, if not in all, fiction.[25] The difficulty here is that this book requires exegesis all of its own. A few observations may be appropriate, however. As in Schreiner and Lessing, the madness of Elizabeth, the central character of *A Question of Power*, relates to a fundamental *alienation* from her environment—but not as a white, since Elizabeth is a "coloured" who has felt at home neither in South Africa, where she was born, nor in Botswana, where she has settled. As in Peter Abrahams's book, also about "coloureds," she too faces a crisis of identity, but *not* in relation to whites: Elizabeth's anguish lies in the fact that she does not feel properly African; and, according to all the patterns we have seen so far, she is also consequently

25. Bessie Head, *A Question of Power* (London, 1974); page references are given in the text.

susceptible to all sorts of projections, distortions, fears, and fantasies about African men particularly. These are manifested, again, in the form of her own obsessive monologue, rather than in any real dialogue with the characters who seem to plague her. As in Schreiner or Lessing, the fact that Elizabeth is a *woman* then is crucial, but in this case not because she is an oppressor or even half an oppressor. On the contrary, as someone who is not white, not African, and is a woman emerging out of the half-life of South Africa, Elizabeth is trebly a victim. Indeed, it becomes clear that Elizabeth's madness is inseparable from an entire social ethos and history of victimization—that the rawness of her exposed inwardness is the internal *incarnation* of external realities. Insofar as the novel offers a diagnosis for all of this it is that unwarranted assertions of power produce madness; but so too does unwarranted subservience to it, or too much goodness or oversensitivity in response—which may equally be tempted by a form of psychic power. The solution, interestingly enough for the patterns we have been describing, is one of ordinariness and *belonging*. The final lines of the book read as a prescription to remedy all the ills we have seen so far: "As [Elizabeth] fell asleep, she placed one soft hand over her land. It was a gesture of belonging" (p. 206).

The question, and I say this without trying to sound too ironical, is how we all can achieve that state.

III

At the outset I said that I would be raising certain hypotheses regarding the recurrent appearance of the theme of madness in southern African fiction. Some of these should by now be clear, from questions of alienation from the colonized environment for the colonizing culture, to alienation in working relationships. From Olive Schreiner to Bessie Head, issues of gender have been crucial. The syndromes associated with the theme of madness in these settings have included patterns of projection, displacement, and symbolic association—for instance, of the colonized people with the colonized continent. We have seen how an oppressive mental framework is subject to the threat of a return of the repressed, which signifies on political and psychological levels simultaneously. For the oppressed we have seen what relegation to the "unconscious" of a dominant culture signifies, and the difficulties and ambiguities involved in any "return."

To these ideas I should like to add that the concept of limits or limitation seems crucial. For this is what defines a framework of reality, what lies inside its boundaries and what outside, what is counted as sane and what is counted as mad, how far coherency is maintained and where it begins to break down; what exactly is *beyond the limit*, as it were. Indeed, one might say, following Michel Foucault, that the concept of madness is inseparable from the concept of a limit: as he sees it, "madness," as the object of policy and knowledge within Western culture, is the product of a historical division at the end of the Middle Ages which separated out the specter of the mad from the enclosure of the sane. Even as far as an analysis of this "madness" is concerned, Foucault remarks that "what is constitutive is the action that divides madness, and not the science [of psychopathology] elaborated once this division is made and calm restored."[26]

While broad references to Western culture may appear rather sweeping, nonetheless it does seem that in the colonial setting the analytical consideration of madness is intrinsically connected with a search for significant limits. Thus, as a partial explanation for the recurrence of this theme in the fiction, one might point out that seldom has the idea of limits been so important as it was in colonial cultural formations in Africa. Mannoni suggests that the incipient colonial consciousness is, on the contrary, characterized by its quest for *limitlessness*. In other words, in the colony the (usually male) colonizer seeks a world of limitless play and power unchecked by customary moral authority or any other form of reality principle.[27] While this may be the case in the *prospective imagination* (Mannoni draws interestingly on Shakespeare and Defoe to make his point), on the other hand, it may be argued that once the colony is in operation it depends profoundly on the idea and reality of limits. Indeed, the colony is founded upon delimitations that divide the colonizers from the colonized. This is true in terms of land ownership; of economic and political rights; of living areas and forms

26. Michel Foucault, *Madness and Civilization: A History of Insanity in the Age of Reason*, trans. Richard Howard (1965; New York, 1973), chap. 1, and p. ix.

27. O. Mannoni, *Prospero and Caliban: The Psychology of Colonization*, trans. Pamela Powesland (London, 1956), pt. 2, chap. 1, "Crusoe and Prospero"; to this extent the colonial project is also, for Mannoni, inherently infantile.

of social interaction; of cultural patterns of behavior, attitude, and response. Without this the whole raison d'être as well as modus vivendi of the colony falls apart, if one thinks of anything ranging from the extraction of surplus value (land appropriation, the control of resources, control of labor) to forms of local, global, and strategic power. In this context, for those within the colony, it is no surprise that lines of symbolic demarcation form an integral part of these other kinds of delineation.

Any number of examples, both general and particular, reinforce this understanding. In his discussion of the "invention of tradition" in colonial Africa, Terence Ranger points out that what character-ized colonialism on that continent was that it was a colonialism of *settlement;* therefore what it required in order to establish both legitimacy and effectivity were traditions of mastery and control. Implicitly and explicitly this involved the setting up of boundaries where the symbolic dimension was significant: thus, there was a need for white farmers to represent themselves as "gentlemen farm-ers"; even lower-order occupations in the home countries, such as those of hunters, traders, storekeepers, policemen, and missionaries were gentrified in this way in the colony.[28] As well as inventing traditions of control, dialectical consistency meant that traditions of *subordination,* too, needed to be invented:

> Embedded in the neo-traditions of governance and subordination, there were very clear-cut requirements for the observance of industrial time and work discipline—the neatly, even fanatically, prescribed segments of the schoolboys' day at Budo; the drill square as source and symbol of punctuality. On the other hand, the invented traditions which were introduced to Africans were those of governance rather than of production.[29]

The fact that these rituals were of "governance rather than pro-duction" does not contradict the point being made here: that the symbolic economy of the colony is productive in its own way; more-over, that it is one that puts a premium on limits, boundaries, and order in time as well as social space as part of an extended, over-

28. Terence Ranger, "The Invention of Tradition in Colonial Africa," in Eric Hobs-bawm and Terence Ranger, eds., *The Invention of Tradition* (Cambridge, 1983), pp. 211–12, 218.

29. Ibid., p. 228. The school referred to was the famous King's College, Budo, Uganda, especially established for the sons of the Baganda aristocracy, pp. 221–23.

arching, everyday allegory of control. Ironically, even in terms of indigenous African "tradition," Ranger points out that colonial administrators were induced to invent all sorts of fixities of identity and social hierarchy—for instance the concept of a tribal identity itself—where the reality had been much more fluid in the past.[30] Again the logic of subordination produced the compulsion of delimitation.

If these generalized accounts seem too broad, one might turn to more particular analyses. Thus, through Charles van Onselen's discussion of the social history of domestic servitude on the Witwatersrand at the turn of the century (although set in a different time and place, this is of some relevance for *The Grass Is Singing*) it becomes evident that the idea of limits (or, conversely, transgression) was central to it as an institution. Where white female servants were meant to work alongside black males, the logic of racial boundaries overrode those of gender and class: the females were soon supervising the blacks at their labor. Where, because of demographic necessity, white children were initially looked after by black male nurses, as soon as conditions changed the symbolic limits were erected once again, and the feeling became that "the Kaffir is not the person to be placed in charge of young children." In any number of ways servants were marked off from their employers: degrading uniforms and names, even a degraded language of command and response (the kitchen-language of *fanakalo*), demarcated zones and forms of interaction.[31] The fact that these limits were significant is attested to by the response when they were transgressed. One letter to a Johannesburg newspaper complained about the behavior of domestic servants on Sundays, "attired in the most up-to-date costumes, and carrying canes and sticks... swaggering along using English lan-

30. Ibid., pp. 248–51. Some of Ranger's more categorical statements on the extent to which colonial administrations "invented" the African cultural past should perhaps, however, be treated with caution.

31. Charles van Onselen, "The Witches of Suburbia," in his *Studies in the Social and Economic History of the Witwatersrand 1886–1914*, vol. 2, *New Nineveh* (London, 1982), pp. 24, 28, 38–39. Uniforms for domestic laborers were introduced later than the period van Onselen deals with, but he demonstrates a manifest anxiety on the part of employers over the symbolism of "equal" clothing. His account also suggests that one of the limits in this setting had even to do with speech and silence: "masters and mistresses spent an endless amount of time talking about their servants—and not infrequently... in the presence of an apparently deaf-mute 'houseboy'" (pp. 39–40).

guage of the most appalling description"; this sort of pastiche seems
to have been common in many colonial settings.[32] Almost inevitably, however, the greatest symbolic weight was attached to the
boundaries around white womanhood. So-called black peril scares,
concerning the rape of white women by black men, were as regular
as the economic crises that attacked the Witwatersrand; and where
sexual relationships across the color line did take place (usually
between white women and black men), a Commisssion of Enquiry
in the wake of one black peril scare put these down to "sexual
perversion on the part of the female."[33] The only way, it seems, in
which white women could transgress the limits set up to protect
them was through abnormality and deviance.

It is at moments such as this that one senses the *anxiety* underlying the enforcement of limits in the colonial or developing apartheid situation. Indeed, it seems that we can speak of an *anxiety of
limits* in general, both promoting and then reinforced through these
demarcations. If the colonial powers contracted and rigidified indigenous African identities, they certainly did the same for themselves: one senses the potential repression and self-alienation
that attend such processes and which, we might say, emerge in the
fictions of transgression and limitation we have discussed. If
white farmers felt themselves ipso facto "gentrified," what emotional and psychological pressures were put on those who were de-
monstrably *not* gentry, such as the couple that Lessing depicts in
her novel? An understanding of this dimension of symbolic action
adds to our sense of the intensity of the struggle over limits in that
book.

In a different context George L. Mosse has shown that nationalism
and sexuality, when yoked together by bourgeois morality in the
guise of "respectability," have constituted an alliance of tremendous
social and cultural force in Europe since the late eighteenth century.
In nationalist movements the idea of womanhood was held up as
the epitome of virtue; but where an unlicensed sexuality threatened
the respectability of the status quo, this was also a mode of social
control.[34] How much worse it was then in the colony, where the

---

32. Bertie C. Simes to the Editor, *The Star*, May 8, 1912, quoted in ibid., p. 33.

33. Van Onselen, "The Witches of Suburbia," pp. 45–54.

34. George L. Mosse, *Nationalism and Sexuality: Respectability and Abnormal
Sexuality in Modern Europe* (New York, 1985). Though Mosse's book is, as it states,
about modern Europe, when applied to the colonial situation the patterns he dem-

fervor underlying the symbolic allegiances of nationalism was intensified, and where the constrictions upon women, enforced with greater rigor because of the greater need to be respectable and *uphold* limits, were correspondingly increased. This would help explain the fact that it was in the form of her womanhood that Olive Schreiner experienced her colonial alienation (unredressed in both respects, of course, when she went to London). Indeed, if sexuality is where desire is active and transgression controlled, it becomes a key symbolic marker for colonialism, not only because it upholds the boundaries preventing miscegenation, but because it represents also the limit and shape of a whole order of being. Yet, if there is such intensity about the limit, one may surely posit a sense of potential crisis that underlies it—the ever-present threat of transgression in the colony—usually displaced, in the symbolic order of things, onto the role and position of women.[35]

From this point of view everything about colonialism was ambiguous and self-contradictory, promoting its own anxiety at the same time as it enforced its dominance. Indeed, there was a contradiction at the heart of the nationalist endeavor in the foreign environment. Mosse points out that European nationalism drew heavily on ideas of nature: "Nature symbolized a healthy world. . . . Indeed, nature was perceived as the native landscape, its mountains and valleys inspiring the members of one particular nation but alien to all others."[36] To this one might add that the three keywords associated here, "nation," "nature," and "native" all come from the same Latin root "to be born." Yet if nationalism attached itself to a *native* environment in the home country, hence its doubled anxiety in the colony, where *nature* was in fact *alien*. The logic of nationalism, which by extension is the logic of colonialism, contradicts itself in the colony: here the natives were not the European nationalists, and vice versa, and nature was certainly not perceived

---

onstrates are extremely suggestive. "If a woman was idealized, she was at the same time put firmly into her place. Those who did not live up to the ideal were perceived as a menace to society and the nation, threatening the established order they were intended to uphold" (p. 90).

35. I am partly indebted for this point to a discussion with Donna Harraway. For a recent article exploring this issue, see Dorothy Driver, " 'Woman' as Sign in the South African Colonial Enterprise," *Journal of Literary Studies* 4 (March 1988): 3–20.

36. Mosse, *Nationalism and Sexuality*, p. 183.

as healthy. Instead of an autochthonous, self-verifying identity, European nationalism had very shallow roots in the colony; hence the symbolic slippage, identifying the "natives" with *their* local nature, which so threatened the hierarchies of the colonists. By its own symbolic rules, then, the colony conceded its illegitimacy on foreign ground (an illegitimacy clouded over by generations of bluster, which did not of course necessarily reduce the anxiety underlying it). Ironically, the colony was excluded externally and threatened internally through its own initiating and inspiring sense of limits. The deep-seated crises associated with this pattern come to light in the fiction because fiction works in this symbolic territory, mediating between the conscious and unconscious, limit and transgression, the unsaid and the sayable, and because one of its primary functions is to activate potential history as a sense of what might occur.

Finally, one might take from Mosse the point that what European nationalism did attempt to set up outside its limits were interchangeable categories: the inferior races (Jews, blacks, and so on), homosexuals, the criminal, and the insane.[37] Where inferiority, deviance, or insanity defined within a whole mental framework what lay outside its boundaries, is it any wonder that fictions that approached the edges of those limits should appreciate the stakes in terms of an allegory of (or in some cases the reality of) madness? Or that works approaching these limits from the "other side," as it were, should be traversing, in a different direction, the same ground? From this point of view the notion of limits is crucial to our theme.

IV

It will be a matter of exploration to see whether the limits of particular texts—defining their unconscious, so to speak—will always coincide with the limits of the broader frameworks of which they are a part, and define accurately questions of madness. For the moment, however, I want to develop the idea of limit in one more sense—the *historical* sense. For the question becomes, What happens to a society in conflict as a dominant framework of reality

37. Ibid., chap. 7, "Race and Sexuality: The Role of the Outsider," esp. pp. 133–40; see also Gilman, *Difference and Pathology*, chap. 5, "On the Nexus of Blackness and Madness," and chap. 6, "The Madness of the Jews."

reaches its limits *in time*, and begins to break down? In conclusion I want to address this question briefly by bringing the story that I have been tracing up to date, suggesting what is happening in South Africa today and indicating some notable patterns.[38]

As far as white writing is concerned, the pattern is roughly as follows. In the 1970s, as Mozambique and Angola were liberated, and the war in Zimbabwe began, a phase of resistance in South Africa was initiated that has lasted to the present day. In these circumstances it became apparent that the dominant order was beginning to crumble. Once again the theme of madness entered South African fiction, and what it signified now was the ending of that order. Gordimer's *The Conservationist* linked the notions of political oppression and psychological repression, and foretold the doom of its white-capitalist central figure, Mehring, who ends up in total crisis and/or mad.[39] In J. M. Coetzee's *In the Heart of the Country* (again *that* sort of title) his central character Magda lives out a psychofantasy on a deserted white farm, having reached, among other things, what appears to be the end of a white mental line.[40] In both novels, written in the mid–1970s, there was an interesting shift. Whereas the dominant form of South African fiction up to then had been realism, both writers were now fusing this with a hauntingly symbolic kind of vision. We might say that realism represented the world as it existed, while the symbolic was coming to signify the repressed, the unknown, or the future. Madness was always presented in a symbolic mode.

Black writing was beginning to tell a different story. Thus, in Mongane Serote's *To Every Birth Its Blood*, it is the framework of the *present* which is madness.[41] In the first half of that novel its central character, Tsi Molope, is caught in a world of degradation and breakdown from which there appears to be no escape. In the second half, however, there is a shift. There the book focuses on a *group*, who work *collectively*, as members of the underground, to-

38. This section draws on Stephen Clingman, "Revolution and Reality: South African Fiction in the 1980s," in Martin Trump, ed., *Rendering Things Visible: Essays on South African Literary Culture* (Johannesburg, 1990).

39. Nadine Gordimer, *The Conservationist* (1974; New York, 1975). For extended commentary along these lines see Clingman, *The Novels of Nadine Gordimer*, chap. 5, "Prophecy and Subversion: *The Conservationist*."

40. J. M. Coetzee, *In the Heart of the Country* (1977; Johannesburg, 1978).

41. Mongane Serote, *To Every Birth Its Blood* (1981; London, 1983).

ward a new political dispensation. This appears to be the recovery of sanity and humanity that was foreclosed to Peter Abrahams. Significantly, this novel displays a modal reversal compared to the white writing. Symbolism conveys the madness of the present—the "unknown" present for blacks—but it is a new *realism* within and toward which the second half of the book moves, signifying, I think, the idea of a new and rational future.

I should like to end with one observation. For all South African writers at present, black and white, their fiction has shifted from representations of mental conditions to a focus on physical realities or resistance: that is, we see a shift from mind to body. In Gordimer's *July's People*, the central character, Maureen, escapes the mental as well as social breakdown of her world by running toward the future; Hillela, in *A Sport of Nature*, finds the future entirely through her body. In both of J. M. Coetzee's latest works, *Life & Times of Michael K* and *Foe*, the fundamental reality of the body represents his last word, so to speak. In Serote's work it is the collective black social body which prepares the ground of its own future; Njubelo Ndebele, in his collection of short stories, *Fools*, combines a sense of the township community as social body with a focus on a new kind of mental interiority which must sustain it.[42] What is the significance of this? I think it is that for blacks as well as whites the limits of a dominant framework of reality have been reached, and there is a need for a new one to be made. The writers suggest in their fiction that under whatever new dispensation emerges, issues of physical and mental liberation will be closely connected.

42. Nadine Gordimer, *July's People* (London, 1981). For commentary along these lines see Clingman, *The Novels of Nadine Gordimer*, chap. 6. Gordimer, *A Sport of Nature* (London, 1987). J. M. Coetzee, *Life & Times of Michael K* (London, 1983); *Foe* (Johannesburg, 1986). Njabulo S. Ndebele, *Fools and Other Stories* (1983; London, 1986).

9

The Subversive Poetics
of Radical Bilingualism:
Postcolonial Francophone
North African Literature

SAMIA MEHREZ

> La France veut que les petits Arabes soient aussi bien
> instruits que les petits Français. Cela prouve que la France
> est bonne et généreuse pour les peuples qu'elle a soumis.
> (France wants young Arabs to be as well educated as the
> young French. This proves that France is good and gen-
> erous to the people it has subdued.)
>
> —Ernest Lavisse
>
> Sooner or later Algeria will become the bloody arena for
> a mortal combat between the two peoples with mercy
> neither offered nor accepted.
>
> —Alexis de Tocqueville

The opening statement in Samir Amin's *The Maghreb in the Modern World:* "Maghreb, in Arabic, signifies the West," provides an
economy for the contextualization of North Africa (that is, the
maghrib) as a geographic, historical, and cultural area. On the one
hand, it situates the *maghrib* in its relation with the *mashriq* (the
Middle East) as the Other: different, distant, and unfamiliar.[1] Such

---

1. The first epigraph comes from the noted French historian Ernest Lavisse's

are the characteristics bestowed upon the area in Arabic lexicography. On the other hand, Amin's statement equally foregrounds the contradictions and tensions that lie within the very etymology of the name *maghrib:* to be at once east and west.

The francophone Algerian writer Nabile Farès further extends and elaborates the other possible significations of the Arabic root *gharaba* (from which *maghrib,* the place name, is derived).[2] *Gharaba* also means to be or become strange, to be or become alien, to be or become in exile, to be or become other. If we consider, along with Farès, that this territory, that is, North Africa, has been the object of consecutive waves of linguistic, economic, religious, and political domination, the last of which has been the French colonial presence; that the word *maghrib* itself is a received designation, given by others, namely medieval Arab geographers, then we may begin to envision the potential double exile, the double otherness of francophone North African writers: all those who by choice or the lack of it have continued to write in the language of the French colonizer.

One of the legacies of the French *mission civilisatrice* in North Africa has been the creation of intellectual elites, products of the French colonial system of education. By way of upgrading the natives on the evolutionary scale, the members of such elites were

---

history textbook, which was taught in colonial North African primary schools well into the 1940s. The quotation appears in Raoul Girardet, *L'Idée coloniale en France de 1871 à 1962* (Paris, 1972). Girardet refers to this history textbook as "le petit Lavisse" to underline both the status and influence of Lavisse, as a historian, and the wide circulation of the text as well. This brief passage, which presents itself as a commonsensical truth for children, is a perfect example of the discourse of colonialism about itself and its Other. Moreover, it exposes the political agenda of the *mission civilisatrice,* as well as the internal contradictions of such an agenda, even as it attempts to disguise and cast them in more readily accepted terms. The French colonial enterprise in North Africa began in 1830 with the fall of Algiers and gradually expanded to include Tunisia and Morocco, both declared French "protectorates" in 1881 and 1912, respectively. The second epigraph is from Melvin Richter, "Tocqueville on Algeria," *The Review of Politics* 25.3 (1963): 362–98, analyzing Tocqueville's contradictory positions on the Algerian question. Richter argues that Tocqueville's views of the French colonial enterprise in North Africa circumscribe the limits of his otherwise penetrating insight as a liberal humanist. This quotation is one of the more lucid observations made by Tocqueville on Algeria, if compared to his comments as regards Islamic societies, assimilation, and colonial rule. See Samir Amin, *The Maghreb in the Modern World* (Harmondsworth, 1970).

2. Nabile Farès is quoted in Luc Barbulesco and Philippe Cardinal, *L'Islam en questions* (Paris, 1986), p. 225.

referred to as *les évolués* (those who have evolved). Contrary to the assimilationist role assigned to them by the French, and in keeping with many other examples of colonial situations, *les évolués* became the vanguard of the resistance to, and contestation of, French politicocultural domination—despite the initial unease, ambivalence, even guilt about their own status as colonial/postcolonial, bilingual/bicultural subjects. In all three North African nation states (Tunisia: 1956, Morocco: 1956, and Algeria: 1962) the decolonization process, both in its political and intellectual sense, was and still is conditioned and shaped, to a great extent, by the writings of such *évolués*.

It is true that literary production in Arabic has increased since independence, and that some writers, like Kateb Yacine and Rachid Boudjedra, have abandoned French for Arabic.[3] Nevertheless, it is equally true that many other writers continue to produce works in French, and in "the metropole." Rather than entertaining the thought of belonging totally to the French literary tradition, these writers have assumed their bilingualism as an effective means with which to contest all forms of domination, and all kinds of exclusion. For, as the Moroccan literary critic Abdelfattah Kilito has remarked in his penetrating article "Les Mots canins," "Le complexe du mutisme vaut celui de la castration.... Ce n'est pas un malheur irréparable de perdre *sa* langue, mais le malheur suprême consiste à perdre *la* langue, le morceau de chair qui se loge dans la bouche."[4]

Hence, the proliferation of francophone North African literature

3. Kateb Yacine is an interesting example of the kinds of adjustments that the francophone North African writer must make once he or she decides to abandon French and start writing in Arabic. When Kateb finally took the decision, he found it necessary to change the literary medium in which he communicated. He moved from the novel to the popular drama which he wrote in the Algerian dialect. His reasons for doing so were twofold: first, he had not been schooled in literary Arabic, the idiom of the Arabic novel, but more important, he felt that his role, as a writer, had changed after independence. During the 1950s it was essential for North African writers to be heard by French public opinion. After independence, however, the urgent message was for the writer's own people. Hence the popular theater which Kateb Yacine started in the 1970s, and which, on several occasions, has been banned by the Algerian authorities.

4. Abdelfattah Kilito, "Les Mots canins," in *Du Bilinguisme* (Paris, 1985), p. 216: "The complex of muteness is no better than that of castration. It is not an irremediable misfortune to lose *one*'s tongue [that is, language]; the ultimate misfortune is to lose *the* tongue, that piece of flesh that sits inside one's mouth" (my translation).

over the past four decades must be read as a willingness to accept the recent past, as well as to confront the actual present.[5] Unfortunately, despite the quantity and quality of this literary production, francophone North African writers have yet to occupy the space and the attention that their doubly significant works merit, both in the context of the Arab world and in Western institutions as well.

Decolonization, as many of these bilingual postcolonial writers understand and define it, is never simply the physical ousting of the colonial presence. Nor is it a recanting of the evils of the colonial period as opposed to the virtues of "traditional culture." Rather, decolonization has been, and continues to be, an active confrontation with a hegemonic system of thought and hence a process of historical and cultural liberation. As such, decolonization becomes the contestation of all dominant forms and structures whether they be linguistic, discursive, or ideological. Moreover, decolonization comes to be understood as an act of exorcism for both the colonized and the colonizer. For both parties it must be a process of liberation: from dependency, in the case of the colonized, and from imperialist, racist perceptions, representations, and institutions which, unfortunately, remain with us till this very day, in the case of the colonizer.[6]

Historically, and because of our conventional and limited definition of decolonization, the colonized have shouldered the burden of the process alone. Decolonization can only be complete, however, when it is understood as a complex process that involves both the colonizer and the colonized. Just as they were

5. Charles Bonn, "Le Roman maghrébin de langue française," *Magazine littéraire* 251 (1988): 34–36. In this article Bonn supplies the statistics for the increasing francophone literary production, based on Jean Dejeux's research in *Littérature maghrébine de langue française* (Sherbrooke, Canada, 1973). Since 1945–50 more than 200 francophone novels have been published. This literary production has multiplied since 1973, from more than 5 novels each year in 1969 and 1970, to an annual average of 10 to 20, not to mention the re-prints.

6. Several Arab intellectuals have undertaken projects that dismantle hegemonic institutions by exposing their ethnocentric, Eurocentric, and even racist attitudes toward the "object" of their study. Among such prominent intellectuals are Edward Said, *Orientalism* (New York, 1979); Anwar Abdel Malek, "Orientalism in Crisis," in *Diogenes* 44 (Winter 1963): 103–40; Abdelkebir Khatibi, "L'Orientalisme désorienté," in *Maghreb pluriel* (Paris, 1983), pp. 113–46; Abdallah Laroui, *The History of the Maghreb* (Princeton, N.J., 1977).

both involved in the colonial fact from the outset, so too will they each have a role to play in reversing or subverting it. Indeed, for postcolonial writers to engage in any kind of counterhegemonic agenda, those against whom they are reacting must be prepared to listen. Otherwise, such postcolonial attempts at total decolonization will remain peripheral, and can at best be described as a kind of monologue. For constructive dialogue to begin to take place, the colonizer must be equally prepared to become decolonized. As Barbara Harlow has put it, in a slightly different context, in her book *Resistance Literature:*

> It has become again necessary to challenge the presuppositions and premises of the academic enterprise and the activities which it enjoins and which are used to sustain an internationalization of the issues of development according to western-specific models or patterns. Literature and literary studies themselves, as part of the academic enterprise, are being contested by the cultural and ideological expressions of resistance, armed struggle, liberation, and social revolution in those geopolitical regions referred to as the "Third World."[7]

In the context of our discussion of francophone North African literature, Harlow's message becomes doubly complicated, for here we are dealing with a literary corpus that uses those very same "western-specific models or patterns" in order to subvert them and to create a new literary space that would disrupt national boundries and cultural hierarchies.

Since the true process of decolonization depends on the confrontation with, and the dismantling of, hegemonic structures, it is no surprise that one can discern two types of literary contestation in the development of francophone North African literature. One type is the body of literature that adopts a passive form of contestation, which can be described as a colonial bilingualism. Such a literary production has remained prisoner of Western literary models and standards; it continues to be restrained by the dominant form and language, even as it speaks in the voice of the victim. The other type of literary production challenges its own indigenous, conventional models as well as the dominant structures and institutions of the colonizer. This kind of literary production can be called "rad-

7. Barbara Harlow, *Resistance Literature* (London, 1987), p. 14.

ical bilingualism."[8] By setting itself a double task, a "double critique," radical bilingualism reformulates the whole debate over national literatures and redefines the very nature of postcolonial
bilingualism.[9]

It is this radical bilingualism that will allow us to speak of a
subversive poetics: a poetics that seeks to create a new literary space
for the bilingual, postcolonial writer. It is a space that subverts
hierarchies, whether they be linguistic or cultural; where separate
systems of signification and different symbolic worlds are brought
together in a relation of perpetual interference, interdependence and
intersignification. By so doing, this subversive poetics not only challenges our conventions of reading and writing, but it also questions
the structuring of institutions of learning and disciplinary boundaries. Finally, such a poetics becomes a statement on the process of
decolonization itself, where the latter is to be read as a two-sided
rather than one-sided endeavor; a process in which both colonizer
and colonized are implicated, where both parties are constantly written and rewritten.

It is by adopting such strategies that this subversive poetics actively transforms imposed constraints (bilingualism/biculturalism)
into risky opportunities. In creating a new literary space for themselves, francophone North African writers are imposing challenging
requirements in order for the reader, Western or otherwise, to decode
their texts. Their radical bilingualism demands that Western-
specific models and standards be rewritten to accommodate their
own linguistic and cultural experiences as colonial/postcolonial subjects. Until this demand is fulfilled, the opportunities created by
such writers will remain risky; until we can form readers who can
decode such texts, this radical bilingualism can easily become yet
another constraint, in which the writer will remain on the margins
of literary institutions and disciplinary boundaries.

8. This term was coined by the Moroccan writer Abdelkebir Khatibi. It appears
in an interview in *Les Nouvelles littéraires* 2518 (Febrary 1976), quoted in Jean Dejeux,
Situation de la littérature maghrébine de langue française: 1920–1978 (Algiers, 1982).

9. In one of his articles in *Maghreb pluriel* (Paris: Denoel, 1983), Khatibi sets two
tasks for the Arab intellectuals in order to truly decolonize Arab sociology. In what
he calls a double criticism, Arab intellectuals must deconstruct the Occident's logo-
centrism and ethnocentrism, which affect the whole world, and they must equally
deconstruct and critique the learned discourses that the Arab world has elaborated
around and about itself.

In this article I want to examine the elements for the elaboration of such a subversive poetics in the works of two major North African writers: the Tunisian Albert Memmi and the Moroccan Abdelkebir Khatibi. Whereas Memmi's work provided an early locus for a radical bilingualism that remained constrained by the colonial relationship, Khatibi's literary output has become a remarkable exploration of the parameters for a subversive poetics. My discussion of these two writers, as examples of colonial bilingualism and radical bilingualism, respectively, in no way seeks to establish a kind of linear development in francophone North African literature. Indeed, both kinds of bilingualism(s) coexist till this very day, and examples of radical bilingualism can be traced back to works that predate independence.[10]

Albert Memmi's writing, alongside Frantz Fanon's, has provided some of the earliest reflections on racism, colonialism, and the situation of the postcolonial intellectual. Like Fanon's, Memmi's work has taken the dimensions of a lifetime project, as can be readily demonstrated from a whole range of titles.[11] Both his novels and his long essays have provided important groundwork for others who found themselves in similar situations of discrimination, racism, dependency, and colonialism. Moreover, his experience as a colonized subject was complicated by the fact that he was a French-educated Jew, from a working-class background, with a Berber mother, living in a predominantly Arabo-Islamic society. It is this overcharged personal situation that provided the seed for his critical reflections on the colonial relationship, among other significant issues. Memmi's work is crucial not only for its intellectual value, but also for its portrayal of a social and cultural North African landscape that both colonization, and the eventual creation of the state of Israel, have gradually destroyed.

In his long essay *Portrait du colonisé*, Memmi describes the typical behavior of a colonized people as it is generated within a colonial relationship. For, as he argues, the existence of a colo-

10. I am thinking particularly of Kateb Yacine's *Nedjma* (Paris, 1956) which remains the classic of francophone North African literature and perhaps one of the earliest examples of radical bilingualism.

11. The following are some of the most relevant of Memmi's works: *Portrait d'un juif* (Paris, 1962); *La Libération d'un juif* (Paris, 1966); *L'Homme dominé* (Paris, 1968); *La Dépendance* (Paris, 1979); *Le Racisme* (Paris, 1982); *Les Français et le racisme* (Paris, 1965); *Juifs et Arabes* (Paris, 1974).

nizer requires and imposes a mythic image of the colonized. If colonization is to be at all justifiable then the colonized must be invented as lazy, good-for-nothing, depersonalized, unreliable, and last but not least, mutilated both socially and historically.[12] These are good reasons for being colonized, and thanks to the political economy of colonization itself, the colonized subject gradually internalizes, confirms, and acts out daily, even during and after the liberation struggle, the negative image invented and imposed upon him or her. Thus, the colonized subjects slowly justify the existence of the benevolent colonizer and contribute to the construction of the real image of the colonized, now no longer simply a myth. This mechanism is what Memmi refers to as mystification: "L'idéologie d'une classe dirigeante, on le sait, se fait adopter dans une large mesure par les classes dirigées. Or toute idéologie de combat comprend, partie intégrante d'elle-même, une conception de l'adversaire. En consentant à cette idéologie, les classes dominées confirment, d'une certaine manière, le rôle qu'on leur a assigné."[13]

Needless to say, colonial institutions have played a key role in creating and reinforcing this mechanism of mystification. According to Memmi, two extreme dynamics are generated as a means to contend with these hegemonic structures: to remain grounded in tradition, or to seek total assimilation.[14] In the first case, traditional structures are overvalued as a substitute for an impossible social transformation, impeded by the existence of the colonial institutions. In the latter case, the hopeless attempt at assimilation becomes the only alternative to the colonized's own mutilated past, and their deprivation and gradual loss of collective memory. In this effort to assimilate, perfect mastery of the dominant language becomes a necessity. If the colonized are to be saved from illiteracy,

12. Albert Memmi, *Portrait du colonisé, précédé du portrait du colonisateur* (Paris, 1957), pp. 109–13.

13. Ibid., p. 117: "It is common knowledge that the ideology of a governing class is adopted in large measure by the governed classes. Now every ideology of combat includes as an integral part of itself a conception of the adversary. By agreeing to this ideology, the dominated classes practically confirm the role assigned to them." All translated passages are from Albert Memmi, *The Colonizer and the Colonized*, trans. Howard Greenfeld (Boston, 1965). This passage appears on p. 88.

14. Memmi, *Portrait du colonisé*, pp. 123–30.

if they are to succeed in carving some space for themselves, they must parrot the master. In the preface to *Portrait du colonisé*, Memmi offers himself as a typical example of such behavior: "Si j'étais indéniablement un indigène, comme on disait alors, aussi près que possible du Musulman, par l'insupportable misère de nos pauvres, par la langue maternelle, . . . par la sensibilité et les moeurs, le goût pour la même musique et les mêmes parfums, par une cuisine presque identique, j'ai tenté passionnément de m'identifier au Français."[15]

Memmi goes on to tell us that such identification with the colonizer proves to be impossible. In fact, assimilation would ultimately constitute a disservice for the colonizer, for it would negate the legitimated presence of colonialism. When equality is denied, the colonized begin to assert their difference. Such difference, however, will be articulated in very much the same terms as those originally invented by the colonizer as a justification for the colonial fact.[16]

This self-perpetuating vicious circle Memmi defines as the colonial relationship that enchains both colonizer and colonized: "La relation Coloniale enchaînait le Colonisateur et le Colonisé dans une espèce de dépendance implacable, façonnait leurs traits respectifs et dictait leurs conduites."[17]

In fact, the full title of Memmi's book is *Portrait du colonisé, précédé du portrait du colonisateur*. Memmi's insistence on presenting the two long essays back to back, with that of the colonizer preceding that of the colonized, as the initial perpetrator of this enchaining relationship, underscores the main thesis of the book. If the colonizer created a mythic portrait of the colonized to justify and sustain the colonial enterprise, then, Memmi argues, in their self-assertion, and even in the revolutionary phase, the colonized will create a countermyth, but a myth all the same. Hence Memmi's

15. Ibid., p. 17: "[I was] undeniably [a native] as they were then called, as near as possible to the Moslems in poverty, language, sensibilities, customs, taste in music, odors, and cooking. However, unlike the Moslems, [I] passionately endeavored to identify [myself] with the French" (p. xiv).

16. Memmi, *Portrait du colonisé*, p. 164.

17. Ibid., p. 12: "The colonial relationship which I have tried to define chained the colonizer and the colonized into an implacable dependence, molded their respective characters and dictated their conduct" (p. ix).

colonial relationship is not limited to the physical presence of a colonizer; rather his definition extends itself to encompass a psychointellectual signification of colonization.

Indeed, Memmi's conclusions are not unlike Fanon's in *The Wretched of the Earth*. After having argued that movements such as Negritude, Pan-Arabism, or Pan-Africanism have been racialized reactions to the colonial racist reality, Fanon concludes: "The historical necessity in which the men of African culture find themselves to racialize their claims and to speak more of African culture than of national culture will tend to lead them up a blind alley."[18]

How then does the postcolonial bilingual/bicultural writer break out of Fanon's blind alley? How do such writers unchain themselves from what Memmi has called the colonial relationship? Is it sufficient for such writers to "dare speak" in the master language in order to expose the atrocities of the colonial fact? Or is it more crucial for them to determine *how* they speak in the dominant language? The answer to decolonization or contestation is not simply to wrench away a speaking subject-position. For the crucial questions are what kind of subject-position is being sought, what are the implications of such a choice, which voice(s) do the colonized subjects adopt, where will they position themselves vis-à-vis the dominant language and dominant discursive modes? How will they transform their own stagnant traditions rather than simply reproduce them in the same manner defined by the colonizer? And, ultimately, can the colonized decolonize both themselves and their colonizer as well, while still writing in the master language?

Published in 1953, Memmi's first novel, *La Statue de sel*, provides the seed for an answer to such questions. There is a brief moment in this otherwise linear, conventional, semiautobiographical narrative, written in good, classic French, which could have been the locus for a subversive poetics, a moment that could have turned constraints into opportunities. Unfortunately, this moment of insight, with thought-provoking implications for the bilingual postcolonial writer, remains suppressed, to remind us perhaps of the limitations of contestation within the context of the enchaining colonial relationship.

18. Frantz Fanon, *The Wretched of the Earth* (New York, 1968), p. 214.

The entire text of *La Statue de sel* is presented to the reader as a lengthy, seven-hour, written answer to an examination question, "Analyse the influence of Condillac on John Stuart Mill," which the Tunisian Alexandre Mordekhai Benillouche is preparing in Algiers, the "provisional capital" of the still colonized Algeria, in order to become a professor of philosophy in the colonial educational system.[19] His answer, however, has nothing to do with the original examination question, for he now understands that "ces devoirs ne [le] concernent plus."[20] Hence *La Statue de sel* begins with Mordekhai's childhood on the borders of the Jewish ghetto in Tunis and continues with his years in the French lycée, his revolt against his father and his traditional background, his struggle and failure to become assimilated, the concentration camps in Tunisia during the Second World War, and the consolidation of the Arab nationalist movement against French colonization in North Africa. Finally, the novel ends with Mordekhai's complete alienation and eventual departure for Argentina.

Toward the end of the section entitled l'épreuve," Mordekhai sums up his life in the following manner:

> Moi je suis mal à l'aise dans mon pays natal et n'en connais pas d'autre, ma culture est d'emprunt et ma langue maternelle infirme, je n'ai plus de croyances, de religion, de tradition et j'ai honte de ce qui en eux résiste au fond de moi.... Je suis Tunisien mais Juif, c'est-à-dire politiquement, socialement exclu, parlant la langue du pays avec un accent particulier, mal accordé passionellement à ce qui émeut les musulmans; juif mais ayant rompu avec la religion juive et le ghetto, ignorant de la culture juive et détestant la bourgeoisie inauthentique; je suis pauvre enfin et j'ai ardemment désiré en finir avec la pauvreté, mais j'ai refusé de faire ce qu'il fallait.[21]

19. Albert Memmi, *La Statue de sel* (Paris, 1953), p. 12: "Etudiez les élements condillaciens dans la philosophie de Stuart Mill." All translated passages are from Albert Memmi, *The Pillar of Salt*, trans. Edouard Roditi (New York, 1955). This passage is from p. ix.

20. Memmi, *La Statue*, p. 13: "These tasks no longer concern me" (p. viii).

21. Memmi, *La Statue*, p. 364: "I am ill at ease in my own land and I know of no other. My culture is borrowed and I speak my mother tongue haltingly. I have neither religious beliefs nor tradition, and am ashamed of whatever particle of them has survived deep within me.... I am a Tunisian but Jewish, which means that I am politically and socially an outcast. I speak the language of the country with a particular accent and emotionally I have nothing in common with the Moslems. I am a Jew who has broken with the Jewish religion and the ghetto, is ignorant of Jewish culture and detests the middle class because it is phony. I am poor but desperately anxious

To have answered the examination question would have been for Mordekhai "ce qu'il fallait" (what was necessary) in order to escape even partially the emotional, social, and political controversies of his situation. Instead, however, he looks back upon his past and is transformed into a statue of salt: "Il est interdit de se voir et j'ai fini de me connaître. Comme la femme de Loth, que Dieu changea en statue, puis-je encore vivre au delà de mon regard?"[22]

Despite Mordekhai's conscious refusal to answer the question and to do "ce qu'il fallait," what he actually writes instead is "tout à fait comme il faut!" (entirely proper). His lived conflicts, controversies, and struggles, whether they be linguisic, cultural, or ideoligical, remain something to *tell* about rather than *show;* to write *about* rather than write *in.* The general linear organization of the narrative, the language that is used, the structure of the sentences, the choice of the dominant first person pronoun, all these elements finally converge to exemplify Mordekhai's (and by implication Memmi's) failure to transform the constraints into opportunities. It is true that Mordekhai dares to speak; however, *how* he speaks is in perfect keeping with the dominant; he remains trapped within the constraints of colonial bilingualism.

Nevertheless, there is a potentially subversive moment within *La Statue de sel* that could be seen as a prescription for the bilingual writer in speaking the master language. In the chapter titled "Le Lycée," Mordekhai tells the reader about his alienation from his classmates who all (including the rich acculturated Jews) made fun of his nasal ghetto accent when he spoke French. As part of his effort to assimilate, Mordekhai strives to perfect his French. Finally confident of himself, he asks the teacher's permission to give an oral report on the French poet Vigny. In what initially starts off as an act of defiance, of potential contestation, Mordekhai decides to speak without a written text. But something unforeseen occurs:

> Malheureusement, la fronde m'emportant... je versai dans l'argot... mais je ne pouvais qu'avancer, continuer mon rôle malgré la tragédie muette que je faisais naître....

---

not to be poor, and at the same time, I refuse to take the necessary steps to avoid poverty" (p. 331).

22. Memmi, *La Statue,* p. 368: "It is forbidden to see oneself, and I have reached the end of discovering myself. God turned Loth's wife into a pillar of salt—is it possible for me to survive my contemplation of myself?" (p. 335).

Ma langue était en effet en fusion, un infâme mélange d'expressions littéraires ou même précieuses, de tours traduits du patois, d'argot écolier et d'inventions verbales plus ou moins réussies. J'essayais, par exemple, de nommer les bruits qui, à ma connaissance, n'avaient d'appellation ni en français ni en patois, ou encore forgeais en français des verbes qui n'existaient qu'en patois. Ma langue, tumultueuse, informe, était bien à l'image de moi-même, ne ressemblait certes pas à une source limpide.[23]

It is evident from this passage that Mordekhai has violated the dominant formal and discursive practice in the colonial school. Not only does he speak without written notes, but he mixes the different languages, dialects, and idioms that coexist in his linguistic universe. This violation elicits the following reaction from his French teacher: "Vous avez fait une leçon curieuse; sur tout ce que vous avez dit, sur Vigny, je n'ai pas grand chose à ajouter. Mais pour parler sans notes, ce qui est méritoire, vous êtes tombé dans un langage de concierge."[24]

Interestingly, Mordekhai's report is not critiqued on the level of its content, on *what* he said, for even the teacher has nothing much to add to the student's presentation. Rather, the teacher is specifically concerned with the formal level of the presentation, *how* Mordekhai said what he said. Moreover, the French teacher labels Mordekhai's language with an inferior social category, that of the "concierge," who would normally be excluded from such institutionalized forms of knowledge and whose participation in the dominant discursive practices, like Mordekhai's, could mean the disruption of these very practices.

This essentially threatening and disruptive potential, however,

---

23. Memmi, *La Statue*, pp. 125–26: "Unfortunately, my irreverence carried me away... so that I soon slipped into slang... but I couldn't stop, could only continue my role in the inarticulate tragedy I had begun. ... In effect, the language I spoke was an amalgam, a dreadful mixture of literary or even precious expressions and of idioms translated word for word from our dialect, of schoolboy slang and of my own more or less successful inventions. I tried, for instance, to find names for certain sounds which had not yet, so far as I know, been identified either with French or in my local dialect; or I attempted to create in French those verbs that existed only in my dialect. My language was thus as wild and turbulent as I was; it had none of the qualities of a clear and placid stream" (pp. 110–11).

24. Memmi, *La Statue*, p. 126: "Your report has been most odd. I can add very little to what you've said about Vigny. But, in order to speak without notes, which in itself should merit approval, you've allowed yourself to slip into the language of the man of the street" (p. 110).

remains thwarted, both in the language of the passage just quoted, and in the general structure and discursive modes of Memmi's novel as a whole. For a brief moment, Mordekhai becomes the plurilingual, pluricultural subject that he really is, with all the creative and inventive implications of these terms. He has the capacity to create his own language (ma langue) by translation and invention. He translates, word for word, and with ease, idioms from his dialect and from his schoolboy slang as well. He goes as far as to invent names for certain sounds that exist neither in French nor in his dialect.

And yet, the actual words of the plurilingual are banished from the text. Here is an act of complete compliance with the dominant; an act that totally negates what Mordekhai had initially set out to do: "j'avais violemment envie de manifester, d'affirmer ce que j'étais."[25] The real possibility of self-affirmation, however, is suppressed not only through this process of *telling* rather than *showing*, but also through the negative terms in which the whole experience is articulated. Mordekhai describes his own attempt at self-affirmation as one of irreverence, of inarticulate tragedy, of impertinence, of failure; as proof that he could not expect to speak anything but the language of a "concierge" or "man of the street." In Mordekhai's own words, his report was an "infâme mélange," his language was "tumultueuse" and "informe," but his actual syntax and prose render it as if it were a "source limpide."

What Mordekhai does then, and by implication what Memmi does as well, is to reinscribe himself as a colonized subject, caught in the enchaining colonial relationship (both formally and discursively) throughout the narrative. In writing La Statue de sel, Memmi, like Mordekhai, does not see that the constraints can be rewritten as opportunities, and not just theorized as such. The same man who could *tell* his readers that the only way out of colonial mystification would be a complete rupture with the colonial situation, fails to *show*, in his novel (a literary form that, in the Arab world, was considered one of acculturation) the direction such a rupture could take. The possibilities for contesting the dominant discursive models, the Western literary canon, the whole discourse on the

---

25. Memmi, La Statue, p. 126: "Above all, I was violent in my will to show and affirm what I was" (p. 110).

alienated postcolonial writer, the issues of identity, difference, representation and self-representation, all larger implications of a potentially subversive passage, remain doubly constrained within Memmi's literary text.

Toward the end of *Portrait du colonisé*, Memmi predicted that francophone North African literature would inevitably die out. The future generations, born in freedom, would spontaneously write in their own language. But in the meantime, he added, another possibility could tempt the writer: to decide to belong totally to the literature of the metropole.[26] Even though Memmi, for various political and personal reasons, may have opted for this latter course, the two extreme solutions he once provided do not coincide with today's literary landscape in North Africa or even in France, for that matter.

Most francophone North African writers have come to realize the strength and power of their bilingualism. Rather than speak about themselves as the victims of an alienating historical reality, francophone writers today can see that they have an essential role to play, if complete decolonization is to be achieved. "Le mot est torche qui nous arme d'une attention grave," says the Algerian woman writer Assia Djebar.[27] It is the word that takes precedence over silence, no matter which language the writer chooses to speak. Even if there are constraints, even when there are risks to be taken in writing in the language of the dominant other, there are always means of converting such constraints into opportunities: "L'écriture française nous 'livre' à l'autre, mais on se défendra par l'arabesque, la subversion, le dédale, le labyrinthe, le décentrage incessant de la phrase et du langage, de manière que l'autre se perde comme dans les ruelles de la casbah."[28]

The metaphor suggested by the Tunisian writer Abdelwahab Meddeb in the passage just quoted—to cause native speakers of French to lose their way in their own language (through the use of arabesque,

<hr>

26. Memmi, *Portrait du colonisé*, p. 140.

27. Assia Djebar, *L'Amour, la fantasia* (Paris, 1985), p. 75: "The word is like a torch that arms us with solemn attention" (my translation).

28. Abdelwahab Meddeb, quoted in Jean Dejeux, *Situation de la littérature maghrébine de langue française* (Alger, 1982), pp. 103–4. "Writing in French surrenders us to the other, but we will defend ourselves with arabesque, subversion, labyrinthine constructions, the incessant decentering of the sentence and of language so that the other will lose the way just as in the narrow streets of the *casbah*" (my translation).

subversion, and labyrinthine language that decenters French sentence structures) just as they would lose their way in the meandering alleys of the *casbah*, that is, the old North African *medinas* or cities—is a most appropriate figurative rendition of the new demands of radical bilingualism. Meddeb has defined the principles for a subversive poetics that will turn constraints into risky opportunities. Such opportunities are risky precisely because "the other," unfamiliar with the *casbah*, might lose the way in the elaborate maze, might fail at decoding the text. Meddeb's metaphor has an important function in this context. His use of the *casbah*, as the other pole of the metaphor, has the function of superimposing an unfamiliar model text, which needs to be decoded, if the process of intertextuality is to attain its true significance in francophone North African literature.

One of the most prominent figures in the elaboration of such a subversive poetics has been the Moroccan writer Abdelkebir Khatibi. Having coined the term "radical bilingualism," his work becomes a consistent articulation of it. Professor of sociology at the University of Rabat, Khatibi has been quite accurately described as follows: "Ni romancier, ni poète, ni homme de science désincarnée, ni spécialiste d'histoire de l'art, il fait passer, au travers de la maîtrise de chacun de ces langages, l'inquiétude de l'homme pour qui la passion de connaître, et dire, ne se dissocie pas de la passion de vivre, ni la recherche intellectuelle de la quête de soi."[29]

Khatibi belonged to the group of Moroccan writers who, in 1966, founded the bilingual literary review *Souffles*, which had a most significant role in redefining the space of the francophone writer in the context of national literature. One of the main tasks this group of writers assigned itself was the insistence on renovating literary forms. Distinctions between genres began to disappear, and the word

29. Barbulesco and Cardinal, *L'Islam en questions*, p. 244: "Not a writer, nor a poet, nor a man of science, or art historian, he transmits, through a mastery of each of these languages, the anxieties of a man for whom the passion for knowledge, and communication, is inseparable from the passion for life and the intellectual search for the self" (my translation). Khatibi's literary output, whether it be in the form of articles, essays, novels, poetry, or drama, exceeds the space that one can devote to it in a footnote. Here, however, are the titles of some of his major works in different areas: *La Blessure du nom propre* (Paris, 1974); *Vomito blanco: Le sionisme et la conscience malheureuse* (Paris, 1974); *Le Lutteur de classe à la manière taoiste* (Paris, 1976); *Le Livre du sang* (Paris, 1979); *Le Prophète voilé* (Paris, 1979); *Le Roman maghrébin* (Rabat, 1980).

itinéraire, invented by the Moroccan poet Laabi, came to describe the back-and-forth movement between literary genres and literary idioms.[30] Because of its increasingly leftist ideology, *Souffles* was banned in 1972. But, like many others who belonged to this bilingual literary review, Khatibi has continued to write, always practicing what he preaches, whether it be in his essays, poetry, or novels, if such a clear-cut categorization is ever possible in Khatibi's work.

La Mémoire tatouée, published in 1971, is Khatibi's autobiographical narrative. As the title might suggest, it is simultaneously an autobiography and a narrative on autobiography.[31] In this sense, *La Mémoire tatouée* becomes a mediation that is doubled. This already double mediation is further problematized by the existence in the text of two other characters, besides that of the author's fictitious double. These two characters, namely A and B, who engage in a dialogue toward the third part of the narrative, in their turn assess the narrator's own double mediations on the form, content, and language of his text.

Unlike Memmi's semiautobiographical novel, Khatibi's *La Mémoire tatouée*, as the title indicates, makes no attempt at reconstructing a linear past. Rather, Khatibi actively preserves his tatooed memory; he writes *in* it and not outside it, as a means of representing the torn experience of the colonized subject. Whereas Memmi *tells* his reader about mutilated memory, Khatibi reproduces it, both in his use of the language and in the very structure of his text as well.

Again, a significant difference between Memmi's and Khatibi's first person narrators exists in the roles they attribute to them respectively. In *La Statue de sel*, Mordekhai compares the writing of his own past to the transformation of Lot's wife into a statue, as a punishment for having looked back on the past. Having looked back on his own life, Mordekhai fears that he will fail to live "au delà de [son] regard," which explains his departure for Argentina. In contrast, Khatibi's fictitious double undertakes exactly what Mordekhai escapes, thus liberating himself from the constraints of the past: "La plus belle histoire est de se faire raconter sa propre vie en mourant de rire."[32]

---

30. See Marc Gontard, *La Violence du texte* (Paris, 1981).

31. Abdelkebir Khatibi, *La Mémoire tatouée* (Paris, 1971).

32. Ibid., p. 9: "The most beautiful story is to recount one's own life history while dying of laughter" (my translation).

In *La Mémoire tatouée* paragraphs succeed each other with no immediate causal relationship. The different episodes become reflections from "au delà" on the narrator's childhood, colonization, bilingualism, and so on. The end result is an amalgam of images impressed upon the narrator's imagination as part of his colonial experience: "On connaît l'imagination coloniale: juxtaposer, compartimenter, militariser, découper la ville en zones ethniques, ensabler la culture du peuple dominé. En découvrant son dépaysement, ce peuple errera, hagard, dans l'espace brisé de son histoire. Et il n'y a de plus atroce que la déchirure de la mémoire."[33]

Khatibi's text gains its strength from constraints: "son dépaysement," "l'espace brisé de son histoire," and "la déchirure de la mémoire." All these constraints are transformed into creative opportunities, as the narrative proceeds to represent the imprints of the colonial imagination. Just as Khatibi accepts and parodies his compartimentalized past, so does he accept, and live, his plurilingualism and the layering that must come with it: "A l'école, un enseignement laïc, imposé à ma religion; je devins triglotte, lisant le français sans le parler, jouant avec quelques bribes de l'arabe écrit, et parlant le dialecte comme quotidien. Où, dans ce chassé-croisé, la cohérence et la continuité?"[34]

Near the end of *La Mémoire tatouée*, the narrator encapsulates his attitude toward his bilingualism and biculturalism in the following manner: "L'Occident est une partie de moi, que je ne peux nier que dans la mesure où je lutte contre tous occidents et orients qui m'oppriment ou me désenchantent."[35]

Indeed, the subtitle of *La Mémoire tatouée* is *Autobiographie d'un décolonisé*, where the word "décolonisé" signifies a gesture toward

---

33. Ibid., p. 54: "We well know the colonial imagination: juxtapose, compartmentalize, militarize, divide the city into ethnic areas, sand over the culture of the colonized people. In discovering their alienation such a people will wander, distraught, in the crushed space of their own history. And there is nothing more atrocious than the shattering of memory" (my translation).

34. Ibid., p. 64: "At school, with a secular education imposed on my religious background, I became a triglotte: I read French without being able to speak it, I played with some fragments of written Arabic, and I spoke the dialect as my everyday language. Where in the midst of this confusion is coherence and continuity?" (my translation).

35. Ibid., p. 118: "The Occident is a part of me that I can deny only to the extent that I war against all occidents and orients that oppress and disenchant me" (my translation).

that double movement of decolonization, the beginnings of a radical bilingualism, uninhibited by the constraints of the past; a war "against all oppressive occidents and orients."

In *Maghreb pluriel*, Khatibi sets himself a double task: to demystify and destigmatize the linguistic landscape of the *maghrib* and to map out the future of this region in its plurality. Khatibi's article "Bilinguisme et littérature" begins with what he calls a bad joke: "Nous, les Maghrébins, nous avons mis quatorze siècles pour apprendre la langue arabe (à peu près), plus d'un siècle pour apprendre le français (à peu près); et depuis des temps immémoriaux, nous n'avons pas su écrire le berbère. C'est dire que le bilinguisme et le plurilinguisme ne sont pas, dans ces régions, des faits récents. Le paysage linguistique maghrébin est encore plurilingue: diglossie (entre l'arabe et le dialectal), le berbère, le français, l'espagnol au nord et au sud du Maroc."[36]

For Khatibi, therefore, every writer, especially from the *maghrib*, is at least bilingual. Hence, the crucial question becomes how to transform this bilingualism into creative opportunities. In "Double critique," Khatibi defines the path for the postcolonial bilingual writers, a route that will help them break out of Fanon's "blind alley"

> Sommes-nous destinés à porter la violence contre les autres pour leur faire entendre la voix de la raison? A les menacer de guerre, de destruction et de culpabilité immonde pour que l'Occident se retourne contre son auto-suffisance et son ethnocentrisme, maintenant élevés au niveau planétaire? Et pourtant, nous pouvons, Tiers-monde, poursuivre une tierce voie... une subversion en quelque sorte double, qui, se donnant le pouvoir de parole et d'action, se met en œuvre dans une différence intraitable.[37]

36. Abdelkebir Khatibi, *Maghreb pluriel* (Paris, 1973), p. 179: "We the North Africans have spent fourteen centuries to learn Arabic (more or less), more than one century to learn French (more or less), and from time immemorial we have not learned how to write Berber. Bilingualism and plurilingualism are not, in this region, a recent phenomenon. The linguistic landscape of the *maghrib* is still plurilingual: diaglossia (between Arabic and the dialect), Berber, French, Spanish in the north and south of Morocco" (my translation).

37. Ibid., p. 51: "Are we destined to use violence against others to make them listen to the voice of reason? To threaten war, destruction and vile guilt so that the Occident would renounce its self-sufficiency and its ethnocentrism which today encompass the world. And yet, we of the Third World can follow a third way... a subversion that is in a sense double which, by seizing the power of word and action, accomplishes itself in an uncompromising difference" (my translation).

That third way, that double subversion, that uncompromising difference are indeed what characterize Khatibi's *Amour bilingue.* How does one love as a bilingual? This question becomes the pretext for his theory and practice of being the *bilangue,* rather than the *bilingue.*[38] Khatibi's *bilangue,* like the first person narrator of *Amour bilingue* and his doubles—the second and third person pronouns, who all share the *récit*—must be in constant motion between the different layers of language: "La langue n'appartient à personne.... N'avais-je pas grandi, dans ma langue maternelle, comme un enfant adoptif? D'adoption en adoption, je croyais naître de la langue même."[39]

For the *bilangue,* language is more beautiful, more terrible; what Khatibi calls "la scénographie des doubles. Un mot: déjà deux: déjà un récit."[40] On another occasion, Khatibi had emphasized the fact that "La langue 'maternelle' est à l'œuvre dans la langue étrangère. De l'une à l'autre se déroulent une traduction permanente et un entretien en abîme, extrêmement difficile à mettre au jour."[41]

Rather than simply *tell* about this constant translation from one language to the other, as does Memmi's protagonist in *La Statue de sel,* Khatibi consciously *shows* it. In *Amour bilingue* a constant migration of signs takes place between classical Arabic, the spoken dialect, and French, to mention only the three main layers that Khatibi juggles, in a constant state of interdependence and intersignification in the text. The following is an example of the practice of the *bilangue:*

> Et en français—sa langue étrangère—le "mot" est près de la mort, il ne lui manque qu'une seule lettre.... Il se calma d'un coup, lorsqu'apparut le "mot" arabe "kalma" avec son équivalent savant "kalima" et toute la chaîne de diminutifs, calembours de son enfance:

38. Abdelkebir Khatibi, *Amour bilingue* (Paris, 1983). After the completion of this essay, a translation appeared: *Love in Two Languages,* trans. Richard Howard (Minneapolis, 1990).

39. Khatibi, *Amour bilingue,* p. 11: "Language belongs to no one. Have I not grown in my maternal language like an adopted child? From one adoption to the other I felt I was born in language itself" (my translation).

40. Ibid., p. 11: "A scenography of doubles. One word becomes two, to become a story..." (my translation).

41. Gontard, *La Violence du texte,* preface by Abdelkebir Khatibi, p. 8: "The maternal language is always at work in the foreign language. Between them occurs a constant process of translation, an abysmal dialogue very difficult to bring to the light of day" (my translation).

"klima.".... La diglossie "kal(i)ma" revint sans que disparût ni s'effaçât le mot "mot."[42]

The foregoing passage is an example of how a never-ending and uninterrupted chain of significations and associations coexist in the *bilangue*'s mind and *récit*. What Khatibi demonstrates is the interference and interdependence of the semiotic systems, which are always at the plurilingual's fingertips. The process of translation and association is a constant one, and the traces of both classical Arabic and the dialect are always present.

The title page of *Amour bilingue* offers perhaps the most articulate and defiant graphic and symbolic rendition of the *plurilangue*, which the reader is expected to decipher in the text.[43] The French title appears in bold red letters at the top of the page. At the bottom of the same page is its "translation" written in Arabic calligraphy. This bilingual title page remains only semireadable for the monolingual, just as the text itself would be, if the reader fails to decode its plurilingual narrative. Furthermore, the complete signification of the French title can only be understood in its relationship with the Arabic title: they are interdependent. This is but the beginning of a series of demands placed upon the reader, even as he or she gazes at the title page.

Our full understanding of the word *amour* in the title depends on the unreadable Arabic word *'ishq*, which can signify two things. On

42. Khatibi, *Amour bilingue*, p. 10: "And in French—his maternal tongue—the 'word' (*mot*) is close to 'death' (*mort*): only one letter is missing. Suddenly, he became calm when he happened upon the Arabic 'word' 'kalma' with its classical equivalent 'kalima' and the whole chain of diminutives, puns from his childhood: 'klima.'... The diaglossia 'kal(i)ma' returned without the disappearance of the word 'word' " (my translation).

43. See the Arabic for *Amour bilingue* reproduced above. Also see the article by Reda Bensmaia, "Traduire ou 'blanchir' la langue: *Amour bilingue* d'Abdelkebir Khatibi," in *Imaginaires de l'autre: Khatibi et la mémoire littéraire* (Paris, 1987), pp. 133–60, for an excellent reading of *Amour bilingue*, and Khatibi's work in general.

the one hand, it can mean earthly passion, and on the other, when read within the context of the Islamic mystical tradition, it means one of the higher stages of the mystical experience. The French word *bilingue* is rendered in the Arabic dual form for the word *lisan*, that is, *lisanayn*. Hence the translation that appears on the title page, in Arabic calligraphy, is *'ishq al-lisanayn*. Now, the Arabic title can have more than one meaning, and it is in this respect that the French title will depend on it for full signification.

The word *lisan* in Arabic can convey two meanings: *lisan* can mean tongue, both in the physical and figurative meanings of the word, that is, as both the organ of speech and the language that it utters. Hence the word *lisanayn* in the title can be read as a sign for the two languages (*langues*), French and Arabic, which explains Khatibi's translation of *bilangue* in the text. Or it can be read as a sign for the internal divisions within the Arabo-Islamic culture itself. The division between orthodox, institutional Islamic discourse and the popular, mystical tradition that has always been marginalized, and which Khatibi brings into the text as part of his total makeup as a *plurilangue*. *Lisanayn* can also be read as the division between classical Arabic, which represents high culture, and the dialects, which represent popular culture, and which have always been devalued. To understand the *plurilangue* in the text, one must first understand the intricate interplay on the title page.

Amour bilingue then is a text that challenges our competence as readers and critics alike. When asked about the ideal reader for these works that radicalize bilingualism, the Tunisian writer Abdelwahab Meddeb responded: "Le lecteur idéal de mon livre c'est celui qui partage cette position de l'entre-deux."[44] What is being contested here is the notion of hierarchies, the idea of hegemony, which always implies the ascendency and domination of certain structures and institutions over others.

So long as the institutions that form the reader have not changed, the subversive poetics proposed in the works of francophone North African writers may become constraining. The demands set forth by such francophone writers in their texts have larger implications for Western literary theories and methodologies alike. Otherwise,

44. Abdelwahab Meddeb, "Je est un autre," *Arabies* 7–8 (1987): 87–89. "The ideal reader of my books is one who shares this position of in-between" (my translation).

as Khatibi himself has aptly put it, "Tant que la théorie de la traduction, de la bi-langue et de la pluri-langue n'aura pas avancé, cer-
tains textes maghrébins resteront imprenables selon une approche
formelle et fonctionelle.... Assumer la langue française, oui pour
y nommer cette faille et cette jouissance de l'étranger qui doit
travailler à la marge, c'est-à-dire pour son seul compte,
solitairement."[45]

45. Gontard, *La Violence du texte*, preface by Abdelkebir Khatibi, p. 8. "So long
as the theory of translation, of the *bilangue* and the *plurilangue* has not advanced,
certain North African texts will remain impregnable through a formal or functional
approach. To assume the French language, yes, in order to name this flaw, and this
pleasure of the foreigner who is obliged to work in the margin, that is, for his own
account, alone" (my translation).

10

Literary Whiteness and the Afro-Hispanic Difference

JOSÉ PIEDRA

Hablar de raza española es no saber
lo que se dice...
El lenguaje es la raza.

To speak of a Spanish race makes
no sense...
The language is the race.
— Miguel de Unamuno

Son griegas tus formas, tu tez,
africana;
tus ojos hebreos, tu acento
español;
la arena es tu alfombra, la palma,
tu hermana;
te hicieron morena los besos del
sol.

Your shape is Greek, your face,
African;
your eyes are Hebrew, your accent
Spanish;
the sand is your carpet, the palm
tree your sister;
the kisses of the sun made you
brown.
—from an anonymous song documented
in Mexico in the nineteenth century

Io compré un negro, crespo los
cabellos,
blanco los dientes, hinchado los
beços.

I bought a black man, curly hair,
white teeth, swollen kisser.
—example of synecdoche used by Antonio de Nebrija in his
fifteenth-century book on Spanish grammar

I

Fourteen hundred ninety-two should remind Hispanics of the publication of the first grammar of a modern European language, a fact overshadowed in historical records by the unification of the Spanish nation, the purification of infidels, and the launching of the New World adventure.[1] Antonio de Nebrija's work billed the Castilian dialect as the "companion of the Empire," an appropriate grammatical endorsement of Spain's ethnic assertion, religious and racial bigotry, as well as the ultimate "civilized" weapon for political expansionism among the "illiterate."[2] Spanish grammar became the colonial pretext for the assimilation of otherness and others. Imperial grammarians established a test of literacy for Hispanic citizenship, which, if successfully passed, allegedly provided official entry into the Hispanic "Text of Otherness," a grammatical contract of servitude. Nebrija, in fact, not only announced the imperial qualities of language, but also explained in his text the ability of grammar to assimilate foreign words as well as foreign learners.[3] He proposed a language that would inherit the power structures of other literate societies and in the process would also Hispanicize nonliterate societies. In the final process, Spanish would combine seductiveness with domination. Henceforth the grammatical and imperial "companion" was disseminated by conquerors and bureaucrats who un-

1. The epigraphs are from Miguel de Unamuno, "Espíritu de la raza vasca," in *La Raza y la lengua*, vol. 4 of *Obras completas*, ed. Manuel García Blanco (Madrid, 1968), p. 156; *El Ruiseñor yucateco. Primera parte. Canciones populares*, ed. Galo Fernández (Merida, Mexico, n.d.), p. 36 (song collected in Yucatan by Juan Ausucua as the lyrics of a *guaracha* imported from Cuba); and Antonio de Nebrija, *Gramática de la lengua castellana* (Salamanca, 1492), ed. Ignacio González-Llubera (Oxford, 1926), p. 122.

2. "Cuando bien comigo pienso, mui esclarecida Reina, i pongo delante los ojos el antiguedad de todas las cosas que para nuestra recordacion y memoria quedaron escriptas, una cosa hállo y sáco por conclusion mui cierta: que siempre la lengua fue compañera del imperio." (When in all honesty I think, my enlightened Queen, and place before my eyes all the ancient facts which have been left in writing for us to remember and to keep as memories, one fact stands out and makes me draw a sure conclusion: language has always been the companion of the empire.) Translation is mine. Nebrija, *Gramática*, p. 3. He also leaves up to the queen command over language (p. 9).

3. Nebrija stresses the relationship between imperialism and linguistic assimilation, comparing the imperial position of Spanish to other languages from which it not only inherited power through linguistic assimilation but to which it also owes linguistic derivation ("Prólogo," in ibid., pp. 3–9). He also proclaims the Spanish debt to languages with which it has come in contact (pp. 23–27, 77–78). Furthermore, Nebrija closely correlates the ability of Spanish to conquer and to seduce ("Prólogo," p. 8 and passim). Finally he dedicates Book 5 of the *Gramática* to the teaching of Spanish to foreigners: "Delas introducciones dela lengua castellana para los que de estraña lengua querran deprender" (On the preliminaries of the Castilian language for those who want to learn it as a foreign language); see pp. 141–70.

ified in a rhetorical manner the differences of fate, faith, and race
within the Hispanic empire. The final result was an "impure" but
unified empire, combining aspects of the Latin, Hebraic, and Islamic
models. The fact that the "impurity" of the system was not officially
accepted only served to strengthen the imperial hold. Furthermore,
it would offer outsiders a false sense of accessibility and a similarly
false hope of equality within Spain's implicit, unofficial heter-
ogeneity.

While preparing for an imperial career, Spain, as the dark child
of Europe and the light child of Africa, opted for a linguistic unity
over strictly ethnic, religious, and territorial determinism. Otherwise, national integrity might have lost itself in the long history of
Iberian siege, spanning the Greco-Roman to the Afro-Islamic in-
vasions and passing through what threatened Hispanophiles qualified as Jewish preeminence in commerce. Such interventions,
however, did not forestall the deep-seated Spanish desire to associate with foreigners who were considered ubiquitous and important. Alfonso the Wise, for instance, established elaborate rules for
the exchange between the different groups on Iberian soil. Beneath
the cautionary acceptance of outsiders, Spaniards experimented
with tactical assimilation aimed at national unity. Due to the state
of siege of their territory, national unity could be forged only in
theory, through language and cultural exchange. The work of Nebrija crystallized the most realistic form of unity available under
siege. Nebrija, for instance, briefly discusses the linguistic contribution of Moors and Jews, ignoring their position of preeminence
in occupied Spain.[4] He is chiefly concerned with the unification of
the empire under the aegis of a grammatical mistress. From this
tactical assimilation of the invader's contributions, Spain pieced together a language of survival and domination in both Africa and the
New World. The transatlantic language offered cultural strength for
the occupiers while promising syncretic assimilation for the
occupied.

---

4. Even though in his "Prólogo" Nebrija discusses Hebrew as a "power-language,"
he also points out that the dispersion of Jews around the world has weakened their
civilization because it has eroded their linguistic unity. Moreover, he accepts but
criticizes the influence of both Jews and Moors in the pronunciation and spelling of
Spanish, comparing such "irregularities" to the barbarisms that Latin grammarians
imputed to outsiders' use (and abuse) of their language; see Nebrija, ibid., pp. 122–
24.

A strong common language was essential in the rhetorical war for transatlantic integrity. A unified linguistic front diluted the occupation armies' and master culture's hegemony; their imperial otherness led to a reasonably democratic syncretism of universal pretense. Latin and Castilian Spanish dominated as the vehicles of syncretism, absorbing knowledge from classical European, Islamic, and Judaic sources. Record keeping in Hispanicized languages, whether in Vulgar Latin or proto-imperialist Castilian, enticed the rest of the heterogeneous participants to partake in experiments of translation, teaching, and peaceful coexistence.[5] Columbus, for instance, a recent Italian convert to the Spanish system, expressed himself in these two languages.

Islands of universal knowledge emerged in the budding nation, supported by underground waves of linguistic pride.[6] The imperialist application of Aristotelian views of world unity and Nebrija's grammatical crusade should be considered as the hidden guiding lights for the pioneers of this aristocracy of the intellect with worldwide pretense. Spaniards had, after all, "discovered" Aristotle and the power of linguistic standardization at about the same time, much earlier than other European nations.[7] Under Islamic occupation, Iberian citizens learned the benefits of exploiting the symbiotic rela-

5. Alfonso the Wise used these two languages, Latin and Spanish, as the official ones; see Nebrija's discussion (ibid., pp. 5–6). Alfonso, however, compiled and wrote poetry in Galician-Portuguese. Literature was to be considered a separate linguistic domain.

6. The School of Translators in Toledo, the Center for General Studies in Palencia, and the University of Salamanca were established between the twelfth and the thirteenth centuries. In these centers Latin and Castilian Spanish were the chief working languages.

7. The European rediscovery of Aristotle in Islamized Spain has been thoroughly documented; not so, however, the Greco-Roman legacy of citizens' enslavement to the system, suggested by many classical European writers, especially Plato and Aristotle. See Robert Schlaifer, "Greek Theories of Slavery from Homer to Aristotle," *Harvard Studies in Classical Philology* 47 (1963): esp. 166–70, quoted by David Brion Davis, *The Problem of Slavery in Western Culture* (Ithaca, N.Y., 1966), p. 67. According to Schlaifer, Philemon was most explicit among the Greeks in his opinion that "the entire universe is viewed as a hierarchy of slavery, in which one's place on the scale mattered but little" (p. 190). Curiously, there is a coincidence of names and an affinity of subject matter in Paul's epistle to a Philemon, in which the saint, when pleading to the commoner for pardoning a slave, uses as an example his own "imprisonment" to the kind word of Christ. As for Nebrija's grammar being the "first" in modern Europe, see Nebrija, *Gramática*, "Introduction" by González-Llubera, p. xliii.

tionships with other cultures. The linguistic exploitation of knowledge gave the Hispanic "universities" an edge within "international" pockets of Iberian soil. Knowledge was assimilated as part of the Spanish zeal to control translations of the classics, thus creating a thriving European commerce in humanist books and scholars which is a considerable source for the ideology of the Renaissance. Such individuals as Alfonso the Wise studied and translated the knowledge imported by "barbarians"—Moors, Jews, and to a lesser extent sub-Saharan Africans. Theoretically, Iberians laid claims to Aristotelian thinking on world unity. In restricted diplomatic practices, they also prepared to turn such a thought into apologies for global control thinly disguised as a nationalistic pride in cultural (chiefly linguistic and rhetorical) prowess. The congenial systems of a rediscovered philosopher and a well-placed grammarian laid the groundwork for the exercise of the imperial hold. Europe, Africa, and America became the grounds on which Spain planned to practice enslavement justified as a rhetorical brokerage of universal knowledge.

Spanish interpreters stressed those aspects of Aristotelian theories of world unity and Nebrija's linguistic imperialism which proposed the conversion of outsiders to an official *written* dictum. If one is to follow Nebrija's interpretation, it establishes writing as the natural means of expressing Aristotelian world unity. After criticizing previous empires that spread themselves too thin without having the appropriate grammatical tools to uphold their unity, the Spanish imperial grammarian gives his ultimate endorsement of the power of writing: "Las letras representan las bozes, y las bozes significan, como dize Aristoteles, los pensamientos que tenemos en el anima" (Letters represent voices, and voices give meaning, according to Aristotle, to the thoughts we have in our souls).[8]

Those who opposed the written dictum would be forced to comply as slaves. Enslavement thus comes to be viewed as a harsh form of cultural apprenticeship. Slaves came to deserve a legitimate place in society as their behavior conformed to certain "inherited" rights as potential citizens. The Spanish view of slavery was tactfully disguised as citizen apprenticeship. Furthermore, whether enslaved or freed, every citizen was in fact subject to a degree of enslavement

8. Nebrija, *Gramática*, p. 19.

to the very same bureaucratic system that legitimized him.⁹ Nebrija
endorsed a similar system in his concept of language. He argued that
language becomes a source of power when it provides an official
"home" for the memory of all who contribute to the empire,
and grammarians act as the official guardians of such a home. He
considered grammar the system behind all imperial systems. As a
propagandist extraordinaire, he was personally involved in "grammatical" interpretations of imperialism: official grammarian and
Hispanist, rhetorician and humanist, biblical and secular editor,
apologist and critic of the Inquisition, royal historiographer and
strategist of colonial campaigns. He managed his diverse imperialist
interests while being an advocate of the accessibility to knowledge
through the printing press.¹⁰ Ultimately, he proposed his own book
of grammar as a vehicle not only to conquer enemies, but to stan-
dardize and uphold the rights and duties of citizens and also to make
friends of those who followed in the right linguistic path. Grammar
constituted the core of a citizen's apprenticeship; it guided the recording and the actual making of history as the official channel of
spreading "the truth." Grammar crystallized as the conquering en-
voy to new slaves and citizens. The Spanish empire used textual
participation both as justification and vehicle of its abuses and as
enticement for the abused.

First in Europe and then in the New World, written Spanish was

9. See *Las Siete Partidas del rey Alfonso el sabio, cotejadas con varios códices
antiguos, por la Real Academia de la Historia*, 3 vols. (1807; rpt. Madrid, 1972), vol.
3, pt. 4, title 21, law 1 (p. 117); pt. 4, title 5, introduction (p. 30); vol. 2, pt. 3, title
5, law 4 (pp. 419–20). In these sections Alfonso the Wise discusses the nature of
slavery as an "agreement" against "natural reason," and as a temporary institution
that "should lead toward freedom." In vol. 2, titles 16, 21, and 22, he discusses the
citizenship advantages and the progression of slaves toward free participation in
society. Moreover, newcomers to the Spanish empire had to abide by the conquerors'
proposal to have them "speaking Spanish within six months." See *Colección de
documentos para la historia de la formación social de Hispanoamerica, 1493–1810*,
14 vols., ed. Richard Konetzke (Madrid, 1953), 1:237–240.

10. Among his most prestigious posts was that of Royal Historiographer. He was
probably responsible for the introduction of the printing press into Salamanca, of
whose university he was an influential young professor, or at least was involved in
the editing and printing of the earliest Spanish books, including a few of his own.
He was editor of the Polyglot Bible under the supervision of Cardinal Cisneros,
Inquisitor General, to whom he wrote an *Apologia*. He was also involved in the
creation and administration of universities and the introduction and management of
humanist education in general. See Nebrija, *Gramática*, "Introduction" by González-
Llubera, pp. xiii–lxii. He also took active part in Spain's African campaigns.

projected as a centralized, self-consistent, and self-righteous textuality that invited outsiders to participate. The invitation glossed
over potential differences—such as origin, faith, social standing,
reason, and race. On paper, but not in practice, differences were
minimized as alliances were maximized. Nebrija provided the New
World with the justification for a cohesive Hispanic Text; he unified
"otherness" under the grammatical self-righteousness of the colonial letter. Henceforth, the discourse of "the Hispanic Self" disseminated within the discourse of Others (Moors, blacks, Jews) in
occupied Spain was transformed into a unified discourse of Others
within the Imperial "Self"—as Spain subjected the "blood," "faith,"
and "letters" of previous settlers on the Iberian Peninsula as well
as native Americans and African slaves in the New World to a bureaucratic test of Hispanic worth. Thus, by virtue of this assimilation
and incorporation, the Others found themselves in a position of
tactical compromise that was never to be forgotten in subsequent
literature of Latin America. It was only those who considered themselves mediators between the extremes of the master culture and
the potential slave who dared to challenge the uneasy compromise
spun by the Hispanic Text.

Afro-Hispanics were among the mediators most profoundly affected by the Hispanic textual compromise. Arguably they were the
most precarious and challenging participants in the Spanish melting pot, having entered Spain as conquerors with the Arabs and as
conquered with the slave traders. Furthermore, as I hope to prove,
they defied the linguistic stability of the empire. The unification of
all races into the Text was propelled by many social, religious, and
historical circumstances, chief among which were Spain's own racially ill-defined origins, its occupation by lighter- and darker-
skinned conquerors who imported their own black slaves and citizens, and the rest of Europe's prejudices about Spain's imprecise
racial heritage. This constellation of circumstances led to a theoretical welcoming, on paper, of black newcomers under the far-
reaching umbrella of a "Hispanic" race. This welcoming, however,
was predicated on the supposition that knowledge and practice of
the Hispanic ways would dissipate the more blatant differences
when transcribed into writing, primarily through official syncretism and legal miscegenation. After these prerequisites for assimilation were satisfied, marginals were permitted a place in the world
structure designed and led by Spaniards. Syncretism and miscegen-

ation remained pages of theories that were liberally distorted by interpretations and chiefly practiced unofficially. Even for those who gained access to the bureaucratic means of swearing off their differences, there were far too many implicit variants that could be shed merely by explicitly declaring oneself Hispanicized. Spaniards, who had for centuries known Islamized Negroid peoples as conquerors, had now successfully transformed them into collaborators. In justifying its expansionist policies, the empire applied a parallel rule to its conquest of sub-Saharan blacks under the guise of transforming them into political allies. The newcomers would serve a period of slavery while aiding the Hispanic search for new frontiers. It was the blacks, who, among all the mediators "officially" welcomed, experienced the most difficulty in proving their allegiance to the Hispanic—presumably blind and equitable—form of literary whiteness.

The concept of Hispanic "race" grew as a myth in print, rarely believed but mostly accepted as the unifying principle for the dissemination of Hispanidad. The voice of marginals was traditionally included in, but seldom allowed direct manipulation of, the printed page. And yet, enlightened Afro-Hispanics soon learned to use as publishing vehicles the very bureaucracies that monitored the integrity of printed materials. I have uncovered a significant number of these writers in official religious and secular records throughout the Spanish colonies; their works now come to light after centuries of burial as manuscript depositions for "crimes of difference."[11]

The issue of race has never subsided, solved only in the most fictional of rhetorical solutions. To this day, Hispanic unity is celebrated among Spanish-Americans as Día de la Raza ("Day of [the?] Race") on the date of Columbus's first landing. The race in question is a grand metaphor for unrealized promises of universal harmony offered by the Linguistic Mother of the Spanish New World. A "Grammar Day" would be a more appropriate celebration, albeit with caution, since it refers to the enlightened despotism of rules that set the terms of inscription for all Hispanic subjects.

11. I am indebted to the Menil Foundation, and particularly to Dominique de Menil and Karen Dalton, for giving me the opportunity and the encouragement to pursue the research which has yielded a movement of eighteenth-century black writers and artists in Latin America, as well as sporadic but important examples as early as the late sixteenth century.

Traditionally, all the peoples lagging behind the mythical Spanish-speaking race had to prove allegiance to the model in some court—a test required in particular from those "burdened" with visual differences. The ensuing tests of Hispanidad became cruel performances acted out by newcomers needing to partake of the world empire. Most newcomers desired to be counted, recorded, and declared *gente de razón* ("persons of reason"), a difficult trial for those adventurers who arose from the most uncertain strata of Iberian society.[12] From the outset, however, these future citizens found linguistic loopholes for the swearing-in.

At the turn of the fifteenth century, alongside the birth of the nation, the Spanish instituted the proof of *pureza de sangre* ("purity of blood") for those who wished to be Hispanic. In this way, the state attempted to ensure for each citizen a place in the imperial "genealogy." The issue of "purity of blood" involved a trial of faith, race, and national origin, depending on the issue in doubt. The end result was usually an auto-da-fé. This was the theatrical Spanish way to declare oneself faithful; the auto-da-fé, in fact, derived from the Spanish medieval plays that were secular adaptations of religious matters. Thus, the proof of Hispanic worth had become a theatrical production, words on an inquisitorial stage. The trial was no less staged; the suspected individual was publicly tried with all the pomp and circumstance of a pageant.[13] In fact, many prominent black citizens "dramatically" accused themselves of crimes that could be proven untrue during the trial.[14] Their reason for this legal

12. The category "gentes de razón" became a bureaucratically difficult issue toward the end of the seventeenth century, as the children of miscegenation openly demanded to be included. Some suggest it was easier for the offspring of Latin American Indians alone or with Spanish partners to obtain such a classification; this seems to correlate with the fear of a black, as opposed to a native American, middle class. See Jonathan I. Israel, *Race, Class and Politics in Colonial Mexico, 1610–1670* (London, 1975), chap. 2.

13. For elaborate descriptions of the Inquisition as theater in which the word *teatro*, "theater," is used in the description, see *Documentos inéditos o muy raros para la historia de México*, ed. Genaro García (Mexico City, 1974), pp. 31–41, 92–93, 145.

14. Most of the self-accusations are of being Jewish, and it remains difficult to separate fact from fiction, particularly because many blacks enjoyed a symbiotic cultural relationship with Jews. See, for example, *Documentos inéditos*, pp. 150–51, and Solange Alberro's discussion of several examples in "Negros y mulatos en los documentos inquisitoriales," in *El Trabajo y los trabajadores en la historia de México*, ed. Elsa Cecilia Frost, Michael C. Meyer, and Josefina Zoraida Vázquez (Mexico City, 1979), pp. 144–49.

maneuver was to gain access to an official audience, often for their writing, or for defending rights that could not otherwise be brought to court, much less to the approval and/or mercy of the public at large. Significantly, the first item expected from the state in such trials was a genealogical account, intimately connected with the suspected individual's service to the Crown. Through the centuries, the suspect who could not pass such a trial would be denied in turn "reason" or "citizenship" until the eighteenth century, in which the trial was often relegated to a *prueba de hidalguía* ("proof of nobility").[15] After the Age of Enlightenment, a difficult combination of credentials could permit a marginal to qualify for citizenship: a letter of manumission (or other proof of freedom) and willingness to abide by mythical whiteness as incorporated by the pronouncements of the Spanish Royal Academy of the Language. These metaphorical dictates undermined the issue of race and, more broadly, of differences. Hence, acceptance into the system of Hispanidad was a far cry from an invitation to join the scores of "persons of reason" who occupied the elite positions in the dictatorship.

A light-colored nobody or an exceptional Moor, Jew, or Afro-Hispanic could, to some degree, swear off impurities and gain a fictional genealogy and a grammatical standing in the New World. Latin, the Law, the Faith, and the degree of Hispanic honor and nobility were claimed by the elite as badges, either automatically due in recompense for services rendered to the Crown or laboriously litigated in trials. Castilian and literature, parody and magic constituted the arsenal of the exceptional marginal person. Thus, most reasons for Inquisitorial trials against marginals were linguistic and/or magical in nature; that is, individuals were accused of substituting for the official logic and written letter of the law some other form of expression. Even ventriloquism was considered a crime: *hablar por el pecho* ("to speak through the chest"); the accused was often charged with the ability to produce objects through words.[16]

15. Even a descendant of Nebrija went through a *prueba de hidalguía* during the eighteenth century, which served as a source of much of the biographical information on the famous ancestor. See Nebrija, *Gramática*, "Introduction" by González-Llubera, p. xvi and n. 14.

16. There are many examples of such a crime in the manuscript collection "Ramo

Ventriloquism—a form of expression that bypasses the linguistic strictures of the Hispanic system—serves as a metaphor for the birth of literature in Spanish America. Before the discovery of the New World, it was primarily the highborn who were supposed to produce literature in moments of idleness. After the discovery, adventurers seeking nobility, honorary citizenship, or just freedom impersonated the voice of the idle rich as *littérateurs*. Nebrija sets an extreme example of prediscovery literary attitudes by ignoring the "official" example of the poetry of Alfonso the Wise. The intellectual king, however, made a good case for biases against the official status of literature by compiling poetry written not in Castilian but in Galician-Portuguese. Nebrija not only denies by omission the existence of literature in languages that coexist with Castilian on the Iberian Peninsula, but he also puts in question the worth of literature. He declares in the "Prólogo" of his *Gramática:* "I por que mi pensamiento y gana siempre fue engrandecer las cosas de nuestra nación, dar alos ombres de mi lengua obras en que mejor puedan emplear su ocio, que agora lo gastan leiendo novelas o istorias embueltas en mil mentiras y errores, acordé ante todas las otras cosas reduzir en artificio este nuestro lenguaje castellano, para que lo que agora y de aqui adelante enel se escriviere pueda quedar en un tenor, y estenderse en toda la duracion delos tiempos que estan por venir." [And due to the fact that I put my intellect and desire to work toward the exaltation of our country's products, and that to give those who spoke my language works in which they would best use idle time, which they now waste reading novels or stories wrapped in lies and errors, my priority was to reduce the artifices of our Castilian language, so that whatever is written in it now and henceforth would fit into a mold, and would last forever into the future.][17]

According to Nebrija, fiction in the Hispanic empire was in peril. And yet, Hispanic-American fiction was born precisely from the elasticity gained by the official language. The creation of a Hispanic mold allowed the assimilation of viewpoints into "grammatically correct" writing. Orthography, syntax, and rhetoric were allies not just of historiography, but also of fiction. Discovery and conquest

---

Inquisición" of the Mexican *Archivos de la nación:* few transcriptions, however, have been published. For a published example, see *Documentos inéditos*, pp. 60–61.

17. Nebrija, *Gramática*, p. 6.

by force and by word cooperated without success in the attempted assimilation of differences. While the New World was created at the edge of an empire, discovered and named, conquered and renamed by outsiders, Hispanic-American fiction was born on the margins of what was officially accepted as grammatical writing. The same adventurers and marginals who manipulated Nebrija's codified Castilian employed techniques of fiction to convey facts never experienced before. Columbus, who was not even a Spaniard, coated his unexpected finds in the New World with official-sounding words of consolation.[18] Such a tactical coverup allowed him to experiment with fictional techniques without jeopardizing the semblance of truth and the power of convincing. On the contrary, fiction aided the rhetoric of truth devised by grammarians of imperialism such as Nebrija. Columbus's "mid-Atlantic" viewpoint creates a rhetoric of compromise aimed at preserving American differences within the Spanish textual molds.

From the outset, Hispanic-American fiction recorded the opinions of extraordinary adventurers and relatively ordinary citizens who expressed themselves in the imperial language of tactical obedience. The emerging literatures walked a thin line between compromise and resentment in order to recreate a fictional Hispanic self within the factual mold. The recreation summarizes the sacrifices suffered by outsiders who "took advantage" of the Empire's offer to "cover" them with a utopian blanket of purity. This compromising offer translated into action Spain's own universal quest, under whose aegis the nation upheld a blind literary and Catholic whiteness.

In the New World, Hispanic discourse is reborn as a fictional manipulation of a rapacious grammar. Nebrija's textual guide yielded a new grammar assimilating nontraditional reality in instantly accepted, faithful words. The same could be said of historical records, the laws of the Indies, and the dictates of the Inquisition, which included local variants and fictional interpretations. Imperial grammar, history, law, and religion forged a wordy colonial bureaucracy, but the largesse of the mother language disguised a linguistic dominatrix that condemned dissident values to hierarchical classifications and stages of unpleasant conformity.

New World practitioners of the language of bureaucracy claimed

18. See Christopher Columbus's *Journal*, trans. Cecil Jane (New York, 1960).

rights as Creoles and as Christians almost as soon as they were willing to forgo their national or religious differences and officially join the Hispanic system. Conformity was sealed as a superficial, written allegiance; bureaucratic records provided labels for the pretender that indicated the degree of declared and feasible imitation of the official norms. Racial differences demanded a much greater commitment to imitation: either slow miscegenation toward the Hispanic model or an instant "certificate of whiteness" ensuring a place under the blind domination of the imperial grammar.[19] The present effort aims to trace the origins of Afro-Hispanic writings to factual and fictional differences within the model of literary whiteness.

II

Traditional literary history has it that black writings of literary significance began in the Spanish-American world in the nineteenth century. At that time, the causes of abolition and liberation were well under way, presumably spurring Hispanics of all races to embrace the defense of the "darker" Others in their midst. The drive paralleled the legalization of a general Creole otherness against the one empire, echoing, further back in history, the Hispanic drive for a single national unity. With vicious circularity, texts embedded in literary whiteness mounted a rhetorical defense of black characters, who were used as the fictional mediators for ideas too daring for whites, such as surrendering to suppressed factual differences. The "rhetorical defense" placed black characters between fact and fiction, a convenient limbo to which newcomers were often confined by the dictates of the Old World. In the New World, the black mediators eventually emerged from their textual limbo to aid other Hispanics in common adventure: as interpreters of the nature, lan-

19. Elaborate miscegenation tables have existed at least since the early seventeenth century, as documented by Inca Garcilaso de la Vega, *Comentarios reales*, ed. Angel Rosemblat (Buenos Aires, 1943). The "certificate of whiteness" refers to the *documentos de gracias al sacar*, mentioned by Alexander von Humboldt, *Political Essays of the Kingdom of New Spain*, 4 vols. (London, 1814), 1:246–47, but in existence since at least 1789. See discussion of Pedro de Ayarza in the text.

guage, and work orders of the conquerors for the native American terra incognita.[20]

Recent discoveries place the incipience of Afro-Hispanic literature early in the colonial period, although such finds confirm the preponderance of a system of black mediation aligning itself with the general cause of Creole liberation.[21] Historians of Spanish America traditionally trace the ferment of Creole unrest to as early as the eighteenth century; black characters and writers joined in the projected restructuring of the rhetorical unity. Whereas the growing wave of underground syncretism between white, black, and native values surfaced as a new enlightened unity, however, only the black characters', but not the black writers', mediation was considered acceptable. Creole rhetoric continued the campaign of the imperial language against difference, particularly from the pen of the openly different.

When the New World divided into new independent worlds in the Americas, the rhetorical empire was the first to show signs of unrest and the last to admit these signs or to crumble under the ensuing rebellious texts. To this day, language remains the relative dictator of Hispanidad. Nonwhites could write as long as they did not address the issue of difference, a stricture that practically denied them self-conscious literature. The first black writers who published in

20. Many free black Spaniards are represented in the early New World adventure; the chief occupation among these was that of "interpreters": of "virgin nature" (such as possibly Prieto, the pilot of one of Columbus's ships), of barbaric languages (such as Estebanico, who "translated" for Cabeza de Vaca in Florida, and who also discovered what is today the Southwest of the United States), of fate (such as the "soothsayers" who appear in colonial chronicles and other documents, for instance Juana García from Freyle's *El Carnero*), and of leisure (such as Juan Cortés, the poet who improvised for the conquistador Cortés).

21. During the eighteenth century, the emergence of the Latin American Creole class as a political force changed the panorama of black slavery. Both members of loyalist and independentist camps attempted to attract Creoles to their ranks, and individuals of black ancestry were often included. A number of Hispanicized slaves were offered freedom in exchange for military and political support. Therefore, many of the freedom papers obtained were not necessarily associated with humanitarian views of abolitionism, but rather sought as a selective form of payment for services rendered. The European-born Enlightenment brought new euphemistic labels for categories of miscegenation, or *calidades* ("qualities," implying "castes"), whose chief purpose was to encourage free children of miscegenation to join the ranks of tax-paying and law-abiding citizens. Loyalists and independentists fought with rhetoric and other forms of coercion to enlist these new citizens in their causes.

Vulgar Latin or in Castilian Spanish argued eminently neutral or white issues before they addressed their own difference.

Blacks who wished to write at all were encouraged to climb the imperial ladder of Hispanidad toward a rhetorical whiteness. Such whiteness stood as a symbolic acceptance of the system, where differences were reduced to rhetorical participation, in other words, loyalty and allegiance to a piece of paper. The monstrous system paid in bureaucratic complexity what it gained in plasticity and availability. Writing standards tacitly permitted tactical differentiations and a reserved form of racial "passing" for the imitators of the written norms.

The increased specificity of miscegenation tables and the proliferation of certificates of whiteness bespeak the tragic "opportunities" available to black applicants desirous of rhetorical conformity. The tacit attempt to differ or the explicit desire to fail could produce the same result for the resentful imitators of Hispanic norms. The systematic impositions of such norms, however, could not erase certain differences. Those who failed could opt to revenge themselves against the white goals by exploiting the elusive opportunities that distinguish enlightened despotism from prior racial dictatorships. At the end of the eighteenth century, a substantial number of Afro-Hispanics asserted themselves beyond the alleged opportunities offered by the official discourse. But even before the peak of such a substantial wave of assertion, society was already "listening" while it brought to trial the first black writers openly resenting whiteness. In fact, Afro-Hispanics found in the trials of the Inquisition an unusual forum for their ideas; black writers even found judges ready to become their first literary critics.[22]

Before giving examples of the forbidden literature of the Afro-Hispanic Enlightenment, it would be expedient to compare its authors to exceptional predecessors and successors. An example of the former category is a late sixteenth- to early seventeenth-century Afro-Spaniard, and of the latter a late eighteenth- to early nineteenth-century Afro-Peruvian. Both writers dramatized the enslavement of marginals to the word, exemplified by their own names and careers. They also demonstrate that literary whiteness was, second only to

22. Records of Inquisitorial trials that contain writing, such as the one concerning Baltasar de Esquivel (discussed later), contain comments on the meaning and value of such writing; see the *Archivo general de la nación* (Mexico City), Ramo Inquisición, vol. 988, folios 392–417.

pride in black aesthetics, the most difficult subject to communicate for the Afro-Hispanic *littérateur*. The examples serve to put in perspective other alternatives in establishing a mutually agreeable compromise between unofficial differences and the official model: either by progressive syncretism and miscegenation or by instantaneous certificates of whiteness.

The first example emerges from Spain's habit of conferring rather loose labels on newcomers during their "imperial apprenticeship." Citizens considered to be "low class" were enrolled under the uniform social label of *ladinos* (which disregarded race, creed, and national or civil status), as soon as they spoke the rudiments of the official languages. Castilian Spanish and Vulgar Latin were considered as a progressive linguistic unity for this purpose. The rhetorical license was conferred upon black slaves who learned Spanish "within six months," and one black *ladino* became Juan Latino, the Latin grammarian and poet.[23]

For Latino, marrying into a "noble and white" Spanish family was simply a personal and social achievement, rather than an act of tactical miscegenation. Before his marriage, Juan had already experienced the scale of personal labels that named the stages of his acculturation. He had changed his slave name of "de Sessa," indicating his belonging to a "noble and white" Spanish master, to Latino, or "Latin," which lent the former black slave an old imperial bloodline and genealogy based on his own linguistic merits. Juan's Hispanicization took him a step beyond the middle-class Spanish meritocracy; he climbed the ladder of whiteness, nobility, and grammatical proficiency leading to the highest Latinesque strata of the imperial chain. A noble, solicitous Spaniard, he served the Habsburg dynasty and honored them with his literature.[24]

Within his restrictions, Latino manifested his defense of blackness when he viewed, with cautious anonymity and resentment, the African differences within the rhetorical blindness. In his own words:

Obvious Aethiopem Christum docet ore Philippus...
Ne Aethiopi iusta haec forte Philippe neges...

23. The quote is a "campaign motto" issued by the Crown of Spain as an ordinance, collected by Konetzke in *Colección de documentos*, 1:237–40.
24. Latino dedicated an epic poem in Latin to the Habsburg dynasty; see Ioannes Latinus, *Fernandi Principis Navitate... Austrias* (Granada, 1573).

Phillip [II, Habsburg King of Spain] instructs the found Ethiopian
about Christ...
Do not deny, Phillip, to Ethiopians these just rights...

And more explicitly:

Quod si nostra tuis facies Rex nigra ministris
displicet, Aetheiopum non placet alba viris.

If our black face, King, displeases your ministers,
Ethiopians do not like white ones on their males.[25]

The warring blacks, usually known in Spain as Moors and not
by the effete cultural label of Ethiopians, are bound to learn the
word of the Crown and Christ regardless of Latino's ironic plea
on their behalf. The author's plea discreetly challenges the discourse of assimilation by taking the initiative and the official word
in hand. The second excerpt suggests the limits of assimilation by
contrasting aesthetic prejudices from both sides. Furthermore, Latino underscores the pursuit of whiteness as a weakness, considered unmanly among Ethiopians. In the Latin inscription he
ordered for his own tomb, he cites among his accomplishments
the dedication of his considerable knowledge to the service of the
Hispanic ways as much as his *niggerrima* (blackest) origins.[26] Posterity was to judge him as much for his black origins as for his
Hispanic goals.

The second literary figure of our concern wrote much more directly of the war of veiled assimilation and prejudices waged by Afro-
Hispanics. José Manuel Valdés, the Afro-Peruvian physician, scientist, historian, and writer, lived during the transitional period after
the Afro-Hispanic Enlightenment, when white writers attempted to
manipulate the defense of blackness in their antislavery textual campaigns. Valdés witnessed his country's independence from Spain and
assumed a low and bitter profile for his racial difference; his life
vehemently unveils the imprints of marginality disguised by his
writings. He bore the surname usually given by Latin American
states to bastard children, one that is often found among writers
born out of wedlock by one black parent. He wrote himself out of

25. Ibid., p. 10.
26. Valuarez B. Spratlin, *Juan Latino, Slave and Humanist* (New York, 1938), p.
21.

blackness by assuming an invisible self even when he addressed issues of marginality, as he did in his scientific and historical treatises.

It has been suggested that he received a certificate of whiteness to become a priest and a theoretician of medicine, even though he would not have needed it for practicing medicine, since many low-order ecclesiastical brothers and many surgeons in pre–nineteenth-century Peru were black.[27] In order to write, however, the same individuals had to reject symbolically all variables disturbing the empire's whitewashed, pure singleness of text. Valdés took to heart such a rule by carrying out the ultimate textual commitments to racial blindness. Not only did he receive and then renounce a certificate of whiteness, but he also refused to have his portrait painted.[28] Curiously, the only likenesses that remained were painted by Pancho Fierro, a black contemporary. The two watercolors by Fierro present the doctor obscured by a cape very much like the veils used by the *tapadas*, or women who hid their identities in the street. He also wears the sandals worn by the poor, in contrast to the rest of his clothing and the setting, which indicate the life of a gentleman.[29]

In spite of his self-imposed invisibility, and perhaps because of it, Valdés was able to deal in an impersonal fashion with the issue of minority-status people—women, the poor, and blacks. He intro-

27. The black majority among pre–nineteenth-century Peruvian physicians is suggested by many statistics. See Manuel A. Fuentes, *Lima: Apuntes históricos, estadísticos, administrativos, comerciales y costumbres* (Paris, 1867), pp. 167–71. The work of black surgeons in Peru and Valdés's practice as a *cirujano latino*, that is, "Latin-conversant surgeon," is also discussed by J. A. de Lavalle, *El Dr. José Manuel Valdés (apuntes sobre su vida y sus obras)* (Lima, 1886), pp. 3–4.

28. Information about a possible "certificate of whiteness" is discussed by J. A. de Lavalle, in ibid., p. 10. Paraphrasing Mendiburu, whose *Diccionario histórico y biográfico del Perú*, 11 vols. (1874–90; rpt. Lima, 1935) I have not been able to consult, Lavalle notes that Pius VII signed a bull to exempt Valdés from "irregularidades de su nacimiento y el inconveniente de su color" (irregularities of his birth and the "inconvenience" of his color) in order to admit him into the sacred orders. Lavalle concludes that Valdés decided not to make use of this bull (pp. 10–11). Lavalle quotes from what he claims to have heard as a child about Valdés, who was then in his seventies (p. 26). Valdés, according to Lavalle, refused to be portrayed because "los negros salían muy feos en pintura" (blacks came out very ugly [badly?] in paintings).

29. Of the several portraits by Fierro mentioned by Lavalle, I have viewed two similar watercolors in the Museo de Arte del Perú, Lima, in which Dr. Valdés's face is covered and he is wearing the sandals typical of the poor. One of the images includes a horse-drawn carriage and coachman waiting in the background.

duced blackness into his more personal endeavors by fictionalizing the life of Saint Martin of Porras, the Afro-Peruvian saint from the turn of the sixteenth century. Actually, he received an official ecclesiastical commission to write his work. Only in his testament does he focus on his black genealogy—his posthumous wish conveniently tears the veil from his tactical pretense of racial neutrality.

By virtue of their language skills and controlled exertion of their differences, Juan Latino and José Manuel Valdés, children of at least one black parent, lived as virtually neutral Hispanics and only recreated their "selves" as Afro-Hispanics for posterity. For their pains and accomplishments they wore the letter of the empire written in blood over their identities and psyches. Both set important precedents in the history of black pride, making subtle but sure gestures of proud differentiation. Latino writes about anonymous *Aethiope* ("Ethiopian") warriors, Valdés about an illegitimate *pardo* ("brown") saint; both do so with awe and with sadness, against a background of rhetorical inequality. As a meager compensation for their efforts, less marginal interpreters of the Spanish language extended to them the honorable classifications of *Aethiope* and *pardo*, respectively.

III

The Enlightenment produced a new vocabulary of race and a fresh look at the mediating role of the different in the Spanish empire. This new vocabulary ultimately changed the European approach to otherness. Most enlightened Europeans, chiefly the French, considered Spanish-speaking people as their "wards," including white Spaniards and Spanish-Americans. The French justified political takeovers as ways to "enlighten" the minds of Hispanics on issues such as liberty, equality, and fraternity—which ironically permitted French hegemony in both Spain and Mexico. The paradoxical wave of ideas divided Spanish-American elites who supported either Spanish conservatism or French liberal ideology as cultural alternatives. Both extremes attempted to rally marginals to their cause. The attempts were either direct—recruiting the outcast as a tax-paying citizen and/or cannon fodder—or indirect—linguistic recruitment through elaborate tables of miscegenation, promising a place for everyone in the realm of the official word. The only difference between conservatives and liberals might have been their attitudes toward servitude. The pro-Crown conservatives promised improved conditions for the "slaves of the king"; the Francophile liberals promised improved conditions for the "slaves of the nation." The rhetoric, however, began to take a new turn as the institution of freedom from national boundaries or from international occupation now required a social choice from free citizens. The war of words came to be fought on the bases of the sociopolitical and economic advantages of recruiting supporters.[30]

Marginals, for instance dark-skinned individuals, confronted the very classifications which allowed them to be counted as citizens in positions more advantageous than that of the lowly, pure black. It was clearly not enough for enlightened blacks to be labeled with archetypal terms such as *Aethiope* or *pardo*, labels that covered a multitude of differences under the guise of "taming" a black ancestry into Hispanic conformity. In the enlightened New World, a detailed subdivision of categories of miscegenation and the proliferation of opportunities to become officially white became official policy. Both options steered clear of extremism in racial rankings by generating a contrived linguistic system. Nonwhites were encouraged to remain at a racially safe midpoint, indicated in the rhetoric of the empire by the term *moreno*. The etymological origin of this term is the conquering-conquered *moro*, or "Moor," a term that thus substituted for the concept of blackness one of an alleged neutrality.[31]

Afro-Hispanic authors must have been aware of the enlightened vocabulary's new ploy to "tame" them. I have found no evidence for their own use of such a vocabulary, or, for that matter, no evidence of any practical use by the authorities—in either birth certificates, censuses, or Inquisitorial records. We cannot assume, however, that the new vocabulary was solely a theoretical issue, particularly because of the proliferation, during the eighteenth century, of the so-called *pinturas de castas* ("paintings of castes," or

30. See note 21.

31. The word *moreno* has been in use since at least the early thirteenth century in Castilian (ninth century in Catalan) to indicate a Moor-like person. The implication of a proud, dark person became popular in Spanish America in the eighteenth century, however. For the usage in Spain, see "Moro," in Joan Corominas, *Breve Diccionario etimológico de la lengua castellana* (Madrid, 1980), p. 404.

"miscegenation paintings").[32] These paintings represented the consequences of miscegenation by comparing the physiognomies and
lifestyles of father, mother, and child. We cannot assume either that
these paintings were only aimed at enticing nonwhites to climb the
socioracial ladder of whiteness. Along with the euphemistic, hair-
splitting racial classifications we find in these paintings overt representation of "regressive" racial traits—such as *torna atrás* and
salto atrás ("turn backwards" and "jump backwards").[33] I suspect
that these paintings were used by ecclesiastical authorities for the
purpose of marriage counseling. Each racial classification was portrayed with its parental source and the type of job, food, clothing,
and other corresponding social benefits. A couple would thus become aware of the advantages or risks of their union vis-à-vis the
white model race. The relative whiteness of the Spaniards themselves might have diminished the rhetorical "excellence" and "purity" of the model. Only at the time of marriage could the
ecclesiastical authorities exert their influence. That would explain
why the elaborate caste system does not appear at other times, such
as in birth certificates, censuses, or during trials. At these other
times ecclesiastical authorities consistently assigned very straightforward terminology to blacks. The aim was still assimilation under
broad categories.

In documents of the Mexican Inquisition, for instance, one rarely
finds qualifiers other than *negro. Mulato* is in fact the rare second
choice, and *lobo* (the offspring of a black and native American union)
follows.[34] During the eighteenth century, however, words that at
one point had been considered defamatory nomenclature when applied to the national origin of whites became points of pride for
black writers of Hispanic literature. The fact of the matter is that
many whites themselves no longer considered such terms as derog-
atory, but rather as labels that identified them either as loyalists
(for the *gachupín*, or Spanish-born immigrant) or advocates of in-

32. See Johanna Faulhaber, "El Mestizaje durante la época colonial en México,"
in *Antropología física: Epoca moderna y contemporánea*, ed. Javier Romero Molina,
Alfonso L. de Garay, Johanna Faulhaber, and Juan Comas (Mexico City, 1976), pp.
69–119.
33. This classification was assigned to several racial combinations; see ibid., p.
117.
34. Ibid., p. 112.

dependence (for the *criollo*, or New World-born).[35] When black writers were brought before the Inquisitorial tribunals, debates arose about their national rather than their racial classification. Despite such elaborate, and even idealized, categories of miscegenation, nonwhites struggled to be classified according to social and political standing, rather than race. There are even cases of individuals brought to trial at the Mexican Inquisition who refused all forms of citizen classification.

Two writers of color from the eighteenth century, one from Mexico and the other from Colombia, illustrate the marginals' adamant attempts to name themselves as they pleased. The known autobiographical writings of these two people still exhibit the high price paid for their efforts at self-assertion. The texts of the Mexican are known through Mexican archival depositories, such as the Inquisitorial records; those of the Colombian appear in papers from secular tribunals. Although they both legally won their cases, chiefly by presenting essay-length letters to the authorities, the former was eventually declared a misfit, and the latter declared himself one.

José Ventura, an author who was officially declared "white," is one of the unsung defenders of true racial blindness during the Enlightenment. Even though brought before the tribunals of the Mexican Inquisition as a "Spanish heretic," his heresy was chiefly a linguistic one: he refused to be classified in terms of differences— racial, religious, or social.[36] Due to this refusal, his exact heritage still remains a mystery, and his effectiveness as an antiracist campaigner was greatly enhanced by his self-declared racial anonymity. He argued selflessly in favor of an impure and unorthodox image of Mexican selfhood, in which differences were admitted in reality but obliterated on paper for the sake of a democratic meritocracy. The Mexican Inquisition tried unsuccessfully to assimilate this humble man, an embroiderer by profession, into an imperial system which deprived him of the most elementary of choices: the definition of his self-image. Then the courts sought to find a legal

35. For a discussion of the etymological implications of these words see "Cacho I" and "Criollo," respectively, in Joan Corominas, *Diccionario crítico etimológico castellano e hispánico* (Madrid, 1980), pp. 725–27 and 243–45, respectively.

36. The biographical information about Ventura, his writings, and drawings are part of the records of his trial. See the *Archivo general de la nación* (Mexico), Ramo Inquisición, vol. 1505.

cause for punishing his refusal. In fact, his many infractions against Church law became insignificant in comparison to his refusal to be cast as a member of a specific Hispanic caste. Thereby he created a formidable obstacle for a bureaucracy whose custom it was to introduce each case brought to trial by recounting the genealogy of the individual to place him or her in the proper socioracial category.

Ventura further jeopardized his fate by creating designs for embroidery in which he depicted social injustice, using himself as an example. Many of these sketched the rebellious message by presenting nude figures acting out their "sins" and revenge against society under the embellishment of an overlay of clothing or the suggestive bluntness of a prurient setting. The message was further driven home by his filling in some of the sketches—possibly not for sale—with volatile poetic captions, very much in the style of twentieth-century comic strips. For this complex of cultural heresies, Ventura was finally convicted by the secular legal system as a Creole pornographer. Ultimately, however, he was left relatively free to continue the expression of his moral violations, having been declared an "ethical" outcast and sentenced to life in an asylum for the insane. In spite of this tragic end, Ventura succeeded in making his antiestablishment points more than clear. His greatest victory may have been to point out for posterity that he could not be condemned for his refusal to remain racially neutral by the very system that promoted the caste system as a mechanism of assimilation pretending neutrality.

By means of his 1789 trial, through the writings and drawings included in the official record both in his defense and for the prosecution, José Ventura became a public self. The unabashedly Mexican writer assailed racial prejudices that were crucial to the definition of Mexico as a melting pot. The Mexico he portrays in his work was then barely a formed nation with a forced united front—a single mythical race, a single faith, and a single nationhood. After ironically accepting the inevitability of such a unilateral front, he proposed to base it on a tactical unity that openly incorporated plurality.

Perhaps no other text of Ventura's is as concise an example of the suffering experienced by Mexicans for claiming differences in writing as this letter to his daughter:

Querida hija de mi estimación, te remito esta carta en la cual verás el desengaño de la sanguinidad que por herencia te corresponde. Es cierto que Dios separó las formas de la naturaleza del hombre y también apartó las de la mujer. A unos los hizo blancos, a otros Amarillos, a otros Negros, a otros Pardos y cada generación a sus principios les daba vergüenza estar juntos y se fueron apartando: el blanco tenía su Rey, el Amarillo tenía su Rey, el Negro tenía su Rey y cada cual se hallaba en su lugar gobernando su cuerpo, el blanco en su blanca, el Negro en su Negra y el Amarillo en su Amarilla.

Mas esto asentado, tenemos por cierto que si queremos saber o indagar quiénes fueron nuestros Padres y la sangre y calidad que le asiste, hallaremos por nuestro Rey y Reyes anteriores que bajo de su corona hay blanco, hay Negro, hay Amarillo, hay Pardo, consintiendo los Reyes anteriores que el blanco se case con una Negra, el Negro con una blanca, el Amarillo con blanca y la blanca con un Pardo. Y así la Información no me cuesta ninguna dificultad el despacharla, bajo de cuyo supuesto te digo que bajo de este Imperio todos los que estamos somos españoles, porque el Rey de España a todos nos ha avasallado y avasalla....

Dear daughter of my heart, I am sending you this letter by which you will experience disillusionment with the blood line which is yours by heritage. It is true that God separated the forms of man's nature and also distinguished the forms of the woman. Some he made white, others Yellow, and others Black, and yet others *Pardo* (Brown). And each generation in the beginning was ashamed to be together and they distanced themselves from one another: the white man had his King, the Yellow had his King, the Black had his King and each remained in his place governing his body, the white man in his white woman, the Black in his Black woman, the Yellow in his Yellow woman.

But once that has been settled, we know for a fact that if we want to ascertain or to investigate who were our Parents and the blood and quality (caste) which identifies them, we will find out that under our present and every previous King there have been white people, Black, Yellow, Brown, consenting such previous Kings for the white man to marry a Black woman, the Black to marry a white woman, the Yellow a white woman and the white woman a Brown man. And it is not difficult to dispense such Information, under whose aegis I can tell you that all of us here are Spaniards, because the King of Spain subjected and continues to subject us to servitude.[37]

Ventura proceeds to attack native Americans who refused to become Hispanic while they lived under the control of the Spanish

---

37. I have used the partial transcription of Ventura's letter, respecting his original choice of capitalization and emphasis. The original is in the *Guía de forasteros: Estanquillo literario* 1 (January 1984), 8–9.

empire and suggests that the Indians, the original "citizens," act as the latest "newcomers" to the empire. In Ventura's view, they should realize their inability to claim "purity of blood" just like the other peoples gathered under the New World umbrella. Finally, the Mexican writer questions the justice of a bureaucratic system that supports one arbitrary and unjust God, one color, one government, and one standard of aesthetics without properly accounting for the "marginal" contributions.

Ventura's argument against the concepts of purity of blood and genealogy unveiled miscegenation as a historical fact that was part and parcel of the imperial system, while others opted for a meta-phorical acceptance of whiteness. Whereas Ventura was persecuted by Church and Law for his overt choice to defend miscegenation, other individuals were rewarded by the Crown for their strategic and more acceptable desire to become officially white.

The second example in question is perhaps the most famous petition for "extinction of color," that of the *pardo* captain Pedro Antonio de Ayarza from Colombia, who petitioned the king of Spain on behalf of his son's rights. Ayarza's son had attended school and learned the basics of the humanities, as prescribed by the educational system of the time. By virtue of his race, however, the son could not obtain a formal degree or continue his professional studies. The king responded directly to Ayarza, bypassing the courts that normally interpreted the laws of the Indies, and yet adhering explicitly to the letter of those laws. The king's written permit circumvents racial differences in favor of an act of rhetorical blindness, whereby "the character of mulatto [a less desirable term than *pardo*] being held extinguished in him, he be admitted, without its serving as a precedent, to the degrees he may seek in the university." Thus José Ponciano de Ayarza became an honorary white lawyer by act of the royal pen, on March 16, 1797.[38]

Whiteness was granted to Ayarza through a *documento de gracias al sacar* ("document of grace upon receipt"), a curiously legal and religious-sounding title for a Spanish certificate of whiteness. This

38. The text of the "certificate" was published by John Tate Lanning, "The Case of José Ponseano de Ayarza: A Document on the Negro in Higher Education," *Hispanic American Historical Review* 24 (1944): 432–51. See esp. p. 439. For more information about this case, see James F. King, "The Case of José Ponciano de Ayarza: A Document on *Gracias al Sacar*," *Hispanic American Historical Review* 32 (February 1952): pt. 2, 640–47.

type of rhetorical circumvention reveals much about the history of the people who devised it. The issue of "grace" euphemistically addresses both the rights and honors conferred upon a citizen that should already belong to the citizen, at least according to utopian Spanish and Catholic principles.[39]

Unlike these representative examples of the black middle class, poets of the Afro-Hispanic Enlightenment remained reluctant to accept compromises with literary whiteness. The conciseness of form and looseness of message that poetry could convey served to disguise the effrontery of its authors. Although many poets were brought to trial for failure to toe the official line, others enjoyed the relative freedom of the paid itinerant improviser. The resulting self-assertive writing by all Afro-Hispanics is characterized by a parody of the very fabric of the imperial grammar. Citizens of all types read or heard this poetry, were prompted to cry or to laugh with or at the artists. Yet the reader's emotive response was built upon the writer's tacit indictment of the linguistic system.

An important documented trial of an enlightened black poet was that of Baltasar de Esquivel by the Mexican Inquisition.[40] This author, somewhat like his compatriot José Ventura, tactically avoided a clear definition in terms of race, religion, and nationality. Unlike Ventura, however, from whom he learned to sew, Esquivel is much more candid about his blackness, his lax Catholicism, and his even laxer Mexican nationalism. His trial in 1753 records fragments of a fictional autobiography. He invented several selves, names, and origins, all of which enhance and ridicule a noble but illegitimate birth in an invented Spanish town full of heretics. The versions of his life narrated to the judges further coincide in describing a New World escape with a wet nurse, first to Havana—where he learned how to read, write, and sew—then to Mexico, where he was determined to serve the system as best he could.

The puzzled Inquisitors were at odds to formalize an accusation against Esquivel, whom they called at first a *gachupín*, then of *cal-*

---

39. As an implicit honor or *honra*, and a state of grace or *estado de gracia*, to which individuals were entitled as soon as they were declared Catholic believers and citizens by the respective forms of "naming," and as long as they behaved according to the principles they had "signed into."

40. I uncovered the trial of Baltasar de Esquivel, including his autobiographical and biographical sketches, letters, and poetry intercepted or voluntarily given as depositions, in *Archivo general de la nación*, Ramo Inquisición, vol. 988, folios 392–417.

idad desconocida ("unknown quality or caste"), and eventually a *criollo*. His assimilation into the text of the Inquisition, and thus of the official word of the Hispanic world, depends on his novelistic depositions. And yet, amidst the pages of his only known official record, his poetry transcends the ambivalence of his autobiographical narration:

Negro se te vuelva el día
negro por sus negras horas
y negros trabajos pases,
pues de negros te enamoras.

To black shall your day turn
in the black that the hours bore
and black labors you shall bear,
for it is blacks whom you adore.

Con repetidos clamores
falsa, leve y sin fe
le suplico al cielo que
todas las tres pascuas llores
y con crecidos dolores
por tu infame tiranía
nunca tengas alegría
y para mayor quebranto,
pues a lo negro amas tanto
negro se te vuelva el día.

Once more my claims have burst
falsely, lightly, without faith
begging heavens for you to face
in tears every biblical first
and with pains at their worst
under your tyrannical concern
may happiness you never earn
and to your even greater sadness,
having loved so much blackness
To black shall your day turn.

Quiera Dios que con afán
no tengas ningunos gozos
y que des tiernos sollozos
cuando otros cantando están,
y pues negro es tu galán
y negro el amor que imploras
ese negro a quien tú adoras
con voluntad tan veloz
lo mire como a un reloz
negro por sus negras horas.

May God set as a stubborn ploy
for you to lack in every pleasure
and to sigh softly under pressure
while others are singing with joy,
and as black is the man you enjoy
and black is the love you implore,
the black man whom you adore
with such a fast staying will,
as a clock you'll see him fill
in the black that the hours bore.

Nunca del floreado pan
gustes sus blancas dulzuras,
sino unas semitas duras,
y por los días de San Juan;
más pobre te veas que Amán
y cuando a casarte haces
sea un negro con quien te cases
que de él mismo vivas harta
y que te traíga a la cuarta
y negros trabajos pases.

May you never of the finest bread
taste the sweet white at its core
but hard seeds that come to the
    fore
by the feast of Saint John led;
more than Haman having shed
by the time that marriage you
    dare
if a black choice you declare
for you shall live full of him
and he will fill you to the brim
and black labors you shall bear.

Cuando el verano en primores
vista el campo de alegrías,
entonces con melarquías
lágrimas tengas por flores,
ansias, penas y temores
tengas por minutos y horas;
pues a lo blanco desdoras,
quiera Dios por tu apetito,
el que paras un negrito,
pues de negros te enamoras.

When the gala of summer
  showers
dresses the ground with joys
just then melancholy annoys
you with tears instead of flowers,
anxieties, sorrows and fear of
  powers
filling up hours and minutes
  galore
as the white you begin to abhor,
may God feed your eager ploy
with the birth of a black baby
  boy,
for it is blacks whom you adore.[41]

A critical lesson to be derived from this poem is the manner in which Esquivel defends "sacrificial blackness" as a rivaling part and intimate partner of the "victimizing whiteness" from which a mixed product emerges. The metaphorical usage of black and white as rivals is parodied by the incidence of intimacy between two representatives of the respective racial groups. No one is to blame for either the rejections in theory and the attraction in practice. The poet wishes for the partners of his portrayed affair to take full responsibility for their acts. Tradition as portrayed by Esquivel already contains an indication of cooperation between the races, often with tragic as well as triumphant consequences. For instance, the three "biblical firsts" Esquivel suggests as dates to recall the responsibility of miscegenation correspond to official feasts of "naming" among Hispanic Catholics not ordinarily associated with such responsibility: January 6, the Feast of the Epiphany; June 24, the Feast of Saint John the Baptist, and the floating feast of Resurrection, often in March, when Christ acted out His divine role in God's name. The Feast of the Epiphany is implicitly interpreted as the feast of the mysterious conception of the global family. The Feast of Saint John is suggested as an improvised baptism of a new faith. The Resurrection was most likely suggested to be the decisive rite of faith toward the promise of an afterlife. These dates are, as it were, at the point of convergence between Judaism and Christianity, and thus are cruel remembrances of ethnic strife and the apparent triumph of one group over another. Furthermore, Esquivel sees both conflict and compromise from a

41. Ibid., folio 400 and verso; my own translation.

relatively neutral perspective, until at the end of the poem the birth of a black baby boy serves as a reminder of the sacrifices still to be made for the blind acceptance of love. Both actors in this birth, the "black" man and his "white" lover continue to share their responsibilities. Esquivel, however, gives an added twist to the poem's social message by writing it from the perspective of the "white" or lighter-colored woman who falls in love with a black man.

Esquivel endows the symbols of officially white, Western tradition with black responsibility, and vice versa. The offspring of interracial lovemaking certify the union of races and remind everyone of a painful joint responsibility. The poet elevates a love poem to the category of a racial model for society by "sanctifying" miscegenation with allusions to the Scriptures. Through his poetic manipulation of language the feasts of birth, baptism, and resurrection relate the culmination of Judeo-Christian tradition with the evocation of a biracial Christ. In fact, the Judeo-Christian feasts live in symbiosis with Africa in Latin America. The subtext of this poem evokes the three most popular dates for Afro-Hispanic carnivals during colonial times. Esquivel's poem mimics and mocks the religious liturgy and official calendar by announcing their relationship with blackness.

In one last stroke of linguistic manipulation, the poem forces the reader to deal with an outsider to both the black and white codes vying for attention. Haman, the biblical figure who acted against the Jews, appears as a metaphor for one who pays a high price for one's xenophobia. Haman's financial and social greed is the true motivation behind his attack on Jews. The feast of Purim celebrates a singular triumph: the miscegenation between a Jew (Esther) and a non-Jew (Xerxes, the Persian king) serves to save the rest of the bearers of the tradition. Esther, who appears in the Bible as a reluctant wife of Xerxes, asked her husband to put a stop to the massacre of her people as a favor to her. The biblical subtext suggests that Xerxes stops the Jewish massacre in exchange for the love of his wife. Purim, the celebration of this triumph of compromise, is in fact a carnival-like affair in the spring, a token celebration of freedom negotiated in a cross-ethnic compromise by Jews. Thus viewed, Purim is, beneath the official discourse, a feast of negotiated ethnic recognition through "miscegenation" and also through syncretic convergence with such pagan rites as Saturnalia.

Esther and Esquivel, Purim and the Christian "carnivals" of naming, have much in common. The biblical character and the Afro-

Hispanic writer make a compromise with "the one" power structure to save their respective people's lives and works. Haman and the other threats become assimilated into a concentric metaphorical language in Esquivel's poetry. The superstructure of whiteness, whether in the accepted Catholic or "unacceptable" Jewish manifestations, becomes both the subject and object of a text of blackness.

Esquivel's parodic participation in literary whiteness is a subtle indictment of the rhetorical system. Such a system never envisioned itself as an "opportunity" for the assertion of "differences"; on the contrary, it built itself as a "companion of the empire" in the assimilation of outsiders. Esquivel's autobiographical poetry follows the legacy of a discourse grammatically legalized by Nebrija on the verge of the Spanish empire, unsuspecting that its very effort of assimilation had its limits. The empirical grammar's proposed thoroughness in accounting for the variables of the others was based on a precariously obtained enlightenment that "lightened" the differences. Instead of total assimilation, the linguistic system created an all-encompassing bureaucracy large enough to encourage multiple interpretations and thus loopholes. Esquivel's poetry exploited the bases of the Hispanic tradition on faulty racial, ethnic, and cultural compromises. While he "lightened" his grammar of direct allusions to difference, he kept a rhetorical eye on the rebellious interpretations easily overlooked by the official bureaucrats. In fact, it appears that the Inquisitors saw the racial tragedy rather than the triumphs of Esquivel's poem about miscegenation. Esquivel's ultimate triumph remains that this and other poems were kept for posterity by the Inquisitors in its original booklet format attached to the records of his trial.

In a suite of poems included in his booklet, Esquivel reveals another angle of the implicit "blackness" of his poetic language versus the utopian "whiteness" of the model, that is, between the unofficial subtext and the official text. This time, the subtext of his work appears to be sanctioned by the formulas of courtly love against a background of Christian textuality. Esquivel manipulates such dual formulas in a style reminiscent of European courtly poets who subverted the standard metaphors of Western poetry in order to deal with forbidden love. The author purportedly overcomes the racial obstacle to the object of his desire by disguising his love in deliberately opaque language. His object of love is a *morena*—or dark Hispanic woman— whose ambivalent racial definition derives from a double etymology:

treacherous fish of the depths or Moorish, that is, a proud and feisty Afro-Hispanic woman.[42] The worth and beauty of this *morena* is in the eyes of society as well as in the interpretation of a gluttonous language. The suite, buried in the Inquisition records, reads:

Amante es más justiciero	Lover is far more judicious;
aunque me anima el amor	although I am moved by love,
si le miro como amante	if I see him as a lover
le respeto como a Dios.	I respect him like God.
Amante de las almas	Lover of all souls,
esposo verdadero que sólo tus	true husband above all
piedades	for whom only your pity
al suelo te trajeron.	brings down to earth.
Como tan compasivo	Because of your compassion
por mi divino dueño	toward my divine master shed,
te cargas de mis culpas	you assume my load of guilt
y pagas lo que debo.	and pay what I owe in debt.
Señor sacramentado	Lord by sacrament delivered
que encubierto debemos	under cover we support
y descubierto muestras	while uncovered you exhibit
que eres señor inmenso.	your wide acceptance as lord.
Trigueño estás por el sol	From the sun you have darkened,
más que mucho sol bello	darker in beauty than any sun:
si es morena la madre	he whose mother is a *morena*
que el hijo sea trigueño.	should have an equally dark son.[43]

Parody still remains a disguise for frustrated action. The Afro-Hispanics who wrote literature, particularly poetry, suffered like no other Hispanics for their difference both on and off the record. On

42. A singular metaphorical association occurs early on in Spanish between the words "negro" and "fish," particularly in literature. For instance, since the thirteenth-century *Cantigas* of Alfonso the Wise there are many occurrences of the expression "negro[a] como un pez" ("black as a fish"). Is this a veiled allusion to the *morena?* Possibly, if one accepts the double connotation of the word *morena* as the "dark and treacherous" fish (Latin *muraena*, English *moray*) and as a "low-lying" Moor or a Moor lying low in order not to be recognized. This play on words can be found in Afro-Hispanic writings as late as the eighteenth century. An example of the Afro-Mexican Vasconcelos will be discussed later in the text.

43. The trial of Esquivel, in *Archivo general de la nación*, folio 402ᵛ.

record, Afro-Hispanics allied themselves with the false compromises promised by the Imperial Grammar of the conquerors; hence, the results are reminders of a literature of resentment. This literature is heroic as much in its effort to transcend as in its skill to be assimilated by the enemy without calling attention to its differences. Of the Afro-Hispanic heroic acts, the most lasting is the visionary expression of blackness as an important element *within* the Hispanic culture. Transatlantic black culture in the Americas distills a philosophy of self-protection adaptable to the needs of nonspecifically black Latin Americans in search of their own "space" in the Hispanic world grammar. Afro-Hispanic writers learned to write "black" poems in Spanish, exploiting the built-in openness of the cultural proselytism and uncovering the built-in prejudice of literary images of blackness. Euro-Hispanics adopted this philosophy of writing when they argued in favor of their nationalism as a kind of "blackness."

National freedom and black liberation have traditionally coexisted as parallel aims in Latin America. Perhaps the ultimate proof is the employment by whites of black troubadours of freedom. Thus, many Afro-Hispanic writers tried by the tribunals of the system were free citizens who exploited the dubious liberal tendencies of their compatriots and won their cases. If at times the Inquisition intercepted their texts while they were likely being distributed from hand to hand among a select group, more often it was the writers themselves who brought their written materials before the judges. Those accused of violating some legal code often used their literature as a proof of worth, even though in fact they had to disguise or deny the contents of such literature.

Among the few known writers not tried by the Inquisition, two were itinerant performers who earned part of their livelihood from their "trade"—a further proof of their having become black heralds of liberal causes. The price they paid for their trade was the need to lighten the social implications of their black verse and their human worth as threats by the deliberate use of self-deprecating humor. As buffoons, they engineered public displays of their oral talents and limited "publication" as graffiti artists or comic counterparts of white straight men. The best known are Meso Mónica from the Dominican Republic and José Vasconcelos from Mexico, respectively known as "the little black Dominican poet" and "the little black

Mexican poet."[44] It is fitting to end this essay by quoting their views of racial and social justice against the myth of one Hispano-Catholic whiteness.

Mónica comments on a basic source of rhetorical unity for the Spanish empire:

Aristóteles decía	Aristotle used to trace
(filósofo muy profundo)	(being in philosophy profound)
que en la redondez del mundo	to the fact the world is round
no existe cosa vacía.	the absence of all empty space.
Falsa es su filosofía	His philosophy I shall deface
según lo que a mí me pasa,	according to my own pleasure,
le discutiría sin tasa,	arguing without measure
y al cabo él se convenciera,	I shall undoubtedly win,
en el momento que viera	the instant he will have seen
las cazuelas de mi casa.	at home my cooking pot's treasure.[45]

Finally, Vasconcelos comments on the main racial image for rhetorical unity in the Spanish empire:

Calla la boca, embustero,	Your boasts, oh liar, do quench,
y no te jactes de blanco	by whiteness you cannot abide,
saliste del mismo banco	since you bear the same hide
y tienes el mismo cuero.	from the same working bench.[46]

Before the time of these two black poets, the Royal Academy of the Spanish Language had been founded as a bastion of the Imperial Grammar. The illusion of one pure, constant, and splendorous whiteness for all Hispanics exudes from its founding motto: *limpia, fija y da esplendor*—"cleanse, steady, and shine."

44. For an introduction to the controversial careers of these two poets and examples of their works, see Eduardo Matos Moctezuma, *El Negrito Poeta Mexicano y El Dominicano ¿realidad o fantasía?* (Mexico City, 1980).

45. Ibid., p. 131.

46. Nicolás León, *El Negrito Poeta Mexicano y sus populares versos* (Mexico City, 1912), p. 229, my own translation.

11

Drawing the Color Line:
Kipling and the Culture
of Colonial Rule

SATYA P. MOHANTY

Analysis of the "culture" of colonial rule is a fairly recent development in scholarship. It would not be too unfair to say that until the discovery of "daily life" as a conceptual and analytical problematic—the discovery of culture as the realm of everyday habits and actions[1]—historians of colonialism could only perceive the narrowly

---

1. The radical implications of this "discovery" are most clearly evident in Marxist thought because of Marxism's focus on the interchange between "culture" and the "sociopolitical." For many contemporary Marxists, the culture of "everyday life" becomes the site in which social power is both deployed and resisted, hegemony produced as well as contested. Thus the study of "culture" (which is defined broadly as the way we live our daily lives as social creatures) deepens our understanding of the ways in which political and social relations are reproduced or changed. For an informative account of these issues, see Karl E. Klare's essay from the early seventies, "The Critique of Everyday Life, the New Left, and the Unrecognizable Marxism," in *The Unknown Dimension: European Marxism since Lenin*, ed. Dick Howard and Karl E. Klare (New York, 1972), pp. 3–33. Klare indicates how this kind of critique relates what might appear to be "superficial" phenomena to "deeper," systemic processes: "The critique of everyday life proceeds by creating a subtle and rich description or phenomenology of the forms of alienation in daily life: in the family, sexuality, the work situation, cultural activity, verbal and other forms of communication, social interaction, institutions, and ideology. The analysis does not limit itself to the description of the immediate appearances of daily life, or the level of false-consciousness, but attempts to go beneath them to reach a dynamic historical understanding of broader social and class forces (the 'macro-social' system)" (p. 6). Klare considers this analytical emphasis on everyday life a "methodological departure" for

political (thus writing "cabinet histories," with exclusive emphasis on the formulation of administrative policy) or else focus on the narrowly intellectual (examining ideas and their contexts).[2] Generally speaking, the earliest anti-imperialist historiography produced in India implicitly assumed that colonial rule was coercive. Perhaps seeing this assumption as a "nationalist" oversimplification, many scholars (the most prominent of whom were located in Cambridge, England) began to emphasize the collaborative process whereby rule was secured and political hegemony established. The political analysis of colonial rule thus oscillated between two competing claims: (1) colonizers ruled by force and coercion, against the will of an essentially homogeneous and more or less (that is, in fact or in principle) united nation of the colonized; and (2) colonizers and significant members of the colonized society collaborated to create the colonial polity, and the colonized were not one nation but rather divided into factions and mutually hostile subcommunities.[3]

---

traditional Marxism. For our purposes it is important to note two related points about this methodological discovery: (1) culture is granted a new kind of significance, for it registers and makes available for analysis social and political currents and tendencies that might otherwise be invisible; but (2) that redefinition does not lead to the simplistic "culturalist" claim or analytical assumption that all significant political processes and relationships that map and define a social formation can be deduced from, or evident in, the sphere of everyday life.

2. For a sampling of the variety of such competent but methodologically limited studies, see S. Gopal, British Policy in India 1858–1905 (Cambridge, 1965), R. Robinson and J. Gallagher, Africa and the Victorians: The Official Mind of Imperialism (London, 1961), L. H. Gann and Peter Duignan, The Rulers of British Africa, 1870–1914 (Stanford, 1978), and Philip Mason's two-volume study, The Men Who Ruled India (London, 1953–54). That the new kind of social and cultural history of colonial rule needs to be resolutely interdisciplinary was stressed by Bernard Cohn in his 1970 article, "Is There a New Indian History? Society and Social Change under the Raj," which the reader would do well to consult for the earliest incisive formulation of questions of method. That piece, as well as another on African and Indian historiography written in the mid-seventies ("African Models and Indian Histories"), should be of interest to most students of colonial history and culture. Both have been reprinted in Cohn's An Anthropologist among the Historians and Other Essays (Delhi: Oxford University Press, 1987), pp. 172–99 and 200–223, respectively. Cohn combines the methods of the anthropologist with those of the historian, and his analyses have immense value for the study of colonial culture. The student of the "new" African colonial history is ably served by the excellent volume edited by A. Adu Boahen, Africa under Colonial Domination 1880–1935 [vol. 7 of the UNESCO-sponsored General History of Africa] published in 1985 by UNESCO (Paris), Heniemann (London, Ibadan, and Nairobi), and the University of California Press (Berkeley).

3. The "collaboration" model was most clearly articulated in R. Robinson and J. Gallagher's influential 1972 essay on imperialism in Africa, "Non-European Foun-

Both the coercion and the collaboration paradigms (and if we call the former the "nationalist" model, we have to call the other the "neocolonialist" one) understood by politics the activities related to the state on both the central and the local levels. Both paradigms confined themselves to power relations among groups and classes of people as they were mediated through recognizable institutional practices: voting and representation, the delegation and sharing of power, the formulation, reformulation, and enforcement of the law, and in a less direct way the dissemination of ideas about these institutions.

The significance of "culture" was first made evident in fact in that most extreme of coercive colonial formations, New World slavery. John Blassingame and Eugene Genovese, writing in the late 1960s and early 1970s, corrected the earlier scholarship's emphasis on complete dehumanization and the psychological decimation of the slave. They resurrected, following the suggestions of writer Ralph Ellison, the daily life of the plantation. We learned much from these landmark instances of colonial historiography about the culture the slaves drew on, created, and transformed in order to resist and survive this most brutal of social and economic systems. We learned also—and this is more important from the perspective of this chapter—about the racial meanings, values, and images whereby social actors constructed themselves, fabricating personas, subjectivities, indeed supremely functional selves that served to make possible subjugation, consent, domination, and resistance.[4]

At the most basic level, it is my contention that colonial rule in contexts as different from New World slavery as, for instance, nineteenth- and twentieth-century India and Africa, provide crucial examples of analogous processes of racialization. Here, I will examine such racialization of the culture of colonial rule in late nineteenth-century British India, to show how culture can serve to

---

dations of European Imperialism: Sketch for a Theory of Collaboration," in *Studies in the Theory of Imperialism*, ed. R. Owen and B. Sutcliffe (London, 1972). Sumit Sarkar provides a useful survey of nationalist South Asian historiography as well as a selective acount of the Cambridge School in his *Modern India 1885–1947* (New Delhi, India, 1983). See chap. 1, pp. 1–11, and the bibliographic essay, pp. 455–78.

4. See John Blassingame, *The Slave Community* (New York, 1972), and Eugene Genovese, *Roll, Jordan, Roll!* (New York, 1974). Full citations for Ellison's writings on this subject are available in Stanley Elkins's 1974 essay, "The Two Arguments on Slavery," in his *Slavery*, 3d ed. (Chicago, 1976), pp. 267–302.

lubricate the machinery of rule through the production of new mean-ings and identities, some of which in fact survive in many of our postcolonial encounters. Such an analysis might indicate, in fact, the ways in which our current discourses of "race relations" embody problems and concerns in areas as diverse as ethics and political theory; these problems can only be understood if we approach them genealogically, beginning with our current questions and analytical issues and tracing them back in history.[5] That, at least, is my guiding hypothesis. It may well be that relations of rule, deeply ingrained habits, attitudes, even images of self and world, pervade our own current social practices, and the ways that we conceive of, rethink and indeed live what W. E. B. Du Bois called the "color line," the "problem of the Twentieth Century."

The analytical concept of "racialization"[6] suggests, moreover, that the color line does not merely divide and separate; it also involves a dynamic process through which social groups can be bound, de-fined, and shaped. This process not only creates stereotypes of the colonized as "other" and as inferior; by a continuous logic, it may be suggested that the colonizer too develops a cultural identity that survives well past the formal context of colonial rule. Racialization involves not just the denigration of "black," then, but also in crucial ways a less obvious definition of "white"; racialization narrates conditions of political and ethical possibility, defining and reshaping ideas, ideologies, and interests.

In British India of the nineteenth century, we can discover much about the general process of racialization of cultural iden-tity. We realize that colonial rule generated a dominant image of the white man as spectacle, as so many historians of colonial Af-rica and India—Helen Callaway, Terence Ranger, Bernard Cohn, among others—have demonstrated.[7] But Kipling's writings also

5. This genealogical approach would then be fundamentally different from the one proposed in Anthony Kirk-Greene, "Colonial Administration and Race Relations: Some Research Reflections and Directions," *Ethnic and Racial Studies* 9 (July 1986): 275–87. Readers may wish to consult Kirk-Greene's article for evidence of the way the British academic "race relations" industry depoliticizes racism in contemporary metropolitan societies. Its purely antiquarian interest in colonial rule follows nat-urally from its political conservatism.

6. I adapt this term from Michael Omi and Howard Winant, *Racial Formation in the United States* (New York, 1986), esp. pp. 64–66.

7. See the chapters by Bernard Cohn and Terence Ranger in Eric Hobsbawm and Terence Ranger, eds., *The Invention of Tradition*, and Helen Callaway, *Gender*,

reveal another, seemingly contradictory imperative: the white man as simultaneously invisible, or at least capable of invisibility in a context that renders him eminently spectacular. The public sphere in the colonial context seems to contain within it both of these opposed modes of existence, modes reserved for and articulated as the imaginary of the white male colonial ruler: eminent visibility, the ability to command respect and fear in the subject race, on the one hand, and on the other, the ability to blend in, to be no different from the colonized and their society. The domestic sphere, the world of the memsahib, is only now beginning to be analyzed in any detail. In the metropolitan context of England the home was the site of the invisible; the domestic sphere was ideologically coded as the realm of private sentiment and feeling. But in the colonial world, the domestic sphere is a doubly marginalized space. If the reading I am about to offer is even minimally convincing, we need to reorient our inquiry into the public-private dichotomy by examining the complicating fold that colonial relations add to the social construction of gender.

Kipling's Children: Innocents Abroad?

But why focus on the children, as subject and audience, in Kipling? In the first place, Kipling's work reveals the emotional value he placed in childhood and its unique world of perceptions. T. S. Eliot, in a useful essay on Kipling's verse, in fact talks about "two strata in Kipling's appreciation of India, the stratum of the child and that of the young man." Kipling the young man, writes Eliot, "observed the British in India and wrote the rather cocky and acid tales of Delhi and Simla, but it was [Kipling the child] who loved the country and its people."[8] Kipling, we know from his correspondence and his autobiography, *Something of Myself*, considered his early years in India to have been indescribably glorious, especially in contrast to the next few years he spent in England away from his parents and with an affectionless and indeed cruel family. One of Kipling's recent

_____

Culture, and Empire (Urbana, Ill., 1987). Cohn's chapter is reprinted in his *An Anthropologist among the Historians*, pp. 632–82.

8. T. S. Eliot, "Rudyard Kipling," in *A Choice of Kipling's Verse Made by T. S. Eliot* (Garden City, N.Y., 1962), p. 26.

biographers, Angus Wilson, deems this contrast a formative one, with significance for all of Kipling's later writings: "Rudyard Kipling was a man who, throughout his life, worshipped and respected... children and their imaginings. He took part in children's games, as many witnesses make clear, not as many adults do in order to impose his own shapes, but to follow and learn as well as to contribute." Wilson sees in Kipling's relationship to childhood a source of some of the writer's deepest moral and cognitive values. Kipling's descriptions of his memories of Bombay, where he was born and lived until he was six, give Wilson a clue to "the elusive magic" that defines his work. Wilson explains: "That magic, I think, came from the incorporation into adult stories and parables of two of the principal shapes which are to be found in the imaginative world of children. The first is that transformation of a small space into a whole world which comes from the intense absorption of a child. The second is the map-making of hazards and delights which converts a child's smallest journey into a wondrous exploration."[9]

There is much to support Wilson's point about the centrality of the world of childhood in Kipling's work, and in particular of the kind of perception that his work often celebrates. Indeed the only way we can consider T. S. Eliot's odd and sentimental comment that Kipling was perhaps "the first citizen of India" even remotely plausible is by looking at those moments in *Kim* when the central character's relationship to the environment reveals a unique mode of perception—a mode of perception that suspends social codings and even intellectual categories in order to reveal the pure energy of movement and diversity.[10] Part of the novel's irresistible charm lies in the cultural and political possibilities that blossom in certain passages, when Kipling's profoundly renewed and vital perception almost veers into a utopian assertion of pure *becoming*, a suspension of coded meanings and ritualized social existence. The following description takes place on the Grand Trunk Road, that great artery running through northern India, site of much of the social and economic activity of the region since the time of the Moghuls:

> The diamond-bright dawn woke men and crows and bullocks together. Kim sat up and yawned, shook himself, and thrilled with delight. This

9. Angus Wilson, *The Strange Ride of Rudyard Kipling* (New York, 1977), pp. 1–2.
10. Eliot, "Kipling," p. 27.

was seeing the world in real truth; this was life as he would have it—bustling and shouting, the buckling of belts, and beating of bullocks and creaking of wheels, lighting of fires and cooking of food, and new sights at every turn of the approving eye. The morning mist swept off in a whorl of silver, the parrots shot away to some distant river in shreiking green hosts: all the well wheels within earshot went to work. India was awake, and Kim was in the middle of it, more awake and more excited than anyone.[11]

The power of this passage consists as much in its syntactic modulation of all the different activities—in visual and aural terms—into a rhythmic explosion in the present moment, as in its crucial suggestion that it is Kim's open and receptive consciousness that makes this celebration of the present possible. Indeed, this stylistic celebration has implications that are almost metaphysical: not only a leveling of "men and crows and bullocks," then, but an implicit valorization of their "together[ness]" as well. Description blends into a subtle shading of value: to perceive in this way is an act of will, or at least of consciousness: it implies a kind of agency, not simply passive contemplation. But the "approving eye" does not forcibly *organize* the "new sights" around it; it embodies, rather, a desire to pay attention, creatively discovering the world's "real truth," learning to participate consciously ("India was awake, and Kim was in the middle of it, more *awake...*").

However, there are clear limits, or at least further specifications, to be recognized if we are to read Kipling's text in terms of this perceptual reorientation. For in the very chapter where this moment occurs (and there are several such moments in the novel) we are also made aware of a distinction between Kim and the Indian priest (the lama) whom he accompanies. Faced with this richness of existence, the lama unfortunately never quite measures up. After a particularly vivid Chaucerian description of the social diversity of the travelers, our attention is directed quietly to the fact that even in the early stages Kim perceives more than simply the motion and the energy. It is not simply the capacity for "making new" that Kim's modes of perception reveal. The abstract utopianism the novel suggests is accompanied by the character's more specific faculty of perceiving unities and differences as *interpretable* social facts. And

11. Here, as elsewhere in this essay, I quote from the Bantam paperback edition of *Kim* (New York, 1983). The quote is from page 66. Further page references to *Kim* are given in the text.

it becomes gradually clear that the distinction between Kim's incipient consciousness of detail and the lama's blissful and soporific
inattention to such things is crucial for the narrative. Kim will later
effortlessly become what the lama—and for that matter most of the
Indian characters in the novel—cannot quite become: a competent
and reliable reader of texts, ultimately, in fact, of society as text.
Consider in the following passage how the distinction between the
lama and Kim is subtly but firmly established, while the novel ostensibly busies itself with providing a description of the land and
the people:

> The lama never raised his eyes. He did not note the money-lender on
> his goose-rumped pony, hastening along to collect the cruel interest;
> or the long-shouting, deep-voiced little mob—still in military for-
> mation—of native soldiers on leave, rejoicing to be rid of their
> breeches and puttees, and saying the most outrageous things to the
> most respectable women in sight. Even the seller of Ganges-water he
> did not see, and Kim expected that he would at least buy a bottle of
> that precious stuff. He looked steadily at the ground, and strode as
> steadily hour after hour, his soul busied elsewhere. But Kim was in
> the seventh heaven of joy. The Grand Trunk at this point was built
> on an embankment to guard against winter floods from the foothills,
> so that one walked, as it were, a little above the country, along a
> stately corridor, seeing all India spread out to left and right. It was
> beautiful to behold the many-yoked grain and cotton waggons crawl-
> ing over the country-roads: one could hear their axles, complaining a
> mile away, coming nearer, till with shouts and yells and bad words
> they climbed up the steep incline and plunged on to the hard main
> road, carter reviling carter. It was equally beautiful to watch the peo-
> ple, little clumps of red and blue and pink and white and saffron,
> turning aside to go to their own villages, dispersing and growing small
> by twos and threes across the level plain. Kim felt these things, though
> he could not give tongue to his feelings, and so contented himself
> with buying peeled sugar-cane and spitting the pith generously about
> his path. (pp. 56–57)

These are then not merely descriptions of the Indian landscape and
the countryside; they also mark *potential* distinctions and dis-
criminations in ways of seeing and knowing. The "money-lender"
is not merely a man on a pony, since he is connected to his social
function. The visual markers that might identify the individual are
here tied to a basic understanding of the man's social role, and the
seemingly casual mention of "the cruel interest" indicates, in
much the same way that the native soldiers' "leave" does, that the

social world is structured and differentiated by work and play, indeed by various kinds of work, by roles, functions, activities, and meanings. The lama is content to ignore these, and through this contrast we realize that this is indeed Kim's world, where he comes into his own. He finds "beautiful" the "little clumps of red and blue and pink and white and saffron," and he is, we are told a page or so later, able to "[dive] into the happy Asiatic disorder" of India (p. 58), but this capacity to dive in, in effect to belong, is not based on ignorance of social meanings. It is tied to his capacity to know, or more precisely, to attain a certain kind of *social* knowledge. Indeed, this capacity is signaled for us through details that seem gratuitous at first but later take on a strategic meaning. Kim's roving about the Indian countryside, for instance, is predicated on a very specific mastery. We remember that he speaks the native languages of North India as well as the native boys; indeed, if the prime test of social proficiency in any language were to be considered—some authorities consider this the capacity to swear naturally in it—Kim is better at it than all his Indian friends! Kim might be a child, but he is a special kind: it is easy to forget in these moments that he is in fact white. That he is able to belong so effortlessly to the Indian landscape, and belong more intelligently and consciously than the lama himself does, is perhaps not incidental. In the context of colonial India, as we shall see, Kipling's novel seems to embody a general cultural project, imagining and elaborating forms of selfhood that have a particular racial inflection as well as a larger historical resonance. It is through the prism of "race" that we begin to grasp some of the essential cultural lineaments of this "history."

Kim's marvelous facility in inhabiting India—in being able to navigate its social mores just as easily as the narrow and confusing corridors of its urban bazaars, to score points over a small-town policeman by outdoing him in verbal abuse—is underscored from the beginning. Indeed, we miss the force of the novel if we read in it simply the magic of innocence and childhood. The crucial difference is that Kipling's hero is a white boy who can discard his color at will or whim. He lives and sleeps and eats in the open social world of colonial India, against a backdrop of an interimperial war between Britain and Russia, but his identity is never something that ties him down. He is in fact a political abstraction: cunning and beguiling enough to outdo and fool the natives, yet always implicitly and securely on the side of Empire. The pleasure he takes in India and his adventures can thus never quite be mere pleasures; it seems that something else must also be at stake. Even the initial descriptions seem to be seeking out a certain *personal capacity* that is more than that of a boy who can play innocently, and be a world unto himself. Kipling tells us that "his nickname through the wards was 'Little Friend of all the World'; and very often, being lithe and inconspicuous, he executed commissions by night on the crowded housetops for sleek and shiny young men of fashion. It was intrigue, of course, ... but what he loved was the game for its own sake—the stealthy prowl through the dark gullies and lanes, the crawl up a water-pipe, the sights and sounds of the women's world on the flat roofs, and the headlong flight from housetop to housetop under cover of the hot dark" (pp. 2–3).

But where did Kim learn all this, one is tempted to ask—who taught him to prowl without being caught, spy without being seen? In some ways this is an unfair question. For we know that although his parents were white he grew up as a street urchin in Lahore, in the care of a half-caste Indian woman. We know how boys learn to survive in a difficult world; they learn, like Huck Finn, to value the hardship of an unsheltered life over the privileges of "sivilization." But in one sense our question is appropriate. For when we begin to take Kim's cultural identity seriously and when the character becomes real in our imagination, we pay attention to the narrative's elusive and mystifying cultural vision and wonder about the sources of its motivation. The question about Kim's "education" directs us to parallels in Kipling's earlier fiction. Kim's immediate ancestor was Mowgli—again, a child living with strangers who love and take care of him, and from whom he learns to survive in the harsh world. Mowgli, adopted by wolves and befriended by all the other animals of the jungle, is taught to inhabit the jungle by the natives themselves. Here, too, the child lives a charmed life: the world of the other, potentially the enemy, opens up to him as if by magic. I think it is this unexplained possibility on which is predicated what Angus Wilson calls "the elusive magic" of childhood. Here is the moment of Mowgli's (and later, Kim's) necessary education, an education as strategic as it is miraculously effortless. Mowgli grew up with the cubs, though they, of course, were grown wolves almost before he was a child, and Father Wolf taught him his business, and the meaning of things in the jungle, till every rustle in the grass, every breath of the warm night air, every note of the owls above his head, every scratch of a bat's claws as it roosted for a while in a tree, and every splash of every little fish jumping in a pool, meant just as much to him as the work of his office means to a business man.... When he felt dirty or hot he swam in the forest pools; and when he wanted honey . . . he climbed up for it, and that Bagheera showed him how to do. Bagheera would lie out on a branch and call, "Come along, Little Brother," and at first Mowgli would cling like the sloth, but afterward he would fling himself through the branches almost as boldly as the grey ape. He took his place at the Council Rock, too, when the Pack met, and there he discovered that if he stared hard at any wolf, the wolf would be forced to drop his eyes, and so he used to stare for fun.[12]

As in the case of Kim, Mowgli too belongs without ever leaving any doubt in the reader's mind about his alien status. Mowgli can stare down any wolf, and even though he learns the ways of the jungle from his adopted family he remains superior in clear-cut ways. In effect, after his education, he is an accomplished insider without having given up any of his privileges as an outsider. Kim's attempts to disguise himself are similarly effortless; he moves in and out of his roles as native and British, black and white, with only as much work as it takes to put on makeup. Much of the pleasure of Kim's narrative derives from this "intrigue," where the danger remains muted; situations that could potentially represent tense race relations are transformed into an innocent game of play-acting. One may see how the *Jungle Books*, written in the mid–1890s, invite an allegorical reading, with the jungle representing the political stage of colonial India.

Colonial Culture, Racial Identity

If there is anything that characterizes the political climate of British India in the latter part of the nineteenth century, it is the tense state of race relations. Many historians have noted the impact the 1857 rebellion had on the metropolitan British imagination. Indeed,

12. Rudyard Kipling, *The Jungle Books* (Baltimore, 1987), pp. 43–44. Further page references to this work are abbreviated *JB* and are given in the text.

the Empire and colonial rule of India suddenly became an issue for the cultural imagination precisely because they were threatened. While traditional imperialist historiography has played down the anticolonial sentiments that shaped the revolt by calling it a "mutiny"—a purely intramilitary bureacratic matter requiring administrative solutions—popular opinion among the ruling and the middle classes was decidedly changed by the event. In fact, the rebellion made the issue of Empire an urgent racial one, and it was no longer possible to go on believing that the British Empire had been "acquired in a fit of absence of mind" (a sentiment J. R. Seeley was later to formulate and make immensely popular) and that it could be maintained in the same way. Thomas Macaulay wrote, for instance, "The cruelties of the sepoys have inflamed the nation to a degree unprecedented within my memory. Peace Societies, and Aborigines Protection Societies, and Societies for the Reformation of Criminals are silenced. There is one terrible cry for revenge. The account of that dreadful military execution at Peshawar—forty men blown at once from the mouths of cannon, their heads, legs, arms flying in all directions—was read with delight by people who three weeks ago were against all capital punishment."[13] It has been noted that the use of racial terms such as "blacks" or "niggers" to refer to Indians became more common around this time, and such expressions appeared in personal correspondence even in the highest government circles. Anger was generally directed at the Indian soldiers who took part in the rebellion, and even though the atrocities of the British retaliation are well documented, such atrocities were considered fair and just. Even though the earliest instances of anticolonial revolt—for example, the sepoy uprising in 1806 in Vellore, Madras; the extended "paik" or peasant-soldier rebellion in 1817 in Khurda, Orissa; and the various rumblings through the 1820s in Bareilly, Barrackpore, and Rohilcund—had been registered by the British-Indian community as seriously disturbing, the perceptions of both British-India and the metropolitan population joined for the first time after 1857 to define a political situation in terms of a racial opposition. Here is an extract from the personal correspondence of a well-known contemporary in England:

13. Cited in Francis G. Hutchins, *The Illusion of Permanence* (Princeton, N.J., 1967), p. 85.

And I wish I were Commander in Chief in India. The first thing I would do to strike that Oriental race with amazement...should be to proclaim to them in their language, that I considered my holding that appointment by the leave of God, to mean that I should do my utmost to exterminate the Race upon whom the stain of the late cruelties rested; and that I begged them to do to me the favour to observe that I was there for that purpose and no other, and was now proceeding, with all convenient dispatch and merciful swiftness of execution, to blot it out of mankind and raze it off the face of the Earth.[14]

The blustery prose and sentiments were those of Charles Dickens. All evidence suggests that popular opinion echoed Dickens's. But at the top, where rulers rule and make crucial decisions, it is well worth remembering that there was recognition of the deeper threat that the 1857 revolt posed. Viceroy of India Lord Canning, in a letter to his Secretary of State in London, was less sure that this was simply a local matter, attributable to the depraved native character. In 1859 he wrote: "The struggle which we have had has been more like a national war than a local insurrection. In its magnitude, duration, scale of expenditure, and in some of its moral features it partakes largely of the former character."[15] Recent historians have discussed the ways in which British colonial rule consolidated itself gradually over the nineteenth century, stressing at the same time the perennial resistance it encountered in the countryside. As the modern Indian peasantry took shape over the course of the century, particularly during the second half, the radical forms of political and economic change—forced patterns of migration and settlement, dispossession and relocation—led to both explicit and mediated kinds of anticolonial rebellion. Thus among most British officials and military men, even when Canning's idea of a "national" uprising was not in evidence, the sense of danger would have been pervasive. Since what was difficult to acknowledge and name openly was the anticolonial nature of the revolt and its long-term implications, racial categories were used to shape the issue in purely administrative—and judicial—terms.

If this elementary kind of racialization of the issue helped contain the moral and political dimensions of the revolt, race also provided

14. Cited in B. J. Moore-Gilbert, *Kipling and "Orientalism"* (London, 1986), pp. 75–76.
15. Cited in S. Gopal, *British Policy in India* (Cambridge, 1965), p. 1.

the basis for formulating the vague and generalized sense of threat. The Indian landscape teems with danger for the whites, and there was a feeling that even though future revolts might be averted, colonial rule had become precarious. H. S. Cunningham writes in a book subtitled "A Vacation Idyll" (London, 1887), "A chapter of accidents, among the strangest and most romantic that history records, has resulted in an equilibrium of transcendent forces. It has its own law of stability; once disturbed, it may defy the universe to restore it, and its crash may mean a second chaos."[16] Notwithstanding the vague suggestions of "transcendent forces" and mystical laws here, the fear was real, as were the suggestions for administrative control. The provincial governments recommended that magistrates be allowed to search people's homes for arms at whim, and that if arms were found in one house, the entire village be held culpable. A Mr. Mayne, magistrate of Banda, wrote to the commissioner of Allahbad, C. B. Thornhill, in October 1859: "If we ever wish to govern the natives of India effectively, we must treat them as they are and not as civilized and intellectual beings. The laws which we make for them should be adapted to their understanding and contain rules of the most simple kind and easiest to be obeyed."[17] Similarly, a Mr. J. Vans Agnew, magistrate of Saharanpur, after asserting that "we can never again trust" either Hindus or Muslims, went on to propose a rather elaborate method of colonial rule: Indians should be prohibited from possessing or bearing arms, he argued. "In their place we might import foreigners, white and black . . . and we might raise regiments in India from the tribes who possess neither of the proscribed creeds. . . . The effect upon India . . . would undoubtedly be very great. Respect for the European would increase, and the absurd pretensions of the high-caste Hindoo, and bigotted Musalman would be lowered." With such a foreign army, he goes on to argue, "we should be rid forever of the bugbear of mutiny or rebellion . . . and be in a position to pass whatever laws, and impose what taxes we choose, without the slightest misgiving or regard for the opinion of the whole native world."[18]

In diaries, memoirs, and private correspondence, as well as in

16. Cited in Moore-Gilbert, *Kipling*, p. 86.
17. Cited in Thomas Metcalf, *The Aftermath of Revolt* (Princeton, N.J., 1964), p. 307.
18. Cited in ibid., p. 307.

official memoranda and reports, similar judgments are pervasive, suggesting that for the British-Indian of the last decades of the nineteenth century, the Indian landscape is not one teeming with the simple joys of diversity and variety, of God's plenty; it is rather a hazardous and threatening environment, an environment that needs to be tamed, controlled, at the very least to be mapped and understood. It is difficult to see Kim and Mowgli frolicking all over the countryside, then, and not think of these dangers. For neither boy is simply a child; and neither simply belongs. The story of "belonging" is significant only to the extent that we keep in mind how difficult it is for the British to belong to rebellious India at this moment, and what range of possible meanings belonging could imply.

Recent historical research helps us specify the particular social and racial status that boys like Kim had in colonial India. Correcting the general notion that most if not all the whites in nineteenth century India consisted of high-level bureaucrats, military men, and business people and their families, David Arnold has shown that there were in fact numerous "poor whites" who lived close to the natives and often even in the streets. Unable for obvious reasons to keep up the ideals of physical vigor and youth, and the kind of social dignity that comes from maintaining a distance from the natives, this class posed a threat to the racial image the colonial whites wished to present to the India they ruled. The origins of this awkwardly intermediate class can be traced back to the latter part of the eighteenth century, Arnold argues, and as they increasingly became vagrants and embarrassing to the colonial order they were either shipped back to England or, more frequently, confined to workhouses and made "invisible" and "useful" at the same time.[19] Most of these "poor whites" were not "half-castes," that is, of mixed Indian and British origin (as Kim's ayah is, for instance); their incorporation into the colonial social and political order seemed therefore to be more urgently necessary. And as children, even less easily categorizable at first glance, poor whites must have raised considerable anxiety and concern in the mind of missionary and administrator alike. Their education, in particular their moral and political education, was a crucial challenge for British colonial civil society

19. David Arnold, "European Orphans and Vagrants in India in the Nineteenth Century," *Journal of Imperial and Commonwealth History* 7 (1979): 104–27.

as well as the state. In this context, and given the kind of textual concerns we have just been discussing, Angus Wilson's interpretation of Kipling's children seems partial and a little too abstract. It tells us about what such children's stories *might* mean, in a social vacuum, but not about what historical and political anxieties, desires, and motivations these texts—composed a few years after Kipling left India for the last time and in the context of the emerging anticolonial movements—suggest. For restored to their colonial context, Kipling's Mowgli and Kim tell a distinct and specifiable political story in which adventure is indistinguishable from surveillance, pleasure is intertwined with power, and the values of childhood are but a thin allegory of imperial ideology.

In his fiction about India, Kipling creates children who embody values and qualities that are essential for white colonial rulers and their agents if they are to survive in and *manage* a racially tense social and political world. The danger of their existence is first fantasized away by the narrative, as the children's ability to live and move about in a hostile world is presented as a magical, miraculous gift. But the Mowgli tales, just as much as *Kim*, contain enough of a clear sense of danger for the historically informed reader to know what is at stake, to understand the general context of threat which frames and enriches the significance of the childlike play. Nothing is more vivid in this context than the opening of "The King's Ankus," when Mowgli and Kaa, the python, are playing together: the fantasy is here not so much a wish for pure freedom as it is for involvement without any real implication. Kaa could crush Mowgli with the slightest slip; and what Mowgli plays with, in fact, is precisely this. Their inequality is reduced to a game. Indeed, as we know from the beginning of the story, Kaa acknowledges the human boy as the Master of the Jungle, and brings the boy all the news that he hears. Here is that breathtaking description of the game that Kaa and Mowgli play—breathtaking to the extent that we find ourselves attracted and compelled by the very sense of danger that would in real life keep us wary:

> "I will carry thee," said Mowgli; and he stooped down, laughing, to lift the middle section of Kaa's great body, just where the barrel was thickest. A man might just as well have tried to heave up a two-foot water-main; and Kaa lay still, puffing with quiet amusement. Then their regular evening game began—the Boy in the flush of his great strength, and the Python in his sumptuous new skin, standing up one

against the other for a wrestling match—a trial of eye and strength. Of course, Kaa could have crushed Mowgli had he let himself go; but he played carefully, and never loosed one-tenth of his power. Ever since Mowgli was strong enough to endure a little rough handling, Kaa had taught him this game, and it suppled his limbs as nothing else could. Sometimes Mowgli would stand lapped almost to his throat in Kaa's shifting coils, striving to get one arm free and catch him by the throat. Then Kaa would give way limply, and Mowgli, with both quick-moving feet, would try to cramp the purchase of that huge tail as it flung backward feeling for a rock or a stump. They would rock to and fro, head to head, each waiting for his chance, till the beautiful statue-like group melted in a whirl of black and yellow coils and struggling legs and arms. (*JB*, p. 257)

But Mowgli, like Kim, reveals the capacity not only to inhabit the jungle through this wishful allegorical fantasy, but also to chart and track it as well. Central to Kipling's conception of both characters is their ability to read the world around them. Here, too, they are perfectly schooled—indeed, often better than most of the natives. Notice, in "The King's Ankus," for instance, the way Mowgli learns as he participates in the hunt for the thieves. Here is one typical moment: " 'Now he runs swiftly,' said Mowgli. The toes are spread apart.' They went on over some wet ground. 'Now why does he turn aside here?'.... It is the foot of a Gond hunter,' he said. 'Look! Here he dragged his bow on the grass" (*JB*, p. 268). Kim, for his part, knows how to read maps better than the lama, but the native boys he is naturally compared with somehow lack the very faculty that makes "reading" possible. In Simla, when Lurgan Sahib teaches Kim and the Indian boy how to observe people's faces and reactions, to interpret behavior and identify motive, and then to disguise themselves as other people—in other words, to assume others' roles, Kim seems to learn it quickly, while his native friend is left mysteriously handicapped. The narrator explains why the Hindu child played the game clumsily: "That little mind, keen as an icicle where tally of jewels was concerned, could not temper itself to enter another's soul; but a demon in Kim woke up and sang with joy as he put on the changing dresses, and changed speech and gesture therewith" (*Kim*, p. 143). There is a continuity, then, between learning to observe carefully, to observe without being observed (as Kim often does), to interpret people and situations, to move stealthily and unnoticed, and to assume roles. Both Mowgli and Kim learn through their narratives the value of doing these things—to inhabit perfectly without being tied down to the place of their habitation; like their roles and disguises, they discard these places at will.

To understand this project of self-fashioning, it might be useful to recall that the nineteenth century is the period when colonial rule consolidated itself through a phenomenal increase in its "scientific" knowledge of the various populations of India as well as the land itself. This is the age when the census was introduced, and a preliminary colonial taxonomy was established and solidified in the process of being "discovered"; this is also the century when the great land surveys (an operation involving engineers and military and revenue officials) mapped and codified much of the subcontinent not only topographically but also in terms of land "quality," making possible the settling of nomadic populations and the conversion of the "rough pastoral" countryside into—taxable—agricultural land; and finally, this was the age of the railways and the telegraph lines, and the expansion of the road networks, which facilitated revenue administration as much as military control.[20] In varying degrees, these things happened in the portion of India under direct British control and in the territories called the Princely States, which were ruled indirectly through political agents or "Residents." Accordingly, this era was the context for the discourse of control and surveillance that pervades all colonial societies and cultures, a context in which knowledge and politics, the scientific objectification of a social world and its subsequent manipulation, were intertwined in very specific ways.[21] And the racial discourse I have been tracing, examining the various modalities of a politically necessary and functional selfhood, provides a "cultural" barometer of this specificity.

Hunters and Real Men: A Genealogy
of Whiteness

Kim's instruction in the Great Game of espionage is little more than a continuation of the kind of child's play that involves

---

20. See C. A. Bayly, *Indian Society and the Making of the British Empire* (New York, 1988), esp. chaps 5 and 6.

21. I develop this point in a slightly different way in the following discussion of the significance of the "hunt" in colonial and imperial history. For the fullest elaboration of the themes of knowledge and power in a colonial context, see Timothy Mitchell, *Colonising Egypt* (Cambridge, 1988).

observing and interpreting while remaining conveniently invisible oneself. A few years after Kipling's novel was published, another best-selling book—this time a nonfictional work, a manual for young English boys that was to prove immensely influential—cited Kim as the prototypical young hero of the Empire. Lord Baden-Powell's *Scouting for Boys*, published first in 1908, was an explicitly ideological book: it sought to induct children into the cause of Empire. Echoing the pervasive feeling that the Empire was in danger— as much from anticolonial movements (registered as mutinies or criminal acts) as from the appalling weakness of physical and moral constitution of English working-class boys—Baden-Powell sought to educate the country's boys to "BE PREPARED," in body and in mind, to fight for the Empire and to rule.[22] "We have all got to die some day; a few years more or less of our lives don't matter in the history of the world, but it is a very great matter if by dying a year or two sooner than we should otherwise do from disease we can help to save the flag of our country from going under" (p. 331). The scout's duty consisted in the following: "Woodcraft. Observation without being noticed. Deduction. Chivalry. Sense of Duty. Endurance. Kind-heartedness." But this is no abstract list: *Scouting for Boys* also contains instructions for scout masters in training boys. This is what they must be told:

> You belong to the Great British Empire, one of the greatest that has ever existed in the world. (*Show on the map.* [Baden-Powell's instruction for the scout instructor])
> From this little island of Great Britain have sprung colonies all over the world, Australia, New Zealand, South Africa, India, Canada.
> Almost every race, every kind of man, black, white, or yellow, furnished subjects of King Edward VII.
> This vast Empire did not grow of itself out of nothing; it was made by your forefathers by dint of hard work and hard fighting, at the sacrifice of their lives—that is, by their hearty patriotism. People say that we have no patriotism nowadays, and that our empire will fall to pieces like the great Roman empire did, because its citizens became selfish and lazy, and only cared for amusements. I am not so sure about that. I am sure that if you boys will keep the good of your country in your eyes above everything else she will go on all right. But if you don't do this there is very great danger, because we have

22. R. S. S. Baden-Powell, *Scouting for Boys: A Handbook for Instruction in Good Citizenship* (London, 1908), p. 48 ["Camp Fire Yarn" no. 4]. Further page references to this work are to this, the first, edition, and are given in the text.

many enemies abroad, and they are growing daily stronger and stronger
(pp. 28–30).

By the turn of the century, when Kipling and Baden-Powell were
both writing however, the world itself had changed. Now one needed
not simply hardihood but also stealth—a capacity to be invisible,
to blend with the surroundings, to watch without being watched—
in short, to be a good spy. As Michael Rosenthal argues in his valuable book, *The Character Factory*, Scouting remained a kind of pre-
paratory training, as well as a substitute: "If a boy can't be a spy,
Scouting still remains important as a technique in solving the various murders he might tend to come across in his daily activities.
Early in *Scouting for Boys* Baden-Powell recounts the tale of the
Elsdon murder, in which a brutal murderer 'was caught, convicted,
and hanged through the scoutcraft of a shepherd boy.' The value of
the tale is clarified in a note Baden-Powell appends for the use of
the potential Scout instructor: '[The following story, which in the
main is true, is a sample of a story that should be given by
the Instructor illustrating generally the duties of a Boy Scout].'"[23]
The Scouting tradition relied on such tales (or "Camp Fire Yarns")
for their pedagogic effectiveness. And as we have seen, notions of
duty and chivalry were valued less as general human virtues than
as practical, political ones. It is no paradox, then, that the specific
politics of imperial conquest and colonial rule enabled a morality
that was only abstract and decontextualized. Indeed, even cognition
and ratiocination were reduced to formulaic and easily transferable
practices, and selfhood was rendered purely functional. This reduction is one of the essential elements of the racialization of culture,
the inherent logic of the color line, then as much as now.

Kipling's project was different from Baden-Powell's insofar as it
works out, in fictional terms, a fantasy and a narrative of a kind of
sentimental education. *Kim* and the *Jungle Books* are not explicit
political tracts as *Scouting for Boys* is; but then the latter, we tend
to forget, has often been considered a mere manual. My analysis
indicates the extent to which children's fiction might function in
this context to fashion the imperial self from within, simultaneously

23. Baden-Powell quoted in Michael Rosenthal, *The Character Factory* (New York,
1986), p. 165.

shaping and articulating desires, patterning images of self and world not only in terms of value, but of possibility and necessity as well. Kipling's texts work as fiction to the extent that they enact an allegory of desire in which we can participate as readers. This is a desire to be invisible, to belong, to contain the threat of any real encounter, to observe without being observed—in short to rule colonial India without seeming to do so. One of the marks of this specifically colonialist desire is that white men are seen in a purely abstract and funtional relationship to their world: the capacity that Mowgli and Kim must develop to "read" the world around them is not simply the capacity to understand more deeply. Rather, what is involved is a specific kind of reading in which the object being analyzed is reduced to something that can be manipulated. It is there only to be deciphered, read, and interpreted, without any significant cost to the reader. The white man learns only so much from the world as is necessary to rule or subjugate it. The hunterlike discipline that is exemplified in the Mowgli tales is a Western and colonialist art. It might appear to be no more than the childlike desire to "go native," but in fact that discipline brings to mind the long history of colonial myths of the (white) hunter who must learn from the natives in order to defeat and rule them.

The earliest contact of the European colonists with Native Americans is an interesting case in point. The pervasive mythology that surrounded the image of the white hunter who lived comfortably with the indigenous people and learned to embrace the wilderness cast him as a utopian alternative to the Puritan who feared nature as the antithesis of civilization. At the same time, however, as Richard Slotkin has shown convincingly in his study of the "mythology of the American frontier," the archetypal white hunter almost always had a peculiarly inflected relationship both with the wilderness and those whom he often accepted as his teachers.

The spirit that rules the wilderness is embodied in the native persons and animals of the wilderness. . . . The hero's mode of interaction with these beings is that of the hunt. He tracks them, learns from them the secrets of their skill, and brings to the surface that latent sympathy or consonance of spirit that connects him with his prey. But his intention is always to use the acquired skill against the teachers, to kill or assert his dominance over them. The consummation of his hunting quest in the killing of the quarry confirms him in his new and higher character and gives him full possession of the powers of the wilderness.[24]

The North American myth of the hunter fuses a religious narrative of conversion and regeneration with the colonist's fantasy of knowledge, control, and domination of the native population. But this fusion is achieved through a spurious claim of kinship with the natives and their world. For the "skills" of hunting were, for most Native Americans as well as for most preindustrial peoples, not to be abstracted from a deeper relationship with the natural world. This relationship varied according to culture and period, but what underlay it was respect for nature and its other inhabitants, a respect based on recognition of the complex interchange that continually exists between human and nonhuman. The Native American hunter was often also a saint and a seer; and he mourned the death of the animal he killed in a ritual expression of solidarity with his natural kin, thanking nature for what the hunter must do of necessity. "The Euro-American," Slotkin argues, "having no such connection with the earth he possessed, destroyed the balanced world in an attempt to remake it in the image of something else, and among the balances he destroyed was that which sustained the Indian in his universe. ... The white mythology of the Indian dimly recognized that the Indian's feeling for nature was of a different quality from that of the colonist. Yet the mythology insisted that the Indian's essential character was that of the hunter who exploits the land and that he was by nature opposed to the spirit of the farmer who cultivates it. In fact, no such dichotomy existed for the woodland Indians, who were sometime farmers and who in any case envisioned hunting as an appreciative cultivation of certain spirits inherent in nature."[25]

It would be a mistake to interpret the colonial mythologies of the hunter as the innocent act of "going native." For peoples whose relationships with their world is not Western or colonial, that is, for most traditional cultivator or hunter-gatherer societies, hunting must have been the locus of a complex variety of experiences common to which would be a recognition that humans are *dependent* on nature. Compare, for instance, the Native American hunter-hero I have just alluded to with the ordinary, distinctly unheroic character

24. Richard Slotkin, *Regeneration through Violence: The Mythology of the American Frontier* (Middletown, Conn., 1974), p. 551.
25. Ibid., p. 559.

Mandia Jani in the 1945 Oriya novel *Paraja*. This classic of modern Indian literature focuses with remarkable lack of condescension or sentimentality on the lives of members of the aboriginal people, the Paraja, who live in the Koraput district of Orissa. Sukru Jani and his children live, like most people in the village, a life of destitution at the barest level of subsistence. The Paraja and other "tribal" people of the region have barely settled to the lives of agriculture, for much of their food comes from what they can gather from the forest. Governed by the rhythms of the seasonal harvests and backbreaking labor, the ritual hunt that is described in the novel is a distinctly festive and social affair, experienced by Sukru Jani's son Mandia as anything but high metaphysical drama. Mandia is talented and strong, and a reasonably capable hunter, but he is hardly the image of the "primitive" abstractly in search of his quarry. His senses are alert, but thoughts of his daily life creep in. The narrator's emphasis is on Mandia Jani's complex social existence, and the way a network of ethical and political entanglements situates him in his world:

The hunters selected suitable spots overlooking the ravine and posted themselves in readiness. Mandia Jani had taken the post furthest ahead, and sat with his ancient matchlock loaded and ready.... Moss and ferns grew luxuriantly here, and other small plants with yellow flowers had sprung up in the damp soil, forming a little jungle of their own. Mandia Jani made a screen for himself out of some twigs and leaves, behind which he crouched and kept a sharp look-out.

The voices of the other hunters were faint now, and the jungle was quiet, almost sinister in its silence. From time to time Mandia Jani was startled by what sounded like snapping twigs, but he could see nothing; most of the time the only sounds were the bubbling of the stream, the whistling of the wind through clumps of prickly bamboo and the drone of honey-bees in their hives in the trees. The scene was one of peace and beauty, and yet Mandia expected a tiger to charge out of the thicket at any moment. Once he had seen one scampering effortlessly, almost gaily, up a sheer hillside, with a nearly full-grown buffalo gripped in its jaws. There were bears in the forest too; they liked to feed on termites, and he had seen several ant-hills, or what remained of them, scarred with the claw-marks of bears. But the killing of bears was taboo. Tigers were another matter, however; besides, his own mother had been killed by a tiger, and revenge would be sweet. But what if the tiger should kill him? He saw himself stretched out on a bier of yellow flowers, with Kajodi [his betrothed] grief-stricken at his side, tugging disconsolately at one of his dead arms. And the other arm was being pulled by the Sahukar [the money-lender]. Mandia laughed when he saw the look of utter frustration on the Sahukar's face: the thick lips pulled back from the teeth, the corners of the mouth dribbling with saliva, the eyeballs rolling. So much money gone to waste![26]

Unlike the Euro-American mythical hunter-hero, Mandia Jani is implicated in his environment. Attentive to the "silence," which he can interpret as "sinister," and to the sound like that of "snapping twigs" which could mean an approaching animal, he is at the same time aware of the code that shapes his relationship to the bear (whom he should not kill), the tiger (whom he wants to kill, as an act of vengeance), as well as Kajodi, his betrothed, and the local money-lender for whom he is obligated to work as bonded laborer. The passage quoted depicts both the humor and the pathos in Mandia's life, and it is difficult to abstract from this complexity a goal-directed pure activity called "the hunt," an activity exemplifying the hero's relation solely to his quarry, man pitted against the treacherous wilderness.

Unlike Kipling's Mowgli or Baden-Powell's Boy Scouts, Mandia Jani knows how to read and interpret the signs of the jungle, but he is not concerned about mastering the natural world. Mowgli and Kim learn from the natives the secrets of their ways, the lore of their world; not unlike the white North American hunter Slotkin describes, they learn in order to rule and dominate. They will accomplish this, however, only if they can, in varying degrees, extract the lesson to be learned as a pure technique, ignoring the way in which it is part of a larger way of living. The practical and ideological framework to which they adapt such technical lessons is one of ruling, of an entirely different relationship of subject and object, self and world. Mandia Jani, on the other hand, is content with his relationship of interdependency with his world; there is room in his narrative for both valor and weakness, since each is defined and situated in relation to a larger human and nonhuman community. Right before Mandia spots his prey, a jackal appears as if by magic, with a sign, a pointed and meaningful look. And here is how the sign is read, as the narrator suggests the ways the world of the hunt is similar to the social world of the village.

26. Gopinath Mohanty, *Paraja* (Cuttack, India, 1983); English trans., Bikram K. Das, *Paraja* (Delhi, 1987), pp. 162–63. The British edition is published by Faber with different pagination.

Presently he heard a rustling in the trees. He looked up to see a jackal standing not a dozen yards off, staring intently at him. Their eyes met; the jackal disappeared.

But why had it come? There was sure to be some game around; he hadn't seen a hare so far, and that was a good sign. But the jackal? There had been a familiar twinkle in its eye, as though it were trying to say something to him. Where had he seen that look before? Then he remembered: long ago, when he had gone stealing ears of maize from the Sahukar's [money-lender's] garden, and there had been sounds of the watchman approaching, someone had given him just that wordless look of warning. It had been his mother, Sombari.

Mandia Jani shivered. He tried to see which way the jackal had gone, but it had disappeared. At that moment a huge stag leapt straight out of the clump of trees on the water's edge and stood poised on a slab of rock, surveying the scene majestically. (P. 163, translation modified)

Here, as in the case of Native Americans, there is no gulf that separates the social world from the natural. Unlike the Puritan settlers who saw the wilderness as the antithesis of civilization, the indigenous people often saw nature as the place of freedom and uncorrupted values. This opposition should not be seen as an absolute cultural divide between the colonizing West and the colonized societies, however, for that would be historically simplistic. Yet there is in the history of modern colonialism, at the most general level, a confrontation between the values of preindustrial native inhabitants of a land and an alternative approach that the Euro-Americans embody. What I have been analyzing as "racialization," the process whereby whiteness becomes constructed and formulated as the "cultural" cement of colonial ruling relations, suggests that at the level of cultural identity specific values and categories are displaced or ignored, revised and rewritten. This history of appropriation is an essential aspect of our modern colonial encounters, and a genealogical study of such processes will have much to tell us about not only the hegemonic cultural norms and identities that exist today, but also historically relevant alternatives to them.

The white hunter is, then, an ideologically specifiable phenomenon. Since the eighteenth century in particular, his identity has increasingly been carved out of the European colonial imagination as emblematic of racial (and gendered) values. By the early years of the twentieth century, his status as culture hero of the Empire is reflected in Baden-Powell's *Scouting for Boys*, which distills the various contexts of hunting into an image of imperial masculinity, conflating a wide variety of people and activities to create a racially focused moral narrative.

> These are the frontiersmen of all parts of our Empire. The "trappers" of North America, hunters of Central Africa, the British pioneers, explorers, and missionaries over Asia and all the wild parts of the world, the bushmen and drovers of Australia, the constabulary of North-West Canada and of South Africa—all are peace scouts, real *men* in every sense of the word, and thoroughly up on scout craft, i.e., they understand living out in the jungles, and they can find their way anywhere, are able to read meaning from the smallest signs and foot-tracks; they know how to look after their health when far away from any doctors, are strong and plucky, and ready to face any danger, and always keen to help each other. They are accustomed to take their lives in their hands, and to fling them down without hesitation if they can help their country by doing so.[27]

The hunt was not merely a generalized cultural image; we know that big-game hunting in India and Africa was an elite ritual. It isolated a sphere that was essentially masculine, moreover, for only in the rarest cases were (even white) women allowed to accompany the hunters. The connotations of virile masculinity (compare Baden-Powell's "real *men*") were, however, inflated to formulate national stereotypes among the colonizing Europeans. Thus the "effeminacy" of the Spanish and the Portuguese was evident in their lack of prowess in hunting, and for some observers it contributed to the decline of their empires. "Masculine virility," which the hunt both demonstrated and developed, had become, by the end of the nineteenth century, one of the *seminal* values of European imperial culture.

In our analysis of Kipling's tales, we have seen that some of the personal capacities such children as Mowgli and Kim either possess or are taught have dense racial and political meanings. The children are thus part of a general cultural history of colonial conquest and rule, and as such embody and refract larger meanings than is immediately evident. Mowgli and Kim's significance in this history lies, however, in their seeming innocence, the way in which they naturalize certain political values, incorporating them into the reader's everyday consciousness. The stories are also significant for the way they flesh out the details of a compacted cultural image, elab-

27. Baden-Powell, *Scouting*, pp. 12–13.

orating in narrative form (in the form of a pedagogical narrative) its implications and its emotional investments. Both of these processes, the naturalizing of values and the elaboration of their meanings in the form of a narrative, are the hallmarks of *ideology*, not "ideas" in the abstract but rather the fabrication and dissemination of social meanings.[28]

Consider, in this context, the layered way in which racialization takes place in these simple tales. It is not just that Kim and Mowgli are taught to be certain kinds of selves, situated ultimately in a moral narrative in which they must rule and control (as in that of the North American hunter myth, or the colonial parable of Baden-Powell's Scouting movement). The tales further reveal that the ruling subjects must learn to be above any kind of specific desire, anything that can be identified as *interest*. Thus they must rule without seeming to want to do so. For if it was Providence that chose the British to rule the world (as was commonly believed and stated), then that mission was above politics, beyond interest and self-interest. Indeed, it needed to be made clear that they—as rulers—had no interests at stake. Consider the way Mowgli can desire the jewel-studded ankus while being able to rise above his desire, to throw it away at crucial moments in the narrative without a second's hesitation. The text drives the point home by reenacting the attractiveness and desirability of the ankus for the reader. The description is one of Kipling's most effective:

> [Mowgli] found something really fascinating laid on the front of a howdah half buried in the coins. It was a two-foot ankus, or elephant-goad—something like a small boat hook. The top was one round shining ruby, and eight inches of the handle below it were studded with rough turquoises close together, giving a most satisfactory grip. Below them was a rim of jade with a flower-pattern running around it—only the leaves were emeralds, and the blossoms were rubies sunk in the cool, green stone. The rest of the handle was a shaft of pure ivory, while the point—the spike and hook—was gold inlaid steel with pictures of elephant-catching." (*JB*, pp. 263–64)

Mowgli is attracted, the narrative goes on to specify, but it does not lead to a desire than can inhibit him or tie him down. We recognize this as significant to the extent that as readers we have responded

28. For the use of "ideology" understood in this way, the most important work in recent criticism is Fredric Jameson, *The Political Unconscious* (Ithaca, 1981).

to Kipling's evocative description, and have been introduced into this elementary economy of desire and scarcity. Indeed, it is then that we appreciate the fact that unlike those who steal the ankus, and who are punished by fate for the act, Mowgli can both desire and not desire: in fact he is the only character in the jungle who possesses this capacity to both belong completely and yet remain above it all.

If the readings sketched here suggest anything, I believe they indicate the extent to which the separate world of childhood that many have seen as the unique charm of Kipling's fiction is not all that insular after all. In fact, if the Indian tales are read with the colonial context in mind, they point to what may be an essential ideological concern and indeed to a political project. They reveal a subterranean mapping of imperial subjectivity as abstract, unspecifiable in its contexts, floating above desire and ideology. They trace the narrative outlines of a desire not to desire, an insistent desire to remain vaguely defined. Indeed, they reveal a crucial pedagogical project; molding desire and training the sensibility, they "map" the ruling subject's selfhood *racially*, that is, ultimately in terms of an inflexibly *general* relationship with the colonized and their world. Kim's anxieties about his identity—"I am Kim. I am Kim. And what is Kim?"—resonate with no real cultural situation at all, with no identity crisis that I can imagine. For his relationship with the lama leaves him essentially unchanged. Contrast this with Huck Finn's encounter with Jim, for instance, and it is possible to see how culturally vacuous Kipling's hero's relationships are. And the lama's own otherworldliness is quite convenient for the narrative: the (moral and religious) Law he follows is left sufficiently undefined by the end of the novel for it to blend into the Great Game, spying in the service of the Empire. Racial difference is constructed here to sublimate the political world, enabling an abstraction of personal definition. The ruling self is not only positioned in relation to the world it rules as though the latter were a pure object for interpretation and manipulation, it is itself also formulated as an impossible abstraction. The crucial redefinition of the ruler's self-interest as either benevolent or nonexistent is a necessary element of the project of racialization. It has the advantage over, for instance, Baden-Powell's "real men," in that it is less vulnerable to attack, since it is less easy to track down and define. The line that divides does more than separate in this text and in this context; it creates a distinct racial identity for the British colonial rulers of India. Needless to say it is an open question whether—and to what extent—these identities and relations inform our present contexts, and we might have much to learn from focused genealogical accounts of current racial discourses and attitudes.

Edward Said says in his *Orientalism* that Kipling and his white man emerged from complex historical circumstances. I have suggested some of the specific ways in which understanding these circumstances can help us trace a distinctly political project shaping racial meanings, identities, and possibilities. Fiction, I have argued, might have played a crucial role in this project. The other major cultural manifestation of colonial rule that one needs to consider for a more complete historical analysis involves the contradictory desire to fashion the self—the British white self—as a spectacle. As numerous scholars have suggested recently, the ritualization of colonial culture, the adoption and adaptation of the native North Indian *durbar*—or royal display—by colonial British administrators, was an essentially new feature in the late nineteenth century. Bernard Cohn has argued that the *durbar*'s adapted forms can be seen anthropologically as the elaboration of a "colonial sociology," a creation of new hierarchies and divisions in the Indian social order. Immense value now resides in the new project of rendering the rulers *visible in a certain way*. From dress and physical appearance to the determination of when to be visible, how much, and to whom, colonial culture becomes obsessively concerned with marking difference with ostentation.[29] At one level, then, we are presented with a contradiction between two images of the ruling self: one tends toward the invisible, the other toward the eminently spectacular. They seem to mark the two extreme modalities of an imperial subjectivity at this historical and political moment, both perhaps tracing the outlines of an abstract form.

What can we say about this contradiction in general terms? It seems to me at this point that we cannot—and should not—say much in a purely *theoretical* way. Recent scholarship, drawing on the resources of both anthropologists and historians, has emphasized the spectacular dimension of all European culture in the latter part

---

29. See Edward Said, *Orientalism* (New York, 1978); Bernard Cohn, "Representing Authority in Victorian India" in Hobsbawm and Ranger, eds., *The Invention of Tradition*, pp. 165–209.

of the nineteenth century, and indeed the ways in which specifically imperial themes predominate as images for mass consumption in the 1880s and 1890s. If my suggestions about the thematic of invisibility are convincing, we need to look carefully at the cultural levels at which these two competing imperatives operate. They might in fact be complementary imperatives, with different and geographically distinct audiences in mind. Spectacles—exhibitions, *durbars*, the ritualization of the monarchy and its public activities— seem to be confined to the cities, both in England and in colonial India, while the concern with invisibility reveals itself in the contact with the colonial countryside, the world of the peasant and the sepoy (often the peasant-sepoy), now insistently unreadable as political constituencies. Both invisibility and spectacularization seek to comprehend and rule, as I have said, and push the image of the ruling self into forms of necessary abstraction. In what ways these different forms coincide in their political significance is a historical question, to be analyzed and elaborated in specific contexts.

Culture and Race: Learning from History

Let me conclude with a few words on questions of method. My analysis of racialization, the process by which the color line gets drawn, has been based on a definition of culture as both dynamic and layered. The definition of culture as a dynamic social element is nothing new in the field of cultural studies, which has continually stressed the way in which cultural meanings and values reflect and refract larger historical forces, and hence serve as barometers of historical change. Such an understanding of the relationship between culture and history is, it seems to me, necessary if we are to understand the complex phenomena associated with modern colonialism. In the early 1950s, Philip Mason, in his monumental *The Men Who Ruled India*, explained why books like his were necessary. He wished to record the experiences of men like himself who served in the colonial civil service and lived for several decades in India. It is a significant experience, Mason argues justly; but the reason he considers it significant is curious and telling. "In the years betwen 1914 and 1940," Mason writes, "India was a problem not yet solved that lay on England's conscience; now [that is, the early 1950s] that it is India's problem not ours, we can begin to look back with detachment." And this "detachment" is predicated on the following view of what is to remembered as significant, on the following view of what "culture" is:

> And there are things which should be set down before they are for-gotten, the smell of dust thirstily drinking the first rain, the spicy peppery smell of a grain-dealer's shop, the reek of mangoes, marigolds and lush vegetation when the sun breaks through the clouds in August and the earth steams, things too that fade more quickly such as the sounds of men's voices in petition, the look of a man's face when he is found guilty, a peasant's emotion when a wrong has been put right.[30]

Mason slides effortlessly from the reek of mangoes to the "peasant's emotion," from the land to its inhabitants, precisely because he sees himself implicated by both in more or less the same *kind* of way. Culture is the space of smells and sights that persists in one's mem-ory; several decades of experience as a colonial civil servant, what one British-Indian poet calls a "fostering despot," seem to have left no other traces in him. We have seen in the foregoing analysis, however, how this very image of the ruling self capable of "detach-ment" is a historically specifiable cultural value, and how with a deeper understanding of culture Mason's very comfortable detach-ment can itself be reinterpreted. It suggests a paternalism that the exercise of near-absolute power breeds, the kind of power that was embodied in the very rituals of daily life as "ma-baap" (mother and father) of the people. Compare the following description of Thomas Twining, who served in India in the late 1700s and the early decades of the nineteenth century, of his own (quite typical) ex-perience:

> I moved about with the parade and display of former times, being accompanied with a large number of attendants, civil and military. Wherever I encamped I held a court; received the homage of the prin-cipal inhabitants; the petitions and compaints of all; granted redress; distributed pensions; ordered the execution of public works, and the formation of villages for the reception of retired sepoys from our army, whom Lord Wellesley had been pleased to place under my protection.[31]

---

30. Philip Mason, *The Men Who Ruled India*, abridged one-volume ed. (London, 1985), p. xi.

31. Quoted in L. S. S. O'Malley, *The Indian Civil Service 1601–1930* (London, 1965), pp. 177–78.

It is hard to imagine that two centuries of this kind of experience left no more trace than the memories Mason evokes. Indeed, it is hard to imagine a colonial cultural studies today that can afford to ignore Mr. Mason's own text as a symptomatic cultural document in its own right, to be read as evidence of that very complex history of racialized subjects and their own densely ingrained habits of telling and forgetting. But to recover this history we need a conception of culture (not just of colonial culture) that is open to the claim that colonial relations persist even today, in our "liberal" postcolonial sentiments, embodied in our daily habits of gesture and thought.

For what I have called "racialization" consists not simply in the creation of new meanings and values, new patterns of cultural behavior. Rather, "culture" marks the site of a profound political process. As we saw, the racialization of colonial rulers arose in direct relation to the threat that anticolonial sentiments and revolts posed. The process I have been describing, focusing at least in part on Kipling's tales, involved the shaping of the subjective interests of British-Indians around the color line, giving ideological shape and weight to their imaginations, their habits of living. But these subjective interests were also significant because they were related to the real material interests of the colonial rulers as a collective body, their investment in the continuation of colonial rule. The analysis of historically specific processes of racialization can show us the extent to which the development of racial ideologies are tied to the ways latent social antagonisms come to the fore. "Race" is often the form in which these antagonisms are lived and imagined, the way the "social" is mapped and reunderstood.[32]

Can we, today, in our various postcolonial contexts, go beyond the image of the benevolent, all-seeing, unimplicated ruler—the image I have been tracing through Mowgli and Kim, Baden-Powell and Philip Mason? So much depends on how much imaginative and philosophic resonance we are willing to grant to this image of colonial rule. That this image is a fundamentally gendered one is historically demonstrable; most colonial rulers (and imperial adventurers) were men. It is not *in principle* a male image, but it is a masculinist one, historically and ideologically coded as such. But this vision of rule is also a vision of an epistemology, an ethics, a politics in which we aspire to the universal only by obliterating—

---

32. See Omi and Winant, *Racial Formation*, pts. 2 and 3.

or denying—our specific locations, our changing but nonetheless locatable social identities and activities. If in our postcolonial contexts (and at this point in history, "postcolonial" needs to refer metaphorically as much to gender, sexuality, and class as it might to "race" or "nation"), we seek to escape the limiting forms of this universalism, this search for a prehermeneutical, uninvolved and unimplicated objectivity, I think we would do well to resist the false options of a romantic particularism or a cultural relativism.[33] If racialization is a process of historical coimplication of the colonizer and the colonized, our contemporary projects of decolonization cannot be based on a denial of racial relations. We have no "cultural" holes to crawl in to, to escape from this history. It is in some ways a little too soon to begin dreaming of many spaces, of plural identities. It is a little too soon, that is, until we begin to take seriously one another's histories, and the ways we have been shaped by them.[34]

33. See, on these issues, my "Us and Them: On the Philosophical Bases of Political Criticism," *Yale Journal of Criticism* 2 (Spring 1989): 1–31. For a critique of "colonial discourse" as a methodological position, as well as a consideration of what an analysis of the political economy of colonial society and culture could look like, see the review I have coauthored with Chandra Talpade Mohanty, "Contradictions of Colonialism" (review of *Recasting Women*, ed. Kumkum Sangari and Sudesh Vaid [Delhi, 1989]), in *The Women's Review of Books* (March 1990).

34. I would like to thank the American Council of Learned Societies and the Society for the Humanities, Cornell University, for fellowships that enabled me to begin work on this subject. Versions of these arguments have been presented to audiences at Cornell, Berkeley, Oxford, and the University of Pennsylvania; I learned much from their criticisms and suggestions. I would also like to thank David Goldberg, Biodun Jeyifo, Dominick LaCapra, David Lloyd, Kenneth McClane, Chandra Talpade Mohanty, and Hortense Spillers for helping me think through some of these issues.
This essay is dedicated to Audre Lorde.

Notes on Contributors

KWAME ANTHONY APPIAH previously taught at Yale University and at Cornell University and now teaches in the Philosophy Department at Duke University. He is author of *Assertions and Conditionals* (1985), *For Truth in Semantics* (1986), and *Necessary Questions* (1989). He is preparing (with Peggy Appiah) "Bu Me Bé: The Proverbs of the Akan."

STEPHEN CLINGMAN is Assistant Professor of English at the University of Massachusetts, Amherst. He is the author of *The Novels of Nadine Gordimer: History from the Inside* (1986). He also edited and introduced *The Essential Gesture: Writing, Politics and Places* by Nadine Gordimer (1988).

HENRY LOUIS GATES, JR., is the W. E. B. Du Bois Professor of Humanities at Harvard University. He is author of *Figures in Black: Words, Signs, and the "Racial" Self* (1987) and *The Signifying Monkey: A Theory of Afro-American Literary Criticism* (1988). He is the recipient of the American Book Award and the Anisfield-Wolf Award.

SANDER L. GILMAN is Goldwin Smith Professor of Humane Studies at Cornell University and currently Senior Research Historian at the National Library of Medicine, National Institute of Health. His books include *On Blackness without Blacks: Essays on the Image of the Black in Germany* (1982), *Difference and Pathology: Stereotypes of Sexuality, Race, and Madness* (1985), and *Sexuality: An Illustrated History* (1989).

MICHAEL GOLDFIELD is Assistant Professor in the Government Department at Cornell University and Senior Research Associate at the Center for Labor-Management Policy Studies, City University of New York Graduate Center. He is author of *The Decline of Organized Labor in the United States* (1987). He is preparing a book-length manuscript titled "That Magic Moment: Class, Race, and the Possibilities for Radicalism in the United States During the 1930s."

DOMINICK LACAPRA is Goldwin Smith Professor of European Intellectual History at Cornell University. His books include *Rethinking Intellectual History: Texts, Contexts, Language* (1983), *History, Politics, and the Novel* (1987), and *Soundings in Critical Theory* (1989).

FRANÇOISE LIONNET teaches French and Comparative Literature at Northwestern University. She is author of *Autobiographical Voices: Race, Gender, Self-Portraiture* (1989) from which her contribution to the present volume is drawn. She is currently working on a study of subjectivity and history in postcolonial women writers.

ANNE MCCLINTOCK teaches cultural and women's studies at Columbia University. Her forthcoming book is titled *Maidens, Maps and Mines: Making Feminist Sense of Race and Gender in Victorian Britain and South Africa;* her contribution to the present volume is drawn from it. She is currently working on a book on women and the sex industry as well as on an edited collection of writings on the politics of sex work by sex workers, feminists, AIDS activists, and film-makers.

SAMIA MEHREZ is Assistant Professor of Arabic Literature and Thought in the Department of Near Eastern Studies at Cornell University. She has published on modern Arabic literature, francophone North African literature, and *Beurs* literature in France. She is currently working on a biography of the Nobel Prize winner Naguib Mahfouz.

SATYA P. MOHANTY teaches in the English Department at Cornell University. He is the author of *Literary Theory and the Claims of History*, forthcoming in 1992.

JOSÉ PIEDRA is Associate Professor of Romance Studies at Cornell University. He has completed a book-length manuscript titled "Shadow Writing: The Neo-African Aesthetics of Alejo Carpentier," and he is preparing two others: "On Paper: Latin American Overview of Anthropoetical Space" and "Letra en sangre: Literatura neoafricana y la inquisición de la Nueva España."

HORTENSE J. SPILLERS previously taught at Haverford College and at Cornell University and now teaches English and Women's Studies at Emory University. She has published essays on African-American literature and theory and on issues in feminist criticism. Her book, *In the Flesh: A Situation for Feminist Inquiry*, will be published by the University of Chicago Press.

NANCY LEYS STEPAN is Professor of History at Columbia University. Her publications include *Beginnings of Brazilian Science* (1976), *The Idea of Race in Science: Great Britain 1800–1960* (1982), and *"The Hour of Eugenics": Latin America and the Movement for Racial Improvement 1918–1940* (1991).

Index

Library of Congress Cataloging-in-Publication Data

The Bounds of race: perspectives on hegemony and resistance / edited
with an introduction by Dominick LaCapra.
p. cm.
Includes index.
ISBN 0-8014-2553-0 (alk. paper). —ISBN 0-8014-9789-2 (pbk.:
alk. paper)
1. Race in literature. 2. Afro-Americans in literature.
3. Blacks in literature. 4. Blacks—Race identity. 5. Ethnicity.
I. LaCapra, Dominick, 1939–
PN 56.R16B68 1991
809'.93355—dc20   91-11896